More praise for

# Howard Cosell

"The treatment this controversial giant in sports journalism deserves."
—*New York Post*

"The first thoroughly researched and effectively framed biography of Cosell and his times. . . . Beyond its poignant depiction of a flawed, paranoid and narcissistic character with the uncanny talent to immerse himself entirely, almost supernaturally, into emerging events, Ribowsky's *Howard Cosell* makes crystal clear the entwined path of Cosell's epic career within the world of Big Time sports and its broadcasting partners, as they quite literally created the monstrosities they are today."
—James Campion, *Huffington Post*

"A sportscasting giant is interpreted for a generation that never knew him. . . . Mark Ribowsky's clear-eyed take on the broadcaster who built his career on 'telling it like it is' reveals the insecurities that fueled Cosell's bravado, charting his ascension from growing up in a middle-class home in Brooklyn to a short-lived career as a lawyer before elbowing his way into radio and TV and becoming the most influential—and controversial—sports commentator in America."
—*Sports Illustrated*

"Ribowsky's book is not a glorification of Cosell. In fact, it is often unrelenting in showing just how egotistical, bombastic, highly unpleasant and extremely insecure he could be. Although the personality on display here is definitely unpalatable, Ribowsky is not only concerned with likability. He constructs a good case for thinking that the tough journalism of Cosell's earlier years shifted the future of sports coverage (and it certainly appears that Cosell was a lonely pioneer)."
—Mark J. Miller, *Salon*

"Mark Ribowsky reveals the obnoxious broadcaster who transformed sports reporting." —Sherryl Connelly, *New York Daily News*

"Ribowsky has deftly captured this complicated figure, and anyone who cares about sports and how we talk about sports will find this book well worth the time, no matter how off-putting its subject was to many." —Steve Kettman, *San Francisco Chronicle*

"An entertaining read and a thought-provoking portrayal of the multifaceted Howard Cosell in all his glory and enmity. It is based on voluminous, well-sourced research into print and electronic material, coupled with numerous interviews with Cosell's contemporaries. . . . The book vividly depicts Cosell as a brilliant meteor that soared through the electronic sky before ultimately fading, dimmed by controversy, age, exhaustion, and perhaps his own obstreperous personality. Warts and all, there has never been, and may never be again, anyone quite like Howard Cosell." —Don Ohlmeyer, *Wall Street Journal*

"A rich read. Famous for his bark, Cosell comes off as far brighter than the current ilk of sportscasters, with a deeper understanding of the crossover points between sports and society." —Chris Erskine, *Chicago Tribune*

"Ribowsky has produced a mighty epic here, a loving, loathing and lingering portrait of Cosell. It is a book that reveals what drove a master media showman, what devils possessed him and how he transformed sports and media at the same time." —Harvey Frommer, *Bleacher Report*

"A powerful biography . . . well researched and well written." —*Jewish Journal*

OTHER BOOKS BY MARK RIBOWSKY

*He's a Rebel: Phil Spector, Rock & Roll's Legendary Producer*

*Slick: The Silver and Black Life of Al Davis*

*Don't Look Back: Satchel Paige in the Shadows of Baseball*

*The Power and the Darkness: The Life of Josh Gibson
in the Shadows of the Game*

*A Complete History of the Negro Leagues, 1884–1955*

*A Complete History of the Home Run*

*Crazy and in Charge: The Autobiography of Abe Hirschfeld*
by Abe Hirschfeld and Mark Ribowsky

*Eleven Days of Hell: My True Story of Kidnapping,
Terror, Torture and Historic FBI and KBG Rescue*
by Yvonne Bornstein and Mark Ribowsky

*The Supremes: A Saga of Motown Dreams,
Success, and Betrayal*

*Signed, Sealed, and Delivered:
The Soulful Journey of Stevie Wonder*

*Ain't Too Proud to Beg: The Enduring Soul
and Troubled Lives of the Temptations*

# Howard Cosell

## THE MAN, THE MYTH, AND THE TRANSFORMATION OF AMERICAN SPORTS

## MARK RIBOWSKY

W. W. NORTON & COMPANY

NEW YORK LONDON

Photograph credits: frontispiece, Lane Stewart / *Sports Illustrated* / Getty Images;
Part One, Bettman/Corbis; Part Two, AP Photo / Joe Caneva;
Part Three, Bettmann/Corbis.

For information about permissions to reproduce selections from this book,
write to Permissions, W. W. Norton & Company, Inc., 500 Fifth Avenue,
New York, NY 10110

For information about special discounts for bulk purchases, please contact
W. W. Norton Special Sales at specialsales@wwnorton.com or 800-233-4830

Manufacturing by RR Donnelley, Harrisonburg
Book design by JAM Design
Production Manager: Devon Zahn

Library of Congress Cataloging-in-Publication Data

Ribowsky, Mark.
Howard Cosell : the man, the myth, and the transformation of American sports /
Mark Ribowsky.
p. cm.
Includes bibliographical references and index.
ISBN 978-0-393-08017-9 (hardcvover)
1. Cosell, Howard, 1918–1995. 2. Sportscasters—United States—Biography
3. Sports—United States—History. I. Title
GV742.42.C67R53 2012
070.449796092—dc23

2011027501

ISBN 978-0-393-34387-8 pbk.

W. W. Norton & Company, Inc., 500 Fifth Avenue, New York, N.Y. 10110
www.wwnorton.com

W. W. Norton & Company Ltd., Castle House, 75/76 Wells Street, London W1T 3QT

1  2  3  4  5  6  7  8  9  0

*For my son, Jake,*
*who patiently explains to me what*
*pop culture is all about these days*

In one year I traveled 450,000 miles by air. That's 18 times around the world—or once around Howard Cosell's head.

—Grand Prix race car driver Jackie Stewart, 1978

Brain in neutral, mouth in gear.

—Anonymous

# CONTENTS

## Part Three: Turn Out the Lights (1976–1995)

# Howard Cosell

# INTRODUCTION
## A GIFTED ONE

I
N ENDLESS variations and permutations, jokes about Howard Cosell's outsized ego and nonstop verbosity proliferated during much of his lifetime. It may be surprising to those who were not alive then, or were too young to know, but his presence so dominated popular American culture that it was virtually impossible not to know who he was. During those heady times, especially during the late 1960s and 1970s, it was hard, in fact, to find someone who *didn't* take a whack at the world's most inflated ego. Yet nobody laughed more than Howard Cosell did himself, knowing full well the hold he had on the media-driven culture he had helped define and cannily exploited for thirty or so years. Indeed, the more Cosell's detractors twitted him, the bigger he became. Too big, way too big. If, in the modern vernacular, Wall Street is too big to fail, Howard Cosell was exactly the opposite—he was too big to *not* fail, which is why this biography isn't merely an examination of the media phenomenon called Howard Cosell but something of a modern fable, complete with shadings of Greek tragedy.

The main reason I decided to undertake this work was to fill a vacuum that has existed for the last two decades since his final, and surprisingly quiet, exit from the stage. It doesn't seem to make much sense, given the

giant that he was. That a mainstream biography of his life hasn't been previously undertaken might be construed as inevitable: Perhaps Cosell dug
his own historical grave, ensuring neglect of his achievements, because
what he did he did so well, and so obviously, was outrageously singular. In
retrospect, it's easy to dismiss him in the epitaphic words of one of the few
sportswriters he held in high regard, Red Smith, who said, "Howard Cosell
doesn't broadcast sports, he broadcasts Howard Cosell." Guilty as charged.

We can call his time the Age of Cosell, so total was his saturation of
American sports and popular culture. Now, in his absence, it has been far
easier for people in the sports universe to treat him as if he were a passing freak show: fascinating, but in the end just a circus performer who
overshadowed the athletic purity of the games. This may or may not be
true, but such an assumption seems to be a way to grant themselves
immunity for their lack of conviction, perspective, and stomach for fighting the fights he did. That mindset has surely meshed with the post-
Cosell times, when network sports executives have pretty much
determined that a Howard Cosell not only is no longer possible in the
world as we know it, but is no longer needed. That is the unkindest cut in
the legacy of Howard Cosell. What's more, they are wrong. Clearly, we
do need a Howard Cosell. In fact, we need one real bad.

WE ALWAYS need people like Cosell, people who are not only transi-
tional but *transformational* figures. Through them, old dissolves into new
in response to a cultural void; the new order is hammered into place and
given its character. There are a blessed handful in the modern sports
culture who made and left those kind of transformational traces, most
notably Muhammad Ali and Joe Namath, both of whom challenged the
norms and confines of their sports, which required challenging the norms
and confines of the world beyond the stadium gates, at a time when such
sedition was actually a risk. And then there was Howard Cosell, who
transformed sports despite, as he was never loath to point out, the fact
that "I never played the game," a condition that he knew may well have
been the biggest obstacle he had to overcome as a sportscaster. For this
reason, Cosell's transformational influence, while not as important in the

sociopolitical context as Ali's, was just as broad—and, for him, just as risky. Boil away the endless layers involved in the transformation he created and ponder a simple question: Has any other sports announcer ever needed armed guards, as he did, to protect him from avowed death threats upon entering and exiting a stadium, or as he did his work inside it? In this light, Cosell wasn't a sports announcer; he was an *outlaw*. That was what "telling it like it is" could get you back then. Little wonder we see and hear so little of it today.

That the generations that came after him have only hazy memories of Cosell borders on tragic, considering the blood, sweat, and tears he contributed to his art, but it is understandable given the truncated attention span of postmodern culture. The irony is that sports—a business so big and so inextricably bonded to the bigness of TV because of the transformation Cosell helped bring about—is by its very bigness a circumspect, a too comfortable beast, itself too big to fail. By contrast, never during Cosell's time did anyone, least of all him, *not* fret that failure was right around the next corner. It gave those men a brazenness proscribed in today's timid TV corporate sports environment. A major objective of this work is to acquaint younger sports viewers with those intrepid times that made sports-watching not merely routine but *daring* and, might we even add, fun, and this when sports events were a lot fewer in number and actually *important*. To appreciate the tone and texture of, say, an Ali fight during the years he was deemed an enemy of the state, or of the upstart Jets' 1969 Super Bowl win over the proxy of NFL invincibility, the Baltimore Colts, one needs to appreciate who and what Howard Cosell was, how important *he* was, and his story is. Through his voice, the hard yielding of individual freedom in the outside world began to seep into sports. At a time when America was being torn apart by issues like war and racism, he walked a delicate line as a representative of a major corporation with the power to frame images and debate on its airwaves. He did it, nimbly but not without being branded as subversive himself by many sports fans and recalcitrant media voices. Some of us can remember that; too many of us have no clue about it, and for that, the blame lies with a culture all too willing to forget him and his times. As this book will demonstrate, that omission is damn near a crime.

As a mission statement, it should be obvious that this work is far more than a biography of a dramatically important, even heroic man. It is no less than the story of the transformation of American sports, and the media through which it has grown to corpulent corporate dimensions. There never was before Cosell, or has been since him, anything of his sort in sports, media, or the culture—by way of quick clarification, loud voices do not mean *brave* or *intelligent* voices. It is as if, with Cosell having bared claws and fangs to turn sports broadcasting from a lap dog of network TV to the tail that wags the entire dog, this instinct is somehow irrelevant now, when heroism and importance are not part of the job description of a sports announcer. Cosell would not have stood easily for these terrible ironies. He would crave paving the way for another transformation, challenging the new reality that there simply could not be room for him today—indeed, there wasn't room for him late in his life, in the late 1980s and early 1990s. Things had changed by then, beyond his control and to his chagrin. By then, he could only look back. And that is what we all should do, to the Age of Cosell, when a sports announcer could be a king.

WHEN COSELL was entrenched, he was thundering, blustering, utterly compelling proof that TV had become not a silent Cycloptic eye on the world but the cynosure of Marshall McLuhan's "hot" medium, the message in itself. What was not, however, in the McLuhan theory was the missing link that was Howard William Cohen, who would achieve fame and fortune as Howard Cosell, his name change being not insignificant. His voice itself, for those too young to recall him, was like a pealing, staccato diesel engine, driving you nuts as you drove on the highway. For three decades, it was the very soundtrack of sports, so omnipresent, so omni-hated, so omni-riveting, that within the general societal framework little was heard or seen that didn't bear some trace of him. In fact, when *The New Yorker* got around to noticing this phenomenon in the mid-seventies and presented a very highbrow treatise about the new, egocentric media, the avatar was one Howard Cosell.[1] It was why Woody Allen always found him so fascinating. In fact, Allen was so taken with Cosell that he put him in three of his movies, in which he played nothing but himself, to stupendous effect.

Of course, Cosell's life stretches far, far beyond caricature and mere ego. It was an endless churn of self-serving playacting intertwined with a ferocious conviction that he was on earth to set things straight in a Potemkin village of bogus norms and heroes with clay feet. The classic outsider, as clownish as he was loud, Cosell was never boring or ignored, and he was rarely wrong. At a time when sportscasters were pleasant, nice-looking gents who bowed to the royalty of sports leagues and the sanctified memories of Babe Ruth and Knute Rockne, his views, emanating from a deeply entrenched stand of great moral offense, rewrote the narratives of sports. Sports could be corrupt, he said, the province of bloated corporate sultans stealing their athlete employees blind while posing as men of leisure. He had seen men just like this keep other men, like Jackie Robinson, out of baseball back when he was an ambitious lawyer in Brooklyn. Indeed, his image of team owners—at least until he began to see them as elitists of his own cloth—was carved in stone when Walter O'Malley smiled, assuring Brooklyn that he wouldn't take the Dodgers away, and then did just that.

When Cosell first turned his sights on sports in the late 1950s, no one was supposed to be angry at the things he said on the radio or on that nascent invention called TV. At that time of his genesis, he was a lonely voice in the wilderness, so it was safe to regard him as a crank. Yet decades later, he felt it had been almost all for naught, after he had taken his leave. And he was right, as usual, because what remains now of Howard Cosell is not the advanced evolution of sports fused to advocacy journalism. What remains, simply, is the singular voice of Howard Cosell.

Such becomes evident in current times, in small, disjointed ways. During the researching of this book, there was an endless stream of visits to the microform room of the New York Public Library, in which a hardworking, underpaid librarian became very well aware of the guy with the salt-and-pepper hair and sunglasses, which never came off, who was there to cull every piece ever written about Cosell in the newspapers or magazines, plundering the microfilm argosy contained in sturdy filing cabinets that lined three of the walls. Finally, this librarian who had per-

formed the archival searches on Howard Cosell looked up from her com-
puter monitor to ask a pressing question.

"Are you going to write about the *Odd Couple* he did?" asked this
kindly woman in her fifties, quite earnestly. "I remember he was with a
kid who won a 'Why I Want to Be Like Howard Cosell' contest." She
laughed easily. "I don't know why I remember that. I don't know a thing
about sports. I just remember him on *The Odd Couple*."

Actually, he did three *Odd Couple* episodes, each screamingly funny,
as was always the case when he moonlighted across the media corridors,
for no other reason than that he always played himself, and nothing was
funnier than that because he did it so well—his parting in one prefaced
by this flawlessly turned valediction:

"And so, another long day's journey into night for the gifted one, when
he had to surmount the mediocrities around him. But at least on this
occasion, the exposure to the whole American public of the utter paucity
of talent of a given sportswriter and a given photographer. To paraphrase
John Keats in his final letter to Fanny Brawne, 'Fare thee well, friends. I
could never gracefully bow.'"[2]

It was a line he wrote himself—but then, who else could have?

GIFTED, INDEED. He was likely the most overcaricatured human ever
seen on a television screen—a "ferret-faced man" (*Sports Illustrated*)
with a "pipestem neck," a "drooping face and stooping figure" (*Newsweek*), a "tail of a pony" (Muhammad Ali) glued on his bald head, a voice
"like a clogged Dristan bottle" (*Encyclopedia Britannica*) or that of "a
guy behind a Brooklyn delicatessen counter reciting Leviticus" (*Baltimore Sun*). No one ever caricatured him as well as he did it though, and
when he did, he could never quite inject enough satirical leavening of the
hardening crust of the character he had created to keep away the tragedy
that lay within him. Normally, overachieving and overarching men like
Howard Cosell get to watch themselves anointed, aggrandized, and cop-
ied. This has happened with a handful of high-visibility TV lions who, as
did he, left the broadcasting universe bigger and bolder than when they
arrived. Cosell, though, was not anointed but cursed by his own ineffable

success; he was, in the parlance of mythology—a realm where he actually belongs—Icarus flying into the sun.

No one else in his feral business ever flew that high, or receded so quickly into a hazy mnemonic memory. Always monumental, he was never anointed by his peers for his work when he was living, and rarely since. Some never forgave him for sticking his proverbial big nose where it didn't belong, mainly on the side of what the larger population considered uppity black men who weren't satisfied making lots of money by the good graces of the sports overlords. But that he made such things part of the sports dialectic was a remarkable feat, and one that made people want to hear him, *need* to hear him, and that was everyone. Beano Cook, then a CBS publicist, nailed it in 1981 when he observed that "the two biggest liars in the world are the people who tell you they don't watch [the CBS prime-time soap] *Dallas* or listen to Howard Cosell."[3]

Granted his license for oratorical excess by his sapient ABC Sports boss, Roone Arledge, Cosell delivered numbers, big numbers, no matter the sport—and he broadcast pretty much all of them—no matter the trivialized melodrama. Unlike the fictional character much like him, Peter Finch's mad newsman Howard Beale in Paddy Chayefsky's serrating satire *Network*, he never gave anyone a chance to kill him off for the crime of "lousy ratings." He could only kill himself, which he did, slowly but surely.

SOME OF US may be unaware of his lingering presence, but the truth is that he never really went away. For example, when ESPN's Chris Berman goes into his "He . . . could . . . go . . . all . . . the . . . way!" shtick, or growls something about "the *Raid*-ahs!" while showing football highlights, he is paying intentional homage to Howard Cosell, who did precisely the same shtick narrating halftime highlights on *Monday Night Football*, the program Cosell stamped into the American cultural identity. There was, too, the 2007 ESPN miniseries *The Bronx Is Burning*, its title said to be cropped from one of a thousand and one memorable Cosellisms, this during a 1977 World Series game at Yankee Stadium when an aerial camera found a blaze raging a few blocks away and, reaching for apocalyptic alluvium, Cosell supposedly intoned, "There it is, ladies and gentlemen, the Bronx is burning." The last seven words would be used as the title of Jonathan Mahler's 2005 book on which the TV film was based, retro-codifying New York City of that era as the ninth circle of Dante Alighieri's descent into hell. Just as Cosell intended it when he said it—or rather, as the producers of the 1972 documentary *The Bronx Is Burning* intended it, literally, in their mosaic of fires in the Bronx in the early seventies.

But *did* he, in fact, say these lyrical words? Or did the words find their way into his mouth because Mahler put them there, where they just seemed to belong, given that Cosell was the perfect metaphoric prophet of his times? There seems to be no surviving videotape of the moment, and Mahler has since admitted that—like myself, people who were in the booth with him, and the executive producer of the film—he never heard Cosell say it nor found any witness who could back it up, but he went with it anyway. Not that it matters, because Mahler wrote a fine book, and the phrase is now owned by Howard Cosell, even if in myth, too much him for it not to be.

Like Freddy and Jason and all those other scary pop culture mutants, he has a habit of reappearing in sequels. For a decade after he died on April 23, 1995, his memory lived, albeit decreasing in intensity, in the ongoing legacy of *Monday Night Football*, which had prospered for over two decades in no small part due to his gargantuan presence—if only because millions wanted to yell at their screens for him to shut the hell up. In his tenure, *MNF* was finite. There was no football on Sunday or Thursday nights, no satellite game, no NFL Network; until the seventies no cable, much less an iPad. *MNF* was the royal crown of the sport, of *sports*, of TV. *That* was must-see TV. But the cosmos changes, and that was underscored when ABC could no longer in an endless sports universe afford to broadcast the network's longest-running show. It was also a sentimental evergreen: one of the biggest gambles in television history that had become the rocket fuel of ABC's rise from last to first in the ratings. But on that day, *MNF* went to ESPN, as a reduced-calorie product.

That day, it can be argued, was when Howard Cosell died a second time.

———

"Oh, this horizontal ladder of mediocrity. There's one thing about this business: there is no place in it for talent. That's why I don't belong. I lack sufficient mediocrity."[4]

"The networks [have] forfeited their rightful prerogative in the field of sports by allowing agencies and sponsors to dictate which announcers would be used, what might be said—and not said. Let the announcers violate those laws and his departure is imminent."[5]

He said those seditious things in 1967 and 1968, respectively, just as the vast majority of America was coming to know who he was. Not yet completely secure in his job, he had no qualms about letting the world know that he was spectacularly different (read: better) than the rest of the mediocrities in the sportscasting crowd. In truth, he was exactly the same guy he would become decades later, when he wrote proudly, "Arrogant, pompous, obnoxious, vain, cruel, persecuting, distasteful, verbose, a show-off. I have been called all of these. Of course, I am."[6] Shy and retiring fellow that he was, Cosell once ventured that he belonged in a kind of holy trinity with Carson and Cronkite as the biggest TV icons of his time. (At other times, it was he, Carson, and Richard Nixon who were the most recognizable names in the country.) The lingering mystery is: How? How did he get there? He was, after all, a performer with no acting skills, a sports denizen who boasted that he never played the game, and an ex-attorney who used magniloquence in describing how grown men beat on or tackled each other or hit horsehide balls with sticks.

His contradictions, creating a balancing act between audacity and parody, made him compelling, and explain why people felt guilty about enjoying him so much—we were supposed to hate Cosell, so we did, while always making sure we tuned in to hear what he said. Because he was that different. He had the highest Q rating in television, always sitting atop lists of America's most known, most liked, and most hated people, which might be hard to fathom now, when his fame seems almost ephemeral and he is so unknown to a younger generation. Back then, it was the kind of schizophrenia only a Howard Cosell could fashion. He was inspired and/or insipid, but always with perfect timing and delivery— "I tell it like it is"; "Witness the adulation" (upon seeing the stir he had created in a crowd); "My footprints are cast in stone" (upon being told his footprints were cast in sand); "I'm impressed by the continuity of his physical presence" (of a certain quarterback). He meant every one of them, though his swagger lasted only until someone of inferior stock insulted him, as everyone did. There were the jaw-gaping constructions and misconstructions of the English language—or, as Jonathan Yardley once dished it back, "his penchant for sesquipedalian oratory"—that worked only for him yet baffled everyone else, to his delight. There was the pompousness, the name-dropping, the presumptuous overfamiliarity ("My guest today, Alvin 'Pete' Rozelle"). There was the confrontation. There was the heavily nasal intonation that began with the profound, needless prologue, overly slow, staccato syllables punching the air: "This is HOW-id Cyo-SELL . . ."

Everyone tried to imitate him; no one really could. Even *Mad* couldn't satirize him any better than Cosell satirized himself. In a 1972 spoof, the Cosell character harangued a fictional washed-up quarterback, "I want you to tell me, once and for all, straight from the shoulder . . . exactly why do you stink as a passer?"[7] Yet this was tame by the standards of the real Cosell, who once pressed an immortal but aging Johnny Unitas, "People want to know if you can still throw the long ball." Worse was his merciless browbeating of embattled U.S. Olympic track coach Stan Wright in 1972 for the screwup that kept the best sprinters off the track, which was reviewed as "cruel and unnecessary."[8]

TO CALL Cosell a sportscaster is to call Muhammad Ali a prizefighter. As Ali dwarfed any fight, Cosell dwarfed any sports event. Little wonder the two men, both reflexively labeled "big mouths," made such a perfect marriage. Many are vain, self-important, narcissistic, solipsistic, any or all of the above. Cosell was all of them, but not enough of any to think he could get by on bluster—he was, as we now know, a helluva sports journalist and a helluva sports celebrity, somehow interweaving the two. But he was also arguably the most insecure man in the public eye, and one given to fitful bouts of depression and self-erected isolation, with constant anger toward critics he claimed were dim-witted louts who made him doubt himself. And all of it caught up with him. As his most knowing observer, his near-sainted wife, Emmy, once foretold, "Howard will go to his grave thinking that he never accomplished all that much. He's satisfied only that he provided well for his family."[9]

Preposterous, yes. But also layered with many impulses, derivations, and ingredients that helped make him both preposterous and grating, and preposterously and gratingly brilliant. And, as he well knew, absolutely a product of and a necessary commodity for his times. At his peak, he must have felt invincible. Only he could have started a commercial—with the sponsor's blessing—by saying, "I'd like to tell you about a snack you may not like." Though the analogy wasn't his—but rather the stately sports columnist Red Smith's, cribbed by Cosell—only he could have said, "Sport is the toy department of human life in this sense: It doesn't really matter who wins or loses a game. The contest in the arena fulfills the primary function of sport, which is escape. In the face of the stress and complexities of daily existence, people have to have escape." Or, at considerable risk, "I think that every time they run up the flag and fly the airplanes and everything else, they should also hold an antiwar demonstration on the field. I don't buy any of it. I don't equate professional football, major-league baseball, or any other sport in this country with motherhood, apple pie, and patriotism."[10] In 1975, he wrote a piece for *Ms.* entitled "Why I Support the ERA." Try finding someone, anyone, in a sports capacity who would say or do things remotely that audacious today.

It is often said that Cosell changed the face of broadcasting—but the truth is that he merely changed it for himself, and in his own time, one that has been called, rightly, the golden age of network sports. The irony is that while it might actually be *easier* to take stands like these today, given loosened media boundaries, examining broad issues in sports seems not to be worth the effort, if it is done at all. Have all the battles been won? One suspects that if he were around, Cosell would find a few. Back then, he found them all over the map. Indeed, that he thrived during a new age of social tumult and questioned authority was not incidental. "The '60s," he once said, "were really my birth. The time of the anti-hero. The '60s were just right for me,"[11] though hearing him, a product of an earlier generation, spout things like "Let it all hang out" and "What you see is what you get" was downright painful. His signature "I tell it like it is" credo seemed not hip but mocking, of those he implied neither could nor did.

He surely was capable of audacity—such as when he told Ali to his face that he had no chance against George Foreman in Zaire. So too was he capable of farce. As Cosell would admit, needlessly, "There is a good deal of put-on in my personality." But both he and Ali would win out— big-time—when things turned very serious. That, of course, was when Ali refused to be drafted into the army in 1967 and Cosell joined the liberal literary cognoscenti and backed him, with passion and cogent legal reasoning about the Fourth Amendment. This posed a monstrous dilemma: maintaining the relationship at the risk of imperiling his career. ABC was deluged with hate mail and telephone calls, including several threats on his life. Cosell once described some of the letters as an attempt to "get that nigger-loving Jew bastard off the air." In time, ABC had to assign bodyguards to Cosell and his family. It was hairy, and yet to a country—and a broadcast industry—in transition, it likely made Howard Cosell a man of high importance, who really *mattered*. The effect was seismic. It still is, although the irony was that as his star became cosmic because of *Monday Night Football*, the celebrity began to outweigh, and suffocate, the journalist.

IN HIS prime, he roamed freely across the media meridians, leaving his mark on TV, radio, movies, and print. He didn't get to that level of pop culture on his own. Cosell's career would thrive on the whims and mercies of Ali and Arledge, both of whom welded his future to boxing's mercantile explosion in the sixties and seventies. As a blow-by-blow man, his frenetic calls gradually became the gold standard. His call of the Joe Frazier–George Foreman fight in Kingston, Jamaica, on January 22, 1973—a quaking Cosell's gritty-throated "Down goes Frazier! Down goes Frazier! Down goes Frazier!"—was Cosell at his peak, proving just how good he was on his feet at ringside, and it is among the greatest calls sports has ever heard. By then, he was of such altitude that the new champ's first words were "I'd like to credit this championship to Howard Cosell," who had predicted Foreman would win. He also called the Ali-Foreman "Rumble in the Jungle," the Ali-Frazier "Thrilla in Manila," and all of Ali's remaining bouts. But when Ali began a sharp slide downward in the mid-seventies, even the hardheaded Cosell seemed to understand he was going down with him.

Cosell lived in anger and agony, it seemed, but never more so than during the 1972 Summer Olympics in Munich, an epiphany on many levels for him that, typically, also caused him some embarrassment. He had finished up his boxing duties on September 5 when word broke that five "Black September" Arab terrorists had taken eleven Israeli athletes hostage, holding them in their rooms for almost a day. Throughout the tense siege, while the tersely dramatic Jim McKay related events in a calm and professional manner, an agitated, inebriated Cosell continually urged Arledge to put him on the air. Roone, however, wouldn't let him get anywhere near an open microphone, and Cosell brooded about it, never more self-pitying and insensitive.

He never forgave Roone for it, the man who had allowed him to go to the summit in sportscasting and even allowed him, against all reason, to host a Saturday night variety show, an epic disaster. But no defeat could ever knock him off stride. On December 8, 1980, during an *MNF* game, Cosell was informed through his earphone that John Lennon had been murdered. Now it would be Howard Cosell, not Jim McKay or Peter Jennings or anyone else, who would break the news to the country, and he did so with an economical, pitch-perfect elegy. There were some in the media who gave him his due. One, Frank Deford, wrote in 1983, "Cosell isn't television. He's not audio. Howard Cosell is sports in our time. Feel sorry for the people who turn off the sound [on *Monday Night Football*]. The poor bastards missed the game."[12] But encomiums like that were always too few.

BECAUSE SO much of quotidian sports paled next to these epochal battles he had fought, he grew bored by much of what he saw from the broadcast booth. In 1980, referring narrowly to *Monday Night Football* but with a much broader context, he said, "Do you think I take any of this seriously?"[13] Not long after, by the early eighties, his mind and body in serious deterioration, he was pretty much done—as was Ali, whose last few bouts Cosell could barely watch from his broadcast perch at ringside. Then, at the mike on November 26, 1982, in Houston, when Larry Holmes gave Randall "Tex" Cobb an unmerciful battering for fifteen lopsided rounds, Cosell vowed never again to call another fight, the inevitable riposte to which, voiced by Cobb, was that "I'd go 15 more rounds with Holmes if I thought it would get Cosell off football broadcasts."[14]

That wouldn't be necessary. The infamous, and absurd, contretemps about him calling Redskins receiver Alvin Garrett a "little monkey" on September 5, 1983, dogged him until the end. Never able to laugh off criticism, he felt a sharp knife behind every inference that the man who had put his neck on the block defending Ali was somehow racist. Angered, bored for years with his football chores, seeing conspiracies against him in the booth, he was drinking heavily, affecting his work. He now had his opening to get out, and he left *MNF* shortly before the start of the 1984 NFL season, but not before justifying the exodus by claiming that the NFL had "become a stagnant bore." His duties were greatly reduced, his sports news program called *SportsBeat* canceled after a four-year run in which the show won three Emmy Awards, though not for himself; the only one of those he ever got came just after his death, perhaps easing the consciences of those who had neglected to honor him when he was alive. That was a posthumous Sports Emmy Lifetime Achievement Award in 1995.

Arledge allowed him the customary "retirement" rather than an outright firing just before the 1985 World Series, baseball being the only sport he would consent to do now. ABC released him shortly thereafter. It was quiet news, if for no better reason than that he had ridden the act to painful redundancy, and also because he had alienated just about everyone he'd ever known, leaving himself without courtiers.

Nonetheless, Cosell did have his radio show and the love of his life, the woman who could reduce him to a little boy with one cross look. As trite as it sounds, he still had his Emmy, and she had him. Remarkably, even with cancer, a serious heart and kidney condition, Parkinson's, and a long pattern of alcoholism, he could get himself together and hold spirited group discussions on his radio shows. But in 1990 Emmy died, and he began to live out his life as a sad recluse in his apartment on Manhattan's East Side. When he died five years later, beyond the mandatory obituaries few mourned his passing with great emotion. If there was a sense of loss, it was for one's own youth, not Cosell, who for many had been dead for years.

Thus began a decade of devolution that preceded this book, which, beyond the story of how transformational a force he was in the cultural and media evolution of his time, is a primer of a career far more brilliantly conceived than the caricature he craftily concocted, and that others concocted around him. There are, indeed, many branches to the story; one aspect, for example, is how Cosell agonized over the smear that because he changed his name he somehow had turned his back on his Jewishness. In part, that was true; as a young man he rebelled against his father's religious litmus tests, even marrying out of his faith. But "Cosell" was actually a form of the original family name, even if his return to it was no more than a favor to his grandfather. Also true is that while he was hypersensitive to anti-Semitism all his life, he never embraced Judaism until the horror of Munich; even then, he never really did beyond contributions to Jewish philanthropies, and never had the stomach to confront the anti-Semitism he stared down. One more truth is that as fearless as he was about Ali, he was so invested in him that he refused to call out Ali for not rejecting rising Black Muslim militancy. Sometimes, playing it safe was more prudent than telling it like it was.

He was, to be certain, a complicated man. Something that Emmy once told him about Ali—"As long as you know him, you'll never really know him"[15]—actually applies more to Cosell. Certainly the enormous viewing audience he bred didn't. Not even two of the nation's finest actors, Jon Voight and John Turturro, each buried under layers of prosthetic clay and a beaver of a toupee, could get him right. In Will Smith's

*Ali* he was a surly, macabre cadaver; in the TV movie adaptation of the 1988 book *Monday Night Mayhem*, a gumbo of psychoses. In neither case was he human. Yes, he was strange, he did make people uneasy, even unhinged, and despite the hippodrome he played there was nothing really lovable, or even much endearing, about him. The erudite writer David Halberstam renounced his esteem for him in a 1982 *Playboy* profile that alleged Cosell endured as a mere "clown" and a "bully" who had become the very beast he had railed against; that "his insecurities, which had once made him interesting and irrelevant, now made him seem heavy and ponderous."[16] More sadly, Cosell probably knew all this was true.

In his writings, Cosell stamped himself heroic; he was, he said, "a unique personality who has had more impact upon sports broadcasting in America than any person who has yet lived," although one reviewer of his last book called it out for "paranoia, condescension and hypocrisy." What else, after all, could explain how Cosell could have the gall to dub Don Meredith in that book as "Texas Cruel" for his "mean streak"?[17] All of those failings can be gleaned from these pages, but so can the fact that his most noble quality, his heroism, is, even if it can be found, hardly a qualification for employment in the sports media these days. This is partly because his generation is dying out. Roone Arledge, Jim McKay, Don Meredith, and, at least in its historic incarnation, *Monday Night Football* are all gone. So too is boxing, not only from ABC but from all except the cable networks, and the sport itself, especially the heavyweight division, is moribund, dwarfed in popularity by kickboxing, a sport that once would only have been low-grade fodder for *Wide World of Sports*—which itself is now no more than the name of a theme park in Florida. Sports journalism is fairly moribund—night and day is the difference between his eloquent defenses of Ali and those shrieking ESPN hosts cast in his image.

Muhammad Ali bears the cruelest irony he or Cosell could have imagined, almost as grim as death: the inability to speak, having taken too many blows Cosell described so vividly. And at a time when no one on the sports beat is either loved or hated, just sort of there, the "jockocracy" in the broadcast booth that Cosell railed against is very much alive—with not a single non-ex-jock, besides the play-by-play man, in any broadcasting booth. It is as if Howard Cosell never existed.

He lives again in these pages, the vital center of American cultural history, a man almost eponymous with post-fifties sports and its media confluence. The not insignificant conclusion is that he was as great as he said he was. After all, being adored and abhorred at the same time was no small achievement. An era that taught us so much about ourselves and our clay-footed heroes irrevocably ended when the gifted one finally went off into the good night, with not so much as a graceful bow.

## PART ONE

# Black and White

## (1918–1964)

# 1

## "INSECURITIES IN YOU THAT LIVE FOREVER"

I N THE matter of Howard Cosell, there is perhaps nothing as remark-able as the realization that whatever his stage in life, whatever his professional or economic status, whatever the direction of his future, there was never the smallest measure of deviation in his comportment. In bearing, in attitude, in degree of pomposity and self-aggrandizement, he was always rigidly, belligerently, narcissistically, and unforgettably, Cosell.

By the time he first made it into print, in the Eisenhower summer of 1955, he was for example already so much and so indelibly Howard Cosell that even as a nobody to the public at large he had managed to get himself noticed by no less than *The New Yorker*. This was back when a place in the favorite magazine of cultured society swells was normally reserved for topics of leisure class amusement and profound intellectual thought. All one need do to know he was more than qualified on both counts was ask him, though it rarely got that far before he had already convinced someone in some position of authority and influence how amusing and intellectual he was.

Clearly, someone on that level at the haughty magazine had gotten wind of him, and was amused. Because in the June 11 issue, there he was in a "Talk of the Town" tidbit that began:

> The other day, we had lunch at Bob Olin's restaurant, on Central Park West, with Howard Cosell, a busy, erudite man who handles most of the legal problems that come up to harass Monte Irvin and Willie Mays of the New York Giants, and Wally Moon and Alex Grammas of the St. Louis Cardinals, and has given business advice to Bobby Thomson of the Milwaukee Braves, and Gil Hodges and Don Hoak of the Dodgers.[1]

If this sounded, in the modern context, as if he were a real power broker looming large over a galaxy of star ballplayers and lucrative deals, he was anything but. At the time, long before lawyers or agents held much sway in the hidebound caste system of pro sports, almost no players had any idea they *had* any legal problems, and business deals were confined to appearing in print ads or TV commercials for cigarettes, chewing tobacco, and razor blades for maybe a few hundred dollars. Cosell, a Brooklyn native and rabid Dodger fan whose idea of an idyll was to haunt the grandstand at Ebbets Field back in his early years, was primarily known to athletes for haunting the locker rooms at all three New York ballparks, scrounging up player interviews for an obscure five-minute radio show on local radio that had him moderating questions for ballplayers from Little League kids. Walruslike, he would lumber in carrying early recording equipment the size of a Buick, to the inconvenience of most everyone in the room, newspaper reporters and players alike.

Being at the junction of player usury and legal advocacy, he had already been nurturing the seed of a cockeyed dream—a kind way of describing the urge of a successful thirty-seven-year-old attorney with two young daughters to be some kind of multimedia sports broadcaster/reporter/gadfly. It mattered not that, at the time, there really was no such thing, and if there had been, it would have been on a pay grade any lawyer on his level would cackle at. He was absolutely unrelenting, and stage one of the fanciful flight was to talk his way into the good graces of whatever players would hear him out.

Of course, that was the easy part—the talking. He could have talked his way into piloting a nuclear submarine if he'd had to. All he had to do here was wax eloquent for indentured ballplayers about opening up mercantile avenues for them—though he never actually came through on his boasts. Still, barely pausing, he left them in his dust as he moved on, and up, gaining beneficial associations with a handful of other athletes, allowing him the pretense of claiming in later years that he had been a kind of forerunner of the modern sports agent—forgetting to add that he did exactly nothing for any athlete he ever advised in this role.

Doing this pro bono was a concession he could easily afford, with a comfortable $30,000 a year salary. More valuable than money, this strange rise of an obscure lawyer as a sports consul of sorts was getting him places, important places, where he could go on, and on, with stuffy eloquence about players' severely limited rights, as in this oratorio in *The New Yorker*:

> Ballplayers are apt to approach business propositions *a bouche ouverte* [literal translation: with open mouth]. Because they're gregarious, if an agent sells one player he can generally sell the entire team. The result is players are apt to fall victim to hornswoggling and pettifoggery on a huge scale . . . They are likely to be sold bad insurance, make bad realty investments, and sign away their legal rights *a maximus ad minima*. In their search for financial security, they may unwittingly pauperize themselves. If something worries them—debentures, tax laws, amortizations—it probably affects their fielding and hitting as much as a sprained ligament would. An attorney can act as a kind of *voorloper*, or vanguard, guiding them through the veldt of agents constantly besieging them with questionable propositions.[2]

*Voorloper* or not—and it seems not—the sports labor revolution was history he desired to report, not help make. His eyes were on another prize, a different stature. The constructions and applications of case law would not become his concern; too boring, too out of the limelight. Even though he had the ear of people ranging from the high tea set at *The New Yorker* to the sweatier editors at the *Sporting News*, he wanted the ears of thousands, millions, glued to their radios to receive his blustery narratives about sport and society. Even more, he wanted to do it on the new, star-making medium of TV, something to which anyone familiar with his hangdog ears and jowls and cawing voice would have raised a strenuous objection. Yet those same nay-sayers had sworn that he was too outspoken. Well, too Brooklyn—as he knew, a euphemism that was an all too normal refrain for TV honchos who meant "too Jewish"—but certainly too *Cosell* to get himself on radio, or, God forbid, TV.

If it all was clear to him, any future move of that magnitude could only have been on a drawing board inside his head, not visible to others. One day that winter of 1955, at Mays and Irvin's soon-doomed liquor store, a man named Ray Robinson encountered him for the first time. Not the inimitable champ "Sugar" Ray Robinson but the future author of the brilliant *Iron Horse: Lou Gehrig in His Time*, among other important sports books. Today, recalling how as a hungry young sportswriter he came to interview Irvin for *Sport* magazine, he described a similarly young Cosell entering the premises.

"He burst in, came over, and sat down. Didn't even ask if he could sit in on the interview, he just did, like it was his privilege," Robinson recalls. "I was a little bit upset about it. I wanted some amount of privacy, but he just sat there listening. I don't think he even introduced himself, I think Monte said he was his lawyer. I think at the time he had some *meshugena* radio program with about five listeners, which I'd never heard. I wasn't overly impressed. In fact, very little about him was impressive, other than the fact that he was instantly memorable, for reasons that weren't entirely good."

What strikes Robinson about that first acquaintance was that the Howard Cosell of then, a man indelible for no good reason, was exactly the same creature who would become indelible for a million and one reasons.

"He was someone with whom you couldn't have just one brief, fleeting experience, not if he saw in you something that could benefit him. Howard was what I call a collector of people. Anyone he thought might do some good for him, he collected. After getting to know him a bit, it was obvious he was very bright, very ambitious, driven, and I guess you could say egomaniacal but also very insecure. His bluster was a cover for his insecurities; all that bloviating was a giveaway. It's surprising that a man as smart as Howard didn't see that."

If he didn't, it was because he simply became addicted to playing the role of Howard Cosell. Later that day, as he and Robinson rode the subway back to Manhattan, their small talk was interrupted when he shifted into full Cosell mode.

"He began saying things like 'I'm going to be the most famous name in all broadcasting,' in that way he spoke—I always thought he sounded like W. C. Fields. It was kind of amusing because he was saying this while sitting in a subway car but he was perfectly serious. And then he went on a rant about the sportscasters who were on TV. He said, 'They're all a bunch of assholes' and, in a more eloquent passage, 'They are sons of the wild jackass,' which is an expression only Howard could have used, with that aureate pretension, biting off and drawing out each syllable. That was what made what he said memorable, even then. He could have made a Chinese menu sound memorable."

Robinson, hardly convinced he was riding the subway with a future broadcasting titan, and trying not to sound condescending, kibitzed him, "So I guess that means you'll be the biggest asshole of all."

Cosell quickly replied, without a hedge, "Yes, I will."

Robinson, with a wry grin, adds the mandatory footnote.

"I don't think anyone would disagree that he was absolutely right," he says. "Because in the end, that is exactly what he became."[3]

Not that Cosell had a problem with that. To get to where he wanted, he knew, he would *have* to be the world's biggest posterior aperture.

WHETHER A fruitcake or a Cassandra, he would have no reason to look back, not to the years before he left Brooklyn. But there would never be a day when Brooklyn would leave him. In fact, back across that remarkable bridge connecting it from lower Manhattan lay the clues to both his ambition and his insecurity, by dint of his desire to both please and rebel from his father, Isidore Martin Cohen, a Polish immigrant who was less than a year old when he arrived with his parents in the great wave of immigration from Eastern Europe.

According to family history, they landed in 1890 at the immigration processing center on the southern tip of Manhattan Island called Castle Garden, where no fewer than eleven million immigrants streamed through in seventy years of operation before it was supplanted by Ellis Island in 1892. As was commonly the case, the family's ancestral identity was instantly altered by a harried, Anglo-speaking customs agent. Unable to make out what they were saying through their thick accents when asked their surname, he scribbled "Cohen" on their papers and stamped them as official. However, exactly what the original surname was is a matter of confusion. "For the record," Cosell noted in his eponymous 1973 memoir, his first book, "Cosell—once spelled with a K—*is* the family name." His daughter Hilary believes it was "Kozel." His older brother, Hilton, who was the first to accede to his grandfather's wishes that his American-born scions restore the family heritage, once ventured that the name was "Kozel or Kassell or something like that."[4]

The family patriarch, the newly minted Harris Cohen, settled in immigrant heavy Brooklyn with his wife, Esther, and their infant son, Isidore—whose name his son spelled in *Cosell* as "Isadore" but which appears on his death certificate, 1930 census forms, and other public records with an *i* and not an *a*, though it *is* spelled with an *a* on his 1920 census entry. He had been born in Russia on October 12, 1889, a year before his mother and father bundled him up and fled to Poland to escape the Cossack pogroms against Jewish peasants. In Brooklyn, they moved into a cramped apartment in a public housing project within the crowded knot of eastern Brooklyn known as Brownsville, bordered by other neighborhoods like Bedford-Stuyvesant to the north, Bay Ridge to the south, East New York to the east, and Flatbush to the west.

Only one square mile, it was a tight-knit community of hardworking men and their thankless wives, as well as a hotbed of restless political activism; both the Socialist and American Labor parties, their tents of working-class rights and wealth redistribution having been borne on the waves of European emigrants, made such inroads in Brownsville that by the 1920s and later in the 1930s, in the wake of the Bolshevik Revolution and the desperation of the Depression, its voters elected members of both parties to the New York State Assembly.

Within this maw of head-in-the-clouds idealism was bred Isidore Martin Cohen. Though the neighborhood was predominantly Jewish, the young men of Brownsville learned early to either fight or strike an accommodation with the Irish or Italian mobs who bled in from places like Flatbush or Ocean Hill; even on their own streets, anti-Semitism was virulent, with Jewish kids regularly targeted—the risks of wearing a yarmulke or being seen coming out of a synagogue were obvious. Those who fought hardest or bought their own safety by paying protection money— or who just ran the fastest—lived to see the next day, in one piece. Not by coincidence, Brownsville in the 1930s would be where multiethnic gangsters godfathered by Jewish Mob kingpins Benjamin "Bugsy" Siegel, Meyer Lansky, and Lepke Buchalter formed that charitable organization known as "Murder Inc."

"IZZY" COHEN was able to dodge the pressures and perils of streets already mean in his youth. To no one's surprise, when he grew to manhood and set out on a career in the early 1910s, he intentionally chose one that would take him frequently from Brownsville. He became an accountant for a chain of credit clothing stores—sometimes calling himself a "supervisor"[5]—requiring him to spend most of his time on the road. On one trip in 1911 he did accounting for the owner of a store in Worcester, Massachusetts, Ahrins Rosenthal, a part-time rabbi who with his wife, Dora, fled the congestion of Passaic, New Jersey, to move their brood to the oasis of New England, to a hamlet called Hampshire. During the job, Izzy met Ahrins's daughter Nellie, the sixth of ten children. The Rosenthals, too, were an immigrant Jewish family, having made their way from czarist Russia in the early 1880s. Nellie, born in 1894, was seventeen, four years younger than Izzy, and she and Izzy quickly fell in love. Only a year later they married and moved into his small apartment in Brownsville.

The Cohens were a winsome couple, he tall, wavy haired, and, if no matinee idol with his long nose and narrow eyes, wearing a look of a man very sure of himself. As Cosell would recall in his 1974 book *Like It Is*, "My dad was not a good-looking man, but he had great dignity in his bearing and in his face." To him, Isidore resembled the patrician "Henry Morgenthau, Franklin Roosevelt's secretary of the treasury, with the same rimless, pinched-nose glasses"[6]—an irony to be sure, since Izzy's own treasury was normally in a state of depletion.

Nellie, he said, was pretty and precious—"strikingly attractive," he wrote of her, with a "positively beautiful complexion"[7]—as well as properly subservient and encouraging; all in all, the perfect wife for a young Brooklyn man who needed all the positive reinforcement he could get. Living their own rendition of the American Dream, they had their first child, a son named Hilton, in 1914, the same year Izzy became a naturalized U.S. citizen—though he told the census taker in 1920 that Russian was his "mother tongue," his parents never having learned to speak English fluently or spoken it around the house. By the time Nellie became pregnant again four years later, Izzy, who was not called up and did not enlist in the military during World War I, gave in to her wish for more breathing room for his growing family and moved them to a small house in Winston-Salem, North Carolina.

At the time the town was populated by only forty-eight thousand people, a good percentage of whom worked at the R. J. Reynolds tobacco company, the largest cigarette manufacturer in the world. Winston-Salem was where millions of Camels, Prince Phillips, Winstons, and Salems rolled out each year. It was also where, on March 25, 1918, another instrument that would involve an oral fixation was conceived. On that early spring day, eight months before the end of World War I, Howard William Cohen was born. He came into the world with lots of dark brown hair and long limbs, and no doubt with his mouth open and in midsentence.

His future, needless to say, would not be on Tobacco Road. Before he had turned two, a homesick Izzy and Nellie moved back to Brooklyn. They rented a two-bedroom flat in a 110-unit apartment building at 489 Sixth Street in Park Slope, just down the street from the green oasis of Prospect Park. A few years later, they would move north and east of the park, first to 329 Lincoln Place, then 852 Classon Avenue in the Adelphi section, a few blocks north of the bustling expanse of Eastern Parkway and a short walk from the Brooklyn Museum of Art. A little longer jog down Flatbush Avenue bordering the park's eastern end was the junction of Sullivan Place and McKeever Place—where stood the state of the art if slightly lopsided mecca called Ebbets Field.[8] It was a route Howard Cohen traversed so often he could have managed it in his sleep.

Everything seemed to happen in a great confluence here; all up and down Eastern Parkway the trolleys ran day and night along their tracks, threading through an increasing flow of automobiles rolling west to Grand Army Plaza or on a winding path northeast toward Atlantic Avenue and the sprawling nexus of cemeteries in the crook of land where Brooklyn met Queens along Union Turnpike. For all the unsettling aspects of the old neighborhood, middle-class Brooklyn bustled with shops and museums, and a stroll down Eastern Parkway offered a smorgasbord of ethnic delicacies and scents, where a row of stores—a pizzeria, an Irish pub, and a kielbasa shop, one right after the other—could pull a stroller in with its piquant smells.

Despite the ethnic diversity, most everyone was lured by dreams of upward mobility, though success was relative; most young families continued to live rather humbly even when times were better for them, tempered as they were by immigrant ancestors who had had nothing and reminded them that tomorrow could wash away everything—which it did for many during the Depression. Another commonality was that Brooklyn was breeding not only businessmen but ballplayers. Baseball and football were the standards, but it was the relatively new indulgence of basketball that caught many a kid's imagination. In their high-top sneakers, they honed their skills on asphalt playgrounds, in airless church and synagogue basements, and in school gyms. It kept them away from the hazards of the street, but how they played, with tricky feints and eye-popping passes, came to define "the City Game."

Brooklyn soon would develop a reputation as the incubator and home turf of the country's best and toughest athletes, making it almost mandatory that every kid play competitive sports. Some would display not only skill but a near warlike competitiveness. Born in 1929 in Brockton, Mas-

sachusetts, but brought up in an apartment on President Street right off
Lincoln Terrace Park in Crown Heights, a couple miles east down the
parkway from the Cohens, a kid named Allen Davis would ride middling
skills and ferocious ambition a long way; by the time Howard Cosell
would land a job in network television in the early sixties, Al Davis was
an assistant coach of the Los Angeles Chargers in the new American
Football League, and three years later head coach and part owner of the
Oakland Raiders. To the south, in Sheepshead Bay, a squat football player
named Vincent Lombardi gave up studying for the priesthood the year
after Davis was born and was soon on his way to Fordham University,
and football sainthood.

Howard Cohen took to sports, too, telling tales through the years,
perhaps apocryphally, such as being "the last kid picked" in a punchball
game, being stuck in left field, and making a great catch of a "screaming
liner" hit by a kid he recalled as Jack Storm, only to make two errors the
next inning and be kicked out of the game. Then there was the time,
allegedly, when he drove in the game-winning hit in a stickball game for
his team, who called themselves the Eastern Parkway Jews, against a
team of Irish Catholics. Funny how whatever game he was in, there had
to be a heroic moment, or even one that foretold future greatness—if not
for him, then for an opponent. Once, he said, during a pickup game of
tackle football at the Manhattan Beach pool, where he spent many a hot
summer day, he was smashed to the asphalt by the lifeguard, who during
the school year played at Fordham with Lombardi—Alex Wojciechowicz,
who would go on to become a college and pro football Hall of Famer.[9]

Regardless of his participation, he was like all Brooklyn kids a rabid
Dodger fan, their perpetual finishes in the second division of the
National League only engendering stronger emotional attachment to
"Dem Bums." All games were of course played in the daylight then, but
there was no live coverage of them on the radio yet. And so if the team
was out of town, meaning that no neighbors could tell him of the day's
game by word of mouth, the young man would wait at the local candy
store for the evening edition of the paper to come in and ferret out the
score. His favorite was fleet center fielder Johnny Frederick, who broke
in in 1929 and proceeded to hit .300 over six seasons, leading off a game

with a homer ten times. The guys who scratched and clawed just seemed to dovetail with his own skewed view of life.

HE PLAYED sports, too, but seemed more intrigued with sports broadcasting—an avocation that in the twenties and thirties could seem as exciting as playing center field for the Dodgers. When Howard Cohen turned twelve in 1930, it had been only thirty-four years since Marconi was awarded the first British patent for the invention of the radio, and only twenty-four years since what is purported by some historians to have been the first-ever radio broadcast, on Christmas Eve 1906, from Ocean Bluff–Brant Rock, Massachusetts—a live performance of "O Holy Night," which was heard only by a few ships at sea.

It would not take long for the new medium to catch on. In 1920, news was broadcast by what are now considered the first nonamateur stations, WWJ in Detroit and KDKA in East Pittsburgh, Pennsylvania, the latter of which charted a historic first providing coverage of the Harding-Cox presidential election in November. Most pertinently for the fortunes of the young man in Brownsville, the first known sportscast happened on November 13, 1920—when a station called 2ADD at Union College in Schenectady, New York, did a Union-Hobart football game. By 1922, using a field telephone set, play-by-play accounts of games were regularly being transmitted on a "network" to opposing colleges.

The novelty of radio as something more than an amateur dalliance gave way to serious business by the mid-1920s, cheek by jowl with the technology of wireless wave transmission exploding. With money to be made, stations proliferated all over the landscape, filling up virgin bandwidth space, with different wavelengths for lower- and higher-powered stations. In New York, four high-powered stations had popped up, WBAY, WEAF, WOR, and WHAZ; by 1927, there were no fewer than fifty-seven of them swarming the bandwidth, mandating creation of the Federal Radio Commission that year to sort out the chaos.

Newly formed by the Radio Corporation of America, the National Broadcasting Company network—nineteen stations linked together by telephone lines—hit its stride on June 11, 1927, when Charles Lindbergh returned to America after his flight to Paris and it offered all-day and -night coverage of the festivities and parades given Lucky Lindy in Washington, D.C. About six million listeners tuned in that day, and sales of radios (most manufactured, of course, by RCA) spiked, even though a set was not cheap—going for anywhere from $69.50 to $895; the most popular model, the sleek Radiola, sold for $157.50, and demand for it outpaced production.

For curious listeners there was much to hear. The 1930 census forms specifically inquired whether one owned a radio; nearly everyone on the long page that listed the Cohens and their neighbors did. By the midthirties, the big vaudeville performers such as Eddie Cantor, the Marx Brothers, Burns and Allen, and Ed Wynn had their own shows. *Amos 'n' Andy* was on every night at 7 P.M. However, an obvious omission from those Radiolas in New York City was live coverage of the games of the three local baseball teams, all of which were so alarmed by the popularity of radio that they imposed a blackout, fearing attendance at the park would be undercut. It took until the 1939 season for the blackout to be lifted, by the Dodgers, who hired a soft-spoken, eloquent southern gent named Red Barber to call the games from the Ebbets Field catbird seat.

Howard Cohen would catch the fever of sportscasting from an earlier trailblazer, Graham McNamee. In 1923, McNamee, an opera singer, had taken a job as a staff announcer at WEAF in New York, then owned by AT&T. His savory sports news reports, in mellifluous, authoritative tones buffed by rich detail, caught on. In 1926, when WEAF became the flagship station of the NBC network, he was assigned the World Series, which had previously been called by moonlighting sportswriters. He was also put to work calling the Rose Bowl and championship fights, political conventions and presidential inaugurations. The way he opened his broadcasts practically wrote the manual for generations to come—"Good afternoon, ladies and gentlemen of the radio audience. This is Graham McNamee speaking."

McNamee made a visceral impact on young Howard Cohen, with his voice and style, his omnipresence and versatility. But Howard also would glean much from Clem McCarthy, who took over many of McNamee's sports duties when the latter moved on to mostly showbiz gigs such as being the sidekick on Ed Wynn's program. McCarthy's style was punch-ier, grittier, delivered with a frenetic, sandpapery voice. There would come a day when the creature later known as Howard Cosell would be an almost perfect hybrid of both men. Which was only logical, since at the beginning, not just the medium but the art and craft of play-by-play was new and infectious, and a generation of young Americans descended from Pilgrims and peasants alike could claim it as theirs, it being some-thing their parents had never heard or done. As Hilton Cosell remem-bered, his very impressionable kid brother "always had a mouthpiece. Even when we were kids, living near Ebbets Field . . . he'd sit in the bleachers and broadcast the whole game."[10]

AS HE and his vocal cords got older, the voice became resonant, if strik-ingly nasal, and his vocabulary remarkably expansive; he also had a pho-tographic memory for events and names. Most of all, he had an eye for advancement, a hunger for money. Living so close to Eastern Parkway, where they said you could smell money along with the pastrami, opulent townhouses and modern apartment buildings spread out with an élan that led him to think of himself, in the parlance of the times, as an "East-ern Parkway Jew," meaning those who had class and poise and made something of themselves. The young man had little use for the masses in Brownsville, where his father had matured. On the parkway, he wrote in *Like It Is*, there were "fine, modern, doorman-attended, elevator-equipped, six-story buildings."[11] To a Brooklyn kid, that was another way of saying it was Arcadia.

But the best he could do was "feel" like an Eastern Parkway Jew. The reality was that, as he recalled, "Eastern Parkway was for the rich people. We were not that." Making friends with high school classmates from that hallowed turf could alter reality, a bit. And so he made it his business to tag along with the kids whose fathers owned some of those stores. With their acquiescence, "I became part of Eastern Parkway. I was 'in' with the crowd . . . Hamilton became my torch, Eastern Parkway my arena."[12]

No matter that he actually did not make it to the parkway proper until Izzy and Nellie made that huge leap years later, taking an apartment at 175 Eastern Parkway. It would be there where Izzy, in fact, was living when he had the heart attack that killed him in 1957. Of course, their younger son would rise a long way above and beyond the fading glory of Eastern Parkway, and by the time he did he considered himself the ultimate example of postmodern Jewish upgrading.

Frank Deford, arguably America's finest sportswriter of the last half century with his work in *Sports Illustrated* starting in 1962, was that rarest of creatures: a sportswriter who enjoyed a long, uninterrupted affinity for and from Cosell. Knowing him as well as he did, which is about as well as anyone could have, Deford looks back today and says, "I always got the feeling Howard's life belonged in *Our Crowd*"—meaning Stephen Birmingham's signal 1967 book, which traced the Jewish American aristocracy, notably the German-Jewish aristocracy, Manhattan's *"other* Society" of mercantile barons like Carl Loeb, Herbert Lehman, and Bob Sarnoff, all of whom transcended from humble roots to palaces and private parlor cars.

"Howard believed that was *his* world," Deford continues. "I'm not Jewish, but it's the same with all ethnic groups who face bigotry. There are different *kinds* of one's own group. There are the rich Irish and the shanty Irish. You're not only part of an ethnic group, you're part of an economic class. And Howard, look, Howard was middle class growing up. It wasn't like he was from the slums. His father was a white-collar guy. The family was lower middle class, at worst. Howard was not deprived. I'm sure they must have had hard times, but there wasn't any deprivation in Howard's life. But, the thing was, he had to see it in that light if he was going to go over the rainbow and be that *kind* of Jew he wanted to be."[13]

Proud of being a Jew, he would be constantly reminded of what he was up against. "As young as you were you knew, by God, that you were Jewish, and you knew every restrictive boundary and every thoughtless slight," he wrote in *Cosell*.[14] The dilemma, as with the patricians of *Our Crowd* he sought to emulate, was that, class distinctions aside, he would have to figure out *what* kind of Jew he was going to be.

HILTON, THEN HOWARD, attended elementary school at P.S. 9, on the corner of Sterling and Vanderbilt, where two previous students included composer Aaron Copland—who grew up above the family furniture store on nearby Washington Avenue—and Clara Bow, who had gone from a Brownsville tenement to Hollywood fame as the saucy "It Girl" of the silent movies. From there it was on to Alexander Hamilton Vocational and Technical High School on Albany Avenue a few blocks north of Eastern Parkway. This was an all-boys school that, for obvious reasons, was not his first choice—that was the coed Erasmus High, south of Ebbets Field on Flatbush Avenue, which had already spawned Mae West and would crank out future stars in sports (one being Al Davis) and show biz (Barbra Streisand). But he had no say in the matter; his mother thought girls would be a bad influence on his studies; he put up his best arguments to the contrary, in vain.

English had to serve as his main interest; fellow students remembered how he memorized the great poets, and how he would recite Keats's "Ode to a Nightingale" in the hallways. Sports also crept more and more into his purview, both as an athlete and writing for the school paper, the *Ledger*, where he became sports editor and penned a column entitled "Speaking of Sports." All this was pretty much based on his own word—archival material, yearbooks, the *Ledger*, and the like perished; none exists prior to 1942 today (the school itself closed in the eighties), and all his teachers and likely his classmates are now gone. Not to worry, though. The blanks about Howard Cosell's academic and athletic strides achievements were through the years filled in by . . . Howard Cosell.

The athletic record he wrote for himself is particularly savory. For example, he wrote in *Like It Is,* "Year in and year out, P.S. 9 had held the PSAL track and field championship of New York City. I, myself, had finished second in the city championship meet in the standing broad-jump"—his wife, Emmy, he added, "still has the silver medal" from the event. He also told of the Hamilton football coach, one Tony Bove, being so impressed with his work covering the team in the high school paper that this Bove sent him a note reading: "You may be doing this the rest of your life." And that the 1936 yearbook carried the prediction "He'll be a reporter for the Brooklyn Dodgers."[15] These chestnuts may be accurate;

only the long-deconstructed walls of the school would know. But one thing that would become clear about this kid named Howard Cohen was that he could *embellish*.

BEYOND ARGUMENT, he was the neighborhood version of a Renaissance Kid, soaking up the diverse milieu of Brooklyn—its movie houses, candy shops with freely flowing egg creams, verdant parks, and, just a short hop on the elevated subway westward, Ebbets Field, where if he couldn't afford a ticket in the bleachers he would be content haunting Bedford Avenue, trying to find a knothole to peer through. There were also the crowded vaudeville theaters such as the Loew's Metropolitan, Loew's Kings, RKO Albee, Brooklyn Paramount, and in 1928 the Brooklyn Fox. On these boards he would see Jack Benny, Eddie Cantor, and Jack Oakie, gushing years later, "What shows we saw!"

Yet to hear him tell it in later years, those formative years were rough and tumble. Nearly by the day, he would claim, he was constantly tangling with gangs of Irish bullies. Those were years, he would say, when the "age of Hitler hovered over anyone who was Jewish," even in Brooklyn, and on any given day he would be "fighting a group of Studs Lonigans and running away from them, to get to school safely." As he would "climb a back fence and run because the kids from St. Theresa's parish were after me," his ears would be burning with anti-Semitic epithets— "sheeny," "kike," "Jesus killer," "prick cutter."[16]

He told the same stories with such relish that victimization became part of his character, as did an I'll-show-you sense of mission—as well as a rare admission in one recollection of those street scrapes, when he practically defined himself by telling *Esquire* in 1972: "I think these things create insecurities in you that live forever, and your drive to offset them is a drive to accumulate economic security."[17]

But it was those insecurities that he preferred to drown out with bombast—and hyperbole. For instance, he would shamelessly link his mundane travails of youth with far more profound bigotry. Mickey Herskowitz, the now retired *Houston Chronicle* sports columnist whom he chose to coauthor *Cosell*—to the writer's regret—recalled that "Howard felt in a personal way that he had gone through a little bit of what Jackie Robinson had. I believe he had the sense of proportion not to equate them, but it shaped his belief as a future journalist and a person."[18]

Actually the analogy made little sense, other than that with Howard Cohen, as with Howard Cosell, everything he did, and evangelized about, was all about overcoming persecution, religious, intellectual, cultural, economic, whatever. However, his greatest persecutor wasn't the gangs he ran from. That was simply the one he could speak of the easiest. A far greater hurdle was something he could never run from, no matter how far and how long the years took him from it.

That stain was closer to home. In fact, it was *in* his home.

ONE CAN decipher between the lines of Cosell's carefully clipped recollections of childhood that Howard William Cohen would morph into Howard Cosell with a good amount of disgust and shame about his mother and father. As much as he tried to shield that reality, by turning his life in Brooklyn into a cliché of finding his way through a Depression-clobbered badlands, he couldn't help but tell a more intense, personal narrative, with a tone of scorn, resentment, and enduring pain.

First, there was the delicate matter of his Judaism, the cause of so much angst later in his life. On its face his maturation recalls something of a *Jazz Singer* dynamic, such was the culture clash that went on within the Cohen family. In fact, this must have occurred to the man who went through life as Howard Cosell, who when he was cast as an unlikely Ed Sullivan as host of a seriously ill-conceived TV variety show in 1975, one episode featured a skit called "Howard's Bar Mitzvah." In it, on the day he became a man, he crushes his parents' will to live when he tells them he wants to be a sports color man. That was something like art imitating life.

Further underlining that theme is that Izzy adhered to his ancestors' old-world rule that the family must keep a kosher home, and that Nellie's father was a rabbi. But the story becomes much more tangled and contradictory because in truth Izzy's religious commitment had lapsed by the time his sons were born, and he would not return to it, too busy was he with trying to keep his head above water during the Depression. And so while Nellie's father gave young Jewish boys tutorials in their Bar Mitz-vahs, his own grandsons were not among them.

All Cosell ever had to say about it was that he had not been "formally reared" as a Jew, "not even Bar Mitzvahed."[19] Amazingly for a proverbial mouth that roared, he seemed not to know what else he could say on this subject, not even whether he regretted his forgoing of the ceremony. Even when he would "rediscover" his faith years later, he found no rea-son to close the circle by arranging for himself a symbolic, belated Bar Mitzvah, though he was not beyond using that holy ritual of manhood to underscore his religion in a bad TV skit. Something about his diffidence makes one wonder if he believed it was up to Izzy to see to it that he went through the proper rituals of his faith, and thus any inner conflict about religion was his father's fault.

If so, it wasn't the only thing for which he blamed Izzy. There is indeed much ugliness about the early years of his life. While he didn't belabor the point, it is clear that he almost never saw Izzy, who was on the road endlessly, as much as eleven months a year. It was as if he didn't even *have* a father, and the strains of that loss were surely pulverizing to his psyche. After all, he *needed* someone to protect him from the street gangs, someone to toss a ball around with and kibitz with about the Dodgers. All he really had to do that was his brother, who being older had his own circle of friends. Howard Cosell would in future years relate how he stood at his window for hours, peering out aimlessly into the darkness.

When Izzy did appear through that blank window, his youngest boy would feel elated. One cannot today read Cosell's recollections of child-hood without feeling the self-pity about being denied a full-time father; the moments he did share with Izzy lingered as warm, fleeting breaks in a long, cold winter of childhood. To *Cosmopolitan* in 1974, he peeled back time, saying, "Every Sunday when we were kids he'd get out his violin to play Victor Herbert songs like 'My Hero,' and my mother would yell, '*Stop* it already!'"[20]

He also recalled that "he'd take us rowing in Prospect Park." Because of Izzy's fervent belief in Franklin Delano Roosevelt, Howard, preco-cious child that he was, became arguably the youngest New Deal fanatic, and a Democrat for life. In sum, he could distill the experience of being Izzy and Nellie's son and present a broad framework in which his parents, as he told *Cosmo*, "gave us a sense of values, of morals, and it sank in. Dad was a beautiful guy . . . a good guy." But clearly not, in his eyes, something like "'my hero."

As liberal politically as Howard Cosell was, he was as conservative as a man could be later in bringing up two daughters—and that was directly traceable to Izzy, in ways both good and bad. Good because he was so strict, demanding that his sons bring home A's on their report cards and insisting that they had no choice but to turn themselves into good professional men. Howard Cohen made him that promise, and he would not go back on it, even if Izzy was less than the best role model in the world—that was the bad part, causing his son to grow up and away from him so as not to be like him as a father, though Howard too, because of the nature of his job, would not be there enough for his two daughters. But his *presence* would always be there, in the love he professed to them and the rules he imposed on them.

Nellie had much to do with his strictness as well. Oddly, but perhaps tellingly, in *Cosell* he dispensed with her rather quickly, and less fondly than he did Izzy. As if realizing this many years too late, he self-consciously ladled praise on her as a saint in *Like It Is*. This is not to say he did not love and adore his Yiddishe mama, as all good Jewish boys supposedly do, but his original memories of her dealt mainly with how she caused him neurosis; he wrote in *Cosell*, "I am a hypochondriac today, no doubt, because my mother, for as long as I can remember, was either sick, on the verge of being sick or thinking about being sick." Indeed, years later, Emmy Cosell would remark that her husband had "spells of borderline hypochondria. He had a rash, a nervous eczema, but a marvelous dermatologist cured him."[21]

Not for public consumption was that the marriage of Izzy and Nellie Cohen was cleaved by infidelity—*her* infidelity.

It was one of the many things they fought about, along with money and Izzy spending more time with his parents than with his own wife and kids. The young Howard overheard their battles through the apartment's paper-thin walls, their brutal savaging of each other carving deep psychological scars. The worst was that Nellie, unable to stand being alone so many long, lonely nights, took up with other men, whom Howard would see from the window dropping her off at the front door. However Izzy found out, either because Nellie 'fessed up or his boys spilled the beans, he and Nellie would have it out. In time, it became almost a ritual.

Cosell kept on the periphery the darker details of his childhood family life, yet in one rare, fleeting moment, he told the *Saturday Evening Post* in 1974 that the ironfisted discipline he imposed on his own household was a way of overcompensation. "My family is everything in my life," he said. "This is probably psychological as much as pure love. I'm sure my view on deep family ties is predicated on the fact that my parents' marriage wasn't particularly good. I was determined that mine would be." Another time, he said: "The family, as far as I'm concerned, is the whole bag. I've never lost my own sense of family. It's all I've ever cared about. And no, sports teams are *not* families. They're bunches of loosely strung individuals at odds with each other, with very little paternal guidance." Adding one more element, Hilton Cosell would say that Izzy being away so much "was a big reason Howard and I are both so attached to our wives. Our own parents didn't have such a great marriage."[22]

The upshot was that, until death took Emmy from him after nearly a half century, there was undeniably pure love between them, but also very nearly a psychological codependency that necessitated them *having* to stick together. As had Izzy and Nellie, who despite all the ugliness stuck it out to the bitter end, until Izzy's death in 1957, albeit not with anything resembling pure love. Not that their vow to stay together impressed their younger son. In his memoirs, their union he damned with faint praise, writing: "My mother and dad didn't have the best marriage in the world. Not the worst, either, for when people suffer together something does develop between them, and there was a bond, a reliance."[23]

He would never allow his own marriage to descend to the level of faint praise, though there would be times when he would put Emmy through hell. As he wrote in *Like It Is*, "When I would hear and see my parents quarrel I would cringe. I made a vow, then and there, that when I married, my children would never witness an argument between my wife and me. That has turned out to be the case almost, not quite, but almost."[24]

For his daughters he would allow little slack to come and go as they pleased. "Howard is the disciplinarian," Emmy admitted in 1975, "and I felt that sometimes he was unreasonable. He insisted, absolutely insisted, that the girls get excellent marks in school. I had to keep explaining to him that you can't make a law about things like that. You may even create such tensions that you produce bad marks."[25]

High marks they'd get, and while the girls would have their own problems being the daughters of Howard Cosell, they would never waver in nor apologize for their devotion to him, even long after he was in his grave. That was something he never could muster for Izzy or Nellie. Indeed, according to his elder daughter, Jill, there was a moment of hard and heartbreaking truth when Emmy once asked him why he had to be so overly strict with the girls. Sadness came into his eyes and his voice.

"I'll tell you about my mother," said Howard Cosell.[26]

CRISES IN the Cohen household were many. Hilton, for example, contracted tuberculosis as a teenager, not only a serious illness then but one that families tried to hide, stigma that it was. For months he lay on his back, rising only to be taken to the doctor for treatment, which involved, gruesomely, having his lung collapsed, then reinflated. But what hurt more for both of the Cohen brothers was that their father wasn't around for the events, good and bad, of their lives. For that, Howard Cosell would neither forgive nor forget.

Recalling his father in conversation and in the print of *Cosell* in the coming years, there would always be an awkward ambivalence in his words. He would dutifully issue props that Izzy, for all his absences, acted in his son's best interests, doing all he could to keep him on a straight path. "I remember my dad going to the bank every three months to renew the loan that sent me through college and law school," he wrote in *Cosell*. But such praise seemed grudging and perfunctory, and would be countermanded by other recitals of an Izzy failing to provide for his wife and children. The Depression, he said, was "difficult for my dad. I remember the electricity being turned off in our house for nonpayment of rent and my dad fighting with the janitor to try and get it turned back on."[27]

Such examples of misfortune he turned into a homily; that "growing up this way, with all of the insecurities attendant to it, you develop a drive or you simply cease to exist . . . That is your quest. You don't *ever* want to have happen to you what you have seen happening in your home."[28] There is an undertow of remonstrance in that passage, aimed at a home he came to loathe. The implication was that he made it on his own because he was different—*better*—than Isidore Martin Cohen.

Through the decades inestimable pairs of ears would have no choice but to hear his tales of tarnished youth. One was the now venerable and waggish sports columnist Jerry Izenberg, who began a long personal and professional kinship with him in the late fifties when Izenberg was a young sportswriter at the *Newark Star-Ledger*.

"I don't know how many times he subjected me to the stories about that there was no electricity in the house, they couldn't pay the rent, Jewish ghetto, yada yada," Izenberg says, echoing Frank Deford. "I'm not saying it wasn't like that. I didn't know how poor they were, how they had a house or how he was able to go to a big-time college under those circumstances, which didn't seem entirely logical. But it was as if Howard believed he was the only one who could have suffered like that. His life had to be the worst. He had to have come the farthest, beaten the longest odds. The father was always tied in to these poverty stories, and he was very harsh about it. Howard did not say nice things about his father to me, that's what stood out."[29]

Buried within those reproving words were the clues to what took him beyond Brooklyn—the promise of being a better man than Izzy Cohen.

# 2

---

# AN OBVIOUS MAVERICK

DESPITE THE tensions between them, Howard Cohen matured into young manhood just as the prodigal father had dictated he must, to the point of seeming like a savant, scaling summits previous Cohen men could not have dreamed of. While Hilton followed in Izzy's footsteps and cast his lot in life as an accountant, getting a degree attending night classes, his kid brother accumulated sky-high grades at Alexander Hamilton High and was quickly accepted by New York University in 1936. For Hilton, the divergence between them, which would grow wide as a continent, caused some understandable envy fueled by his own wistful fancies lost in time.

"Listen, my brother's a fine young man," he would say when neither was young anymore. "I wish for him what he has, which is what he wants to do in this world. He got to go to day college, at NYU; I had to go to night college, at St. John's, because it was the Depression. I wanted to be a doctor, do medical research. But I don't begrudge Howard. He's brilliant, and he always was."[1]

The gifted one—one might even say the chosen one—advanced beyond his brother only because Izzy had scraped together every penny he could so that the brainier of his two sons could achieve more than anyone in his lineage had. To Izzy, this was a nonnegotiable demand, and even if he couldn't always keep the lights on at home, he would put up his home as collateral to send his boy to a top school. For that, Howard Cosell would be grateful, but it meant following the path Izzy charted for him, something he was ambivalent about.

That feeling became more acute after, to his great relief, he was out of Brooklyn and on the NYU campus in the Fordham section of the Bronx known as "the Heights." He majored in English literature, his beloved area of expertise, and within two years had compiled sixty-six credits (though with a rather mediocre grade average of 77), enough for him to make a decisive decision. At the time, a student with sufficient credits could leapfrog from a bachelor of arts curriculum into what was called a bachelor of laws at the NYU Law School, a kind of abbreviated but perfectly accredited law degree earned in the four-year undergraduate tenure.

The decision to go for a bachelor of laws was not his—it was Izzy's. Howard had never thought about law as a career—and would say he didn't want one—but his English lit degree had no place in Izzy's blueprint for him as a professional man. As he saw it, he had only two choices, law and medicine, which meant there was no choice: With his preternatural gift of gab and grasp of the language—not to mention the art of overstatement—his future had to be in the courtroom. Not overly thrilled about the whole thing, he nonetheless threw himself headlong into his studies, on the premise that, as he wrote later somewhat grudgingly, "I owed it to my dad, because of everything he had done for me."[2]

He would rack up a remarkable academic career. Already, he had been accepted into the Pi Lambda Phi fraternity, which was founded at Yale in 1895 and previously had as a member the great composer Oscar Hammerstein. He was quite a sight, too. While he was still up in the Heights, his visage graced the 1936 and 1937 editions of the school's yearbook, *The Violet*, in Pi Lambda Phi group pictures, in each one standing slim and ramrod straight in a dark suit, ears sticking out like jug handles, hair piled high on his head, looking haughty and almost grim. If there was a word that could best describe him, it might have been arrogant.

At NYU Law, a four-story brick building with a circular courtyard on the southern edge of Washington Square Park in Greenwich Village, he flourished. Haunting the law library until late evening most days and bowling over his professors, he was taken onto the editorial staff of the prestigious *NYU Law Review* in his final year, 1940. How much *that* further inflated his already swollen ego can be imagined; one way to judge was how high his pronounced proboscis was stuck in the air. Another was that in the future his admirable credentials would not seem quite enough. For years his ABC biographical sheet included the claim that he had been "elected to Phi Beta Kappa" and that he "edited" the law review. Both of these claims made their way into *Who's Who*.

But they are tenuous, at best. In 1978, when Cosell conducted a standing-room-only course at NYU called "Big-Time Sports in Contemporary America," the university archivist, Dr. Bayrd Still, issued a letter clarifying his academic credentials, writing that he had "found no indication of Cosell's election" to Phi Beta Kappa; neither was there any record in the honor society's national office to that effect. As for his role at the law review, technically he *was* an editor, but a lesser one than he made it seem. In the 1939–40 review, the student editorial board masthead lists him only as "Notes Editor," an impressive title but one that had him writing boilerplate reviews of court decisions about such issues as "Agricultural Marketing Agreement Act—Milk Regulation" and "Collective Bargaining Agreements as a Bar to Proceedings Before the National Labor Relations Board"—the latter topic, labor law, being one in which he had become expert. A sample of his writing from the latter summary reads like this:

> To completely envisage the power and scope of the Board's actions, it is necessary to determine the nature of contracts involved in labor problems, the experience in view of which the powers of the Board were granted, and the implied limitations impressed upon the Board by the Act.[3]

Someday, this lawyerly—or, less kindly, torturous—elocution, delivered with a hammy Barrymore-like flair, would find its way into the lexicon of sports broadcasting, both when Howard Cosell was being gravely serious and when he was executing a lighthearted self-parody. And, somehow, it would work either way.

WITH HIS degree in tow, the next step was passing the New York State bar exam. In the narratives presented by Cosell, it happened at the tender age of twenty-one, although the records show differently, that he was still in school from March 25, 1939, to March 25, 1940. Dated even later is the NYU commencement program from June 5, 1940, which meant he got his bachelor of laws when he was twenty-two. Only then, after a prominent NYU alumnus recommended him to a Brooklyn law firm, did he begin his career—as a ten-dollar-a-week clerk.

Even more humbling, he would have to go back to Brooklyn and live at home for a while. But if he owed his degree and lodging to his father's largesse, at least he held his future in his own hands. And, as if to underscore the point, when he set out on his own, it was with a new name. On December 11, 1940, only six months out of school, he went into the Appellate Division of the New York Superior Court in Brooklyn and came out having legally traded Cohen for the surname that would become so inordinately famous. Indeed, in retrospect, though it is possible, it seems implausible that Howard Cohen would have been so transcendent a personality. Fate has a way of delegating unique men with unique brands.

And, who knows, maybe he had an inkling of such matters when with the stroke of a pen he instantly became sui generis, even if he was just a lowly law clerk. In the eponymous memoir that proved his last name was so famous it was the only word needed as its title, he breezed past the subject, writing that the change was made solely to appease his family once more. Specifically, it was Harris Cohen, the aging patriarch of the clan, who made the entreaty of his grandsons by way of honoring their forebears' totemic heritage. The elder grandson was the first to comply, legally becoming Hilton Cosell when he turned twenty. It happened, he said years later, not out of any deeply held conviction but because when he was an accountant in a firm with scads of people named Cohen, Harris had a suggestion.

"Listen," he told him, "Cohen means priest, and we're not priests. Our name should be Cosell."[4]

Thus it was done, with no small irony. Cosell actually sounded less Jewish than Cohen—the latter a profound term in canonical Judaism, derived from *kohen,* or a Jew descended from the biblical Aaron, brother of Moses, and a dynastic thread of the Jewish Levitical tribe dating all the way back to the Tabernacle. But, in the long lens of history, no single act perhaps was more crucial for Howard than this new name tag, even if he, like his brother, had no real commitment to sanctify his primal stock. As it also happened, sounding less Jewish was an option for many like him seeking to secure jobs in a culture cleaved by the uniquely American dichotomy in which its moneyed, ownership class, in large part comprised of Jews, perched atop working-class managers who were freely hostile to Jews in hiring practices. A career in show business almost seemed to mandate a rechristening, it supposedly not being wise to try to make it in the movies or on the radio with the albatross of an ethnic name—even with names like Mayer, Goldwyn, Zukor, Selznick, and Sarnoff at the top of the credits. Lesser mortals, not just actors but screenwriters, were more likely to hide their birthright, one example being Nathanael West (*The Day of the Locust*), born Nathan von Wallenstein Weinstein.

Such a disconnect may not have existed in Howard Cosell's chosen (or nonchosen) field, which was crawling with stereotypical "Jewish lawyers," but if he ever did live out his youthful chimera of becoming a sports broadcaster, well, as they would say in the old neighborhood, it couldn't hurt. In any event, if there was anything about the act that somehow observed the cultural and religious traditions of the family tree, Cosell left it to others to posit such an assumption—and, as it would happen, others did, mainly rival sportswriters who should have known better, and perhaps did but didn't care, than to suggest that he had turned his back on his own religion and heritage.

He was too agnostic to have bothered himself with the religious implications of swapping old and new family identities. But he was indeed turning his back on something—or rather some*one.* As it happened, Isidore Cohen did not similarly reclaim the name he was actually born with, his assigned name already having been too familiar to his longtime clients. Or maybe it was that he simply couldn't care less. But neither did Harris Cohen revert to the name he had carried for his first three decades, believing that at his age such a gesture was without great significance. Whatever the case, their resistance may have been precisely *why* Howard Cohen was so eager to make the alteration, knowing he would go through adulthood symbolically—and, as the years lengthened, literally—estranged from his family and its myriad of torments. When he would begin testifying to Izzy's failings, it was almost as if he were speaking of a stranger. Distance, after all, had been what Izzy had given *him*. Now it was his turn.

AT TWENTY, Howard Cosell was a confident, smoothly eloquent fledgling with a hint of patrician disdain. He was no Douglas Fairbanks, that was for sure. But neither was he plebeian. Tall and bare-boned, he was all arms and legs, and when he would catch his posture slumping, he would recoil into a rigid stiffness. With his full head of black hair slicked back in a pompadour, he seemed to know he looked more handsome with a grim look in his eye than he did when he would smile, something that cast a goofy pall over his curious features. He was similarly self-conscious about his nasal Brooklyn twang, preferring to intone his fifty-cent words in a lower register rather than risking sounding like a shrill, high-pitched duck. That also suited his lawyer's sense of pretension, which grew exponentially when he passed the bar.

He was already in the process of sending out letters offering himself for employment at some of the city's larger law offices, and had honed his self-promoting strategies, when his plans, along with those of the rest of the world, were interrupted on December 7, 1941. On that grim Sunday, when the American navy lay smoldering at Pearl Harbor and people everywhere felt suddenly small and vulnerable, he had to consider how he would serve as a military man, a guise in which he could never have imagined himself. The first thing he did, in February 1942, was swallow hard, march down to the army induction center, and enlist—as Howard Cohen, holding off on using his new surname until after the war.

While he could have been shunted to boot camp, then shipped out to destinations in North Africa or the South Pacific, his big ears sticking out from under a combat helmet, the brass saw something in him that could bolster administrative work on the home front, and he was stationed at the New York Port of Embarkation, an enormous complex of shipping terminals in Brooklyn through which troops would be routed onto transport ships and cargo onto supply vessels headed to Europe. The task was massive and demanding, and in the early days of the war it demanded men with sharp, organized minds to make order out of what seemed like a chaotic rumpus of activity and movement.

The young, officious lawyer had that kind of acumen. And he found himself in a remarkable sinecure, able to help the fight to make the world safe for democracy by commuting on the subway each weekday only a few miles from Eastern Parkway to the port. Izzy and Nellie were thrilled that he was never going to see combat in a foreign land, or see *any* land beyond the border of Brooklyn. What's more, to even his own amazement, he was pegged by his superiors as officer material; by 1943 he had already been promoted to technical sergeant, then offered entrance into Officer Candidate School, which he accepted against the wishes of his parents, who feared he'd have to serve overseas leading men on the battlefield.

They need not have worried. The only time he strayed from Brooklyn was when he was sent to a transportation school at Mississippi State College, part of the OCS process that led to him being commissioned a major in 1943 at age twenty-five, one of the youngest men to ever hold the rank—and solely in charge of sorting out the marching orders of fifty thousand men. The pressures were great on a young man, and greater still the implications of making decisions that would directly affect who would live and who would die in battle. Yet few who knew him, or knew of him, sympathized; to most, the young major had it soft, was lucky, privileged, and he couldn't help but feel a little guilty himself. He would recall decades later, "I well remember how the Minsky widow (her husband had been the burlesque king) couldn't stand the sight of me coming home every day, first with a gold bar, now with a silver, now two silver bars, now a gold leaf. I could understand this. She had a son serving in the Marines on Guadalcanal."[5]

In fact, even the Pentagon was somewhat wary about how fast he was being moved up in rank. Twice the generals proscribed his promotion. They relented only when the port commander, Major General Homer M. Groninger, dashed off a six-page letter calling Howard Cohen pivotal to the U.S. home-front war. Major Cohen would remain at the port long after V-E and V-J days, it being just as important to get the troops home as it was to get them abroad. And the grateful General Groninger would have to intervene on his behalf again, on another matter that would affect his future, his long-term future, it would turn out.

It happened as the result of a plotline straight from a wartime romance movie, which began in 1942 when then-Lieutenant Cohen met a WAC sergeant named Mary Edith Abrams, the secretary of another major on the base, who allowed Howard to call her by the nickname she answered to when used by family and friends—"Emmy." While nobody's idea of a pinup like Betty Grable—he would one day dewily recall her as "a cute, pudgy blonde"—on a base with only two hundred women among four thousand soldiers, she caused Cosell to do a double take, sending him into an imitation of a barking bulldog ordering men about trying to impress her. But when he addressed her, he became tongue-tied, prompting a twinkle in her eye, he insisted in later tellings of the story. Recognizing that she was interested, as he put it, he longed to take her out.

It seemed not to matter that she had a fiancé who was stationed overseas and to whom she was writing every day. She was surprised herself that she felt something for the barking major, whom she would describe many years later as "very outspoken, very forceful, very 'on.' He was an obvious maverick, and I was very attracted to his self-confidence. Of course, there was also a sexual attraction. On both sides."[6]

As for the major, he would recall, as lovesick in the seventies as he was in the forties, "I fell in love with her as soon as I met her, and we still do love each other. I don't see what else there is to life. All the rest is, to use the vulgarity, bullshit. She is a startlingly balanced woman without whose leverage and support I couldn't have existed." As Emmy put it, "Howard relies on me. That's the main thing I'm supposed to have on hand at all times."[7]

The problem in lighting the spark was that army rules enjoined officers from fraternizing with the enlisted subclass. But Lieutenant Cohen, as was already clear, was not one to take no for an answer. Circumnavigating the rules, he appealed to his influential patron, General Groninger—who at war's end would succeed General Dwight Eisenhower as commander of the American occupation zone in Germany—to pen another missive to the Pentagon, asking for a waiver so that his indispensable Brooklyn major could take a blonde sergeant to a Chinese restaurant.

If not love at first sight, it was at least a mutual magnetic pull, based on the laws of polarity. Unmistakably, Emmy Abrams was quite nearly the exact opposite of Howard Cohen/Cosell, and apparently this was a desideratum for either of them to begin a romantic chapter. "Emmy once told me," says Frank Deford, "that she had never grown up with any Jews. If she had, they would have been entirely different Jews on the Mainline of Philadelphia than the loudmouthed one from Brooklyn. And Howard, I guarantee you, didn't know any Presbyterians. How they fell in love is a mystery. It's just beyond me how they did it. But I'll tell you, it was one of the great love stories of all time. They adored each other."[8]

Their daughter Hilary put it this way: "It's very simple. My father can't function without my mother. Of course, in contrast to him, everybody has made her out to be a madonna, which just isn't true. She's a very tough lady—very bright, but with a cynical, sarcastic streak," which matched his own.[9]

Given his filial dysfunction, Cosell may have been primed for someone whose family reminded him of anything but his own. Not that she wasn't much like him in one important respect—she too possessed a steely will and a pouty condescension for people she didn't respect or trust. In that way, Howard knew he had found not just a girl but a retainer who would commiserate with his peeves and defend him against his enemies. Even so, and this was a revelation to him, she was also a *match* for him, in that she had a way of putting *him* in his place, able to shut him up with one cross look of her steel blue eyes. When that happened, he would lay down his arms in complete and unconditional surrender, loving every minute of being relieved of the need to bare fangs all the time.

The potential stumbling block was their religions, since she was a classic shiksa, the product of an eastern Pennsylvania WASP family. Her father, Norman Ross Abrams, was an executive at Congoleum-Nairn, which cornered the market on linoleum and vinyl floor coverings; her uncle a top cat at Weston Precision Instruments; her cousin chairman of the board of Standard Oil. In Howard Cosell's chosen phrase, Norman Ross was "an Old World Republican," which may explain why a decade later, after ascending to executive vice president at Congoleum, he would be appointed deputy postmaster general in the Eisenhower administration. It also may have been a coded euphemism for "anti-Semite," given that Norman, himself a lieutenant in World War I, couldn't abide Howard Cohen, even with that gold maple leaf he earned on his shoulder.

For a man so sensitive to "every restrictive boundary and every thoughtless slight," there was only one conclusion: "Norman just didn't want me in the family."[10] It wasn't just what Norman said—or, more accurately, didn't say, since he usually would engage him with a cold stare—it was that he gave no reason for being so contemptuous of him. That of course promulgated the assumption that the "Old World Republican" was tortured not only because his daughter was about to be taken from him—indeed, after only mere weeks, Howard had proposed to Emmy, and she had said yes, writing a Dear John letter to her no doubt shocked fiancé overseas—but taken by a Brooklyn Jew.

If he did not write that for the world to read, he confided it, bluntly, as if he *needed* to, in more private moments. One of his confidants would be Jerry Izenberg, during the long hours they spent together. "Howard would tell me about the father-in-law, that there was great abrasiveness between them," he says. "One day he started talking about how the old man felt about him, he said, 'Yeah, his daughter married the Jew and she really did badly.' It was obvious there was something there, something deep. He went out of his way to make the point, and the way he used the word *Jew*, it was quite unsettling. Then he said, 'I showed him.' That was the happiest I ever saw him."[11]

To be sure, interfaith marriage was still not common then, and was opposed with equal virulence by Jews and Christians—which is why Izzy and Nellie were just as upset about their son's marriage plans. The prime fear was that the children of such unions would further distill the oneness of religious blood bonds. For his part, Norman Abrams's exclusionary instincts were passed down from *his* ancestral roots, the hidebound Pennsylvania Dutch community, and his disapprobation was so rigid that Howard Cohen could only assume it stretched way beyond his new son-in-law, to his origin, to his parents, to *Brooklyn*.

For that, Howard both detested and appreciated Norman Abrams. Detested because Abrams's bigotry reminded him so much why he was so sensitive to bigotry, and where he had come from. Trenchant indeed was a Jill Cosell observation about her father's background, that "his whole life, Daddy felt like a poor Jewish boy."[12] Yet that was precisely why he could be grateful—because beating people like Norman Abrams could lead him to believe he was invincible, and *better* than any garden variety bigot. It would be why he never would feel he needed to address, much less confront, anti-Semitism with anyone he believed practiced it—a list of people that would grow long indeed. His younger daughter, Hilary, watching him give a pass to more than one troglodytic Jew hater through the years, construed that as proof he was "naive" about the issue—something hard to fathom for a man who attacked racism head-on. But racism he could deal with from afar, with empirical detachment instead of emotion. The extent of his Jewishness removed objectivity; it made him confront *himself*, and that was the hardest thing he could ever do.


THERE IS a curious passage in *Cosell* in which he seems to account for this dichotomy. With typical name-dropping aplomb, he wrote of spending a postwar weekend in Philadelphia with Stanley Kramer, another recently discharged soldier who had spent the war in an army film unit and was a fraternity brother from his college days at NYU. The future Oscar-winning director-producer at the time was still two years from making his first movie. Cosell recalled Kramer, who had planned to go to NYU Law School but chose instead to go after bigger dreams, as saying, "I'm gonna make movies. I can make them cheaper and better than anybody in Hollywood." While they watched the NYU basketball team beat Temple at Convention Hall, Kramer said he was torn between making a movie adaptation of either the Arthur Laurents play *Home of the Brave*, which had a brief run on Broadway in the winter of 1945–46, or Arthur Miller's first novel, *Focus*. Both were seminal works dealing unflinchingly with anti-Semitism, experienced in ways familiar to Cosell, in the former by a soldier, in the latter by the protagonist, Lawrence Newman, a Brooklyn man of English descent who, taken for a Jew because of stereotypical eyeglasses, is bitten hard by bigotry he hadn't conceived existed.

Cosell recalled telling Kramer he thought *Focus* was the better bet. "No way!" the would-be director retorted. "They've already made *Gentleman's Agreement*." He went on to say that he saw in *Home of the Brave* a useful allegory of anti-Semitism, with a crucial alteration. "I'll make the Jewish boy black and I'm gonna deal with the great problem of America to come. The black problem."[13]

That would be just what Kramer did, producing *Home of the Brave* in 1949 as a brilliant psychological drama that won raves and engendered huge ticket sales. And, just as a germ of an idea, it had a profound effect on Howard Cosell. That day in Philly, he came away convinced by Stanley Kramer that racism was a more urgent societal sore than anti-Semitism. Having not encountered many blacks in Brooklyn or within a segregated military pool, he was led by the epiphany to become decidedly attentive to "the black problem," perhaps blunting his sensitivity to "the Jewish problem," or at least his willingness to confront it for fear he might offend the offender—the very hedge that his daughter Jill meant when she said he was "naive" about the problem. In his writings and in interviews, he never would expand about any of this, but the Kramer meeting would seem to be a signal event in his life.

Establishing the chain and the priority that would remain in his perspective, he wrote in *Cosell*: "The 'Jewish Problem' was the major social trauma in this country up to and through World War II. And then it was supplanted by the 'Black Problem.'"[14]

Not that the stain of anti-Semitism would ever recede, nor ever be something he would refrain from ascribing to any number of slights, perceived or misperceived. In his memoirs he told the allegorical tale of how, when he was a major, he was in a restaurant a table away from a bully who used to torment him on the streets, who was now a private. He recalled that he began to consciously fear that the man was going to "come at me," an absurd notion given the difference in their ranks. "But it all ran through me," he wrote, meaning the fears he had grown up with, and "I won't ever forget it."[15]

Anti-Semitism, then, was something close to a phobia. But race would be his cause, his crusade, his sine qua non. Just like Jackie Robinson.


INCIDENTALLY, BUT significantly, the colloquy with Stanley Kramer also provoked in him a certain envy for what Kramer was making of himself, and the crowd he was running in—just making learned small talk about people like Laurents and Miller made him feel he had a place in the new breed of postwar thinkers and trendsetters. He could not help but feel angst that he too could be righting great societal wrongs by bringing to bear his keen powers of perspicacity and persuasion, and of course his voice. Again, all one needed to do for confirmation of these qualities, even then, was to ask him. But he was neither a writer nor a director or a producer. He was a lawyer with the style of a grand inquisitor. He loved literature, of course, but his thing was the poets, his talent florid pontification, his most immediate passion sports. So how in the wide world of postwar American culture was he going to make his voice heard? That was the question.


ONCE EMMY took him up on the marriage, he tried endlessly, but fruitlessly, to come to an accommodation with Norman Abrams. The failure to do that hurt. But at least he had a devoted wife perennially on his side, bringing him serenity in a way few others had or would. She was a pip, for sure. For all of her father's hectoring and scolding, she refused to call it off with the big-eared officer. And he was positively enthralled that this was a sign that Emmy too recoiled from her own family, which while upper class in wealth was just as replete with tensions and lack of communication; as was Howard, Emmy was supposed to do as her autocratic father told her, one example being her enlistment in the army. Having known few Jews, and growing up with her father who painted them as money-grubbing Christ killers, when she met one with no money and a poor family in Brooklyn, he seemed irresistible.

Not really knowing if she was infatuated with him or his world, it was nonconformity as much as pure love that drove them to the altar, the trip made faster because of the static of both sets of parents. Certainly, Izzy had earned no credibility with his hypocritical stand on Jewish conformity, not having bothered to take back the name appended to his heritage. All things considered, neither had he earned the right to pontificate about marriage, on any level. When it came to matters of heart and faith, Howard deemed Izzy an unworthy advisor. And for Nellie, he had only cold defiance. As Jill Cosell tells it, "My grandmother said she was going to kill herself if they married. He said, 'Go ahead, Mother, because I'm going to marry her.'"[16]

The ceremony duly took place on June 23, 1944, a balmy summer evening, before the pastor at the Prospect Presbyterian Church in Maplewood, New Jersey, where she had lived with her parents. The venue was a concession on his part that her religious affiliation was stronger than his, and more important to her given that her parents wouldn't be there unless she married with the sacraments of a church service. Of course, it only further alienated Izzy and Nellie, who came fuming all the way from Brooklyn with their son, a feeling that did not dissipate even as Major Cohen, in his crisply pressed dress uniform, took his vows.

The timing was not optimal. It was barely two weeks since the Allies landed on the beaches of Normandy. The army was slogging through France, and the need for soldiers and supplies was at a peak, meaning that this time around no slack would be cut the major, who was denied leave for a honeymoon. Mr. and Mrs. Cohen—as it read on the certificate, raising the question of whether by some arcane interpretation of the law Emmy was ever technically Mrs. Howard Cosell—moved into a small one-bedroom flat in Brooklyn Heights, with a panoramic view of New York Harbor, where the Cohen clan had arrived half a century before.

It was the first time either of them had lived on their own, and that act of independence added to the storybook idyll that had happened so crazily fast. Fast? Only three months later, in September 1944, the industrious major and his WAC wife learned she was pregnant; on the first day of June in 1945, Emmy delivered Jill at Methodist Hospital in Brooklyn, where he had had his tonsils and adenoids removed when he was six. By Judaic tradition, they agreed that Jill would be raised in her mother's faith. That, of course, left Izzy and Nellie wondering if their son even considered himself a Jew at all anymore. He, on the other hand, thought nothing of it.

Having secured a leave, the new father two days later rewarded her hard labor the best way he knew how, by taking her to a game at Ebbets Field, leaving Jill with her grandmother Nellie. It was the first time she had ever been to a ballpark, and for her Dodger-loving husband, a must. If she wasn't in thrall to the alloyed smell of hot dogs and cigars and the roar of a fanatical crowd, she could tell how much *he* was. While she would long hence forget the minutiae of that game, he never would. Decades later, he meticulously recalled that Emmy watched Luis Olmo hit two home runs that day. She would only remember that she had paid for the tickets.

BARS ON his shoulder notwithstanding, Howard Cosell knew full well that Emmy was his biggest step up in rank. As good as he felt about having found her, however, nothing he could do, no matter what he could make of himself, would ever be good enough for his "other" father, which was all the more irritating given that, by now, Izzy and Nellie had made their peace with the shiksa daughter-in-law. As Hilton Cosell would recall, "Our father got to be nuts about Emmy. He'd go to see her and the kids the minute he'd come from off the road."[17]

When military service ended for Howard Cohen, he could take off his uniform and the bars, adopt the new surname he had held in abeyance for six years, don his blue suit, and go about finding work. Emmy stayed home tending to Jill, almost every day helped by a now doting Nellie Cohen and, when he was home, Izzy.

Howard Cosell meanwhile found no great demand for his services, and that left him incredulous, having come to expect that overseeing a workforce of sixty-five thousand men, and negotiating with unions such as the International Longshoremen's Association, would qualify him for an immediate civil management job. With money tight, the Cosells had to give up the apartment with a view and move in with Izzy and Nellie on Eastern Parkway. At least he could crow about one thing—finally being an "Eastern Parkway Jew," for what that was worth now.

Of course, this descent into the bowels of Brooklyn did nothing to make Norman Abrams any more accepting of his son-in-law. An Eastern Parkway Jew was still just a Jew to him, and in this case a poor Jew; nor was it palliative that Howard deferred to Emmy in bringing up Jill as a Presbyterian, once more displaying an agnosticism about Judaism beyond the birthright. His children, who would have scant freedom of choice when they lived under his roof, would be allowed, however, to determine their own religious affiliations as adults; intriguingly, the younger daughter, Hilary, would choose to become, in her own words, "a raving Zionist."[18]

But for Norman, none of this was pertinent. During the previous years he had hardly been cordial with Howard, but while the latter wore the uniform of his country there would at least be moments of uneasy patter between them. Once the uniform was put in mothballs, Abrams had nothing to say, even to his own daughter for a good two years. During that blackout, Mrs. Abrams had to sneak in and out of Brooklyn to visit her daughter and granddaughter, as such an act would have crossed the line into sedition. He would eventually yield, grudgingly, but for years his relationship with his daughter and son-in-law was, as Cosell put it, "coldly indifferent."[19]

That he could not easily charm the man he took as a failure. Indeed, Norman Ross Abrams was the kind of father figure Howard Cosell had yearned for; he once recalled Abrams as if with starry eyes, calling him "handsome, a fine golfer and tennis player," and "a hard daddy to reject."[20] He of course meant for Emmy to reject, but he might as well have been speaking about himself, because now there was a wall not just between himself and his father but his father-in-law, too. His salvation, however, was that he had Emmy.

Far down the line, as if still with love's first blush, he would regularly pay homage, swooning about the girl who became the woman who was, he would tell everyone, "my life." He would never stop saying things like that, as if he had to leave not the slightest doubt in anyone's mind.

As hyperbolic as valentines like this seemed, people who saw them together would swear it was so. And, that being so, they would give Emmy all the credit. It was no ordinary woman, after all, who would be able to stand Howard Cosell for fifty years.

THERE WAS one ephemeral moment right after the war when Howard Cosell thought he could merge his new identity with the fantasy he had never outgrown since the adolescent days when he'd sat in the Ebbets Field bleachers calling Dodger games. But he was not an impressionable kid any longer; he had grown up, as had radio, an industry that by the midforties was a multimillion-dollar corporate giant, even arguably a cartel, a four-headed, thousand-legged creature owned by CBS, RCA (NBC), the Mutual Broadcasting System, and, beginning in 1943, ABC, which was carved from a second NBC network called NBC Blue.

Like many thousands of others, Cosell's listening habits progressed from *Mary Noble: Backstage Wife*, *The Lone Ranger*, and freaky dramas like Orson Welles's *War of the Worlds* to real-life drama—he, like most of America, having been riveted to the radio when Ed Murrow, bombs falling perilously close, intoned into his CBS microphone, "This is London." That line punctuated the evolving sophistication of broadcast journalism. Now men like John Cameron Swayze, Doug Edwards, and Bob Trout, who had braved bullets to file radio reports from Guadalcanal, Iwo Jima, Normandy, and Bastogne, were household names, the first news "stars" in the information and entertainment combine, the genres unmistakably intertwined.

All this flux caught the fancy of the melodramatic, sentient Brooklyn lawyer. Indeed, as with Stanley Kramer, Cosell was envious of such men rewriting cultural assumptions by not shying away from harrowing truths. He wanted in.

He still believed he could do it somehow in sports, within which the old manicured pretense of Graham McNamee and Clem McCarthy had given way to the grit and gristle of Bill Stern, who came to NBC in 1937 to host *The Colgate Sports Newsreel* and Friday night boxing. Stern, who would soon have his own nightly show interviewing athletes and movie stars, broadcast the first televised sporting event—the second game of a baseball doubleheader between Princeton and Columbia at Baker Field on May 17, 1939—and was the first to do commentary on televised boxing bouts.

The problem, one of many, for Cosell was that he had zero experience in front of a mike. He did not lack for swagger, however. And when a few weeks after his discharge he heard that the local station WOR was holding auditions for an announcer to read news and sports, he applied. This was no small whimsy. The New York stations were the network flagships, and WOR, which headed the Mutual Network, had an enormous audience drawn by a lineup of music and homey talk, and a highly respected sports newscaster in Stan Lomax. But there he was, with Emmy and some of their friends lending support, at the auditions, standing in a long line of announcers with booming voices and impressive résumés waiting their turn to read a script for station executives.

When his came, he stepped up and began to read in a crisp and authoritative manner, only to be cut off in midsentence, then thanked and wished well as he was being shooed out the door. As he recalled, he and Emmy shared his hurt at being told he simply didn't have "an announcer's voice." Not that he didn't agree with that, given his "Brooklyn nasal twang." But that wasn't what he believed to be the *real* problem, which could have been summed up if he had called it "the Brooklyn *Jewish* nasal twang," which is what he held liable for the rejection, as his friends would hear more than a few times through the coming years. That wasn't the first, nor last, time he could epoxy rejection to religion, and in the prism of mainstream radio and then television in the forties, fifties, and early sixties, he was most certainly correct about it. Not just about being a Jew, but on a more visceral level a "New York Jew," to cadge the title of fellow Brownsville expatriate Alfred Kazin's 1978 vita about coming of age in the thirties and forties as a seminal Jewish intellectual. Kazin also meant the phrase to convey a state of being for men who went through life unable and unwilling to hide their Jewishness, the sad coda of which was that the young, dashing rebels of those days—including Howard Cosell—had grown old and establishment.

Back then, Cosell, regardless of the limits of his religious commitment, was most definitely a New York Jew—or, as his daughter Hilary more bluntly recalls what she heard people call him, "a New York kike."[21]

WHAT HE had to run up against was a bigotry far more complicated and subtle than it might seem now in such a radically different world. It is simply too easy to tar the movie, TV, and radio panjandrums of the forties, fifties, and sixties as inherent, unreconstructed anti-Semites and self-loathing Jews. Heroic and fair-minded they weren't. But they operated on fear, reluctant to mess with what was working for them as the cash poured into their corporate coffers from high ratings and box office receipts. Within this timid presidium, the issue was economics, not religion—or race, for that matter, since the same barriers had been in effect for over half a century in hiring, the most pernicious example being the perpetuation of the baseball color barrier. Undeniably, there were virulent racists in the upper echelon of the game, who pandered to racist players, but the justification for exclusion always came down to the imagined devil of a team's "property value" being undercut should a black player be signed, even one of the popular and proven stars from the Negro Leagues like Satchel Paige or Josh Gibson. That comforting sophism was always the most tenacious link in the chain for blacks and Jews to break.

The plain truth few wanted to recognize was that fans never seemed to mind African Americans playing on big league diamonds—witness the large crowds that attended off-season "all-star" barnstorming games between Negro Leaguers and players from the bigs—or Jewish people performing on the silver screen or radio set. The biggest name on theater marquees in 1945, John Garfield, was Jewish, his real name Jacob Julius Garfinkle. Similarly, perhaps the two most popular radio voices in sports were also of the faith: Bill Stern and the New York Yankee and CBS network announcer Mel Allen, he of the indelible "How about that!" yawp. Stern seemed to put the lie to the whole exclusionary practice by not changing *his* name, though few seemed to make the connection because, unlike Howard Cosell, Stern didn't "sound" Jewish. Allen was a bit different; born with the very Jewish-sounding name Melvin Israel, he was ordered to change it by CBS. Still, like Stern, nothing about his magnolia-dipped southern drawl seemed even a little Jewish.

Even what seems like light-years later, the landscape in all media is not materially different. Jews still change their names, and the surest ticket to a big-time gig is to come off as Anglican. Jewish boys try to look like "gangsta white boys" and make rap records. It is not as if Cosell changed the world; in fact, he succeeded in spite of the restraints, which only made him more reviled; never did the scab of anti-Semitism really come off in the industry all around him. As Beano Cook, the longtime ABC Sports publicist and college football analyst, said during Cosell's prime, "You can't avoid the fact that a lot of the anti-Howard stuff is anti-Semitic. All I ever hear is, 'The Jews run television.' And he's such a visible target. People who don't like me on television say I'm irreverent. I know damn well if my name were Goldstein, they wouldn't say I'm irreverent, they'd say I was another wise-ass Jew, like that Howard Cosell."[22]

IN 1946, Howard Cosell, silently nursing his first—but definitely not his last—grudge against the industry he wished so hard to be a part of, let that pipe dream drop, to the relief of Emmy and his parents, especially Izzy. Instead, with his normal quotient of nerve and daring—and the added backbone of Emmy Cosell, whose support made him even nervier—he would later recall his next move by playfully appropriating a famous sixties bumper-sticker exhortation. "With the encouragement of Emmy," he wrote, "I opened my own law office—up the establishment!"[23]

Enabled to put away a nice stash of his army paychecks by living with his mother and father, and willing to let Izzy kick in some seed money, he found office space in downtown Brooklyn late in 1946, as just one of a vast force of downtown lawyers, only to go heavily into debt. However, his rendition of woe as a peon is hard to fathom, given that even in Cosell's self-penned narratives, he suddenly found himself earning $30,000 a year, a handsome salary at the time. In a 1972 *Esquire* profile, writer Joe Marshall said Cosell's first law office was actually not in the depressing urban bog of Brooklyn but across the symbolically emancipating Brooklyn Bridge, at 30 Broad Street in the lower Manhattan financial district.[24] He indeed struggled there, but when he did make a success of himself it was not at his own firm. Instead, by the early fifties, he had closed the doors there when hired at Marro, Pomper, which was located just a few doors away at 25 Broad Street, close enough for Joe Marro and Lew Pomper to have become aware of his skill in labor law cases—or else because he would tell them as much during three-martini lunches at watering holes where the lawyer crowd congregated such as the historic Fraunces Tavern.

Pomper had begun the firm prior to the war, specializing in immigration law through which he assisted German refugees trying to escape the Third Reich. Joe Marro brought his expertise in mortgage and banking law. Now they had a young labor lawyer, but no one in the profession ever mistook him for the big gun of the firm he made himself out to be. With Marro, Pomper, and Cosell one-third his, in name if not in fact, he thought it high time to act and live like it. But the emerging high life of Howard Cosell, attorney, was soon enough going to be nothing more than a means to an end—to get back to the crazy conceit about sportscasting that continued to obsess him.

# 3

## BEING THERE

THE BIRTH of their second daughter, Hilary Jennifer, on March 25, 1952, mandated that the Cosell family finally move to a home of its own. It was overdue anyway, now that he had made a big *macher* of himself across the bridge. And so over the summer that year, he relocated his brood to a somewhat more fashionable slice of Manhattan's East Twenties called Peter Cooper Village, the northern component of a recently erected complex of fifty-six redbrick, high-rise apartment buildings, the southern property being Stuyvesant Town, on grounds where the famous director-general of the New Amsterdam colony, Peter Stuyvesant, had kept his farm in the early days of New York.

Without question, Howard Cosell, at thirty-four, had arrived in Manhattan, and with his salary and the money he had saved after seven years living with Izzy and Nellie Cohen, the Xanadu that had once been Eastern Parkway was now just a decaying street in Brooklyn, a sepulchre of the past where all those memories of youth were entombed. By now he could plainly see that the old-worldly Brooklyn was dying. He wanted not to be a part of it, and he would not be when in 1957 the devil incarnate, the bespectacled Walter O'Malley, spirited the Dodgers away to the West Coast, hastening old Brooklyn's slow death.

With the move, Brooklyn's native son, free and clear of Izzy and Nellie, was living *la dolce vita*, not only a resident of Peter Cooper Village but one of its most social of residents. He and Emmy had a sharp radar for finding the most intriguing and talented neighbors, and in no time their apartment was party central, the place to be when every month or so the lights would burn late into the wee hours and the guest roster would feature the cream of Cooper Village, including New York Giants matinee idol halfback Frank Gifford, actors John Forsythe, Tony Randall, Karl Malden, and Michael Higgins, and writer Mary Higgins Clark. With Cosell's knack for cultivating important friends, one never knew who might be there.

The writer Ray Robinson, who would run across him a bit later, wasn't a neighbor but drew an invitation by dint of making a living as an artisan in letters. He recalls the gatherings as a strange mélange of the people Cosell had "collected" like toys to show off. "By that time," Robinson says, "he'd collected a rather significant group of them. One night the president of Mount Holyoke College was there, Roswell G. Ham. How he and Howard met I never knew, but my wife and I liked him and his wife very much, we even went out to supper with them once or twice. I do remember Gifford being there, with a black eye from the game he'd played that afternoon. My wife, who didn't know who he was, said to him, 'My, where did you get that black eye?' You would go from a top educator to a football player without blinking."[1]

As a new arrival on the scene, Cosell could cut quite the dash. In fact, many women could find him irresistible, especially when he turned on his old-world courtliness and catalog of manners, or trained his aristocratic gaze on them and went off on one of his unending soliloquies bouncing from William Shakespeare to William Blackstone to William O. Douglas to Willie Mays. Years later, as he pushed into his sixties, his younger daughter, Hilary, would insist that "women find my father very attractive. There's sex in his power and charisma. It's only the men who write about his toupee and his big nose."[2] Always, even before tasting real power, he emanated self-confidence, usually with a lot of noise and the ability to command the floor.

What is less than impressive about his social climbing, and perhaps unkindly revealing, is that, contrary to the strongest subtext of his career—his compulsion about race—Cooper Village was off-limits to black renters, regardless of economic status. Maybe it was because of what seemed acceptable at the time. No less than the president of Metropolitan Life Insurance, the developer of the complex, openly opined that "Negroes and whites don't mix." Little was made of it when a Stuyvesant Town resident, a City University of New York professor, circulated a petition to allow blacks in and was fired from his job under pressure from the insurance company. When he subsequently went to teach at Penn State, he tried to circumvent the rules by lending his apartment to a black family, in effect an illegal sublet. Again he was fired.[3]

If it was Cosell's intention to fight from within to undermine the discrimination, or offer any legal advice, there is no record of it—as there surely would have been if he had, with Cosell himself putting it on the record, ad infinitum. Instead, he apparently sat idly by as the controversy brewed and *other* lawyers championed a lawsuit that would go all the way to the Supreme Court, which ruled that a landlord of a private property could "select tenants of its own choice because of race, color, creed or religion." Amazingly, Cooper Village and Stuyvesant Town today are still almost exclusively white, reinforcing the unfortunate trope of a Howard Cosell who was the proverbial limousine liberal, a man whose consternation about racism may not have extended to his own block.

COSELL'S SOCIAL networking was quite active, as was his eagerness to get as famous as his elite neighbors. Doubtful he could accomplish this as an attorney, he would begin to make a connection between the law and broadcasting. The first time this happened was in 1953 when the Little League affiliated with Cosell's American Legion post in Brooklyn needed a lawyer to help it incorporate. As he would tell it, Mickey McConnell, the chief scout of the Dodgers, asked him to organize the league. At the time, such a move was actually the subject of some controversy around the country, when parents grew concerned about the safety of children in sandlot leagues. Some editorials called Little Leagues "reprehensible" and "exploitation of children" staged for the entertain-

ment of bored adults, not unlike "bear-baiting and cock-fighting." Even
the *Sporting News* waded in, on the other side, with its powerful publisher, J. G. Taylor Spink, calling the kiddie circuit "one of the healthiest
developments of recent years."[4]

As a subversive element, the Little League was hardly on a par with
emerging rock and roll, and for Cosell it was plenty safe enough to make a
stand for it. After currying favor with the League's elders, he was hired to
get the charter, which he did, diligently lobbying politicians on the city
council not to turn their backs on the poor kids of the city. By propitious
timing, he had by then become known in the Sixth Avenue offices of the
three TV networks, having represented a group of TV writers asking for
union recognition. While that would seem an odd way to ingratiate oneself
to TV brass, he did, with cogent, passionate—though losing—arguments.

When the Little League World Series championship game in South
Williamsport, Pennsylvania, was carried by the ABC Radio Network that
August, he was taken into the broadcast booth to provide commentary
about the value of sandlot ball in young people's lives. That, history
shows, was the very first time Howard Cosell had a live microphone at a
sports event, notwithstanding that few knew or cared that he was there.
Importantly, too, he was also under the aegis of the American Broadcasting Company, which had created a fifteen-minute Saturday morning network radio program that was a way for ABC to fulfill its FCC-ordered
commitment to produce public service programming. Called *All League
Clubhouse*, it began in July for a prospective six-week run through the
summer, the format being a knothole gang of teenage panelists posing
questions to name athletes. For the moderator, ABC wanted, but could
not get, a sports announcer type; when no one of that stripe wanted the
job, they called Cosell, who was so eager to do it he said he'd take no pay,
a promise they held him to.

But he got more out of it than money. The debut show had Boston
Red Sox manager Lou Boudreau as the guest, sitting before fetchingly
naive kids who, to the shock of Boudreau, asked questions tougher and
more informed than he usually got from veteran sportswriters. Indeed,
only this could have been the case, since Cosell had written them all.
One of the regular inquisitors, Steve Scheffer, recalled that being manip-

ulated in this fashion was not a pleasant way to spend a Saturday morning. "I felt a little uncomfortable at times," he recalled, "because Howard was looking for a story and we were the means of him doing it."[5]

Still, none of the guests were really angered—some, in fact, given an impromptu forum to vent about some issue or grudge they had been keeping to themselves, were refreshingly candid—and the show never degenerated into farce. Smartly, Cosell kept intact the kids' wide-eyed hero worship; some of their quotes even got into the newspapers, one example being when Yankee right fielder Hank Bauer aired his grievance with manager Casey Stengel for benching him. Although few souls who were around then can remember ever hearing it, ABC kept it going for four years, with such stars passing through as Jackie Robinson, Gil Hodges, Harvey Kuenn, and Robin Roberts, as well as sportswriters, announcers, and sundry other sports personalities. In time it was carried by over two hundred stations and Armed Forces Radio. When the show finally ended in 1956, ABC again catered to him, this time giving him a half-hour sports news and talk show late each weeknight on the local affiliate, WABC-TV.

Cosell conceived the show, *11:30 Clubhouse*, with a freelance New York sportswriter named Ed Silverman, one of his "collectibles," useful to him because Silverman wrote copy for Bill Stern's ABC network radio show as well as magazine articles ostensibly penned by Stern. Cosell tried to wangle a meeting with Stern, a man with a terrible reputation within the business—mild mannered as he is, Ray Robinson ventures that "Bill Stern was a fucking asshole"—who went and proved it when he refused to see him because, as Silverman once told writer Dave Kindred, "he absolutely fucking hated Cosell," deeming him "a dilettante with an overtly Jewish voice" (which, to be fair to Stern, was exactly so).[6]

The upshot, of course, was that Stern himself was a Jew, and his attitude a reflection of the institutional anti-Semitism that blinded some Jews themselves. Cosell, given the back of Stern's hand, pitched his TV show not with himself as host, fearing that might kill it, but with Chris Schenkel, the well-regarded New York football Giants play-by-play announcer, who took the job for fifty dollars a week. Schenkel, though, was a bit bland for Cosell's notion of hard-hitting—though just who would *not* be is open to question—and in short order he was replaced by the one human he knew could do that job, one Howard Cosell, which may have been his intention all along. Cosell threw himself into the show, running Silverman, the de facto producer, so ragged that he quit. With all the chaos, WABC indeed killed it before it ever premiered.

As a sop, the network set him up as host of *Sports Kaleidoscope*, a fifteen-minute slice of pre-prime time, from 6:45 to 7 P.M. each Saturday night, meaning he would have two shows on Saturday, along with *All League Clubhouse*. A press release by the station quoted him: "I have some views about what's wrong and what's right with baseball. I see that Commissioner Ford Frick has hired a company to conduct a nation-wide survey. Well, I could help that survey. I have not been asked for this help [but] I may air my views on the *Sports Kaleidoscope*."

The premise was simple, yet daring, considering its host: He would weave issue-oriented narratives with sports news and scores. At the time, no one was doing anything close to that. For better or worse, Howard Cosell and ABC were clasped in something new. But bets were hedged. It was small enough to fail with no one even knowing.

PENDING *KALEIDOSCOPE'S* fate, Cosell's law shingle was active and still tangentially beneficial. More and more, he would hop the subway to Yankee Stadium, the Polo Grounds, and Ebbets Field, where he was easy to locate by his dark suit and tie even on the most blistering of days, bantering and joshing with athletes who didn't know if he was a reporter or a team accountant. When he would mention that he could put them on TV or the radio, their ears would perk up, opening the way for him to offer his legal services, using the enticing argument that he could help them make money off the field. During one of those Polo Grounds sojourns, in May 1953, he trained his sights on Monte Irvin. The veteran Giants left fielder had come to the club from the Negro Leagues in 1949 and then teamed with Willie Mays and Hank Thompson in 1951 to form baseball's first all-black outfield, and also hit .458 in the glorious playoff win over the Dodgers that season. Today, he is ninety-one and clear-voiced, a Hall

of Famer, and living in Florida. When asked about Cosell, he has plenty
to say, very little of it kind.

"Oh man, what an operator he was," he begins. "I didn't know him,
just that he had a radio show with Little League kids, but he walked
around like he owned the ballpark. One day we started talking and he
said he was a lawyer, he could do things for ballplayers. So, as it happened, Willie and I had a liquor store, Willmont Liquors, in Brooklyn,
which was not the place you'd expect a couple of Giants to own a business but it was the only place we could get a [liquor] license pretty cheap.
But all the while we wanted to move to Harlem. Roy Campanella had a
liquor store on 134th Street and Seventh Avenue and did a lot of business
up there. That's what we wanted to do.

"Howard said, 'I got a man who can do that for you guys.' So we gave
him $15,000 apiece to get it done, that was his fee. But after a few months
the man at the State Liquor Authority in charge of leases got caught taking money under the table [in another proceeding] and jumped out a
window, killed himself, and the state froze the transfer of all leases for
two years. So after thirty grand, we were stuck in Brooklyn in an area
where we didn't make enough money to pay the bills. And then Willie got
married and his wife didn't want him to have any outside businesses and
I got stuck with the damn thing by myself. It killed me. Eventually sold
it, lost a lot of money."

Irvin continues: "I don't blame Howard that the guy committed suicide. I blame him for the big buildup he gave me, that he could do anything, when he couldn't do a damn thing! And when he couldn't, he
didn't care, didn't feel bad about it. See, he was on the way up and I was
on the way out [laughs]. All he did was give me a push. But he would still
tell people he was my legal advisor. I said, man, he's full of shit. After the
thing with the store, I never spoke to him. Neither did Willie. We felt
stupid to deal with him, to put up with all his bullshit. He was nothing
but a pain in the neck."

His summation of Howard Cosell is "He sure was full of himself.
He'd say he would invite you to one of his parties, like that was a big deal.
I've been to better parties in a boxcar, man. He was sickening, just sick-
ening, and it got to the point where no one could stand him. I'll say this.

He was the only person I ever met during my career that I disliked, I mean really disliked. Later on, he'd see me and make a big production, you know, 'Monte, my great dear friend.' I'd just walk the other way. If I'd see him on TV, I'd turn it off. Listen, nobody ever liked Howard Cosell. Just his wife, nobody else."[7]

The liquor store matter has stayed with Irvin a long time. But, as he suggests, for Cosell it was a mere blip on the radar screen, though it would be helpful fodder in his bio—as he would tell it, he'd done Irvin and Mays a mighty favor, even reconstructing the "legal advice" he gave them to claim he had secured their original lease in Brooklyn, which was jive. As Irvin suggests, too, Cosell's relationships with players were disposable, each a brief encounter of the Cosell kind en route to someone, something, and somewhere else. It was no way to win friends. But Cosell either would turn a deaf ear to plaints like Irvin's or simply convince himself that he was a favorite of the sports set, any heat merely a form of bench jockeying.

Those rationales were easier to make than harsh words were to take. Never would he understand how it was possible that all his good work and good principles weren't enough for some people. As his daughter Hilary once said, his greatest sense of failure was that not everyone liked him. Yet, without doubt, he had no intention of ever looking back at whatever mess or broken friendship he had left behind. Feeling his oats, in a letter dated April 15, 1954, he easily spoke for the entire organization when he wrote to Walter O'Malley on ABC Radio Network stationery, "May I, on behalf of the American Broadcasting Company and myself, express our deep appreciation to you and the entire Brooklyn baseball organization for the wonderful cooperation and assistance you have given us during the past year in connection with our weekly network public service radio broadcast, *All League Clubhouse*. In our opinion, the Dodgers are not only first in the National League, they are first in the public relations league."[8]

If he would soon enough have cause to alter his opinion of O'Malley, his pretensions about his own standing were inviolate. A year later, he was tooting his horn for *The New Yorker* and, only weeks after that, J. G. Taylor Spink, who interviewed Cosell in his law office and ran a long story about him in his "Looping the Loops" column in the August 10, 1955, issue of the *Sporting News* under the headline "Personal Counsel to Players."

"Howard Cosell is not a ball player. He is a lawyer. But he is going places in the business," Spink wrote, then went over Cosell's "work" with Irvin and Mays and others, and sopped up Cosell's pedantry—e.g., "So many chiselers seek to capitalize on a player's name without paying him for the right. The player needs a lawyer not only to steer him right, but to act as a buffer for him." Spink also ate up a few choice morsels of spoon-fed biographical pabulum—"You should have seen [Irvin] as a high school athlete. I competed against his team. I think he was ready for the majors then," a claim that would have been rather hard to back up since Irvin grew up in Orange, New Jersey, and Cosell never played high school ball.

There was also an intriguing hint about Cosell perhaps buying into the ownership of a team, with him boasting "I can get up the necessary funds if the right proposition comes along" and dropping a name who might help him do it—"Norman R. Abrams, First Assistant Postmaster General, is my father-in-law . . . He has long had a desire to purchase a ball club, and now he and I are more eager about acquiring one than ever before."

However, even as the facsimile of Howard Cosell, "personal counsel to players," was being spread across big national journals, it was actually becoming obsolescent, secondary to Howard Cosell, rising broadcaster. Knowing this, those around him—some, like Izzy and Nellie Cohen, with great horror—could sense that the lawyer part of his being was ebbing. They were right. The truth was, Howard Cosell had gotten all that he could have gotten, and all that he wanted, from being a lawyer.

SOON ANOTHER radio project arose, a weekly sports magazine that was an offshoot of Henry Luce's Time-Life media print dynasty—*Sports Illustrated*. It hit the stands on August 16, 1954, as a vehicle not just for impressionable fans but for literate people of all ages, its articles written not by typical sportswriters but by practitioners of long-form prose, backed by mesmerizing color photography. Some early hires would fuse into fixtures, even titans, of American journalism for decades, such as Robert Creamer, W. C. Heinz, Gerald Holland, and articles were written by Robert Frost, John F. Kennedy, William Faulkner, and A. J. Liebling. Cosell, literary lion that he fancied himself, had had conversations with the publisher, Harry Phillips, not to write for him but to partner up for mutual gain.

The result was a new radio show under the aegis of the magazine, hosted and produced by Cosell, its content much like *Sports Kaleidoscope* but cleaved into five-minute "conversation pieces" featuring Cosell interviewing a news-making athlete, something only Cosell seemed to be able to do pithily in five minutes. The spots would stretch over every weekend, six on Saturday, four on Sunday. He proposed the concept directly to Robert Pauley, president of ABC Radio, who remembered that Cosell came in with a demo tape he had made of an interview with Jackie Robinson and insisted that Pauley hear it. "I liked Howard, so I did," he recalled many years later. "He asked Robinson about being the first Negro in major league baseball. It was provocative. At that time, you didn't ask those questions. But I was honest with him. I said, 'Howard, we have no money to develop untried talent, but if you get a sponsor we'll put it on the air.'

"I assumed I'd never hear from him again. Then a day later he came back with a relative's shirt company as a sponsor. I was good to my word. But I didn't put him on until I sent him to a voice coach to soften that accent of his. The truth is, if you heard Howard as he sounded back then, you'd get a shock. His accent was much thicker. I really was the one who softened it out, made it palatable. He never would have gotten anywhere had he not done that."[9]

The show, *Speaking of Sports*, reprising the title of his reputed column in the Alexander Hamilton High School paper, went on the air in early June 1956, with Cosell earning twenty-five dollars a show, less than scale, less than the lowliest weekend weatherman. All ABC would commit to was six weeks, prompting him to later chide their circumspection—"By God, what security, six weeks!" he wheezed in *Cosell*.[10]

He got off to a promising start when he landed jockey Eddie Arcaro the weekend he was in the saddle for Nashua's last ride. During the first few weeks came a profusion of other timely interviews. He grabbed Phil Rizzuto after the Yankees unceremoniously cut him; had Cincinnati Reds pitcher Hal Jeffcoat just hours after he beaned the Dodgers' Don Zimmer, sending him to the hospital; Sam Snead on the eve of the U.S. Open; Red Schoendienst when he was traded from the Cardinals to the Giants; top heavyweight contender Floyd Patterson, a fresh cast on the right hand he broke beating Tommy Jackson, five months before knocking out Archie Moore with that hand to take the vacant title; Billy Talbert on the eve of Wimbledon; Branch Rickey on the surprising Pirates; Yogi Berra before the All-Star Game; Jim Brown on the day he was taken with the first pick in the NFL draft by the Cleveland Browns. Another guest, Fred Haney, got a call from Cosell half an hour after being hired to manage the Milwaukee Braves. "How did you reach me so fast?" Haney asked in amazement. "I only just found out myself and I'm still talking to [owner] Mr. Perini. Or I was."[11]

Phillips, delighted, ran a "Memo from the Publisher" in the July 9 issue touting the show and claiming, with a bit of blarney, "The idea for *Speaking of Sports* came to Howard Cosell, its producer and announcer, from careful study of *Sports Illustrated* and a conviction that its reporting of sports through leading personalities offered a unique and exciting inside-the-news pattern for sports broadcasts . . . Cosell and *SI*, as usual, have no idea what they'll say. But I'm sure, in speaking of sports, whatever they say will, like *SI* itself, add meaning to events that have happened and understanding to events that will come."

BY THE end of 1956, he had no reason to perpetuate the now-receding pose as a legal advisor to players—or as a lawyer. That part of the equation having played out, with benefits, he came to the momentous decision he had been hoping to make for years. He told Emmy he wanted to give up his law practice and go into broadcasting—his recollection of that moment was that he said, "My disposition demands the immediacy of translation of effort into result." Emmy, ever supportive, if more than a little nervous about him giving up a steady paycheck, said he should go for it. Neither did Marro and Pomper try to stand in his way, perhaps an indication of his atrophying connection to the firm, and their feeling that they had been "carrying" Cosell for years now. In his last mile at the firm, Cosell had even had to borrow money from Joe Marro to be able to sustain his "business" lunches with athletes he was trying to impress. Whatever the case, as he later wrote, "I was infected with my desire, my resolve, to make it in broadcasting."[12]

It was crazy, of course. He wasn't twenty-five with a pretty face and golden pipes, after all. He was thirty-eight, with a wife and two children, stooped, lumpy, and balding, and sounded like the Brooklyn Jew he proudly was. As he neared his fateful decision, his friends told him he was nuts. He thought he was a reformer on the order of a Jackie Robinson, hell-bent to tear down barriers, not just those within sports but docility and cowardice in sports broadcasting. If a vote had been taken among those he knew, nuts would have won. Emmy's support made the point moot. And so he hung up his shingle. Decades later, talk show host Tom Snyder, recapitulating the official back story—including Cosell's cagey reminder that "I did edit one of the principal law reviews in this country"—could only posit that his guest "would have been a fantastic lawyer" had he remained one. It was intended as an orchid, but Cosell looked pained.

"Why do you say *would* have been, Tom?" he said. "I *was*."

There was also the reiteration that he had only become a lawyer because of his family, but he took it a step further, adding, with not any compelling reason other than the conflicting emotions it caused inside him, that the pressures had come from his "*Jewish* parents."

Whatever the ensuing uncertainties, in the end it was his need for instant gratification that carried him downstream from the humdrum tedium of law. "It wasn't for me, dispositionally," he told Snyder, inventing new grammar. "I needed immediacy, inhibitorily."[13]

NO RIFFS of that sort could have mollified the simple accountant his father was. His son would recall that Izzy Cohen, magnificently unimpressed with the sportscasting *mishegas*, would endlessly petition his previously unpalatable Emmy, pleading with her, "Please, dear, have him go back to the profession." When he looked back on those moments, he had the advantage of 20/20 hindsight, knowing he had been undeniably right to chuck the law, and that Izzy was wrong. That had to be satisfying, but it would have been immeasurably so had Izzy lived to see him crowned by success so great as to be quite nearly incalculable. Instead, only months later, on July 20, 1957, his parents were vacationing in Charlotte, North Carolina, when Izzy suffered a massive heart attack. He held on for three weeks in the city's Memorial Hospital before another attack on August 14 felled him at age sixty-seven.[14] The family buried him according to Jewish law a day later in Knollwood Park Cemetery in Brooklyn, but for his younger son lowering Isidore Martin Cohen into his grave did not bury the lacerating memories.

If Izzy's death did lift some of the burdens of the past, Howard still carried the burden of knowing that even now he had not lived up to the old man's expectations. That may explain why his future references to Izzy Cohen came with a skew that Izzy had disappointed *him*, for not believing in him. His epilogue was that his father went to his grave as provincial as he had always been, with the son having gone nearly forty years trying to placate him while being his own man. On that August 14, he figured Izzy had given him his release from that conflict. Now, with Izzy resting in peace, his son could finally go his own way.

HIS FATHER'S death came just as he was finding common ground with his *other* father. Norman Ross Abrams would in fact become a useful tool, as Cosell's tip of the hat in the *Sporting News* made sharply clear. Not because they ever really had any designs to buy a baseball team, that was just a Cosell con, but rather for connections Abrams helped him make.

That same year, 1956, Abrams retired as deputy postmaster general in the Eisenhower administration and moved to Fort Myers, Florida. As Cosell had noted for Spink, Abrams had once been a semipro pitcher and was a baseball junkie. Having once nearly bought a share of ownership in the Philadelphia Athletics, he was on a first-name basis with their legendary onetime owner-manager Connie Mack until Mack's death that very year. Now, living not far from the Pittsburgh Pirates' spring training grounds, he became friendly with the new Pirate manager, Bobby Bragan, and one of his coaches, Danny Murtaugh, who would replace him in 1958. According to Cosell, Murtaugh was a protégé of Abrams, having broken into semipro ball in the Pennsylvania Industrial League when Abrams found a job for him.

Abrams by nature was partial to other men with influence in baseball, one of whom happened to be his broadcaster son-in-law. Whether he had mellowed in his old age, or because Howard Cosell was privy to ballplayers, he now took a different view of the "Brooklyn Jew." Baseball, it seems, was the only agent that could thaw the icy wall between them. Speaking regularly with Abrams on the phone about who knew whom, Cosell suddenly found himself being invited to Fort Myers during spring training. There, he too struck up a friendship with Bragan, who fascinated him, having once been one of the most strident racists in the game but becoming over recent years a changed man who credited Branch Rickey, who now was vice president and part-owner of the Pirates, for helping him see the light.

Bragan was soon a guest on Cosell's various radio shows, as were other players Abrams introduced him to. From then on, he would trek to Fort Myers each March, using it as a base for visits to spring training camps across Florida, recording interviews on bulky recording equipment he strapped to his back. And each year, he would grow closer to Abrams. He might not have conquered broadcasting yet, but he had won over that "Old World Republican." Gloating about it, he wrote that Abrams "was in sportsman's heaven, now that I was a broadcaster and nationally known." By the time Abrams died in 1969, he added, "I had become very important to him. It was a total about-face."[15]

Whenever Emmy would hear him make this claim, she would laugh at how he was gilding that lily. When he went even further, telling *Sports Illustrated* in 1983 that "I became the most important thing in his life," Emmy, sitting beside him, broke in, saying, "That's absurd, Howard."[16] Emmy knew full well that the corollary was more accurate: that Norman Abrams had in fact become very important to *him*; that reeling Norman

Abrams into his world was something to shout about, and reason for him to boast, as he did to more than a few people, "I showed him."

RAY ROBINSON, having met Cosell at Monte Irvin's liquor store, found himself back in Cosell's world on the latter's first spring trip across Florida, as one of those in a growing stable of collectible people. A few weeks before, Cosell suddenly called him with a proposition. Robinson had by now become editor of *Real*, a men's magazine working off the testosterone-surging adventure blueprint of the well-read *True* rather than the cultured man's alternative, *Playboy*. It was the perfect exemplar of what men—so-called real men—craved, as can be gleaned from some of its titles: "I Spy on the Call Girl Racket," "Hemingway: Wine, Women and War," "American Gals: Virtuous Sinners," "I Was an Irish Guerilla," and "The West's Bloodiest Feud," as well as a "Fabulous Female" center-fold with scantily clad pinup (examples: Sophia Loren, Mitzi Gaynor). Yet there was also swashbuckling cover art and an occasional first-person piece by the likes of Jackie Robinson, who wrote a bold article titled "Why Can't I Manage in the Majors?"

Cosell had remained friendly with Ray Robinson, once inviting him to be on one of his radio shows. Now he offered himself to *Real* as a sports pundit. "He sort of conned me into it," Robinson says. "He said, 'You can use a sports columnist.' I mean, we were such bosom buddies, right? So I had to hire him."[17] In truth, Cosell did have the bona fides, and dutifully, for twenty-five dollars each, delivered three six-hundred-word columns for the June, July, and September issues that ran under the rubric "Cosell's Clubhouse" and a head shot stuck atop a stick figure that had him resembling, notes Robinson, an aardvark.

Robinson's memory of that work is vague, recalling that it was "not particularly well written. Let's put it this way. He wasn't an idiot. But he was no Red Smith." Still, the columns were well thought out and exe-cuted, one a profile of Reds manager Fred Hutchinson ("a six-foot, four-inch giant [with] the intelligence, warmth and strength to handle men"), another a treatise about the All-Star Game ("The fans have adopted a spectacle, attached meaning to it and forced the baseball people to do the same—even though the latter know better"), the last a portrayal of NFL Commissioner Bert Bell that reads now like a fable, calling him a "player-minded commissioner."

But these would be the only visits to "Cosell's Clubhouse," possibly because he lost interest in it—years later, he would ask Robinson, "Are you still at that witless magazine?"[18]—or because he and Robinson had a bit of a flap back in the spring. It happened after Cosell asked the editor to accompany him on his periodic five-day trip to the Florida baseball camps, to help him "formulate some interviews and write questions," Robinson recalls. "I thought, yeah, that sounds like fun." When they got to St. Petersburg, "I started working with him and then I realized he was such an egomaniac, he didn't really want me to help on interviews, he felt he could do everything without aid. He didn't even stay in the same hotel with me, he had to have a better one. I ended up carrying his goddamn equipment. He had recorders and other crap like that, which frankly I didn't even know how to use. I wasn't a writer, I was Gunga Din."

Before he left early, Robinson ran into Roger Kahn, who had covered the Dodgers in the early fifties and now was sports editor at *Newsweek* and doing a cover story on Ted Williams. Kahn, who knew Robinson, asked what he was doing in Florida.

"I'm working with a guy named Howard Cosell," he told him.

Drawing a blank, Kahn said, "Who the fuck is Howard Cosell?"[19]


THAT WAS a question asked more than a few times during Cosell's forays to spring training. As in his visits to the ballparks during the season, if he was noticed at all it was not always for the best of reasons. He was, to most, an interlocutor trespassing on the domain of hard-boiled sportswriters who covered baseball but easy enough to ignore since so many had no idea who he was or what he did, his radio shows apparently making little headway among the people he wanted to impress the most—the peers he considered anything but. Despite the lack of notice, Cosell went by a simple credo, one he credited to one of the few sportswriters he could tolerate, Walter "Red" Smith, a craggy-faced, courtly fellow with a discerning pen that, in his "Views of Sport" column in the *New York*

*Herald Tribune* and syndicated nationally, etched keen portraits of athletes and their deeds.

"He gave me two words of advice: 'Be there,'" Cosell once recalled. The result was that "I established friendships and connections that became news sources, without which a reporter is useless."[20] And so wherever one looked, there was a good chance of him being there, sometimes with an ear-piercing, eminently obnoxious peal of "Cosell is here!" Not that anyone wouldn't know it by his behavior in the company of the established sports crowd.

Jerry Izenberg had no idea who he was when he first ran across Cosell in the late fifties, when the former had begun to write a column in the *Newark Star-Ledger* that endures to this day, but knew he had been served notice, for better and for worse. "This was at a Metropolitan Basketball Writers luncheon at Mama Leone's restaurant a block and a half from the old Garden. Howard came in with his Buick-sized tape recorder, and he was so obnoxious. A couple times someone would walk past him and pull the plug out of his recorder from the wall. Or they would stand close to him and utter profanities so he wouldn't be able to play the tape on the radio.

"Dick Young of the *Daily News* did that; he couldn't stand Howard," Izenberg goes on. "But that was mutual. One guy wasn't worse than the other guy. They each went out of their way to provoke the other. But Dick Young was . . . Listen, Dick Young couldn't have run for any office unless it was secretary of the Nazi Party. And Howard had this need to be obnoxious. That's why every conversation with him was a monologue. He was in this great love affair with himself."[21]

NO ONE could doubt he was getting himself noticed, on merit. Those five-minute snatches were almost always diverting. His cachet, such as it was, afforded him the opportunity to get closer to his longtime daemon Jackie Robinson. In late 1956, Robinson provoked a tempest, having agreed to sell to *Look* magazine an exclusive first-person article announcing his impending retirement from baseball—thus running afoul of the sporting press that would be shut out from breaking the story, a clear violation of unspoken protocol concerning such matters. Because he was a naturally sympathetic ear for Jackie, a starry-eyed Cosell didn't even press him over the fact that *Look* had required that Robinson tell no one of his retirement, not even the Dodgers, who had tried to trade him to the New York Giants at the end of the season. Recalling a show he did with Robinson at the time, he labored to deny it was a behind kissing, insisting in *Cosell*, "Privately I agreed that what he had done was right, but as a reporter I was not disposed to take an editorial stand."[22]

Thereafter, and not a surprise, Robinson confided regularly in him, both on the air in other shows and privately. By far the biggest "collectible" Cosell would ever have, Jackie and his wife, Rachel, would often visit the Cosells. Sometimes, the two men could be seen golfing together at a country club in Connecticut—the kind that during Robinson's playing days would have refused him, and quite possibly Howard Cosell, the use of its fairways. It was an irony both of them reveled in.

On a technical level, Cosell's radio work began to feature creative uses of audiotape, which he himself archived—keeping thousands of hours stored and cataloged in his home—and edited, with a technique he later claimed to have invented back in high school. That *really* would have been impressive, since the first practical tape recorder was invented in Germany in 1935 and the first consumer use of magnetic tape recorders came in the late 1940s. As he explained, he tagged his tapes in such a way that he could pull out a part of any taped interview at will, using it as an "abstract interview" to suit any number of topics. He became more streamlined when he began to use a new tape machine, the Nagra, one of the first made, for which he paid $480 out of his own pocket.

Concurrently, his tone moved away from the drone of a lawyer addressing a jury. He was gradually injecting personality, humor, the self-satire of the braggart. Contrary to Robert Pauley's memory, there were no voice coaches; rather, he would say, he needed only to call on his actor friends, men such as his old Peter Cooper Village neighbors John Forsythe and Karl Malden. The former, whom he had actually known in the old neighborhood around Eastern Parkway, had once worked as the public address announcer at Ebbets Field, and had gravitated to the Broadway stage and in the late fifties to Hollywood as star of the sitcom *Bachelor Father*. He helped Cosell understand the nuances of voice, the gradations of decibels, the lyrical flow of a sentence, though Cosell's natural style wasn't to emphasize certain syllables as much as hammer them.

He had heretofore been far from convinced that he could succeed in broadcasting with his natural voice. Now he could dare admit to himself that he was losing some of his insecurity, though even in 1973 he would say, in a rare confession, "I do not now—and never will—feel totally secure. Nothing in my life has conditioned me for it; certainly not in broadcasting. It is a colossal jungle. No one is ever safe in it."[23]

BUT IT had to count for something that he had bark, bite, and even a murmur, if needed. The opening of each radio broadcast set the tone. *Hello again, everyone, this is Howard Cosell speaking of sports.* The sign-off was *This is Howard Cosell reporting*, the last word smartly broadening his context from merely a sports sniffer. The delivery was in an Ed Murrow–like staccato cadence, punching but also jabbing, the bravado and musty cant of Graham McNamee, but with a hint of nose-in-the-air disdain and distance. He was, at the least, entirely inscrutable, since he would careen from hard-hitting reportage to mawkish sentimentality, his droning melting into emotional fluctuations, when he had a human interest story, especially one with a heartwarming family angle.

Once, he began an interview with Iowa defensive tackle Alex Karras, and the "big, heavy, pudding-faced kid," as Cosell would later call him, tearfully wove a wonderful recital about how as a fat, lazy freshman he quit school and came home to Gary, Indiana, only to be thrown out of the house by his mother ordering him, "You go back there and be a man!" Cosell lapped up every syllable, and wanted more of that kind of visceral cheese.

What amazed interested observers was that for a man so ostensibly sensitive, Cosell seemed to have a knee-jerk reflex for cruelty away from the schmaltz of such stories. Says Izenberg: "I would be embarrassed when I was with him, by the fact that he didn't have any feeling for people, even those he knew. The thing was, if Howard didn't know you, he could advocate for you on the radio in ways that could make you cry, you know, about how this boy's father was a drunk and his mother was cleaning floors and he's buying them a house with his first paycheck from the Rams. He really could make you feel for people. But off the air, he wasn't that interested."

From numerous examples that underline that side of Cosell, Izenberg picks one. "We were walking down Sixth Avenue one time and this guy comes up to him and says, 'Howard, you don't remember me, do you? I was your squad leader in basic training.' And Howard gives him that look, like he stepped in shit. The guy goes on, 'It's the first time I've seen you since we got out of the army,' and Howard looks at him and says, 'Then this must be a red-letter day for you.' He made the guy feel two inches tall. I was so pissed off, I looked at Howard and said, 'Fuck you,' and walked across the street. I didn't want to walk with him. It was an evil thing to do. But he couldn't help himself. He was an addict. He was an arrogance addict. Not an arrogant addict. An arrogance addict.

"Sometimes he just didn't get it. I was on the phone with him once and he was haranguing me as usual, and my daughter, who was five, fell down the cellar steps. Blood is coming out of her head in gushes— fortunately, it was just a cut, but I was frantic. I'm holding her forehead and I tell him, 'Howard, I gotta go to the emergency ward, Judy fell down the stairs, I'll talk to you later.' And he said, 'It's not easy being a parent. Jill has acne.'"[24]

IF HE wasn't being cruel, he could be sneaky. Indeed, Frank Gifford's recollection of the first time he ever did an interview with Cosell was in 1956 when he invited him onto the air after a Giants game at Yankee Stadium. Though he knew Cosell from the Peter Cooper soirees—where, Cosell remembered, Hilary once wet her diapers as Gifford was holding her—the superstar halfback was wary. That week an article had appeared in *Life* that called the Philadelphia Eagles—the Giants' next opponent— the dirtiest team in pro football. So as not to provide any bulletin board fodder, Gifford said, that topic would have to be off-limits.

"I absolutely understand, Frank," Cosell assured him. "I won't bring up the Eagles. I would never put you on the spot like that. You know me better than that."[25]

As Gifford recalled, "I went on his show, and after he introduced me, his very first words were, 'Giffer, there's a highly disturbing story out of Philadelphia. The Eagles have been labeled the dirtiest team in football. I would like your . . .' Once I got over my shock, I wiggled out of it with a few we-all-play-hard clichés. And I didn't complain to Howard . . . But I also never went on his show again"—not that the two would not intersect again, not by a long shot.[26]

Another of his young athlete interviewees at the time was a five-foot-nine Columbia basketball All-American named Chet Forte, who averaged 28.9 points per game his senior year, beating out Wilt Chamberlain as college basketball's Player of the Year in 1957. Forte would recall that Cosell similarly assured him before they went on the air that the questions would be soft. When the microphone went live, Cosell wasted no time.

"Chet, is it true that some of your teammates hate to pass to you because you shoot so much?" he asked.[27]

Chet Forte—or, as his questioner would affectionately come to call him, "Little Chester"—couldn't have imagined that there would be a time when he would be waiting with great anticipation for Howard Cosell to badger other athletes with "soft" questions like that. And how amused, and like-minded, both of them would be.

# 4

## MOMENTARY MOMENTS
## OF CHAGRIN

HOWARD COSELL had a new residence in 1958, befitting a family man who deserved being able to stretch out his legs in the lap of suburbia, never mind that he was still only pulling in about half of what he was at Marro, Pomper. Bought with mostly Emmy's family money, the digs were a sprawling ranch house on five acres with a white picket fence around it in Pound Ridge, an affluent, blizzard-white grotto in Westchester County straddling the Connecticut border, with an Irish setter he would take into the woods, along with his two growing daughters and a new set of in-crowd neighbors, such as actors Hume Cronyn, Tallulah Bankhead, Eli Wallach, and Anne Jackson and architect Max Abramovitz. Taking up residence here meant he would catch the New York Central Railroad each morning for the hour ride to Grand Central Terminal. As it happened, that was the means of transit not just for numerous others in his profession but several New York Giants football players who got off at the Yankee Stadium stop. For all involved, being in the same car as Cosell could make the trip seem interminable—a circumstance they tried hard to find ways to avoid.

"Someone who used to ride on that train told me that guys would try to figure out what train Howard was taking that day and switch to another train," says Jerry Izenberg. "Some of those Giants would get to Yankee Stadium three hours earlier just to be safe. They just didn't want to take the chance he'd be there. If [Giant defensive end] Andy Robustelli would get on, Howard would go into his act—'Andy, Andy Ro-bustelli, big num-ber eighty-one . . . Robo!' He'd go through all this shit with each guy he knew, and everyone in there would have to hear and they'd be cringing.

"So one time he was doing this, going through different people, and in comes this guy who sees him and he goes, 'Howard! Howard Cohen!'— which mortified Howard, it was like the guy punched him in the face, he was speechless—and he went on, 'Howard! I haven't seen you since NYU. What's become of you?' And everyone in the car broke into applause. True story."[1]

But not one Cosell ever recounted. Rather, he told of bucolic memories in which his rides to the city weren't in a train but Andy Robustelli's car, shared as well by the Giants assistant coach Tom Landry. Writing of the latter in *Cosell*, he went on: "He had created something called the 4–3 defense. We would talk about it driving in." Those tutorials, he insisted, enabled him to understand and communicate the minutiae of football like no other announcer or sportswriter. With much hauteur, he insisted he could do what few, if any, sportswriters could: keep an objective distance from people he was personally close to, calling it "a mutuality of respect," with the understanding by the jock set that "I was the kind of a guy who was going to speak out."[2]


AS MUCH as he spoke out, in some radio outposts a long way from the metropolis, in places where they had never heard a man, or any human, sound like him, no one heard him. At these affiliates, orders went out not to put Cosell on the air. At WSUN, an ABC affiliate in St. Petersburg, Florida, deejay Donald Kimberlin filled the dead air with canned music. As he recalls now, the gossip at the station was that "ABC has a sports announcer in there who's so bad the station manager won't carry him, Howard Somebody-or-Other from New York. Scuttlebutt had it he's a lawyer who married an ABC vice-president's daughter and they had to give him a job." The injunction seemed wise to Kimberlin, since in his own view, Cosell "just didn't sound like he'd ever be a successful announcer. My instant judgment was that Howard Cosell would never make it."[3]

That the fates would have it otherwise is made plain by the fact that when Lou Volpicelli—who would later work as a high-profile director with Cosell at ABC on series like *Monday Night Football*—landed a job at WSUN in the midfifties, Cosell's lasting imprint was such that people at the station swore to him that Cosell had *worked* there. That may have been the case, because when Cosell would journey to Florida for his spring training interviews with the Yankees in St. Petersburg, he would use the studio to do his daily radio shows. In fact, one of the earliest photos of Cosell shows him perched before a WSUN microphone, looking ever sardonic.

Kimberlin wasn't alone in his negative take on Cosell. And the unkind assumption that Cosell must have married the right ABC honcho's daughter only gained more traction when the summer of '57 rolled around and he was given another shot at national TV exposure, *Sports Kaleidoscope* having expired after only a few months. It would be a six-week summer replacement show, fifteen minutes in duration, a common length in those nascent days, when TV people didn't know for certain if watchers could keep their eyeballs focused on something for any extended time. Called *Sports Focus*, it would occupy the time slot the very popular kid show *Kukla, Fran and Ollie* had ruled for years, 7–7:15 P.M.

As Cosell recalled, however, the job was only his because of one man, John Charles Daly, the longtime and very dignified CBS newsman and game show host (*What's My Line?*) who in 1953 became vice president in charge of news, special events and public affairs, religious programs, and sports for ABC. Daly, who Cosell insisted was "impressed with the kind of topical impact I was making," went up against Jim Aubrey, the vice president in charge of programs, who wanted to hire retired football great Tom Harmon, who was old-school and "safer." Daly prevailed, and ABC inked Cosell, who instantly became something of a heavy, it having been concurrently announced that *Kukla* would not be brought back in the fall, its long run at an end. On June 3, Kukla, Fran, Oliver J. Dragon,

Ophelia Oglepuss, and Colonel Crackle were out and a rumpled, basset-hound-faced New York Jew was in. He sat behind a desk reporting, inter-viewing, wheedling and cajoling, and kvetching under the glare of hot lights, and after the initial shock most viewers liked what they saw and heard of him. *Sports Focus* survived the cut and kept running for eigh-teen months. But it would do little to elevate him to his rightful status, or so he believed, as a household name.

TOWARD THAT end, he kept firing away. His commentary on the radio grew more pointed, such as his recurring disdain for aging dinosaurs Casey Stengel and International Olympic Committee chairman Avery Brundage, the latter of whom he mocked as "William of Orange." His ratings kept climbing, as did his profile. In 1956, he had the last laugh on Bill Stern, who by then was becoming an anachronism and increasingly erratic due to an addiction to painkillers, a result of having a car crash years earlier that necessitated the amputation of one of his legs. When Stern was ordered to take a rest, ABC sent Cosell to host the show. He then became a reporter on the program—a role he continued when Stern returned, and then when Stern was dumped a year later and the show was given to Mel Allen.

Radio, in fact, was clearly his life buoy, keeping him afloat, if not entirely recognizable yet. Unlike in the medium of TV, his loudness was a plus on the radio, which was propelling the growth of teen-fueled rock and roll. Indeed, the station where he was ensconced, smack in the mid-dle of the dial—"Seventy-seven, WABC," went the fizzy jingle that poured every other minute out of transistor or car radios—was the most listened-to Top 40 station in the country. The pace was hectic, manic, highly addictive. Cosell fit right in.

Of more help still was getting the job as producer of the ABC Radio Network's episodic boxing coverage in 1958, a position that would have been unthinkable as recently as a year before when he had yet to see his first bout. It was Ed Silverman who took him to Madison Square Garden, later recalling that at the time it was a sport that Cosell "didn't know from shit."[4] Unlike creatively inclined, rough-and-tumble men's men whose visions Cosell swore he shared, men like Budd Schulberg, Elia Kazan, and Norman Mailer, he had never been smitten with the bold elegies of squirting blood and blackened eyes as the ultimate metaphor of mano-a-mano macho and survival.

Figuring he had better get aboard that train, Cosell began to soak up the color, stench, and romance of pugilism, soon becoming expert in the minutiae of what was a remarkable decade in the ring, one mirrored by its coverage in the media that exploded in the early days of TV when the tube was so saturated with boxing that there were at least six prime-time network fight shows every week. The most popular was NBC's *Gillette Cavalcade of Sports*, broadcast from Madison Square Garden on Friday nights. ABC waited for the midfifties to turn up its interest in the sport, with a prime-time show called *Boxing from Eastern Parkway* telecast only blocks from Izzy Cohen's apartment, though its headline boxing vehicle was the Saturday night *Fight of the Week*, with blow-by-blow duties by the trill-voiced Don Dunphy.

Cosell had no place in these telecasts, but they were advantageous to him when in 1958 ABC began to broadcast fights on radio, with the responsibility for producing given to Cosell. He was supposed to stay behind the scenes, but if anyone expected that to happen they knew less about him than they may have thought. Right from the start he was handling pre- and postfight interviews and occasionally fight commentary. By accident, though perhaps not to him, one side benefit was that he was often present in newsreels of some of the bigger fights of the era. For example, on the eve of middleweight champ Carmen Basilio's rematch with Sugar Ray Robinson on March 25, 1958, a fight carried by ABC Radio, Cosell was preserved for history on grainy celluloid, elbow to elbow with Basilio, wielding his microphone like an épée, not questioning but rather verbally kidney-punching the semiliterate, cauliflower-eared champ.

"Carmen!" he barks on it, loud and nasal as a tankard whistle. "Nine of ten reporters predict that you will be knocked out."

Basilio blinks, then shoots back: "Nine of ten reporters are wrong!" then stalks off, leaving Cosell's microphone stuck into empty air and a smug grin on his face.[5]

Boxing, with its cast of gritty, colorful characters, was a human buffet table for him. It seemed almost an organic fit, the stark contrast in temperament and intellect between the cerebral man with the microphone and the men who took a beating for a living further etching his profile as someone who could boil the essential drama of a *Golden Boy* or *On the Waterfront* down to a few well-chosen remarks.

The revelation for him was that within the fight club there were men of intellectual heft and sensitivity. Prime among them was Floyd Patterson, the heavyweight champ whose extremely introverted, agonistic nature made him an ongoing psychodrama of epic highs and lows. For Cosell, Patterson was a hard nut to crack, given as he was to existential-sounding tripe such as "I won't always be the champ, but I'll always be a man," or that boxing was "like being in love with a woman. She can be unfaithful, she can be mean, she can be cruel, but it doesn't matter . . . It can do me all kinds of harm, but I love it." Because of such philosophizing—which so captivated the erudite writer Gay Talese that he would write thirty-eight articles about Patterson for national magazines—Cosell would say Floyd was "a sociologist's dream and a psychologist's guinea pig." And, for him, something more than just another useful collectible; as he had with Jackie Robinson, there was something close to consanguinity, or as Cosell would say, "I developed an almost fatherly affection for Patterson."[6] Regularly, he spent long hours with the champ while he trained in ascetic isolation at a camp in upstate Greenwood Lake, New York, and overall to the point where he became absorbed with him. During this time, Patterson converted to Catholicism, and Cosell believed he had found a sense of peace and equanimity.

The most fascinating thing about Patterson was that a man so full of self-doubt and with no apparent killer instinct was able to dominate the ring. Granted, most of his fights were against tomato cans carefully chosen for him to beat up on, which he did, sometimes without conviction, as if on orders from his tough-talking trainer Cus D'Amato. And during his reign, he and D'Amato deemed Cosell to be the third of a three-man inner circle. After one Patterson victory, Cus showed up at Cosell's door, a bottle of hundred-year-old Armagnac brandy under his arm.

"Take it," D'Amato said, handing him the bottle, "you've been with us all the way."[7]

Patterson, in turn, became a frequent houseguest in Pound Ridge, and was something like a surrogate family member, with Emmy, Jill, and Hilary growing especially taken with him; sometimes the entire family visited the camp in Greenwood Lake. When Patterson fought abroad, the mailman would bring to the house not just postcards from him but gifts such as a set of sterling iced-tea spoons, a dinner bell, and an ashtray from antique stores in Europe and Scandinavia. If there was reason to believe there was a conflict of interest in being so close to someone whose fights he had to cover, Cosell quickly forgot it. For one thing, he was getting nothing else materially from Floyd except access—that magic word for any reporter—and the chance to study a highly complex athlete. He made no big deal of it, and few knew anything of the friendship. For another, he was far from the only one in the media to fawn over an athlete, and Patterson in particular. For all his independence and professional distance, he would admit later that he had, as he said, "fallen in love with a fighter. So had my family."[8]

His closeness with Patterson did not compromise his objectivity. Patterson, he would tell his audiences, was highly skilled, but his emotional distress level was so low any fight was a potential pitfall for him. What's more, in his unorthodox peek-a-boo stance he also seemed vulnerable to a good, quick right hand. Every word of that analysis proved true, with devastating results, when on June 26, 1959, at Yankee Stadium Patterson defended his title for a fifth time, against the little-known or -regarded European champ, the Swede Ingemar Johansson—whom Cosell derided as "just another handpicked patsy" but who possessed a right hand that the European boxing writers touted as "Ingo's bingo."

For the first time, a sports event would be simulcast on closed-circuit television in movie theaters, returning handsome profits to promoter Bill Rosensohn, who would collect $470,712.25 in gate receipts, the meed from a top ducat price of one hundred dollars and five hundred for "red carpet" ringside seats. As it happened, too, it would also be the maiden fight Howard Cosell would call in real time, as a color analyst, backing up the blow-by-blow commentary of veteran announcer Les Keiter. Cosell also did his usual work interviewing the fighters and VIPs like John Wayne and William Holden, promoting a movie that was the main sponsor of the fight.

After the bell rang, Patterson got the rudest awakening of his life, and one of the sport's most shocking moments, when he was knocked to the canvas seven times in the third round and counted out as he tried to rise, only to fall back down. Cosell then bolted like a fullback into the ring as the count was ending, to reach not the new champ but the old one, who was in a daze. Rather than spew syllables furiously, he shouted at Patterson a simple "What happened?" Floyd could only mutter perhaps the most memorable understatement in boxing history.

"I got hit, Howard," he said.[9]

Cus D'Amato would not leave it there. Grabbing Cosell's microphone, he woofed, "I will tell you right now that for the first time in the history of boxing, you will see a defeated heavyweight champion win his title back!" It was an instant headline, though the overarching narrative was the picaresque Swede, one effusive example being Martin Kane writing in *Sports Illustrated*: "The sports world has a new look today, a fine, delirious look, thanks to the virile right hand of a handsome Viking who scored with it one of the most stunning upsets boxing's heavyweight division has known."[10]

Before the compulsory rematch would take place, D'Amato and Cosell had other business, joining in a campaign to bring to its knees the haughty and hidebound International Boxing Club of New York, the cartel that controlled fighters' rankings, mandated who they fought, and promoted the big championship fights while kicking back considerable change to the Mob. For Cosell, such a cause, waging war against a corrupt, elitist sports federation was a given, and the IBC, as a vestige of boxing's unsavory past, became a juicy target for him. Years later, he would find himself in an uncomfortable web with just such forces. But in 1959, he could take a deep bow when a New York court ordered the IBC be dissolved.

By then, however, Patterson was a mental wreck, his defeat causing him to wallow in self-pity and doubt. Up in Pound Ridge Emmy and the girls had been so distraught listening to the fight on the radio that they cried and Jill wrote Floyd a letter assuring him he'd be champ again. And it fell on Cosell to snap Patterson out of his funk. When D'Amato pleaded with him to go to Patterson's home on Long Island, Cosell on his own asked Jackie Robinson to accompany him. No human in sports, of course, had ever had to cope with more stress and strain than Jackie, and Floyd had often spoken admiringly of him. And, as Cosell had hoped, meeting Robinson acted as a salve for Patterson's troubled soul, initiating a long sodality between them, during which they would participate in tandem at civil rights rallies in the perilous Deep South.

Patterson's comeback came on June 20, 1960, at the Polo Grounds, for the rematch with Johansson. The roles were reversed that night, with Floyd the underdog in the media—Cosell included. But, making good on D'Amato's vow, he took the crown back in round five by uncorking a mortarlike left hook that left Ingo out cold, his foot twitching in a neuromuscular reflex, not to come to for a full five minutes. Once more at ringside as the color analyst and host on ABC's radio broadcast, Cosell when it was over waded into the congested ring with his microphone. He exchanged a few tepid comments with the typically diffident Patterson, then made his way to where Johansson still lay unconscious on the canvas, his trainer Whitey Bimstein standing over him.

"For God's sake, Whitey," Cosell shouted, "is he dead?"

The white-haired Bimstein, a gnomish artifact of boxing's fanciful past, looked up not in concern but anger. "The son of a bitch should be," he said for radio listeners nationwide. "I told him to look out for the left hook."[11]

It was another auspicious night for both Patterson and Cosell, but it would mark the acme of their relationship. Rather than being more comfortable with himself and his craft, Floyd grew only more inscrutable, maddeningly so for Cosell, who watched Patterson loaf through his training for the rubber match with Johansson with none of the rage he had the last time. This could not have happened had Cus D'Amato been there, but Floyd fired him over petty differences and began calling the shots himself, something he was ill equipped to do. Worse, the grim man whom Jackie Robinson had taken out of his brooding shell was now back to his reclusive, antisocial persona. Few, least of all Cosell, could figure out Floyd when he

arrived in Miami Beach on March 13, 1961, for his third dance with
Johansson and began saying weird things. One time he said he'd had a
dream and that if he were a superstitious man he would be worried, then
seemed to dismiss it with a bit of Patterson Zen: "As far as I'm concerned,
a dream is just an empty space looking for something to fill in."[12]

   After he climbed through the ropes—"of little more substance than
an empty space looking for something," wrote Gilbert Rogin in *Sports
Illustrated*—he appeared to be in a trance of some kind. Johansson had
mainly trained for the fight by eating himself into a dirigible, but he put
Patterson down twice in round one, while going down himself once. It
went on, listlessly, with Floyd slipping twice, until in the sixth, trailing on
points, he caught Johansson with a combination, whereupon the Swede
went down, got up, pitched forward in a semisomersault, then was
counted out, a fitting end to a fight that was, said Rogin, "like a bottle of
beer which has been open too long . . . faintly stale and flat."[13]

   From his ringside perch, it was all that Cosell could stand to watch.
Afterward, once more being interviewed as the champ, Patterson told
him he had consciously held back because he had been so vicious in the
previous fight and "it's wrong to hate the way I hated." It was classic
Floyd, but for Cosell such verbal self-torture had lost its flavor, too, and
gone stale and flat. As a challenge far more perilous than Johansson
loomed on the horizon for Patterson—the baleful, scowling ex-convict
Sonny Liston, the number-one-ranked contender who rightly terrified
him—Cosell expected the worst for Floyd, but no longer would he be
there to scrape him off the floor yet again. He began to pull away from
him, not coincidentally just as his image was becoming less sympathetic
to the public at large. Indeed, even while still the ruling champ, Patterson seemed almost past tense as the fateful Liston fight neared. And
Cosell, looking past that fight, already had his eye on a younger, fresher,
louder replacement for his affection.

BECAUSE HE was now being seen and not only heard, Cosell as he
reached forty made a tactical cosmetic decision that he would need to
cover his balding skull, lest he be taken for even older. In retrospect, all it

really proved was that the wigmakers of the day were able to please men who made their living in the public eye simply by seemingly skinning the closest skunk and putting its hide on a waiting head. In 1959, roughly half a million American men wore toupees, spending a hefty $15 million to do so, and unwittingly funny pelts were tacked onto some rather famous bald heads, including those belonging to Jack Benny, George Burns, Bing Crosby, Gary Cooper, and John Wayne.

Cosell, who was at least as tough as Bogie and the Duke, wanted a "natural" look betraying just a slight amount of balding, but so detested the model fitted on him, with its exaggerated and most unnatural widow's peak jutting down his forehead Dracula-like, that he stuck it in his coat pocket, unseen, until he would do an on-air TV appearance. Not for a moment did he expect that such upholstery would be a major part of his very identity. Or that he would need to slap on that rug so often that he would barely have time to take it off.

His public profile, and need to look younger, indeed rose when in 1961 he made it onto TV again, on Channel 7, the New York ABC affiliate, reporting the sports on the early evening news, a post he would hold until 1974. The ABC lifeline was indeed good to Cosell. In the fall of 1959, for another example, it had paired him with veteran sportscaster Chuck Thompson at 11 P.M. Saturdays narrating highlights of a college football game from that afternoon. Granted, ABC was hardly a dominant sports operation, or *any* kind of operation, in the late fifties still only carrying twelve to fifteen hours a week of original programming, none late-night or daytime, and sports that consisted almost entirely of Friday night fights.

In 1960, it did up the ante a bit, paying $2,125,000 a year for a five-year television contract to broadcast thirty-seven national and regional games of the newly formed American Football League. These games, which introduced to TV novelty flourishes such as players being miked on the field and visual angles that moved with the line of scrimmage instead of a fixed camera on the 50-yard line, drew a large enough audience that the other two networks took notice. CBS, which had broadcast the established National Football League regionally, went national, with the NFL aping the AFL's revenue-sharing plan that kept smaller-market teams alive. NBC, with its bigger money and color TV cameras, would lure the AFL away from ABC in 1964, leaving the latter network in the lurch again.

Except that by then it had a verifiable smash hit of its own, one that no one had expected to last beyond the summer of 1961. It was then that ABC began a Saturday late-afternoon anthology called *Wide World of Sports*, the debut featuring the Drake and Penn relays. In successive weeks came a caravan of lesser, cheaply obtained events that would grow to include just about anything that could conceivably be called a sport. As arcane as Irish hurling, Mexican jai alai, a rodeo, or a rattlesnake hunt was, "sports" like these could be dressed up with exotic locales and an opening visual montage of intercut sports scenes, with a narration intoning, "Spanning the globe to bring you the constant variety of sport. The thrill of victory and the agony of defeat. The human drama of athletic competition. This is ABC's *Wide World of Sports!*"

Of course, such pomposity and grandiosity would not have been a bit misplaced with Cosell as host. Instead, the job went to courtly, Philadelphia-bred Jim McKay, who was no stranger to drama, having once been a crime reporter. McKay had hosted the 1960 Summer Olympics in Rome for CBS, from a studio half a world away in Grand Central Terminal. His ability to keep control and perspective during a sports circus led ABC to hire him—wisely, as his fetching way of literately putting sports in broader perspective was far more polished than Cosell ever could have managed.

That is, if he had ever been considered, which was not the case, even though the originator of *Wide World* had taken a liking to him. This was Edgar Scherick, a happy-faced former ad man with thick eyeglasses who had helped bring a televised baseball Game of the Week to TV in 1953, when he got a commitment from Falstaff Beer and brought the idea to ABC, complete with the fractured tongue and homespun homiletics of Dizzy Dean. The financially strapped ABC lost that franchise to CBS two years later, but Scherick—who after CBS bypassed him as head of its sports division formed an independent production company, Sports Programs Inc.—was taken in by ABC, as executive producer of *Wide World of Sports*.

FROM WHAT he had seen of him, Ed Scherick, a native New Yorker, a Harvard graduate, and a Jew, believed Cosell was a rising star—no doubt explaining why, in Cosell's view, Scherick came off as "an extraordinary man, with a fine, creative mind."[14] But whatever Scherick thought of him, the network had the final say. And as the sixties began to pan out, ABC executives seemed less inclined to keep Cosell on board.

What Cosell could not have known at the time was that one of Scherick's hires would have the last word about him. That was Roone Pinckney Arledge, a redheaded, cherubic-looking descendant of hardy Scotsmen. Just turned thirty, he was a Columbia graduate who wanted to be a sportswriter but in the late fifties wound up in local New York TV, producing the kiddie-oriented *Shari Lewis Show* before doing a one-eighty, turning from a puppet named Lamb Chop to a pilot for a show called *For Men Only*, which was based on the very unkiddie philosophy of *Playboy* publisher Hugh Hefner. The pilot went nowhere, but the insights about what "real men" wanted caught the interest of Ed Scherick, who was seeking some stout-hearted men after ABC in 1960 acquired the rights to broadcast an NCAA football Game of the Week—a breakthrough since college football conferences had heretofore been loath to permit anything but regional coverage of their games.

Scherick, playing a hunch, put his new protégé in charge of the production, with a few guidelines that Tom Moore, ABC's head of programming, adumbrated to the entire crew on the eve of the pivotal first game, between Alabama and Georgia. Gathering them in his office, he laid down the gospel that would congeal into the law of the land at ABC Sports for decades to come. "Listen," he began, "we do not want to do a football game like NBC! I want to see the good-looking gals! The chrysanthemums! The cheerleaders! The fans! The players sitting on the bench! I want to see the apprehension of the guy about to go into the game! I want to see the head coach pacing! I want you to capture the story of the moment!"[15]

Arledge, the oration ringing in his ears, ordered extreme close-up camera shots of players, cheerleaders, and fans, and for the announcers to dwell on personal, human interest story lines—the same kind of heavy syrup Cosell poured so well on his radio shows yet was kept from doing on network time. In effect, as Ron Powers noted in his superb 1984 book *Supertube,* paying customers at sports events would accordingly become relevant "largely as ambience" and "paying extras in the vast super-studios . . . that had once been known as stadiums."[16]

Arledge transferred his bells and whistles to *Wide World of Sports,* which he so christened after he noted that Scherick's original suggestion, *Wide World of Sport,* was the name of a section in *Sports Illustrated.* But before the show could go on the air, a deal had to be reached with the Amateur Athletic Union to allow ABC to carry track meets and other amateur sports events, the meat of the show's projected schedule that first year. Nothing less than the existence of the show rode on that deal, for which ABC had set a price limit of a paltry $50,000. Scherick decided to send in Arledge, and he got it done with some intense charming and rump-kissing of AAU officials. Recalling why he had sent Arledge to the AAU poobahs and not himself, Scherick, reconfirming the nature of the business then, boiled it down to a quite simple formula.

"Roone," he said, "was a gentile and I was not."[17]

Howard Cosell, who could relate to *that,* could also relate to Arledge, who like him was a New Yorker, transplanted from North Carolina to Long Island at an early age, but whose comfortable, upper-middle-class background and "gentile" advantages opened doors for him with an ease that a Howard Cosell could only marvel at. His rise was in marked con-trast with the Volga Boatman saga of the Jewish ex-lawyer from Brook-lyn. While in the future Cosell would lay it on thick about Roone, calling him as "a man of impeccable program taste and sensitivity [who] com-bines aesthetic qualities with a toughness that is utterly concealed by a low-key, mild personality and a warmth and humor difficult to resist," in 1961, as smart and aggressive as Roone Arledge was, he had no authority yet to make filet out of a guy who was regarded as a cheaper cut.[18]


INDEED, AS the lineament of a booming network TV culture was being drawn, Cosell felt palpably shunned by his own network, and could see no light in the tunnel. He did have a secure niche on local TV, and on irregular occasions he would go on *Wide World* to ruminate about a fight. But as ABC began to boom, he would recall, "I was a sideline observer. No place to go." The reason for this he wouldn't openly delineate, but many Jews of that era needed only to use a word that Cosell did freely in his memoirs by way of explanation. "Blacklist is a harsh word," he wrote. "Put it this way: When the man who runs the company thinks you can't perform, he has every right not to put you on the air. The man's name was Tom Moore. The company he ran was ABC."[19]

Thus did Cosell in 1973 codify his long and bitter grudge against Tom Moore, a big, moon-faced fellow from Mississippi who was a wartime navy fighter pilot, then a spokesman for the Forest Lawn Cemetery, famously the final resting place for many Hollywood celebrities, before working for CBS Radio in the late forties. ABC hired him as vice president for sales in 1956, and two years later made him head of programming. He was a man few beyond the ABC Sixth Avenue corporate headquarters knew by name or sight, but in Cosell's perspective he was the root of all evil, a man he denigrated as a "Mississippi cemetery salesman"[20]—surely the most imaginative euphemism for "southern cracker" ever coined. In his memoirs Cosell did praise Moore's stewardship in tilting ABC programming toward the younger TV audience, those aged eighteen to thirty-five, who were most receptive to watching the tube and therefore most valuable to advertisers; he also lauded Moore for his ruthlessness in swelling ABC's affiliate roster by requiring local stations to carry the network's regular programming as well as its sports fare.

But that was the rub—that Moore refused to recognize that Cosell was the "against the grain" type he coveted, and which gave ABC its first real success. After all, for one example, who would have been a better salesman for the AFL games than Howard Cosell, who so closely mirrored Al Davis and who in his commentaries expressed an almost missionary fervor for the new league as it tried to keep college players from the NFL? He also was on a first-name basis with David "Sonny" Werblin, vice president of the TV division of the giant entertainment company MCA, who in 1963, with Cosell's encouragement, bought the New York Jets.

That Cosell was being excluded from such a logical gig wasn't his imagination, either. During a meeting he had with Ed Scherick, Cosell would later note, "he was dead honest with me. [He said] Tom Moore didn't want me on the air. I wasn't his kind of image." Scherick was just as honest publicly in future years. Before his death in 2002 at age seventy-eight, he recalled of those barren years, "The word came down to me, very directly from the head of the company, Tom Moore, 'Don't hire Howard Cosell. Don't give him a microphone.'"[21]

For his part, Moore, who died in 2007 at eighty-eight, spoke frankly as well about the circumstances of Cosell's "exile" long after the fact. Deflecting the charge of anti-Semitism, he said his resistance had to do with Cosell having become allied with then–ABC executive vice president Jimmy Riddell, who had emerged as a rival for power with Moore, the latter vehemently opposing Riddell's suggestion that ABC Sports should junk Ed Scherick's outside agency and develop its own sports department. As Ron Powers related in *Supertube,* Tom Moore "believed that Jimmy Riddell should mind his own goddamned business, and ostracizing Riddell's pal Howard Cosell was one way for Moore to put Riddell in his place." Cosell certainly venerated Riddell; in his memoirs he wrote that "I have never had a better friend in the industry," one who happened to be "a great supporter of mine."[22]

The pair even traveled to sports events together, at which times Cosell would freely bounce ideas big and small off him—one perhaps being that Riddell should consolidate sports at ABC, under himself and with Howard Cosell of course a major spoke in the wheel. Coyly, Cosell admitted that this "complicated" his situation at the network, being that he was in the middle of what became "an internecine political hassle."[23] If this was so, it raises the question of whether Cosell was prepared to stab one booster at ABC (Scherick) to curry favor with a potentially bigger one (Riddell). If so, too, he may well have been less a victim of ethnic prejudice at the network than he was of simple office politics when Moore won out, with Jimmy Riddell moving to L.A. to run the network's West Coast division.

As a result, Moore was no more kindly disposed to Jimmy's boy. Indeed, he seemed to have taken from the whole unpleasant episode that he had to keep watching his back, lest Cosell be lurking there with another plot to depose him. This, Cosell later said, created "an intolerable position for me." He recalled a curious instance when Moore drove him home to Pound Ridge and told him flat out that he thought Cosell was "out to get him," an assumption that left Cosell "thunderstruck" and "revealed an insecurity in Moore that I had never suspected. He was running the network, and I was a relatively unknown sports announcer, a nobody."[24]

And going nowhere fast. In his frustration, Cosell briefly felt out the possibility of taking his genius elsewhere, out of the purview of Tom Moore. Keeping tabs as he liked to do on industry people who had aided him along the way, he learned that Don Durgin, who had been an early supporter of his around the time of *All League Clubhouse*, had moved on to NBC television as vice president of sales (in 1965 he would become president of the entire NBC TV division). Because Ray Robinson had known Durgin, he once again opened that door. "Howard called me one day and said, 'Don't you know Don Durgin?'" recalls Robinson. "Maybe he figured I owed him another favor. I called Durgin and asked him if he'd see Howard. I believe Howard went up to see him, but nothing came of it."[25]

Boxed in as he was, he had to be thankful that at least one network had a place for him at all. He would stick it out at ABC, hoping he didn't get too old before someone could talk some sense into Tom Moore. Meanwhile, he still had the local TV sports gig and remained in the good graces of Robert Pauley at ABC Radio, meaning he would be able to go on getting his mug before the public in those fight newsreels. Even so, as he waited for Moore to come around, it could not have escaped him that by now Joe Marro and Lew Pomper had become so successful that they had moved the firm to affluent Huntington, Long Island (Pomper would found Walt Whitman Savings and Loan Association, later to be North Fork Bank and Trust Company). Could Izzy Cohen have been right after all about him leaving "the profession"?

If Cosell had thoughts like that, it would explain some extended wallowing in angry self-pity, blaming Tom Moore in perpetuity for that half-decade "blacklisting," the upshot of which was that, as he treacly lamented years later, he had five years stolen from his career. It would also explain why succeeding wasn't merely a goal for him; it was now a gnawing obsession, and not just for himself but for the nongentiles like him. Defining an epitaphic nutshell that would still apply years later, Jerry Izenberg says: "Howard saw himself as a hook-nosed Don Quixote. He was fighting the armies of the anti-Zionist conspiracy."[26]

Not that he would ever have had the nerve to frame it that way himself, or even close. In a mideighties appearance on *The Tomorrow Show,* asked by Tom Snyder if he had had any frustrations in his career, he breezily began, "There are none, professionally," then, skirting the issue that had always caused him massive frustration, he went on: "I suppose there were momentary moments of chagrin. When I would appear carrying my forty-five-pound tape recorder and be laughed at by other sports announcers saying—'Who is this guy?' And [because of] the high-blown, high-flown language. But those were just momentary irritations of no real import."

He thought a moment. "The real frustration I had was in getting on the ABC television network. I had to scale that wall brick by brick. The whole nature of sports broadcasting is essentially without character, and you have to begin with that premise and lay it on the table—just tell it like it is. Let's not offend a commissioner, let's not offend an owner, let's not say that the contest is dull. And for someone who has something to say, that's not an easy thing. Waves are caused. The more you tell the truth, the greater your problems will be."[27]

AS HE waited, and plotted how to contradict that writ of common broadcasting law, he continued making deeper incursions on the back roads, in unfriendly terrain. He hit the road for Florida again, equipment in tow, for the 1961 spring training season, spending a week at the Yankees' new Grapefruit League base in Fort Lauderdale. If he was easily noticed before, he seemed to be more of a pest now. It was with a perverse sense of pride that he would recall that Ralph Houk, the crusty Yankee manager, finding him in his line of sight so often, told him, "You're like shit, you're everywhere." If so, never had Cosell heard a more meaningful compliment, though Houk was merely spraying the same kind of friendly fire players would exchange regularly with the sportswriting coterie they practically lived with six months every year.

"That line, I can say with certain mixed feelings, has survived to this day," Cosell wrote in 1973.[28]

But the writers appreciated it, too, as a simple and obvious observation, no levity intended. This was especially the case for the older beat writers, who for decades had proprietorship of the press box, the field, and the underside of the stands and had watched Cosell so airily play usurper over the years. Larry Merchant, then a wry young Brooklyn-born sportswriter in Philadelphia, was soon to encounter Cosell at close range when he came to New York to write for the *New York Post*. He recalls that it was possible to identify Cosell in a crowded locker room merely by the "accusatory" tone of his barked questions. "You would just naturally come to remember someone whose questions were more interesting than the answers," Merchant says. "It wasn't quite 'Do you beat your wife?' but it was close."[29]

Oddly enough, it was the writers who seemed to take more offense at his hammerhead queries than the players or managers. For a young sportswriter on the scene at the time, it was easy to catch a whiff of the toxic fumes between Cosell and the older scribes. One, Phil Pepe, another Brooklyn kid who was hired by the *New York Daily News* in the early sixties, says, "I kept hearing things, nasty things, about him from the older guys who'd been around forever, guys like Joe King, Gus Steiger, Dan Daniel, Joe Trimble, Tommy Holmes, Barney Kremenko, and of course Dick Young. They all believed they owned the ground they walked on. And Howard would come in once every two weeks and the players would want to be on TV and they'd fawn over him. Howard would act like a diva, like it was *his* turf, so you had a combustible situation that could only get worse."[30]

COSELL'S FRAYS with Dick Young would make for an entertaining, if pretty juvenile, plotline that tethered them until the latter's death in 1987. On the surface, they were the ideal counterweights, as if sent straight from Central Casting, the contrast between them so pungent that natural law would seem to have dictated that they could not have coexisted on the same planet, much less in the same press room. Though both were from Brooklyn and emphatic in what they were and did, physically and intellectually they shared nothing in common. Where one was long limbed, recondite, bald, and pretentiously white-glove, the other was stubby, street smart at best, and proudly boorish. Young, who for years was identifiable by his bow tie, thicket of silver hair, and sneer, believed that pretty much everyone save for himself was a Communist, or at least pinkish, and as such he was paradigmatic of the *News*'s comically right-wing editorial page that endlessly screamed "Better Dead than Red!"

And yet they were closer in disposition and impulse than they ever would have admitted. Never would either give a thought to the other being more complex in personality than his cartoon facade would indicate. Both were also Jewish, in varying degrees, Young having been born to a Jewish mother in 1917. He began at the *Daily News* as a teenage copyboy, and in 1942 won his first byline in the sports pages. Soon after, he began writing a column. His style was a revelation, perfect prose for a post-Depression, postwar America settling into a comfortable, working-class sensibility. Sports for the masses, in New York and elsewhere, were now played not by demigods but by men of flesh and blood, clay feet, brittle egos, and sometimes more worthy of a verbal slap than a laurel on their heads. As Cosell and Young both knew, sports were a narcotic not for the beau monde but for the ordinary Joe. And both geared what they did accordingly, Cosell from the top down, Young with what the *New York Times* described after his death as "all the subtlety of a knee in the groin."[31]

Each had a ferocious work ethic, fearing that if he slowed down he would lose altitude, which for Young was stratospheric as sports editor of the *News*, a paper with an astonishing circulation of around one million daily and twice that on Sunday. Flaunting his power, he was loud, obnoxious, and unbearably imperious—sound familiar?—and by the early sixties he was the putative suzerain of the sportswriting guild, and worked overtime and then some to keep that status. He would roll out two columns in one day, for both the early and late editions, as well as covering a team six days a week with an overload of game stories and sidebars, all compelling, amusing, acidic. In the press box, he could be heard above the din, often uttering something coarse.

Few could ever figure him out. Fewer got along with him. In the state of mind he called "My America," he was at once a staunch supporter of Jackie Robinson and the fall of the color barrier, and an enemy of player rights. He reeked of contempt for most modern-day players, with none of Cosell's softness for a good sob story. Over the summer of 1961, as the prosaic Roger Maris began to close in on Babe Ruth's hoary record of sixty-one home runs, Young was the first to lobby for an asterisk in the record book if Maris needed more than 154 games to do it, a suggestion scoffed at by Cosell but adopted by Ford Frick, the commissioner and onetime Ruth toady and biographer, although the silly solution was never implemented.

Cosell may have disagreed with practically everything Young wrote, but he read him every day, as he did all the writers, every day since his childhood. The papers were still his lifeline to the world of sports and beyond, and he would have loved to fit in with the newspapermen who believed they were kings, even if many of them were lackeys for team management. If not for the old-guard press corps taking such a dislike to him, he might never have spent as much time as he did obsessing about how to insult them. In fact, early on, he found an ally among them who he believed would do him a lot of good, given that it just happened to be one of the finest sportswriters who ever lived.

This was Walter Wellesley "Red" Smith, the erudite sports columnist who spent nearly two decades at the *Philadelphia Record* before landing in 1945 at the *New York Herald Tribune*, and another three decades later at the *New York Times*, where he would be the first sportswriter to win the Pulitzer Prize for Commentary. With his horn-rimmed glasses and craggy face, he seemed anything but a man whom Ernest Hemingway reputedly called "the most important force in American sportswriting," but he whipped up layered, scenic essays that read like novellas, one seemingly interconnected to the next as a continuing serial. Because of his universally exalted reputation, he could also play the fop as well as the old Brooklyn lawyer could, and though in his bourgeois political leanings Smith was closer to Dick Young than Cosell, this mattered not a whit in their mutual symbiosis.

From Howard's vantage, Smith provided him with a good deal of cover, both as a wayfarer among the literati set and a key constituent of the sporting press. Neither did Smith mind associating with an intelligent sportscaster—a rare commodity, to be sure—who could go toe to toe with him in all the right literary references and quotations. They made quite a pair of fops, dining together at Jimmy Weston's, Jack Dempsey's, Cafe Madrid, or Marianne et Fils. The bonus, maybe even the point, of being seen huddling with the scribe who dwarfed all others was that if the lowercase sportswriters chose to denigrate his credentials as a real reporter, his silent rebuttal was: Take it up with Red Smith.

ON THE lookout for fleeting pets in the press corps, he had no compunction inviting eminent writers like Jimmy Powers, the peerless boxing columnist for the *Daily News*—as well as Dick Young on occasion—onto the ABC Radio fight broadcasts, as highly opinionated and at ease before a microphone as they were. He publicly dropped the name of the clever top-gun sports columnist at the *News*, Jimmy Cannon, whom he quoted now and then on his shows. He would over the years employ a good many other newspapermen to write for shows he hosted.

But if he thought he was bartering for their acceptance, or even tolerance, that never happened, he being apparently unable to keep from belittling their corner of the media. Yet, in the end, all he really did was to fulfill the prophecy he had begun early on to make it all but impossible to retain any enduring friendship or respect within that corps. He could always pretend not to care, but that was a lie. He did care, more than he needed to and, given his fragile ego, more than was healthy for him.

# 5

---

# "LET GO OF THE MIKE,
CASSIUS"

COSELL'S PROGRESS now could be measured in small strides. *Speaking of Sports* was moved from the graveyard of the weekend to right after the news at the top of each hour from early morning all through the afternoon drive time. He was doing all his spots off the cuff, with no notes, not even taping them so they could be edited if he went too long, which he never did. It was as if he had a timepiece in his head, instinctively aware of how much to say. Jingles for his show mirrored his brio and semiparody—*"The gifted one speaks here . . . Howard on ABC . . . Cosell in action!"* By now, too, he was being given the latitude of broadcasting at his whim from a studio he had set up at his home in Pound Ridge, which offered the ease of not having to lug canisters of his archival audiotape with him to Manhattan.

He wasn't a lawyer intoning sports; he was an *entertainer*, with properly manic mood swings and softened inflections, lengthening out his shtick, the chutzpah, the self-effacing insult humor that can only work with a wink and a nudge. He also had a real cachet, such that he seemed able to reach out for a phone and reel in a guest for a show at will, not just one from sports but from politics, acting, writing, game-show hosting, whatever. But sports still had first dibs on him. In 1962, when WABC entered into an agreement with the expansion New York Mets to carry their games on radio for two seasons, duty called. The station, needing someone to host the postgame show, had only to tap its in-house sports director, who approached it not as a pimp for the team—the generic function of people who hold such jobs, often team announcers—but rather as an inquisitor, raconteur, and gadfly, i.e., Howard Cosell. He was paid neither by the team nor its sponsors, and the station cut him as much slack as he required, which for him was always miles since he'd be covering a gong show disguised as a baseball team.

The Mets home games were at the ancient colossus of the Polo Grounds, but he felt no need to soak up the vibes of the team and its emerging fan base. Instead, he merely wove the gig into his daily work-load, camping sometimes all day in the WABC studio on West Sixty-sixth Street, watching the games on TV, then doing the postgame. For a side-kick he tapped one of his old cronies, Ralph Branca, the ex-Dodger hurler who often went to the racetrack with Cosell and Jackie Robinson. Eleven years earlier, in the same Polo Grounds, he had served up Bobby Thomson's epochal homer. Introduced by Cosell as "Big Number Thirteen" or "Big Ralph Branca," the affable Mount Vernon native was taken by how the postgame gig fit so effortlessly into Cosell's nonstop workday, for which Branca had a front-row seat.

"He had this big tape machine and there had to be a thousand feet of tape on this thing, and the tape itself was ten inches thick but he handled it as delicately as a surgeon," Branca recalls. "He knew what every inch of that tape had on it. An engineer would thread it through the machine and Howard would say, 'Okay, go further . . . a little further . . . you're getting closer,' and stop it where he knew something was."[1]

The Mets, composed as they were of aging retreads such as old Ebbets Field favorite Gil Hodges and various and sundry rejects like the magnificently klutzy first baseman "Marvelous Marv" Throneberry, were in every way a joke. But Cosell was not amused, posing a ticklish situation inasmuch as Mets management expected something more than that one of its own cast say how lousy they were. That was certainly not how it was when the general manager, George Weiss, held the same position for years with the Yankees; over there, where winning wrote its own script, announcers behaved as if under orders from a politburo—nothing more than pusillanimous tools, in Cosell's humble opinion.

Cosell, now legendarily, made his first real mark as a scold of Casey Stengel, who returned to the game at age seventy-one not for his managerial skills, most of which he had forgotten, but as a mascot and pitchman, a role he played to perfection that maiden year, cranking out one precious malaprop after another—e.g., "See that feller over there? He's twenty years old. In ten years he has a chance to be a star. Now, that feller over there, he's twenty, too. In ten years he has a chance to be thirty." Stengel could recite lines like that in his sleep—something he allegedly did during games. Seeing the clown show burgeon, Cosell could not excuse what he saw on the field, no matter how many fans streamed in to enjoy a good laugh.

The pith of his Stengel diatribes usually had to do with the pitiful example the old man was setting for a new generation of New York baseball fans; Casey's Mets, he said, were causing "kids to fall in love with futility." Still perturbed about it a decade later, he said about Stengel in *Esquire*, "In the Midwest, kids were being raised on the tenets of discipline and hard work taught by Lombardi; in New York they were regaling futility."[2] His conclusion, as he said on one show, was that "there are those who think that, great as he was through the years, Stengel is not quite the man to lead the Mets to future glory."

It wasn't Stengel's senility that burned Cosell. It was, somewhat contradictorily, that Casey seemed to ridicule the players as well. When Stengel famously lamented that season, "Can't anybody here play this game?" it may have been a great Stengelism, but it turned off even Stengel-friendly denizens like Branca, who says now, "He shouldn't have said that. You can't knock your ballplayers, you gotta pump 'em up. Howard made that point on the air, and I agreed with him."

From what Branca could observe, "Howard had free rein. Howard was Howard. He couldn't be any other way than what he was. That's what you got, and you knew it. Howard knew it, too. He took every inch and turned it into a mile. Even if sponsors of the Mets were unhappy with him, Howard would have said what he wanted to say. He would have told them, 'Get another sponsor.' And they would have."[3] As dangerous as it

was being Howard Cosell, at least according to Howard Cosell, it seemed
he knew how safe it could also be.


IN THE face of dismal failure, a good many within the New York sportswriting corps agreed with Cosell that a clown did not a manager make,
though only Cosell elucidated it clearly and unequivocally. In fact, he was
so blinkered about the writers that he saw no allies. Years later, he would
tell *Playboy* that "the sportswriters loved Stengel because he gave them
copy every day. And what we soon had in New York was a press that celebrated futility . . . creating a legend out of almost purposeful futility." In
turn, his ragging of the team was assumed to be self-serving. "I learned—
by reading the newspapers—that I was being controversial to advance
my career," he recalled, tossing it off as "mindless criticism."[4]

But the press platoon was no longer the monolith Cosell made it out
to be; and ironically it was the younger writers who dug Casey, as a sort
of elder frondeur. One of them, the *New York Post*'s Maury Allen, who
would later write a splendid book on Stengel, recalls, "We were divided
into two groups, those who found Stengel entertaining and liked being
around him and those who said he was a foolish old fart and they ought
to get rid of him. I was young, it was all new to me, so I loved him. Most
of the younger guys did. The older guys were tired of him."[5]

Further complicating the fault lines already forming in the press, on
one side was the old guard, on the other the "new breed"—to use the
sardonic phrase Dick Young coined that summer for the Mets' merrily
masochistic fans—that Young and his confreres held in as much contempt as they did Cosell, who at least in this isolated instance was on the
side of the Philistines. Even though Cosell lined up with the anti-Stengel
crowd, it was hardly enough to override the teeming enmity the old-
guard writers had for him. On the other hand, the new generation of
scribes, who had grown up watching TV, had fewer objections to updat-
ing social and cultural iconography; if it was new and different, it wasn't
threatening, it was cool. With Howard Cosell, the equation was a bit
muddied, even cockeyed. New he was not, nor even all that new on the
scene, but different? Enough so to be a passable progenitor of sixties hip,

even if he was a child of the Roaring Twenties and a spinoff of the protocols of the Eisenhower fifties.

He was also, in a word, strange. Allen remembers a time when the Yankees signed a player and held a press conference at the team's Fifth Avenue office. "Howard and I met somewhere and we walked there together, and on the way we talked about everything but sports. We talked about Vietnam. He was against the war and I was a big activist against the war—and it was a terrific conversation. Then we got to the building and there were fifteen, twenty reporters in the lobby. And as soon as Howard saw them, he went on and on about Mickey Mantle, about how 'Mickey's my best friend' and 'Mickey tells me everything that's happening.' I just sort of stood there staring. It was the damnedest thing. I couldn't believe I'd walked with the same human being. He *became* Howard Cosell, what he thought Howard Cosell had to be. The insecurities rose up. It was pure Freud."[6]

WITH THESE cross- and intragenerational currents bubbling under the surface, both on the field and in the press box, the 1962 season wore on, as did the Mets' ineptitude, culminating with a record 120 losses. And even as fans streamed through the turnstiles, fueling the angle that the Mets were lovable losers, Cosell would not muzzle himself from judging the season as a desecration unworthy of New York. His Mets shows became an ongoing postmortem, though he could become giddy when they did something right—"Mark this day and mark it well," he brayed after the Mets beat the Pittsburgh Pirates 9–1 on April 23, their first-ever win. As *Sports Illustrated*'s Myron Cope would write in retrospect six years later of that bizarre situation, Cosell seemed to be out to do no less than "personally reshape the future of the Mets."[7]

He would bang the same drum again in 1963 when the Mets were just a little less horrid, going 51–111. But the tune was over in 1964, when the team moved to its new home, Shea Stadium, and the Mets, free to switch radio stations, did just that. Although no longer part of the Mets' daily beat, Cosell still had his mike, and did not curtail his philippics against Stengel, who finally quit in 1965. In fact, with consummate

Cosell claptrap, he would imply that he was somehow responsible for hounding general manager George Weiss, whom he regarded as Stengel's enabler, out of office in 1966 and having him replaced by Bing Devine— "one of my dearest friends [who] stayed with me [in] Pound Ridge."

Dripping with unction, he crowed in Cope's *SI* piece, "I went to work on getting rid of Weiss so Bing could get the job. Well, I don't mean I got rid of George, but I poured it on. And I'm sure he stayed on an extra year *because* I poured it on," though just why anyone in the Mets front office would have reason to placate him he didn't say.[8] No doubt because there was no such reason.

ON SEPTEMBER 25, 1962, Cosell was back at ringside as color commentator when Floyd Patterson, gulping hard, defended his title against Sonny Liston in Chicago's Comiskey Park, where the bout wound up after the New York State Boxing Commission denied Liston a license based on his past criminal activity and Mob ties that began at age thirteen. Liston was a palpable bad guy, having in the past done time for robbery and other crimes, and was assumed by boxing people to be owned by Mob-based fight promoters. Accordingly, the NAACP, fearing the image Liston would convey about blacks were he to be champ, asked Patterson not to fight him. The rumor was that even President Kennedy made the same request.

Patterson would have done well to comply. Not two and a half minutes after he entered the ring, the bigger and stronger Liston, a murderous glare in his eyes, caught the curiously inert Floyd with two blinding right hooks, crumpling him to the canvas for the count, the third-fastest knockout ever and the nadir in the odyssey of Patterson Agonistes. Though many had picked Floyd, Cosell would later iterate that "in my talks with Floyd I sensed a preacceptance of defeat." Patterson, who was anything but swaggering prior to the match, saying on Cosell's radio show, "I wonder how it will be when I come out," was typically breviloquent when it was over. Liston, he muttered into Cosell's microphone, "started too fast for me tonight."[9]

Cosell had a great sense of relief at the outcome, that Floyd was spared a longer torture and possible injury. Patterson, meanwhile, fled the stadium in disguise, and promptly went into his latest seclusion, but it wasn't long enough. Coming out of hiding for the rematch on July 22, 1963, in Las Vegas, he invited Howard and Emmy to his training camp, a ranch outside of Vegas. They were not impressed, with Emmy telling her husband, "I get the feeling he's already beaten."[10] She was right. It took Liston only four seconds longer to dispose of him.

Having prepared to divorce Patterson, Cosell now did just that, speaking with him almost never while hoping he would never again see him in a ring; what's more, the feeling was mutual, Floyd having come to believe—with cause, given the timing—that Cosell was a fair-weather friend. That was something Cosell felt he had to deny, insisting that the break was "not because he was losing as a fighter but because of his constant excuses, constant escapes from society."[11] However, he could not deny that, at that crossroads of history, there was another fighter who was a worthier suitor for his absorption, and who was loudly engineering his advancement as sports' first galvanic lightning rod of the sixties.


THAT FIGHTER, in fact, was in a ringside seat that night in Vegas hurling nonstop invective at Liston, whom he habitually called the "Big Ugly Bear" or, for certain audiences, "Big Ugly Black Bear," hoping they'd be fightin' words for Sonny. Many fight observers, though, doubted whether the precocious twenty-two-year-old from Louisville in the ringside seat belonged in the same ring or even the same area code as Sonny Liston. Quicksilver and still growing, Cassius Marcellus Clay Jr.—the poetic-sounding name that of a pre–Civil War Kentucky senator and slave owner—was a young man on the make, boasting Astaire-like feet, lightning-fast hands, a laser left jab, and a killer instinct. But it was his clattering tongue and, as he never hesitated to point out, caramel-smooth "pretty face" that had put him this close to the crown. Though he proclaimed himself "the Greatest," his 19–0 record was built on wins over ring detritus, an elderly Archie Moore, a disputed ten-round decision over Doug Jones, and a victory against a parchment-skinned Brit, Henry

Cooper, who knocked Clay down but was so bloodied he would have needed a transfusion to make it through the fifth round.

Clay was the newest, freshest incarnation of the stereotypical braggart that boxing always seemed to mandate but rarely had seen with such panache—actually, his role model was the professional wrestler George "the Animal" Steele. A boxing bard, he pumped up interest in his mostly middling fights with rhyme no one would confuse with Keats, but recited with a merry froth—he recast himself from the polite, self-effacing light-heavyweight who'd won a gold medal at the 1960 Rome Olympics to the earache-inducing braggart, but he was still stringy and at times awkward at the heavier weight. While he prospered on a famously simple MO—to "float like a butterfly and sting like a bee"—he had an alarming (to everyone but him) tendency to keep his gloves contemptuously low and slip punches by bending backward at the waist, trusting his keen reflexes to keep him safe. They did; there wasn't a mark on that pretty face.

Cosell first met him in August 1962 when Clay blew into New York for a round of self-promotion and he interviewed him on his local TV sports roundup show. At the time Clay didn't know much about the older, rumpled broadcaster beyond that his voice was heard when a big fight came on the radio. Cosell would recall him then as "attractive, outgoing, full of nonsense," with an "irresponsibility about him." About the upcoming title Liston-Patterson fight, he picked one, then the other to win—a ploy the host took note of for future use. Because of the buzz around Clay, Cosell arranged for his match in London against Henry Cooper to be broadcast on the ABC Radio Network. As he told it, Clay took to him, his eyes widening as Cosell displayed his knowledge of the sport—"Gee, you really know about this boxing business, don't you?"—and "there was an instant rapport between us," with Clay "instinctively sens[ing] that the two of us made a very good pair in reaching the public."[12]

As he cooled on Patterson, he began to eye the sleek, antiheroic Clay as a prime protagonist of the cultural reorientation in sports, if not the entire culture, premised by the sixties. It didn't hurt his appreciation for the kid that his playful egomania came with the same muffled gobbling, and even nearly the same locution, as did Cosell's—Clay's "greatest" closely tracking Cosell's "gifted one." They were clearly alike, in all the

Through this portal: 500 St. John's Place in Brooklyn, one of the apartment buildings where Howard Cohen lived, as it looks today. Back then, he would stare out the window waiting for his traveling accountant father, Isidore Cohen, to come home. *(Courtesy of Joe Lops)*

As he came of age in a family struggling to pay the bills, Howard Cohen longed to live on the more worldly, affluent thoroughfare of Eastern Parkway, which some called "the Riviera of Brooklyn" and whose residents Cosell called "Eastern Parkway Jews." Although the borough's glory is long past, the wide expanse of the street is still an impressive sight today. *(Courtesy of Joe Lops)*

Howard Cohen finally did get to Eastern Parkway when he, his new-lywed bride, Mary Edith (Emmy) Abrams, and their baby daughter, Jill, moved into this today unassuming brownstone on the wide boulevard in the late 1940s, sharing the flat rented by a more upwardly mobile Isidore and Nellie Cohen. By then, however, Brooklyn was receding for the young attorney as hallowed ground, and soon he would be headed for greener turf across the Brooklyn Bridge. (*Courtesy of Joe Lops*)

Historic St. Theresa's Church in Brooklyn, still stately after all these years, was in the 1930s a metaphor for the young Jewish Howard Cohen of the anti-Semitism he endured growing up. Walking down the street it was on, he would often be accosted by mobs of insult-hurling Irish and Italian kids who would chase him, forcing him to hop a fence to get away. (*Courtesy of Michael K. Dorr*)

Even at eighteen, he stood out in a crowd. Strikingly tall and with a full head of wavy hair, Howard Cohen looms large, second from the right, second row from the top in this group photo of the Pi Lambda Phi fraternity published in the 1936 NYU yearbook, *The Violet*. One of the youngest in the fraternity, he was also one of the youngest graduates of the NYU Law School when he received his degree in 1940. (*New York University Archives, Photographic Collection*)

## NEW YORK UNIVERSITY
# LAW QUARTERLY REVIEW

Issued in NOVEMBER, JANUARY, MARCH and MAY
By the Students of the New York University School of Law

SUBSCRIPTION PRICE, THREE DOLLARS          ONE DOLLAR PER NUMBER
Unless notice to the contrary is received at the editorial office it is assumed that a renewal of the subscription to the Law Quarterly Review is desired.

### EDITORIAL BOARD
ALISON REPPY
*Editor*

CECELIA HELEN GOETZ
*Student Editor-in-Chief*

RACHEL BUDOFF BACKER          SAMUEL STEINBERG
*Decisions Editor*                    *Decisions Editor*

RICHARD J. NUSSBAUM
*Legislation Editor*

HOWARD W. COHEN          LORETTA I. MARTONE
*Notes Editor*                    *Notes Editor*

The masthead of the 1939–40 edition of the prestigious *NYU Law Review* included Notes Editor Howard Cohen, who soon after graduation would begin practicing law at the age of twenty. Gifted one that he was, it seemed entirely believable when he would imply later that he had been editor in chief of the review. (*New York University Archives, Photographic Collection*)

Living *la dolce vita* after migrating from Brooklyn, the Cosells moved into the still-upscale Peter Cooper Village complex in the East Twenties. In his first Manhattan apartment, the young lawyer hosted regular soirees attended by other rising celebrities such as Tony Randall, Karl Malden, and John Forsythe, all of whom—along with Cosell—would become seventies TV icons. *(Courtesy of the author)*

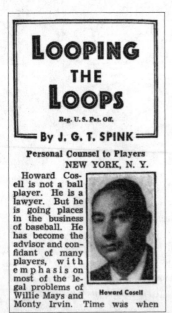

Cosell's forays into representing professional athletes in the mid-1950s, a time when few of them had any such legal advice, won him exposure in the media—such as this flattering 1955 profile in the influential *Sporting News*—and paved the way for his hoped-for career as a sportscaster. *(© Sporting News, used with permission)*

**LOOPING THE LOOPS**

Reg. U. S. Pat. Off.

**By J. G. T. SPINK**

**Personal Counsel to Players**

NEW YORK, N. Y.

Howard Cosell is not a ball player. He is a lawyer. But he is going places in the business of baseball. He has become the advisor and confidant of many players, with emphasis on most of the legal problems of Willie Mays and Monty Irvin. Time was when

**Howard Cosell**

"Howard Cosell, N.Y.C., sportscaster, ABC," as he was identified in this 1956 inquiring photographer newspaper feature, was asked if he admired or resented outspoken people. He answered, "I respect honesty and feel that there is a dismaying lack of it in our present-day society," but added, "However, I do resent people who are outspoken in their social relations for the sake of being cruel"— ironically, a charge that would be leveled at him over the years. (*Bettmann/Corbis*)

The epochal buddy act of Howard Cosell and Muhammad Ali began in the early 1960s when the latter was known as Cassius Clay and boasting about how he would one day become "the Greatest." Cosell, seen here in a fedora and trench coat, covered all of Clay's early fights, knowing how beneficial the men could be for each other if Ali made good on his promise. *(AP Photo)*

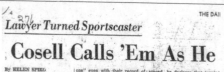

## Lawyer Turned Sportscaster

# Cosell Calls 'Em As He

By HELEN SPIRO

Howard Cosell is a man of opinions.

Some may be right up your alley and some may be ... well, that's what makes a horse race, as the saying goes.

Cosell, who lives in Pound Ridge, started life as a lawyer but today is director of sports for the American Broadcasting Company's radio network. And he has thousands of hours of experience as a sportscaster to back up the opinions he voices unhesitatingly and candidly.

For example, he speaks venemously of Casey Stengel, and abhors the fact that "the Mets outdrew the Yankees two-to-

"almost complete failure."

This record he blames largely on the manager. And he decries the idolizing of these failures by today's youngsters. "Why should kids grow up worshipping total failure?" he argues.

On the cheerier side of the baseball ledger, Cosell, who is the only sportscaster to win an Emmy, calls Willy Mays "great"; Jackie Robinson "most exciting"; Ted Williams, "the best hitter"; Joe DiMaggio, "the greatest ball-player"; Ralph Houk, "the most respected," and Bobby Bragan, "my best friend."

Moving off the baseball di-

amond, he declares that tennis is "the best individual sport, requiring brains, stamina and strategy", and regrets that it is one of the least publicized. He feels track meets are "fascinating". And, treading unconcernedly on thousands of toes, he favors the abolition of big-time college sports because of the "buying" of college athletes who, he claims, are accepted by a school in preference to other applicants.

In reviewing his seven years covering sports, he singled out the heavyweight fight where Floyd Patterson regained the title from Ingemar Johansson as

SPORTSCASTER Howard Cosell tapes many programs from a studio in his Pound Ridge home, where he keeps an extensive sports library. With him here are, left to right, his daughters, Hilary and Jill, and his wife, Mary Edith.

Cosell, his wife Emmy, and their daughters Jill and Hilary struck a warm-hearted *Father Knows Best* theme for a 1964 article in the *Mount Vernon Daily Argus*, when the family lived in suburban Pound Ridge, New York. Because his own parents had a less-than-perfect marriage and he himself a troubled childhood, Cosell made sure his family remained close-knit over the years. *(Bill Mitchell / Photo)*

Cosell likely interviewed more star athletes than any other man in America. Here he enjoys a relaxed give-and-take with Yankee great Mickey Mantle, about whom he produced a brilliant and revealing documentary in the mid-1960s. Another, *Run to Daylight*, about legendary Packers coach Vince Lombardi, is still regarded by many as the finest sports documentary ever made. *(Bettmann/Corbis)*

In this 1965 photo, a year after Cassius Clay "shook up the world" by beating Sonny Liston for the heavyweight title, Cosell chats with the newly renamed Muhammad Ali during a radio interview. With Ali having converted to Islam, the topics turned serious, and would get more so in 1967 when Cosell bravely defended Ali's refusal to enter the military on religious grounds, a stand that would help transform American sports and culture. (*Bill Mitchell / Photo*)

Before the Ali news turned deadly serious and he was stripped of his title, farce often marked his periodic appearances on the air with Cosell. After Ali hinted he might fight seven-foot NBA star Wilt "the Stilt" Chamberlain, Cosell had them "spar" in the studio on *Wide World of Sports*, looking on at the spectacle, which fortunately never came off in the ring. (*Bettmann/Corbis*)

right ways, and Cosell with typical humility saw himself in the exact same light; that he too was about to break out as just such a delegate of a new order, on a different but related plane. As Clay went, so too would Cosell.

But while that may well have been an easy and necessary induction for Cosell, was it for Clay? As precocious as he was—and Cosell would later hail him as "a figure transcendental to sport" and "a native-born genius in at least some areas of his intelligence"[13]—it's tempting to overlook that he was only twenty-two when he fought Liston, and the reason for Cosell subtly qualifying Clay's intelligence is that he was quite naive. Clay approached the world as he did a fight, by forming instant judgments based on what he saw through strictly blinkered eyes and instincts; not from what he knew but what he felt from somewhere within. Later, those instincts would harden through worldly experience, but he would live recklessly as well, too closed off to be able to let anyone too deeply into his life, including wives and longtime associates, any of whom he could quickly turn on.

Cosell, contrary to the impression left by his argosy of interconnected moments with Clay–cum–Muhammad Ali, was not one of those who won his complete trust. He just never fit that way, certainly not the way he fit with the highly intelligent train wreck that was Floyd Patterson. Clay's first impression of him would stand: Howard Cosell was also a corner man of sorts, a useful tool, though not one easily tolerated by other men in the Clay camp. One of those was Ferdie Pacheco, Clay's personal physician, who doubled, at no pay, as one of his corner men beginning with the first Liston fight. Later he would become a longtime boxing analyst for NBC. Now in his eighties, he has a sharp mind and still nurses a grudge against Cosell.

Says Pacheco: "He wasn't anybody then. He was mouthy, ass-kissy, just another New York rat. He wanted to be the center of attention. Cassius was friendly to everyone, he didn't think anything in particular of this New York guy. The prime bullshit was the story Cosell and the rest of 'em put out that Ali wanted to kiss their asses. Listen, he didn't need to do that because they all came to kiss *his* ass. Howard always mistook Ali being nice for being liked. And he created that whole myth about how he 'made' Muhammad Ali. It was so fucking outrageous that he could even say that."[14]

Conversely, according to the man closer to him than anyone else, Angelo Dundee, Clay *did* need to reach out to the media, and even then the "New York rat" with the foghorn voice was a prime get for the Clay camp. Dundee, the brilliant, elfin trainer, ran across him early on, recalling, "The first time I saw Howard, I had a guy fighting at Madison Square Garden, not Ali, I think it was Willie Pastrano, in the early sixties. I went on his TV show so I could brag on my fighter. And I knew this was a very smart guy, and from what he would ask, that he would be good for us.

"When Cassius got to know Howard, it was a matter of respect. They both respected each other. My guy got glib on account of Howard. 'Cause my guy was just a kid with a high school education. Howard really helped to define who Cassius Clay was. Howard was a blessing for us, and boxing. Boxing was my thing, my life. And Howard sold it to the public like it hadn't been sold before. Muhammad always appreciated Howard. He enjoyed Howard. They were two originals, and they knew it. We knew Howard could do things for us. And Howard knew he could go a long way if Muhammad did and if he kept close to him. He was no dummy. Neither of those two guys were. I'd call 'em both geniuses."[15]

Pacheco makes a trenchant point when he metaphorizes Cosell as "Sammy Glick times two," meaning the archetypical parvenu created by Budd Schulberg in his 1941 novel *What Makes Sammy Run?* Like Glick, Cosell ascended as an accurate but unfortunate stereotype of New York Jews on the make, despite the wall of anti-Semitism that he kept running up against. Cosell may himself have wondered at some point whether his "mouthiness" was making him seem as if he, as Schulberg wrote of Sammy, was "running people down" and whether "death was the only finish line, without a single principle to slow him down." Schulberg, a Jew, had to wonder for the next fifty years about what his book had done to the image of Jews. But if Cosell wondered about such things, it would have to wait for later. He was too busy running.

SO WAS Clay. Hard, and upward, as was clear when he commenced an agenda to put himself in position to pick off the title by pricking the brittle ego buried deep beneath Liston's seemingly indomitable facade and fists. For a time Sonny could ignore the babbling of an unproven quantity trying to cut the line waiting for a title shot, but then Clay had vaulted into the role of number-one contender a month before the Patterson-Liston rematch. His taunts became news. To many in the press Clay was the de facto opponent that night, not the devalued Patterson, and the fight merely a warm-up for a more intriguing match. Sonny felt his heat, too. As soon as he'd made quick work of Patterson, Clay was up on the ring apron cawing about how he would tame the "Big Ugly Black Bear."

Had he chosen, the Bear could have repaid the Lip by ignoring him and fighting a couple of bums for easy paydays, while Clay either rose or walked into a right hook against other fighters. But as Cosell tried to conduct an interview with him in the center of the ring, Sonny had had it with the jabbering, sylphlike figure ten years his junior outside the ropes. He began waving a gloved hand menacingly at him, then finally spat out, "You're next, big mouth," which for Sonny was the full tide of eloquence.

For Clay, that was the brass ring; for Cosell, it was the seed not just of a fight but of the next *big* event in sports. As it was, Liston's demolition of Patterson was an afterthought; Cosell had already written off Floyd, his ardor not transferred to Liston—about whom Cosell wrote in his memoirs, "He was a cheap and ugly bully without morality, and I had no use for him. It's just too easy a cop-out to say that Liston was a product of a society in which the black is a second-class citizen. Sonny was simply a bad apple." In real time, he referred to Liston as a "congenital thug" on his radio and TV spots.[16]

Still, his job would be to interview Liston at intervals prior to the Clay fight, a chore few would have even attempted, Sonny's scowl a stop sign to be crossed at one's own peril. Cosell, a man not easily stopped, had tried before the first Patterson fight, driving to where Liston trained, the dilapidated Aurora Downs racetrack outside of Chicago, surrounded by barbed wire. He even took along ex-champ Rocky Marciano, who was just as petrified. Let in by a bodyguard, they encountered a surreal scene in which Liston, dancing with his wife to "Night Train" spinning on a record player, said nothing to them except "I ain't talking." Frustrated, Cosell straightened his spine and challenged him. "I don't give a damn if you hate me; I don't like you either, and I just met you," he said, somehow not wetting himself. "But you gotta do this interview."[17]

A big, and rare, smile crept across Sonny's face. He did the interview, and was even ingratiating at times. There would be others, too, each met by grudging concessions by the press that maybe Cosell was more than a poseur. Boxing people noticed, too. Like Angelo Dundee, who says of the go-getter Cosell, "He got you the nitty-gritty. He spoke to the fighters. And Howard was able to do that because these guys respected him." Dundee, who knew all the subplots of the sport, recalls Cosell's union with Floyd Patterson tellingly, in the same way Floyd put his love and/or hatred of boxing; it was, the trainer says, "like a romance. They were like a married couple. They'd be tight, then they wouldn't be talking to each other, but they always had a soft spot for the other one. When I was training Jimmy Ellis, he fought Patterson in Sweden [in 1968]. And if you watched it on TV—Howard did that fight—Patterson won, because it was Patterson this, Patterson that. You'd never have believed that Ellis won! And then after the fight, Floyd drove Howard to the airport. Howard felt something for Floyd, he saw his humanity. And Floyd saw the same thing in Howard, which not everybody did."[18]

IF SONNY had his foreboding "friends," so too did Clay, in the Nation of Islam sect that had grown in the early sixties primarily because of the advocacy of Malcolm X, whom Clay had met with several times, as well as Elijah Muhammad, the leader of the order since 1935. To be sure, there was nothing casual or unthreatening about such a flirtation during a time when all the public at large knew of the "Black Muslims"—the term regularly used especially by whites for the grim-faced black men in dark suits and bow ties at Nation rallies—was that they seemed threatening, their rhetoric seeming often to be anti-Semitic. Malcolm X by the early sixties was more militant, calling whites the "devil race" and moving toward stricter Islam branches.

To a Sonny Liston, it must have been odd that even his Mob cronies had no ability to terrify his next opponent, or even counterbalance visions of what the Black Muslims might have planned for *him* should he mistreat their new recruit. Indeed, the Clay camp seemed not to have a care in the world about the fading Mob, even if the government still considered the latter a more potent and imminent problem—or at least one that it could go after with safer political cover. Weeks before the fight, FBI agents came to the Fifth Street Gym to ask Angelo Dundee if he knew anything about certain of Liston's alleged associates. "They showed me pictures," Dundee says. "I told them, 'I don't know these guys,' and that was it."[19] Never once, on the other hand, did anyone in authority pose similar questions about Clay and the Nation of Islam—a scab that broke open, perhaps hardly by accident, only days before the fight, when Clay's father, Cassius Sr., told the *Miami Herald* his son had joined the Black Muslims, casting an enormous shadow and a lowery subplot over the entire extravaganza.

Thus, in Cassius Clay there was not only the air of giddy, goofy melodrama but gradations of something much more complicated, dark, discomfiting—and certainly, as Cosell put it, irresponsible. Yet he was utterly irresistible, his wit as rapier sharp as any standup comic's. Some thought he was cuddly, a quality he would nurture even though he was anything but. As with many budding sixties pop culture staples like the Beatles and the Vietnam War—and Howard Cosell—there was much more to him than met the eye and ear. Just what it was, however, wasn't exactly clear.

FOR A time, the Clay-Liston fight, which was scheduled for February 25, 1964, in Miami Beach—fortuitously, where Clay had practically lived the last several years, training at Angelo Dundee's downtown Fifth Street Gym, where Dundee had also trained Carmen Basilio and Sugar Ray Robinson—like all other sports matters fell off the map in the shroud of mourning following the horrific Friday morning of November 22, 1963, when the news broke from Dallas that President John F. Kennedy was gunned down by an assassin's bullet. Cosell mourned, too, but in the midst of grief was compelled to get on his soapbox and rake NFL Commissioner Pete Rozelle over the coals.

That grim weekend, the nation would sit transfixed in front of their TV sets watching in shades of flickering black and white the heartbreaking rites of an American president lying in state in the Capitol, interrupted only by the live murder of Lee Harvey Oswald in a Dallas police garage. Yet the patrician Rozelle, who had come to office in 1960 after Bert Bell died, decreed that the league's games—unlike those of the AFL—must go on, even without TV coverage, lest the owners' investments suffer the loss of one fourteenth of the schedule. For that, Cosell blistered the National Football League as a "national disgrace." And Rozelle, with whom he was yet to become friendly, would come to agree, years later calling that decision the worst he had ever made and the one he regretted the most.

By February 1964 the country was slowly getting its bearings back, the sense of retrenchment aided by the comforts of uniquely sixties entertainment forms—two of which, signally, happened that very month. The first came on the seismic night of the ninth when the Beatles appeared on *The Ed Sullivan Show*. The second, of course, was the Liston-Clay fight sixteen nights later.

As the event drew closer, Clay unveiled his newest rhyme, one he would get tons of mileage out of through the years, only needing to substitute another name for Liston's. This was the one that began "Clay comes out to meet Liston and Liston starts to retreat, if Liston goes back an inch farther he'll end up in a ringside seat" and ended "Hence the crowd did not dream, when they laid down their money, that they would see a total eclipse of Sonny." He would punctuate the "butterfly/bee" riff by booming in unison with Drew "Bundini" Brown, his leather-lunged flunky and corner man, who had written it, "Rumble, young man, rumble. *Haaaaaaaa*. Rumble, young man, rumble!"

Liston wasn't half bad, either, at playing the game. When Clay and his retinue showed up in Chicago to crash a Liston press conference, Sonny seemed to enjoy getting into the swing of the building promotion. Wagging a finger at Clay, he said, "Don't get hurt, little man," meaning in training camp, "'cause I'm gonna beat you like I'm your daddy."

The show was on.


THE "YOUNG and pretty" Clay was everything Howard Cosell wasn't, but the unlikely duo would squeeze every ounce of profit out of incongruity. As usual, Cosell was everywhere. Miami Beach, he seemed to know, would be a key checkpoint. Angelo Dundee recalls: "Howard could turn a guy into a national name. And he knew boxing, he would ask the tough question. He would force Cassius to think. It would be like a shadow box, and they both loved that. Howard could be tough, too. We had nicknames for the writers. Myron Cope was 'Mickey Rooney,' 'cause he was a little guy. Al Buck was 'the Gangster,' 'cause he used to wear a raincoat all the time. Howard was . . . I'm trying to think of what it was. Maybe we didn't give him one. I think we were scared to, 'cause he would have buried us if we did and he didn't like it."[20]

Despite Dundee's efforts to set up his boy with the writers, few—even the favored ones—were taking the long odds that Clay could actually beat Liston, Cosell among them. In retrospect, some of their now-ludicrous prognostications on the eve of the fight seem amusing for their near uniform and emphatic stupidity; by example, Lester Bromberg of the *New York World-Telegram* sniffing, "It will last almost the entire first round," and the *Los Angeles Times*'s Jim Murray cracking, "The only thing at which Clay can beat Liston is reading the dictionary." Jimmy Cannon sized down Clay as a mere "bantamweight who weighs more than two hundred pounds." The *New York Times* was so dismissive of Clay and the fight—with columnist Arthur Daley pointing to Clay's "one trifling handicap. He can't fight as well as he can talk"—that its boxing writer, Joe Nichols, refused to go to Miami to cover it; a young Bob Lipsyte got the assignment.

The fight went off as a putative mismatch, a theme only reinforced for Cosell at the weigh-in the morning of the bout that escalated into one of the most manic and bizarre episodes ever seen by anyone in the fight game. It began when Clay, wearing a shirt reading BEAR HUNTIN', came in screaming like a psychotic madman and never stopped, repeating over and over, "Round eight!"—which had become his mantra in prose and poetry as the time he would remove Liston from the crown—and "Bring on the big ugly bear!" When Liston arrived, the ruckus got worse, Clay moving to within a few feet from him and shrieking, "I'm gonna eat you alive!" and "Somebody's gonna die tonight!"

As Dundee and Sugar Ray Robinson tried to hold him back from leaping on Liston—not an overly difficult task, since as Dundee admits "he was just pretending to get past me. Listen, I could have pushed him back with my pinkie"—the chairman of the Miami Boxing Commission announced he was fining Clay $2,500. The commission doctor, ordered to take Clay's pulse, found it to be 110, more than twice his norm, whereupon, presumptuously for a physician, he pronounced him "emotionally unbalanced, scared to death, and liable to crack up before he enters the ring." As all hell was breaking loose, Liston—who had used previous weigh-ins to intimidate opponents—could only stare incredulously and mutter a few incoherent rejoinders. Eventually, Clay was hauled away, kicking, still screaming.

Cosell would recall the manic scene as "something out of the Mad Hatter" and say that "I, for one, left that weigh-in convinced that Ali had genuinely popped his cork." Before the fight would go on, however, he would realize the whole crazed affair was a sham, its purpose to unnerve an already addled Liston. Early that evening, Cosell was watching Clay's brother, Rudy, a novice fighter (soon to rename himself Rahaman Ali) win a preliminary match when Clay suddenly arose from a ringside seat. "It's my man, Howard Cosell!" Clay yelped while playfully chucking him on the shoulder. "Howard, stand here and watch my brother take care of this chump!"[21]

Said Cosell years later: "I could only think to myself, 'Why, that son of a bitch, what an actor!' Never saw a man cooler and he's about to go up against the most feared heavyweight in a decade. I realized then he'd put on a show that had taken everyone in." He related that when he asked Clay about his freak-out at the weigh-in, the reaction was an impish smile. "Oh, I was scared, man, scared," Clay said facetiously. "I just thought I'd let all those writers see how scared I was." Clay mentioned that he'd done a prefight radio interview with Cosell the day before, and that from what Cosell said, "I was just going to die when Liston stared at me in the ring." That, Cosell seemed to infer, was when the idea occurred to Clay to go into the weigh-in play-acting "scared and crazy," the objective being to scare the pants off Sonny, or as Clay said, "because any man who's not a fool has got to be scared of a crazy man."[22]

At that moment, Cosell professed, he was "convinced that the guy was totally unafraid. I learned early in the game that Cassius Clay is one of the most confusing men in the world; just being in his company one can undergo a series of conflicting impressions. He has the instinct of a honeybee, darting from flower to flower, always looking for the pollen."[23] Believing that he'd played even a minor, unwitting role in forming Clay's stratagem, Cosell would be quite willing to take a bow for that.

NOT THAT he was ready to rescind his prediction of a Liston victory by knockout. That, of course, was the prevailing wind in Miami. On a pre-fight radio show hosted by Cosell, he polled a dozen columnists—Red Smith, Mel Durslag, Charles McCabe, Lyle Smith, Frank Gibbons, Cy Burick, Hal Abrams, Shirley Povich, Murray Kempton, Jack Cutty, Jack Hand, Arthur Daley, and John Carmichael—all of whom forecast Liston in a breeze except Carmichael, of the *Chicago Daily News*, who ventured that "if the fight goes past five rounds, Clay will win it." When Cosell told him he was the only one of that mind, Carmichael said, "I'd rather be right than president, and I have very little chance of being either." Cosell pointed out, with some brininess, that the "sporting press around the nation" had "established the Liston legend of invincibility."

Turning to Liston, Cosell asked what he thought Clay "deep inside" was thinking about. "The payday he gonna make," said Liston, who won-dered if Clay "might jump out of the ring." Then a calm and almost serene Clay proclaimed, "I'm gonna upset the whole world tonight, Sonny Liston is in trouble . . . scared to death . . . At the weigh-in I could see defeat in his eyes. That's his gimmick, scarin' people at the weigh-in. But I got him today." Did he think Liston was a good fighter? "No, Howard, I don't see nothin' to him," adding that Patterson—"a cheese champion" with "no footwork"—had made it easy for Liston to "rabbit hunt." On the other hand, "I'm just like a heavyweight Sugar Ray. It's hard for me to get hit." Was he scared? "After all the talk I've been doing, I'm always wary, but I'm never scared."[24]

CLAY CAME in a seven-to-one betting underdog, and one refrain going around was "I'm betting on Clay—betting on him to live." Yet, attracted by the new-age challenger, the "beautiful people" and literary elite saw it as a "happening." George Plimpton was there for *Harper's*, Murray Kempton for the *New Republic*, Norman Mailer for *Esquire*, Budd Schulberg for *Playboy*. Yet for all the showmanship and melodrama, ticket sales lagged, and on that Tuesday night the Convention Hall, seating around fifteen thousand, was half filled, though a phenomenal 75.3 million listeners did tune in to ABC Radio, which billed it as "the Sound and the Fury," and thousands more were in theaters for the closed-circuit TV showing.

Cosell, again hosting and doing the color beside blow-by-blow man Les Keiter, steered clear of the Black Muslim subplot and defined the fight as a search for "fundamental answers to two naked questions," namely, the credibility of either contestant. When Clay entered the ring, he remarked to Rocky Marciano, "I must say, the kid does look cool . . . buoyant. I'm frankly astonished at his demeanor." Cosell had tipped listeners that Clay would move "clockwise to the left, always looking for the Liston right, then maybe faking once and then coming across with [a] right after slipping Liston's right." And, dissecting Clay's piston-pumping left jabs, he noted that they were executed with the turn of his wrist, sacrificing landing a flush hit to surgically slice his opponent's face. If one had heard no other analysis beyond that, it would have been all that was needed.

Clay, who few realized was actually about as big as Liston, began the fight on his toes, mostly keeping a distance for two rounds, and Cosell was noncommittal, saying after round two that Clay "was gaining in confidence." Then, in round three, those razorlike jabs opened cuts under both of Liston's eyes—his face, Keiter said, looked as if it had "been in a meat grinder." Off air, Cosell now told Marciano that "there's no way this guy can lose. We've been completely fooled, Rock. The kid's a fighter." On air, he said, with a subtle dig at his favorite goblins, "Words don't make a fight, fists do. Clay is making the fight tonight with his fists. We are surprised. So is everybody else in this arena, including the top sportswriters in the nation."

Round four was Clay's crossroads. Late in it, his eyes began furiously blinking—the cause of which, though never confirmed, was assumed to be a burning liniment called Monsel's Solution, which, having been rubbed into Liston's cheek to stem a cut and into his ailing shoulder, then got into Clay's eyes on the clinches. Clay had to evade the stalking Liston without ever really seeing him, but he did, weathering a few big body shots. He then returned to his stool and, looking like anything but the loudmouth braggart, wailed to Angelo Dundee, "I can't see!" and "Cut off the gloves!"—a freeze frame that for many would become a periscope into Clay's vulnerability, or even cowardice.

For Dundee, the frenetic moments in the corner would be a potential Waterloo for him, too, which he avoided when, according to legend, he pushed Clay back into the ring for round five. Dundee, though, downplays the hero's role cut for him, clarifying that after ignoring Clay's pleas he merely stood him up for round seven. Indeed, almost comically now, but not then, several Black Muslim "friends" of Clay seated nearby, seeing Dundee flush Clay's eyes with water from a pail, came to the corner accusing *Dundee* of being the culprit, by using tainted water in Clay's eyes—"They were looking to stick a knife in me."[25]

All the commotion in the corner caused a stir at ringside. Cosell barked over the air, "Something is the matter with Cassius Clay! . . . He is having trouble with his eyes!" At the bell, Keiter added, "One of his trainers yelled that there's something in Liston's gloves." As the round progressed, with an air of doom about Clay's ability to survive, Liston caught up with him and tried to blast away, leading Keiter to burble, "Clay's been hurt" and "Liston is close to finishing it now." But it didn't happen. The few shots Liston landed Clay weathered, and by midround Clay's eyes had cleared and he was further shredding Liston's eye tissue. When the round ended, with Clay intact, Dundee says, "I knew we had it in the bag."

Cosell wasn't as sure, notwithstanding what he told Marciano. After the sixth round, even with Clay feasting on a curiously inert, passive Liston, Cosell could only say, "This is hard to figure out." But not half as much as it was when the bell rang for round seven and Liston remained on his stool, his trainer Jack Nilon waving the back of his hand toward referee Barney Felix, a signal of capitulation. Standing across the ring, Clay raised his arms and began churning his knees in a victory rumba. Cosell, in the middle of a sentence, suddenly began to squeal, his voice close to cracking, "Wait a minute, wait a minute! Sonny Liston is not coming out! He's out! And we have a new heavyweight champion of the world, it's Cassius Clay! Les, I'm going up into the ring!"

As he did, the table at which he and Keiter were seated collapsed under a mass of humanity trying to get into the ring, both reporters and fans. On the radio, Cosell's unforgettably fevered last sentence seemed to reverberate against the pandemonium, his incredulous tone the perfect barometer of the moment—just as it still is nearly half a century later, having grown into one of the most choice of Cosell daffodils (and one that provokes some mimicry from Jerry Izenberg, who recasts it as "I'm going up into the ring where no man has ever gone before!"). Bulling his way through the mob in the ring to get close to Clay, he called out, "Cassius! Cassius!" as Clay, swept up in the crush, was intoning, "I am the greatest! I am the king of the world! I have upset the world! Gimme justice!"

Cosell interrupted him. "Tell the truth, Cassius . . . Did you ever believe it would happen this way?"

Hearing the familiar strident voice, Clay stopped and replied, "I told you. If he wanted to go to heaven I'd get him in seven. I am the king! I am the king! I am the king!" The questions and answers now came in a hail—"What made him so easy for you?" ("Because I'm too fast. He was scared.") "What happened to your eyes coming into the fourth?" ("He had liniment on his glove. I couldn't see all that round. Almighty God was with me . . . I took his best punches and I couldn't even see him.") And, after conducting this operetta done in shouts, Cosell congratulated Clay, then, when he couldn't get his microphone back, said, "Let go of the mike, Cassius"—a small sample of the inspired tomfoolery that would soon become the rule for the two of them.

Making his way to the vanquished Liston, who still sat on his stool, he began, "I hate to bother you at a moment like this," and was able to elicit the scoop that Liston was claiming he had somehow injured his right shoulder even before the fight, making it impossible for him to throw a punch or even lift his arm from the first round on. His last question—would he beat Clay if he had another chance?—brought an answer abstruse enough to be worthy of Floyd Patterson. "I don't know," Liston told him. "I have to think about it." Cosell's last line to Liston was almost like a future condolence: "Thank you, Sonny, and good luck to you, anyway."

Cosell's summation of the night's proceedings went easy on the hyperbole, with none really needed. "That's the history as we have it now in this incredible ring," he began. "They're booing Sonny Liston. You heard the story of his shoulder, what he says happened to it. Cassius is standing in the ring. He's taking his bows . . . This is, without question, no need to pour it on, one of the astonishing upsets in the whole chronicle of boxing."

But it was he, more than anyone except the new Boy King of Boxing, who would keep pouring on about what happened on February 25, 1964. Because with what happened he had found an ace for his sleeve that no one would be able to trump.

# 6

## "BEDLAM, CHAOS, CONFUSION"

IN THE aftermath of the epic and exhilarating, if not troubling, transfer of power in boxing, Cassius Clay only continued to live up to his own self-aggrandizing prophecy. It took mere hours for him to confirm all the rumors about his conversion to the Nation of Islam, a formality that was assumed when days before the fight one of his guests was Malcolm X, but only briefly before he was convinced by the promoters to leave town. But Malcolm, who had recently remarked, openly, that John F. Kennedy's assassination was a case of "chickens coming home to roost," and before that, that American Jews "sap the very life-blood of the so-called Negroes to maintain the state of Israel," was there for the fight, in a ringside seat next to two of Clay's closest bobos, Sugar Ray Robinson and soul singer Sam Cooke, who that December was slain in an L.A. hotel shooting.

On the morning after his climactic victory, after spending the night celebrating with Malcolm and football running back Jim Brown, the new "king of the world" met the press, which kept pressing him on the religion question, with one reporter asking him, condescendingly, if he was "a card-carrying member of the Black Muslims." Exasperated, he decided the hell with questions and went off on a long monologue. "My religion is

Islam, I believe Allah is God. It is the truth and the light." Asking, "What is all the commotion about?" he painted an idyllic scape in service to his religion, the very name of which "means peace. All I want is peace, peace for myself and peace for the world," though his mood darkened when he added he couldn't be a Christian any longer, "not when colored people are being blown up."

In the end, he assured, the Nation of Islam "is no hate group. Followers of Allah are the sweetest people in the world. They don't carry knives. They don't tote weapons. They pray five times a day. Muslims only want to live in peace with their own kind"[1]—never mind that he had made a loud exception by calling one of his "own kind" a "big, ugly black bear" or even an "ugly nigger" at times, and that weapons were in fact commonly carried by Black Muslims, with Malcolm X himself having once remarked that he could not wait to "steal us some guns, and kill us [some] crackers."[2] But then the whole conversion seemed less somber than self-promoting dramatic art; what else could it be when just weeks before Elijah Muhammad had insisted he had no interest in Clay, that sports was "wicked" and that his impending loss would bring shame on the Nation.

In the space of seven rounds, there were suddenly benefits in having him, in publicity and enrollment. He also became a hot potato within the movement when Elijah and Malcolm had a falling-out, partly because Elijah resented how close Malcolm was to the champ—the latter two having realized, as did Cosell and Clay, the mutual benefits of an alliance. For Clay, the kinship made him positively starry-eyed, saying that Malcolm, not he, was "the greatest." But there was darkness on the edge of town. Death threats now began to surface against Malcolm, who in early March split from the Nation of Islam intending to form another Muslim sect, in the Sunni tradition, and thus was "excommunicated" by order of Elijah from the Nation of Islam. Cassius Clay, not by coincidence, announced his own parting of the ways with Malcolm.

Now the fight was on for ownership of Cassius Clay, and legitimate concern arose that he might get caught up in the middle of a tribal, intra-Muslim civil war. One of Elijah's means of controlling him was to rename him. The first choice was Cassius X, or Cassius X Clay, but in March, Elijah decreed a more distinctive identity, Muhammad Ali. Management of his affairs would now be administered by Elijah's son Herbert Muham-mad, replacing the Louisville syndicate that had nurtured him. The musical-chairs game about his new name struck many in the mainstream media as a joke, their general familiarity with such exotic names being from *Ali Baba and the Forty Thieves* and *Arabian Nights* rather than anything in Islamic eschatology and the Koran; nor that Muhammad meant "one worthy of praise"—and being named so was an honor reserved for 1 percent of Nation of Islam members, never even consid-ered for Malcolm X. Historically, Muhammad was the founder of Islam and the messenger and prophet of God, Ali, the cousin and son-in-law of Muhammad who ruled over the Islamic caliphate after his death and wrote the Koran with his own hand.

Few in Judaic-Christian America were prepared to care about the derivations, or call him by his new name, one that many poked fun at. If "Ali" was used at all, it was part of an equation, most often "Muhammad Ali also known as Cassius Clay." The highly respected *Los Angeles Times* sports columnist Jim Murray wrote that "Muhammad Ali—Cassius Clay to you, perhaps," was the "white man's burden." Jimmy Cannon, now with the *New York Journal-American*, hyperventilated that Ali's ties to the Nation of Islam were the "dirtiest [development] in American sports since the Nazis were shouting for Max Schmeling as representative of their vile theories of blood." The high and mighty, and liberal, *New York Times* held off on using "Ali" on the pretense that he hadn't legally changed his name. When Robert Lipsyte would turn in copy using only "Muhammad Ali," he recalled, "some editor would change the copy to 'a/k/a Cassius Clay' . . . Ali didn't get the support he deserved from the media. Attention, yes. Support, no."[3] Dick Young, doing his part to hold back the tide, mocked him as "Muhammad Ali Cassius Clay," or "MACC."

In March 1964, the champ came to Madison Square Garden to catch a stablemate of his, Luis Rodriguez, fight that night. By custom, he was to get a shout-out and walk across the ring, but Harry Markson, the boss of MSG Boxing, would not permit him to be introduced by his new name, on the absurd grounds that "Clay" was on his New York State license. Furious, Ali stormed out, to cascading boos from the crowd. Even Ali's own father and mother went public decrying the Nation of

Islam as a "phony religion," saying that their son had been taken in by "Muslim poison."[4]

On his part, Cosell—who after all had changed his own name—was eager to pat himself on the back in *Cosell* for "instantly" accepting the conversion, with the breezy, noble sophism that "it meant nothing to me because I felt it was the man's own business." Rather than seeing any outrage or danger in it for the fighter, he insisted that at the beginning he was "amused" but nonetheless contemptuous about the "Old World writers [who] wanted [Ali] to live by their code . . . [as] a noble example, in accordance with their concept, of shining manhood . . . [T]hey wanted him to be another Joe Louis. A white man's black man."[5]

The irony was salient: Ali neither drank, smoked, nor used drugs— the standard the moral guardians held athletes to, but which few in the heavy-drinking, smoking, foul-mouthed writing brigade could claim for themselves. Ali was, Cosell said, "the one who was pure," not that it mattered to his detractors, and when their malevolence for Ali would not ameliorate with time, he said, "I grew angry and finally furious."[6]

Still, Cosell never would address the thorny supplemental question that surely resonated with him as a result of the Muslim issue: whether he ever felt threatened as a Jew by the sect's sometimes inflammatory and paranoid rhetoric about Israel and their "enemies" in the American Jewish community—which may have made Cosell more than a bit conflicted, given that many of *his* enemies were Jews in his own industry. Unknown is whether he ever held any of that rhetoric against Ali, though it is relevant that this would not be the last time Cosell would take a pass on such layered issues; in fact, he consciously recused himself from a good many areas related to race, which he of course addressed often, and courageously, but with limited dimension.

For a time, as well, he reflected the knee-jerk hedging by timorous or even bigoted newspaper editors and TV and radio producers by using the awkward appellation "Muhammad Ali, also known as Cassius Clay." He did that as late as Clay's second fight with Henry Cooper in May 1966, when he began an interview with him that way. Ali looked hurt, asking him "Howard, are you going to do that to me, too?" making Cosell feel three inches high and ashamed he'd ever done it.

"You are quite right," he told him. "I apologize. Muhammad Ali is your name. You're entitled to that."[7]

That was the last time he ever conflated the two names, though the reflex to do otherwise remained. As *Sports Illustrated*'s Myron Cope wrote in 1967, "To the disgust or titillation of viewers, Cosell meticulously addresses the heavyweight champion by his Muslim name. Privately he stridently defends the right to be known by the name of one's choice, however exotic, but after tossing off a few Muhammad Alis he lapses into Cassius Clays."[8] Still, he was mortified that even in 1973 when he wrote his memoirs, the *New York Times*, the grande dame of the liberal media, was *still* using that same tortured construction, an act he called not "morally right." That it was an issue for so long within the journalistic fraternity, and as such within the general public, was more than preposterous; it was, he said, "sickening to me intellectually," the worst of ironies being that those writers who were most offended seemed not to know, or care, that the name Cassius Clay was that of a Kentucky senator who before the Civil War had been a slave owner, and that their self-righteous slings were, in fact, "racist snarls."[9]

THE SCHISM over Muhammad Ali's name provided Cosell with one more reason to lambaste "the press." And justifiably, considering some of the ways in which many of the most literate sports journals treated the issue. *Sports Illustrated*, for instance, pricked that the champ—whom it still called Cassius Clay, relenting in 1965 to make it "Cassius Clay (Muhammad Ali)"—would be making "an ill-will tour of Africa and Asia." This, it wrote, was no more than "tragicomic nonsense." Not only did the name and religious conversion meet resistance, the very result in Miami Beach was accepted only grudgingly by many in that crowd, and with conditions attached. Dick Young, for one, deigned in his first postfight column, "If Cassius wants me to say he's the greatest, all right, I'll say it, but I'll also say he scored the greatest retreating victory since the Russians suckered Napoleon into a snowbank. I never saw Joe Louis run away and win, or Rocky Marciano . . . Cassius Clay is the greatest, like he says, but right now that isn't saying much."[10]

Contrived, snide equivocations like that, which were rarely made for other fighters, forever irked Cosell, whose own answer to the "fix" question was direct: that Liston quit when "his spirit had vanished, because he was just a big bully anyway."[11] The media snark intended to degrade Clay's ability curdled Cosell's tenuous relationship with the old-guard news hens. It was heading that way with Young anyway, something that could be discerned late in the Clay-Liston broadcast when he interviewed the pugnacious sportswriter. When Cosell echoed Clay's claim that Liston had liniment on his gloves, Young took issue, saying it came from a sponge in Clay's corner.

"This is entirely true," said Cosell, patronizingly, "but Clay did claim that Liston's handlers did put liniment on his gloves."

"Well," Young sighed, "he's a very distrustful person, I'm afraid."

Breaking into derisive laughter, Cosell ended the session, saying, "You said it, Dick Young of the *New York Daily News*, I didn't."[12]

Young complained for months that Cosell had sandbagged him, putting him on with the intention of embarrassing him, believing that he knew infinitely more about boxing than Young did. Their already shaky relationship was close to meltdown, and it would soon become open warfare, running parallel with the yoking of Howard Cosell and Muhammad Ali. The ascension of both would serve as the fulcrum both of Young's malevolence for the coming future, and of Cosell's for the enduring ineptitude and bigotry of the sports media and the print boys in particular—again, making no exceptions for those who were far more kindly disposed to Ali, such as Jerry Izenberg, who was unqualified in his support of him.

"Howard was not always noble or admirable," Izenberg recalls. "But when it came to race, there was no hypocrisy about Howard. Howard used Ali. Ali used Howard. But the fact remains that Howard really cared about Ali. And essentially that was what Howard was about. He cared about certain things, deeply and irrevocably. That came from a place way inside. He would sometimes lose his way, then he would think of himself as bigger than the great issues, where if you didn't bow to him it meant you just didn't understand anything. He did that to me a lot, and again that was very unfair. It was like the anti-Semitism. If you didn't like him, you were anti-Semitic.

"He also faced pressures from the TV side that he had to appease, which he did very delicately and very well. You cannot take away from Howard that he did a great job on race, and Ali crystallized it. Howard took Ali's side, and that was it. Whatever he did, he never backed down from positions that he really believed. And that was what made Howard Cosell."[13]

BY THE midsixties, ABC was well positioned as a bold operation with a hard nose and even brass knuckles when needed. Tom Moore, as coldly as an undertaker from his days selling those cemetery plots, had not hesitated to confront the other two networks' primacy by playing the game of "leverage," in the industry parlance; for examples, forcing sponsors to make ad buys on *Wide World of Sports* in order to get in on the NCAA football games and luring NBC and CBS affiliates with the carrots of the ABC sports menu; once committed to carrying sports, it was a short step to get them to become ABC affiliates, since the prime-time schedule had hit shows like *My Three Sons, The Flintstones,* and *Ben Casey.*

Such tactics had moved Moore up on the ladder, to president of ABC Television—a development that no doubt kept the martinis flowing to a morose Cosell's table at La Grenouille—and the overall rise of the network made Ed Scherick thirsty to move beyond the sports side as well. In 1964, when Dan Melnick, ABC's vice president for programming, quit, Scherick got the job. Now both of Cosell's main—maybe *only*—underwriters at the company were gone or removed from the sports side, even as it flourished; and Scherick would be on the company payroll only until 1967, when the seductions of Hollywood called.

But what Cosell could not have failed to grasp is that Scherick's exit actually left *him* with some useful leverage, since the three players at ABC Sports who now vied for the seat of ultimate power—Scherick's two rising young protégés, former production assistants Chuck Howard and Jim Spence, and of course Roone Arledge—would progressively amass more power. Howard and Spence, both of whom cut their teeth on *Wide World*, would serve as coordinating producers for it even after attaining concurrent vice president status at the network. But the absolute seat of

power was Arledge, if de facto, since no one at the network felt the need
to codify a formal title for him until 1968, when he would officially be
named what he already had been for years, president of ABC Sports.

It surely couldn't hurt that Cosell kept the stocky, swarthy Spence
and the wiry, sandy-haired Howard favorable or at least neutral vis-à-vis
his prospects at the network, and he worked all the angles to do it. He
dined with Spence and his wife regularly at those fine restaurants. And
Howard, on his recommendation, moved to Pound Ridge, just down the
road; they often came into the city together, willingly on Chuck's part,
not a bad thing considering that he was known to be temperamental and
insensitive—though much of the testimony on this would emanate from
Spence, who endured as his rival—with fixed notions and judgments
about on-air talent. Both men found Cosell quite the charmer.

Still, getting close to the inscrutable Arledge in ways like these was a
tougher chore. Even in the midsixties, Cosell couldn't definitively know
where he stood with King Redhead. Having his two courtiers on his side
was the best he could do; neither did it hurt that a third Scherick protégé,
Chet Simmons, who was not as amenable to Cosell, left for NBC Sports
in 1964 (he would become its president in 1977, then ESPN's first president in 1981). But it was Roone who needed to be convinced to believe
Cosell was as brilliant as Cosell believed he was.

By then, the ABC sports menu had branched out again; the Pro Bowl-
ers Tour, which sprang from periodic coverage on *Wide World* to a Saturday early-afternoon spot, was an instant ratings winner, providing a
key lead-in to the show that spawned it. But as haughty as Arledge had
become at ABC, he still answered to Tom Moore, whose aversion to
Howard Cosell was no secret around the ABC office. Moore's benign
neglect toward the man who mutually despised him had a trickle-down
effect; even if someone in a position of authority at ABC Sports dug
Cosell, the unwritten covenant was clear: Do not hire that man. And
Roone dug him, since the first time he heard him. That was in 1959 when
he was a neophyte producer for Ed Scherick's Sports Programs Inc. and
working ringside at the first Patterson-Johansson fight at Yankee Stadium, which was broadcast on radio by ABC.

Arledge in his 2003 memoir *Roone* wrote of hearing a radio

announcer doing a commercial "in tones that suggested a happening the equal of the Second Coming." Amusingly, he thought it was Eddie Bracken, leading him to wonder "why we had hired the old movie comedian to call the fight for ABC radio." Someone told him it wasn't Eddie Bracken but rather "just a smart-ass from the local station." Acting on some unexplainable instinct, he said, "I jotted down the announcer's name: Howard Cosell."[14]

The Cosell embargo, however, was nothing to trifle with, and it is telling that when Arledge recalled his first five years as a power at the network, he wrote without equivocation that the latter had been "blackballed by Tom Moore for being too New York, too pushy, too all the qualities that made Cosell Cosell." He also recycled Cosell's claim that "anti-Semitism was the actual root of his banning." And so, fairly or not, Arledge too had to wait for the right time and circumstance that would allow him to "sneak" Cosell by Moore, the only way it could have been done. But it was getting close, very close.

THE MEANS to that end would be Muhammad Ali, though for reasons no one could have divined in 1965. Indeed, two weeks after he beat Sonny Liston, when he failed his Selective Service induction exam a second time because of poor reading, writing, and math skills, he was disappointed he was not going to wear an army uniform. Even after his conversion to Islam, he didn't raise the prospect of declaring himself a conscientious objector. Free to defend his title, a Liston rematch was made for November 16, 1964, in Boston—not by decree of Ali but rather the World Boxing Council, the newest international sanctioning body, formed in 1963 as a check on the antediluvian World Boxing Association, which dated back to the 1920s and represented a Byzantine boxing establishment. Neither was fond of Ali. The WBC, suspicious of a fix in Miami Beach, ordered a redo, though it left Ali with the belt. The WBA didn't go along, its rationale about the fight violating its rematch policy a weak dodge for its enmity to the new champ, whom it stripped of its belt, which went to lanky Ernie Terrell, a onetime Ali sparring partner, after he beat Eddie Machen in a bout few knew had even existed, or cared if it did.

Cosell was again a constant during the buildup of the fight, which was remarkable since ABC Radio was outbid for the fight by the Mutual Network. Still, he was tiring of the radio as his main venue, believing the future of sports really belonged to TV. That his overheated radio style had become something of a cliché in the TV era was confirmed when the television and radio critic of the *New York Daily News*, Kay Gardella, wrote that his "speeded-up questioning" in Miami Beach "reminded the listener of the famous I'll tell you what I'm going to do pitchman of radio's early days."[15] Thus, wearing the banner of *Wide World of Sports*, he got all the mileage necessary to perpetuate his presence in the boxing milieu, conducting interviews with fighters and reporting on fights ex post facto.

But he was not in Boston as an Ali retainer. In fact, Liston had trained so hard and looked so mean and lean that Cosell—no matter his epiphany about Ali in Miami Beach—forecast a seventh-round Liston knockout. That set up a mock contretemps with the cheeky champ. Picking him out of a crowd of media congregated at the Boston Garden, Ali initiated a winking diatribe that surely must have sent a tingle up Cosell's leg.

"Stop, everybody," he declared. "I want you to know that this is Howard Cosell. And I'm gonna whup him. He thinks Sonny Liston can beat me!"

The prediction was irrelevant, secondary to the mutual value each had for the other. By now, Ali had come to trust Cosell as a defender at a time when it seemed like the rest of America was against him. Whenever he came to New York, he would either call or walk in on Cosell in the studio, unannounced. Walking down the busy streets together, both men could not help but take notice of the stares that grew into mobs of people all around them. They were, by all measures, a team, complete opposites in every way except for their organic meshing of purpose that seemed to magnify, even elevate, each of them, both separately and in tandem. Only with Cosell could the young black Muslim have perceived that it wasn't just safe but preferable to push the envelope on race and religion.

"Call me nigger," Ali would tell him on those wanderings, "in front of these people. They'll think we hate one another."[16]

Naturally, that was an entreaty that Cosell could never have complied with. Nor was it remotely necessary; not when it was so instantly understood by anyone who encountered them that they absolutely did *not* hate each other. What he saw in Ali, he said over time, was a "complex" and "ambivalent" man, with a highly limited attention span, a kind man, but also a cruel one. These were properties others could lay on Cosell himself, though such truisms usually escaped him. Ali, he said at various other times, was "remarkably dimensional, far above and beyond his absence of literacy and culture."

Ali, in turn, found not just a tool but a kinsman. Quoted by Thomas Hauser in the 1991 oral history *Muhammad Ali: His Life and Times*, he said: "I like Howard Cosell. He was a professional. He knew how to bring out the best in people. He respected the law, and had a sense of right and wrong and history. But he wouldn't have been nearly as big as he was without me, and I hope he knows it. I was big . . . Everyone in the whole country was talking about me."[17]

Cosell without doubt knew it. But there was an undeniable feeling among those who knew Ali—and perhaps Ali himself—that if left to his own devices, he would have flown in a million directions with no fulcrum to center, balance, and humanize him to the public. And as his reign began to stretch out, it was just as undeniable who that force was. According to Robert Lipsyte, "a lot of the [media] attention was focused on the wrong things. But there were several interesting media relationships that developed during that period, and the relationship between Ali and Howard Cosell was one of them."[18]

Actually, that relationship was by far the most significant, its genesis being that Cosell was a propitious conduit, as the only reporter who regularly covered the boxing beat on TV—the medium that was the message. As Jim Spence recalled, Ali "played a very significant part in the early success of ABC Sports. Early on, Ali and Howard Cosell formed a relationship that linked them forever in the minds of the American television viewers."[19] One might even say it was kismet.

Not least of all their mutual attractions was their inability to keep quiet, and to say things that could either amuse and/or anger people. The young fighter had also come to admire the older man's gnawing hatred of the old-guard boxing writers. Just as few of that crowd regarded Ali as a worthy champ, even fewer believed Cosell was worthy of being taken seriously. The synergy between them was one of symbiosis. Like a Coltrane or a Miles or a Dizzy, Ali's mind swung and swayed with certain rhythmic directives, which were actualized by his tongue. The improvised thrust-and-parry charade he could carry on with Howard Cosell fit into the rhythm.

Although Cosell would, partly but not fully in jest, imbue himself with the credit for "making" Ali, Larry Merchant—who began doing boxing analysis for the then-young pay-cable network known as Home Box Office in the late seventies and still does so today, at times as bluntly and controversially as did Cosell—says the relationship was manipulated far more by Ali's skillful guiding instincts. "Ali was good and clever, and it was smart of Howard to latch on to him because Ali was an extraordinary personality. He was a walking reality show before there was such a thing. Everybody in the media loved the guy, because when you spent time with Ali, you got something. But when Howard did his 'I discovered Ali' thing, you know, that was the problem with Howard. He had to be the guy who discovered Ali. Never mind that Dick Schaap was writing about Ali at the 1960 Olympics as 'the King of Rome.' A lot of us had discovered Ali before Howard did. But Howard had the means to use it for self-promotion."[20]

Inescapably, if Ali was something not before seen, Cosell was something not before heard. But their concomitant rise was hardly coincidental for the latter—who clearly could not have fully flowered as he did linked to a Floyd Patterson or Sonny Liston. That case is made in retrospect by Jim Lampley, Merchant's partner on HBO's fight telecasts for over a quarter of a century. Lampley, who began his career as a twenty-something hand at ABC Sports in the midseventies, has the deepened perspective of a former Cosell aide de camp and subsequent boxing play-by-play man walking in Cosell's footsteps, something he points out every boxing announcer to come since, consciously or not, has done. But the progenitor, he says, was Ali.

"Yes, Howard carved the template for us all. Along with all the literary figures who populated the sport, Howard demonstrated that the way to do boxing is from above, working from a limited perspective rather than from down amid the hoi polloi. You don't do boxing in boxing language. You do it in the rarefied language of literature, parenthetically."[21]

What made it work so organically for Cosell was the demand, the need, for greater literary proportions to inform the Ali argosy. But if Ali provided the glue for the mosaic of highbrow and/or lowbrow Cosellian impulses, on a primordial level they were simply damn funny together. Soon, one or the other would be suggesting certain staples for their burlesque—Cosell's toupee, for example—should be incorporated into their act; that's what they called it, their "act." In Boston, the main shtick was Ali's bug-eyed yammer of "I'll whup your hiney!" Noel Coward it wasn't; but it did seem something like a new theater piece opening in the sticks.

NOT AUSPICIOUSLY, however, the show closed in Boston before it could open. Three days before the redux, Ali needed emergency hernia surgery and the fight was put off until May 25, devastating Liston, who could only mutter, "I knew he'd hurt hisself, talkin' so much." The path to the belated rematch now became labyrinthine. First, Boston pulled out, because politicians there suddenly became aware Liston was tied to organized crime or thought the promoters were; not to be discounted, either, was the Black Muslim storm cloud.

For weeks the bout hung in limbo, then found a home seemingly in the only town in America that would take it—Lewiston, Maine, a decaying mill town of around forty thousand on an elevation near the Canadian border known as Skunk Hill. There, the fight would be held in an old high school hockey arena seating four thousand, alternately called St. Dominic's Arena or the Central Maine Civic Center, which had once been used as a sporadic out-of-town home court by the Boston Celtics.

The frivolity of the Ali road show, however, was blown away on February 21, 1965, the day that Malcolm X was gunned down by three very much armed Nation of Islam members as he delivered a speech in Harlem's Audubon Ballroom. When the news broke, the Nation of Islam could barely stifle its joy. Even as black leaders eulogized Malcolm as a martyr, Elijah Muhammad, a self-described man of peace and love, growled, reminiscent of Malcolm's obtuse statement about John Kennedy, "Malcolm X got just what he preached." Ali, given Elijah's opinion on the matter, began to echo it.

Now the open question became whether Ali would be singled out for vengeance. Cosell made the most of every drop of the building melodrama, which became a weekly soap opera on *Wide World of Sports*. Months before, his moxie had scored another nervy, compelling interview with Liston, whom he had, on the air, heavily criticized. When Cosell came calling on him, Liston greeted him with his usual warmth. "You ain't my friend," he said. Cosell readily agreed, then said the measure of a man was "working with people whose company one did not enjoy"—and on that subject, clearly Cosell knew of which he spoke. As he recalled, almost enchantingly, soon "we were walking along a deserted, windswept beach . . . while the cameras rolled." Breaking the idyll, Cosell asked him point-blank, had he thrown the first fight?

"No."

Was he owned by gangsters?

"No."

It was more than anyone else had gotten out of him.[22]

REPORTING ON Ali and the Black Muslims meant that Cosell had to make a crucial distinction. He was, as was empirically confirmed by much of his work, more than a reporter; he was a speaker of truth, unafraid to offend those who might take offense. Ali's very portentous conversion demanded some of that hard crust. That the press by and large had vilified Ali for it would seem to have set Cosell up perfectly to diverge. Instead, he punted, making no real effort to place this or other issues related to athletes involving themselves in social or religious causes into a broader, deeper context. Never, not even retrospectively in his books, did he admonish Ali for being sucked into something he did not fully understand. The repercussions of this dangerous, or at least dangerously misunderstood, alliance were left off the docket.

If asked about these omissions, Cosell could have easily fallen back on the rubric that he was reporting straight news, that his opinion about a man's religious company was immaterial; and he wouldn't have been wrong. However, it could also have been plausibly called a cop-out. Whatever it was, it would be cyclically repeated for other hot-button issues. As it was, only a peck of media people would willingly align on the left side of the social ledger, though not a single one who worked in TV. One who did was Jerry Izenberg, who admits he could enter that territory writing for a newspaper in Newark more easily than a man drawing far bigger paychecks from the American Broadcasting Company.

"It wasn't only Howard. I was pissed off at the time at the television sports guys for being timid. Those guys wouldn't take a stand on anything. Howard was the lone voice in the wilderness. But this was a very tough issue. And I would learn firsthand from working with Howard on some documentaries how hard it was to cross sponsors and network executives. I knew—and he knew—he could have gone further, about Ali and the Black Muslims. I could not abide what was going on with Ali. What he said about Malcolm X made me livid. I thought: 'You son of a bitch. One minute Malcolm is great, then all of a sudden he's nobody, because somebody tells you he's nobody?' That was bullshit and Ali knew it. But Howard had a riskier platform than I did, and he had a more complicated relationship with Ali."[23]

The fact that Cosell was sympathetic to Ali was enough to be a historic milepost. As Frank Deford puts it, "Ali had enormous impact for Howard. The bias, the prejudice he faced, I think that had something to do with his appreciation for Ali and all the criticism Ali got as a Muslim. Maybe that made him hold back on the Muslims, who knows, only Howard did. But with Howard, once he believed in something, or someone, it was set in stone."[24]

Cosell would confirm as much, telling Tom Hauser that Ali was "an index to the bigotry lodged deep within the wellspring of this nation and its people. The only other person to come out of sports who might be as important as Ali was Jack Roosevelt Robinson," though the differences between those two epochal men and the eras they reflected would become clear in time.[25] The irony was that as the Ali saga proceeded, Cosell would take heat from both sides of the racial divide—from Ali sycophants for reproving Ali at times about his gratuitous cruelty in the ring. But his pragmatism about Ali and the Black Muslims was salve for Ali as well, and thus one more reason for Ali to be so gracious to him. After all, if a natural-born yenta like Howard Cosell wasn't going to pry into areas that could embarrass him and ask out loud why the "greatest" heavyweight champ was allowing himself to be led around on a leash by some seriously misguided people, less uneasy would be the head that wore the crown.

ALI-LISTON II, on May 25, 1965—a day before the U.S. Senate passed the Voting Rights Act—was another exercise in primal sixties lunacy. The champ was calm and carefree, happily showing off his new wife, Sonji, whom he would divorce within a year. The only effect the post–Malcolm X frenzy had on him was as a good angle for publicity. Liston, on the other hand, was on edge, and seemingly dissipated. In addition to facing Ali, whom he believed to be absolutely insane, he genuinely feared the Black Muslims. Cosell, on the air, ventured that Sonny looked as if he'd aged ten years in the last six months, though he was still picking Liston to win.

Clearly, the icky overtones of the fight kept the pretty people away this time, and the locals could only fill half the hall on that late-spring Tuesday night; the closed-circuit broadcast—beamed overseas for the first time—would be the only thing that saved the promoters from taking a bath. While Cosell had no place on either the live radio (Russ Hodges and Bill Stern covered it for Mutual) or closed-circuit broadcasts, ABC purchased rebroadcast rights and would show the tape a week later, with Cosell's real-time call, on *Wide World of Sports*, with Ali on hand to offer retrospective comments. As it turned out, there'd be a lot of time to fill, and a lot of explaining to do. To this day, there still is.

Ali, introduced to loud boos, would get no more popular when just before the two-minute mark he unleashed his curious and now infamous "phantom punch" that sent Liston sprawling to the canvas and set in motion a farcical caracole created by the referee, ex-champ Jersey Joe Walcott, who should have sent Ali to a neutral corner. Instead, Ali stood over the supine Sonny, gesturing and yelling at him to "get up and fight, sucka!" Walcott belatedly tried to push Ali away as Liston tried to get up, only to flop back down, but as Ali then vaulted into the air and raised his gloves, the clueless Walcott ushered *Liston* to a neutral corner, then—

astonishingly—left the fighters alone as he fled to get the count. The fight resumed, before Walcott finally stepped in and waved the fight over, some *thirty* seconds after the knockdown, the longest "long count" since Dempsey-Tunney.

As Ali was toted around the ring by his delirious corner men and lackeys, and a dazed but oddly serene Liston stood in the middle of the ring alone, everyone else in the hall either sat silently unbelieving, booing, or crying "fix!" Cosell, barking into his ABC microphone, related a scene of "bedlam, chaos, and confusion" in the old arena. Clambering into the ring, he waded into Ali's lecture about being so fast that the punch couldn't have been seen, though why no one had *heard* it either was a mystery. But he could hardly believe it when Ali made a bad situation worse by attributing the blow—the "anchor punch," he called it—to Stepin Fetchit, the black comic actor of the thirties whose stereotypical "darky" roles were anything but funny to blacks in the sixties. Incredulously, Ali had taken on the old symbol of subservience as an "advisor," and he would back up the tale, saying, "Jack Johnson, the great champion, learned it to me, and I learned it to Ali."

An hour after the debacle, with cries of "fix" and "sham" still piercing the air, a showered and relaxed Ali emerged again, wearing a cardigan and white shirt, for press conference near the ring with surly, skeptical reporters. Behind Ali, a burly bodyguard tried to keep the crowd from getting too close, but somehow there was Cosell's panda face wedged between Ali and Angelo Dundee, his hand raising a microphone under Ali's chin, interrupting, "Muhammad! Was he doing anything differently from the time you hit him, up until the time you hit him, from the first fight?"

Ali never looked behind him; he knew exactly who it was. Stopping in midsentence, he seemed to giggle and hit a riff. "Well, Howard Cosell, what he was doing was, uh . . . ," then, pointing a backward thumb, "This fella makin' all this noise is Howard Cosell." A pause, then, "What he was doing, Howard . . ."[26]

As he went on, the panda kept smiling. Even on this surreal and disturbing night, how calamitous could it have been if there was something to smile at?

AMID THE postmortem, few were willing to swear there had been no fix—including Cosell, who confessed that he never saw the punch and called the fight a "fiasco." Politicians, being politicians, jumped in mouth first, forcing the promoters to hold up the fighters' purses pending investigations, which a grandstanding U.S. congressman, calling the outcome "a fraud" and "a disgrace to boxing," said he'd be only too happy to convene.

On *Wide World* the following Saturday, he was the consummate reporter, giving no quarter to a what-me-worry Ali, who sat beside him perhaps expecting laudation and setup straight lines. Cosell ran the tape of the fight, then broke the knockdown into a series of slow-motion and stop-action replays of different camera angles, none of which could definitively prove there had been a punch, much less one with the sort of force it would have taken to put Liston on his back. Rocky Marciano, an expert witness, said he never saw a punch. Invited on by Cosell, Jimmy Cannon orally redelivered what he had told Cosell right after the fight, "I saw that punch and it couldn't have crushed a grape," a line that would become the most quoted of his career.

Ali, acting highly offended at the premise that the punch and the fight were anything less than pristine, almost pleaded to be believed as he went about his soft shoe about the anchor punch. "I'm glad you're showing this in slow motion," he said, "because I'm so fast you can't see me. You've never seen a man in history move like this." Watching himself stick and move, he purred, "Ain't that beautiful? Notice I'm floatin' like a butterfly and stingin' like a bee." Actually, one clinically slowed-down replay did perhaps back him up, as it showed Liston's cheek shiver and his body abruptly stop moving forward at the precise point the punch would have nailed him. Ali, realizing this, squealed in delight, "See? See? Look at that!" Still, Cosell was unconvinced—and would remain so long into the future, writing in *Cosell*, "People ask me, 'Was it fixed?' I still don't know," and "If there is a secret to the story of Lewiston, Maine, it went to the grave with Sonny Liston." In no mood to clown with Ali, he ended the segment with a sad threnody, sadly and correctly averring that "if boxing can survive this, it can survive anything."[27]

For a time, he had to seriously contemplate whether things would need to change between him and Ali. In addition to everything else, would Ali now be considered a phony, a cheater, just another boxing con? As it was, Cosell had been made instantly suspicious by Liston's demeanor when he left the ring in Lewiston; there was, he would later say, "a look of absolute relief on his face . . . Was he glad just to have it over? Or just to be alive?" given his abiding fears of the Black Muslims.[28] It would be one thing if Ali—as he had shown when Liston first went down—wasn't sold on Liston's flop; but now he was trying to sell the Stepin Fetchit hogwash, which put Cosell in an untenable position. As a consequence, would their budding buddy act go up in smoke?

It helped him no end that the flow of attention moved to Ali's next defense, against Floyd Patterson. No evidence of a fix would turn up elsewhere, and everyone involved with the most tainted title fight in history just wanted to move on. And so the team of Ali and Cosell was on safe ground. By the time Liston made some striking claims years later that he had taken a dive because of his fear of retaliation from the Black Muslims, and another time that it was on orders from the Mob, it grabbed no headlines. The general feeling about Lewiston was that the less said about it the better. That was a break for Liston, too. Though he had to live with the memory of the two most curious fights, he was able to keep fighting until just days before he was found dead on January 5, 1971, a puncture in his right arm, a syringe near his body, bags of heroin in his home, the conjectured cause of death an overdose.

WITH PROVIDENTIAL timing, ABC in early 1965 made its latest strike into the heart of the other networks, NBC in particular, shelling out $5.7 million to take the Saturday baseball Game of the Week from the Peacock Network and back to ABC. The network chose as announcers the likeable veteran Chris Schenkel, the booming play-by-play voice of the Milwaukee Braves and the AFL New York Jets, Merle Harmon—who had been hired for the latter job the year before by Cosell when WABC began to carry the Jets games—and a folksy, phlegmatic Georgian named Keith Jackson, the sports director for ABC Radio West, who had worked some early AFL games for the network and also was the first American to do a sportscast from the Soviet Union. Arledge then made a fateful choice about the man who seemed so perfect to push the hard-edged, colorfully rendered ABC sports template, only to be passed over so often.

The baseball package, Arledge reckoned, was the kind of fortuitous circumstance that would permit him to put Howard Cosell on the network on a midlevel, as he was on *Wide World* reporting on boxing. Making him host of the pregame show on a Saturday baseball game mired in the graveyard shift of the TV landscape was a "safe" gig, and familiar turf for him, though Arledge may have believed he was going out on a thinner limb giving Cosell the job, since in *Roone* he recalled, inaccurately, that Cosell's Mets gig was "terminated when Howard informed listeners that Casey Stengel . . . was taking naps during his team's games," not that Cosell didn't appreciate Arledge perpetuating the notion. About the new job, he twitted, "I have been authorized to say it's great to be back in the big leagues."[29]

To be sure, Cosell had come away from the Mets job with a less than gleaming reputation among the owners, least of all the ones in New York that he nonetheless swore followed his instructions in hiring their general managers. For TV, staying on the right side of the owners was good for business; owners could, and did, make trouble for announcers who deviated from party line to hard truth—no matter that they were being *paid* millions of dollars for the games to be televised. But Arledge was willing to let Cosell do his stuff, prickly though it might be, and let the owners taste what the sixties were like in sportscasting.

A bigger burden was how to, as Arledge put it, "sneak" him by Tom Moore. Keeping Moore in the dark until he could hire Cosell, Arledge literally sneaked him up to his office, looking up and down the hallway as he let him in. Cosell, blissfully unconcerned with how delicate it all was, dispensed a typical gasconade, the kind no one ever knew if he really meant, saying his hiring was "on the scale of Milo T. Farnsworth's invention of the cathode ray tube, the television rebirth of an acknowledged genius. You are to be congratulated, young man, on your sagacity." Arledge still hired him. Saying, "Howard, cut the crap," he laughed at the absurd pomposity, an animal he figured he'd have to live with now that Cosell was on board.[30]

In fact, Arledge wanted that animal prowling ABC's air; as Cosell had proved by his tango with Ali, there was something to be said for an announcer an audience would tune in to see, especially those whom he irritated. Cosell was sharp enough to know how to get people like that to actually like him. But would one of them be Moore? Arledge, who said later he knew Moore would be "purple-faced" mad when he found out, had to bust a gut convincing him of the logic that if the ABC Sports template was to be brash, provocative, memorable, who better than Cosell to voice it?

To his relief, Moore went along. What's more, Cosell worked on Moore, so charming him that he only now began to see the Cosell who was, as Arledge noted, "irresistible, funny, self-mocking, bighearted, a person who owned a room simply by walking into it." The upshot: "He and Tom grew quite friendly."[31] For Cosell, that would be yet another chance to say about someone he thought anti-Semitic—"I showed him."

On the Game of the Week, he showed everybody how transferable the Ali shtick was, though he mainly kept himself to conventional interviewing and reporting the drama of the season that culminated with victories by Sandy Koufax's L.A. Dodgers and the upstart Minnesota Twins. Cosell was even able to call on Jackie Robinson to make a couple of guest shots on the air. However, NBC still had dibs on the World Series, shutting Cosell out of an event he would have killed to cover. Then, the next year, NBC reclaimed the Game of the Week. ABC went dark on baseball for the next dozen years. But Cosell could have every reason to think the next network gig was just around the corner now that even Tom Moore was on his side.

## PART TWO

# Living Color

## (1964–1976)

# 7

## AN ELECTRONIC FIRST

DISPLAYING VERSATILITY few could, Cosell crept further into the network graces by capitalizing on local TV projects, as a behind-the-scenes player, the tangible benefit of which would be to prove his worth as a TV journalist without the distraction of his voice and personality. That seed was first planted in 1962 when he was asked to produce a half-hour late-summer documentary for WABC-TV. Naturally, he didn't go about it halfway. After forming a company production house, Legend Productions, he recalled later that he realized the scheduled air date, August 15, roughly coincided with the twenty-fifth anniversary of Babe Ruth's death; thus a film called *Babe Ruth: A Look Behind the Legend* was born.

For this, one of the first sports documentaries, he recruited Roger Kahn—who a few years before had asked Ray Robinson, "Who the fuck is Howard Cosell?"—to write the script, crusty actor Horace McMahon to narrate it, and appearances by Ruth's widow and some of his surviving teammates, including Leo Durocher, as well as Roger Maris. But there was a snag when Ted Shaker, the ABC executive in charge of affiliate programming, saw it in advance and thought it amateurish and not up to network standards. John Gilbert, who ran the station, broke the news to Cosell: "Shaker says it's a bomb."[1]

He held firm, convincing Gilbert to run it. When he did, the reviews were radiant; one, by Kay Gardella, was headlined "Babe Ruth Hits Another Home Run." Next thing Cosell heard, Shaker, whom he also blamed for holding him back from the network (with some delectable irony, in 1971 Shaker would become chief executive at the Arbitron ratings service that charted Cosell's stratospheric ratings and name recognition that decade), was taking bows at the network; his only huzzah for Cosell was to tell him, "You're a great producer," which while perfectly true was taken by Cosell as a pointed reminder of his place off network air.

The success of the Ruth show mandated more sports films for the station. In April 1964 came the hour-long *The Polo Grounds: Requiem for an Arena*, again narrated by McMahon and featuring no less a cast than Floyd Patterson, Jack Dempsey, Joe Louis, Willie Mays, Leo Durocher, Bobby Thomson, Ralph Branca, and other top-shelf names, the likes of whom Cosell always seemed to be able to rustle up.

But it was the next film, in the fall of that same year, that would swing open the door bolted shut to him for so long. That was the brilliant, cinema-verité-style *Run to Daylight*, which was coproduced and deftly directed by Lou Volpicelli, who had come to ABC Sports in the early sixties. Volpicelli's crew filmed hundreds of hours during the Green Bay Packers' summer training camp at Saint Norbert College in West De Pere, Wisconsin, under the gaze of gruff, sainthood-bound Vince Lombardi, who was himself a partner in the production, it being an adaptation of his 1963 book of the same name, written with W. C. Heinz, which covered a week of Packer preparation during the 1962 season. Cosell optioned it for a small amount of money, then offered the world a rare look at the team's regimentation and the near-ascetic lifestyle in camp.

Half a century removed, one can accuse Cosell of canonizing Lombardi, who was shown strutting, barking, and delivering endless homilies about winning to his spellbound players, even hard-bitten veterans like Paul Hornung, Bart Starr, and Ray Nitschke. Lombardi's corn grew high—examples being "You can't play fatigued. Fatigue makes cowards of us all" and "We're all here only if we win. If we lose, we're gone" (but *not* "Winning isn't everything, it's the only thing"), but a close look reveals not so much a martinet but a brittle, vulnerable man deathly afraid of failing; his core was a soft, sentimental nougat he tried to suppress, but when he had to cut a player, he said, "I don't mind telling you I've cried." During filming one day, the grizzled coach ordered the crew off the field. Cosell was so miffed he was going to call off the project, whereupon a repentant Lombardi implored him to stay.

"You know better," he said, almost gently. "I get so absorbed, I don't even know what I'm saying," which would have made a great scene in the show.[2]

As Cosell would testify, Lombardi was indeed a kind of saint for him. For no one else did he reserve the kind of pious pleonasm that he did for him. "I have never known a man who left more of himself in those close to him," he waxed eloquent in *Cosell*, which was published shortly after Lombardi's death. "No man has ever had a greater impact on me."[3] It was a veneration he seemed only to retain for men so opposite from him that he could see none of himself in them, witness Muhammad Ali. Indeed, that he could be a common denominator in the wide polarity between the new-age black activist and the prissy, old-school, ultraconservative coach pleased him. Cosell delighted telling of when, interviewing Lombardi on one of his shows, the coach ribbed him, "I'm making you famous." Cosell rejoined, "You're beginning to sound like Muhammad Ali."

As Cosell remembered, "Vince didn't like that."[4]

As with Ali, his attachment to Lombardi was visceral, formed at once when it became clear that "he trusted me, and I believed in him." When the coach called him "Coach" one day, it was like a religious experience for Cosell, and he annexed it as his unofficial nickname—this although Lombardi called nearly everyone "Coach," rather than having to remember their names. But as with Ali, this slavish fealty to Lombardi would be cited by his critics as a prime case of crass Cosell opportunism, not to mention a prime name-dropping plum. He also refused to see his own flaws in those of Lombardi, which he preferred to let slide. Only lightly did he touch upon St. Vince's paranoia, which, like his own, centered around being treated unfairly in the press, even when criticism of him was fair, as in 1969 when, after years of decrying players jumping their

NFL contracts to go to the AFL, he broke his own contract as Packer general manager to coach the Washington Redskins.

Certainly, *Run to Daylight* was metaphoric for Cosell, as much so in the context of his career as it was for Lombardi. Because after the film played to critical raves and high ratings, running into the bright daylight of network TV was precisely what he could now do.

IT TOOK Cosell a decade from his notice in *The New Yorker* before the press wrote of him again, though the venue was hardly as chic, or portentous. In early August 1964, the *Daily Argus*, a small newspaper in the suburb of Mount Vernon, ran a profile entitled "Cosell Calls 'Em as He Sees 'Em," which began, "Howard Cosell is a man of opinions. Some may be right up your alley and some may be . . . well, that's what makes a horse race, as the saying goes." Playing the part, Cosell, it reported, "speaks venomously of Casey Stengel, and abhors the fact that 'the Mets outdraw the Yankees two-to-one' even with their record of 'almost complete failure.'"[5] The photo that ran with the story posed him as the embodiment of a family man, perusing sports magazines with Emmy and the two girls, all beaming.

That year was certainly a turning point, such that his gigs with Ali and on the baseball Game of the Week could be construed as a reward for his due diligence in the documentaries he had produced, which drew context and nuance around some of sport's most imposing legends. The documentaries went on, with a regular series of "Self-Portraits," in which Cosell would conduct one-on-one interviews with some imposing sports VIPs: Lombardi, Jim Brown, Wilt Chamberlain, Pancho Gonzales, Whitey Ford, and Mickey Mantle. There was also another documentary, in 1965, *Johnny Keane: The Yankee from Texas*, about the new, ill-fated Yankee manager, who wasn't half as interesting as Cosell and his scriptwriter, Jerry Izenberg, whom he recruited for the job, made him seem. It wasn't easy. During the filming, when Keane, a onetime seminary student, went on about his Christian faith, Cosell interrupted from behind the camera.

"Cut ! Cut! Cut!" he screamed. "I'm not doing a fucking commercial for the Vatican!"[6]

THE MICKEY MANTLE "Self-Portrait" was perhaps the best interview Cosell ever did. It ran on August 19, 1965, by chance when the Yankees' season, and the Yankee dynasty, had crumbled along with their once-great centerfielder. While Mantle's flaws and insecurities were many, his legion of hero-worshipping retainers in the press had for years kept them under wraps. But rather than reduce his legend, Cosell sought to apotheosize him as a real man of real flesh, blood, and pain, not just physical but psychological. Cosell knew of Mantle's alcoholism, as did many who were sworn to keep it quiet so as not to soil his golden boy image, and likewise stayed away from it. Instead, molded by research and questions fed to Cosell by Jerry Izenberg, the content centered on Mantle's ghoulish conviction that he would die young, as had all the male members of his family from Hodgkin's disease. A man of few words normally, he unburdened with simple, quiet, but intense emotion. Cosell was proud of the work, as well he should have been. Some years later, he would swear that, because of the show, Mantle had had a cathartic experience.

While it didn't get on the ABC network, the effect and success of this and his other films on the New York flagship station left his brand in the corporate office and in the sports department, the drama and story lines he created being exactly what Roone Arledge and his minions tried for—only Cosell did it better than anyone else. Indeed, his ongoing interviews with Ali, which might have been filed under docudrama, had provided some of the most memorable programming in the *Wide World of Sports* catalog.

As it happened, the third installment of the Ali serial drama came bare months later, when he defended his title against Floyd Patterson on November 22 in Las Vegas. If by then the foul odor of the two Liston fights had subsided, the ugly racial and religious subcurrents had not. Patterson was partly to blame. So eager to get another crack at the title, he all too eagerly warmed to the role of Great Non-Muslim Hope, saying that the Muslims were "a menace to the United States and a menace to the Negro race" and that "Cassius Clay is disgracing himself and the Negro race," pointedly using that name. In doing so, he was working off the example of other well-known blacks, for instance Joe Louis, who said that "Clay will earn the public's hatred because of his connections with the Black Muslims," and tennis player Arthur Ashe, who averred that the Black Muslims ascribed to "a racist ideology."[7]

But Patterson should have known that all this would stoke the vitriol of blacks and whites hoping for a holy war in the ring he had almost no chance of winning, and that as a fighter it would stoke the wrath of Ali, who in turn belittled Floyd as an "Uncle Tom" and "the Rabbit." Cosell, despite his abiding fondness for Patterson, saw through him, not liking one bit Floyd's refusal to call Ali by his chosen name, seeing it as a crass attempt to cast himself in the role of the "good guy." He also came as close as he ever would to confronting Ali on the controversial reputation of the Nation of Islam, though he was hardly inquisitional about it. Almost defensively, he remarked to him in one interview that "some people" believed Ali had "provided a very bad image for boxing because of your religion."

Ali, prepared for the query, noted with a touché logic that past champs had "come into bars with two blondes on each arm," whereas "I'm strictly a religious person . . . I don't see where I'm such a bad champion."

Cosell, again using the "some people" dodge, then asked if he agreed that Black Muslims were a "hate group."

"No, sir. No, sir," Ali protested, launching into a spirited, positive history of the group—minus its numerous violent acts and incendiary statements. "We are the victims of hate," he said. "Black people in America are victims of hate. We can't be taught to hate."

Cosell was satisfied, perhaps relieved, he had gone where he would not again, and seemed far more at ease massaging Ali's ego than challenging his motives.

"Documentarily," he oozed, seamlessly moving from journalism to shtick, "in your opinion you are the greatest. Is that true?"

"Howie, you're the greatest also," Ali obliged.

"I guess we'd get arguments from a lot of people on both statements," Cosell allowed, putting not an inch of daylight between the two of them.[8]

PATTERSON'S OWN shtick, which had Ali denigrating him as the "Technicolor white hope," did Floyd no good in the ring. Fighting with a bad back, he was a stationary prop for Ali to mete out a cruel punishment, mercilessly punishing him for twelve rounds, barking "What's my name?" before answering with a stinging punch. For the second straight defense, Ali left ample room for slings and arrows from the media; Robert Lipsyte, in the *Times*, wrote that Ali's behavior was that of "a little boy pulling off the wings of a butterfly piecemeal."[9] For Cosell, the fight marked the moment when "I began to get an index to the fact that Muhammad Ali could be a terribly cruel man."[10]

He would not let Ali off the hook for it. When *Wide World* showed the tape of the fight, he expressed his "total disgust" with the bout, branding it a "savage and needless punishment" of Patterson. He then coaxed Ali into admitting that he had "carried" Floyd, though he argued, trying to sound noble, that he had drawn it out because "I didn't want to kill him." But no matter what he had done, he pointed out, correctly, the critics would have made him the villain. "When I knock a man out I'm cruel," he said. "When I don't I can't punch."

Cosell was a bit startled when Ali said he "carried" Patterson, and told him that because of this admission "you might lose your license to fight . . . In effect you have admitted that you didn't put forth your best effort."

"I don't care," Ali came back, unfazed. "It's the truth and I want to say it."[11]

While no one called for a license revocation, Patterson was so offended that he wrote in an *Esquire* article that "Howard Cosell, who used to be my friend," had inveigled Ali to say what he did. Shortly afterward Cosell saw Floyd, who he recalled "couldn't look me in the eye." When he challenged him on the charge, Patterson "tried to avoid the subject."[12] But their "marriage" kept them bonded still. And because Cosell kept pumping up Floyd's status as a contender, it helped Patterson get another, equally painful, date with Ali.

ALI, MEANWHILE, had a proverbial date with destiny, and a gauntlet
to endure for the next three and a half years after, on March 9, 1966, his
draft status was reclassified 1-A—the active-duty status that he had wanted
only two years before, which he now intended to disobey. He was, he said,
a conscientious objector and would not enter the military, famously declaring, "Man, I ain't got no quarrel with them Vietcong . . . they never called
me nigger"[13]—generating instant bold type in thousands of newspapers,
and reams of agitated type from the nation's moral guardians in the sporting press. Red Smith, his generational slip showing, wrote that "Cassius
makes himself as sorry a spectacle as those unwashed punks who picket
and demonstrate against the war." Fellow dinosaur Jimmy Cannon lodged
what he thought was an even harsher charge—"Clay is part of the Beatle
movement," he yowled, along with "kids dancing naked at secret proms"
and "surf bums who refuse to work."[14]

As other overheated reactions billowed—the *Times*'s Arthur Daley
calling for a boycott of Ali's fights, and state legislators offering resolu-
tions condemning him as an enemy sympathizer—a scheduled match
with the WBA cheese champ Ernie Terrell in Chicago was canceled, and
around a dozen cities refused to take it. Finally, it landed in Toronto, but
when closed-circuit promoters begged off, so did Terrell, who was
replaced by Canadian champ George Chuvalo, an easy mark for Ali
though he couldn't knock him out. The fight lost all kinds of money, primarily because of the loss of closed-circuit. Faced with but one option to
sell out a house, or even get a match, Ali could only keep fighting out of
the country, and that yielded a significant development when his management team, led by Elijah Muhammad's son Herbert and a young lawyer named Bob Arum, sold TV broadcast rights for each ensuing fight to
the only willing buyer—ABC Sports.

Through the revolving doors every two months or so now came Brit
contenders Henry Cooper and Brian London in London, then German
champ Karl Mildenberger in Frankfurt. ABC carried them either live or
on tape delay, and they turned out to be the perfect vehicles for the suddenly burgeoning network, its go-to guy Howard Cosell, and a certain
director who had joined ABC in 1963 after a failed pro basketball career
and several years at CBS Sports—Chet Forte, the ex-Columbia All-

American who would now begin what would seem an eternal working relationship with the man who had duped him in that 1959 interview.

Playing off Cosell's braggadocio, Forte's manic temperament translated into his direction, with extreme close-ups and melodramatic story lines that, helpfully to Ali, made the champ into at once a visiting potentate and a man forced from his own country to fight. A good many viewers would object to how sympathetic ABC was to the desecrated champ, but the ratings soared. Cosell did his best to achieve a journalistic balance; on *Wide World*, Ali by his side, he would review each fight and impishly castigate him for having had such a hard time with "nobodies," even with the two Brits whose faces he slashed to pulp, bringing from Ali howls about how underrated they all were, especially the next in line.

Forte, too, was only too avid for Cosell to sandbag these other poor saps the way he once had Forte. Before Brian London stepped in against Ali, Cosell, whom London never heard of, ingratiated himself to the fighter when he trekked to his camp in Blackpool. Then came the interview. "Brian," he began, "they say you're a pug, a patsy, a dirty fighter, that you have no class, that you're just in there for the ride and a fast payday and that you have no chance against Ali. Now what do you say to that?"

London, as if he'd been head-butted, snapped, "I say flip you. I ain't answering the bleeding question." After halting the tape, Cosell explained to him that these weren't *his* judgments, but those of others. "Oh, I didn't understand," said London, who clearly was no Rhodes Scholar. When the tape rolled again, he was asked the same question. "I still don't like the bleeding question."[15] A third take finally produced a usable answer, but the two outtakes would be played for months at ABC parties, a classic marker of the delirious march forward the network had signed onto.

WHEN THE Mildenberger fight rolled around on September 10, 1966, there was something decidedly different about the broadcast. Heretofore, Chris Schenkel had done the blow-by-blow. Now, for the first time, it would be Howard Cosell, alone, with no sideman. Of course, he handled it beautifully, honing in on the confusion caused Ali by the "awkward southpaw" Mildenberger, who lasted twelve surprisingly tough rounds.

The pivotal role of ABC, Cosell, and Forte in melting the solid wall of denial against Ali in the United States cannot be overstated. Inside of a year, these brilliantly covered installments invaluably helped Ali establish credibility, and popularity, earning his keep as a fighting champion, independent of his religious/political beliefs. This happened as opposition to the war began to take hold, still a minority opinion but clearly growing in intensity and numbers as battlefield casualties mounted, making it harder to reflexively chant "USA, love it or leave it" and easier to sing protest songs.

The coming year, 1967, the one known for its "Summer of Love," would mark the hard birth of a "counterculture" melding youth, pacifism, hard rock music, and mind-altering chemicals. It was not something Dick Young or Jimmy Cannon could wish away. And suddenly, bringing home that message even harder, a corporate conglomerate—ABC—and a forty-nine-year-old man of high morals—Howard Cosell—would be in the thick of it. It would require only one more historic event tying the reality of the outside world to the little-boy fantasies of sports—the very ligature Cosell had foretold for years—before all that would become clear.

ALI'S LAST fight of 1966, because of the heightened appetite for him, came at home, in Houston, Texas, on November 14. It was against Cleveland "Big Cat" Williams, a former contender making a comeback after being shot in the gut by a Texas deputy sheriff during a traffic stop. But if Williams thought this was a good career move, on the night of the fight he refused for a time to come out of his dressing room, scared to death by the prospect of facing Ali's guns; Bob Arum had to threaten him with arrest before he emerged, perhaps not with full control of his sphincter.

Big Cat was an oracle, because he and the thirty-five thousand in attendance at the cavernous Astrodome, then the largest crowd ever for an indoor bout, witnessed an Ali primed, ready, and perhaps at his peak as champ, putting Williams away as easily as a tabby cat, knocking him down four times before the ref ended it in the third round, with Williams spitting up blood. Punctuating his performance, he unveiled the "Ali Shuffle," the foot-fluttering fandango designed to distract and confuse the opponent, not that he needed it. So fast was he, so mercurial and decisive were his moves, so pulverizing were his shots, that Cosell would make the case that, on this night in Texas, Muhammad Ali was "the best anyone will ever see him."[16]

It wasn't mere puffery. Indeed, few could have quibbled with his continued rhapsodizing in the wake of the fight, such as marveling about how Ali could administer a beating like that and not once get touched himself. By now Cosell was reaping large public relations dividends for Ali, and had no shame saying that the Ali of that period was like "watching an artist work with oils, hearing Beverly Sills sing an aria, listening to Rubenstein at the piano."[17] And Ali would reciprocate. ABC had a taped package to show before the fight with Cooper, but an early knockout on the undercard accelerated the main event. With network people desperate for time, Cosell banged on Ali's dressing room and pleaded to keep Ali from coming out. Angelo Dundee told him to get the hell out, but Ali pulled rank. "How much time you need?" he asked. In the arena, the lights had been turned off pending his entrance, and the impatient crowd was clapping and stomping their feet. But for eighteen minutes Ali would say, "I ain't ready yet" and "Nobody tells the champ when to go," as ABC ran its taped package.[18]

Not even a seeming misstep by Cosell could breach their bond. After the Cooper fight Cosell cut off Ali when he began to extol the Muslims and Elijah Muhammad, telling him, "We've been through all that before," and adding cheekily, "How about thanking the president of the United States?" Ali, barely reacting, mumbled, "Oh yes, yes. Him, too." On the flight home, on which he allowed Cosell to bum a ride, Ali had not forgotten. Intending to lay down the law, he began, "You know what you said to me in the ring?" but was stopped by Herbert Muhammad.

"Howard was exactly right," he said. "He had to say that. You've just got to stop doing that."[19]

In the past, Cosell was regarded as so interlocked with Ali that a Cleveland newspaper had once called him a "white Muslim." Now some

Black Muslims were angered at his disrespect. But that would pass soon enough, and Cosell knew he was in the lap of Ali's trust, more so than most African American journalists. He was even permitted to tell Ali, at will, "I'm the one that made you" or variations like "Without me, nobody would know your name." People in the Ali entourage, especially Ferdie Pacheco and photographer Howard Bingham, would gag hearing it, no matter if Cosell was less than serious. That Ali let him do it as much as he did may have meant Ali himself believed it, at least to a degree.

THE YEAR 1967 would be frenetic, profound, and challenging. It began with a fairly standard Cosell shuffle, talking out of both sides of his mouth, loudly. Though ABC had no part of Super Bowl I, when the knighted Packers of St. Lombardi met the long-shot Kansas City Chiefs in the Los Angeles Coliseum on January 15, he could reasonably inject himself into the building drama by dint of the fact that he had burnished his football credentials considerably over the past few years, though in the process he also bought himself some added tsuris from his favorite foil in the sporting press.

That interlude began in 1963 when Sonny Werblin bought the Titans—Cosell, his nose buried a mile deep in Werblin's hindquarters, regularly reminded people that his support for the man he cloyingly called "David A. 'Sonny as in Money' Werblin" had somehow been instrumental. If that claim was fiction, Cosell did have a small part in the team's jump-off as a real attraction. That happened when Werblin renamed them the Jets, apropos of what would be their new home-to-be a year later, windy Shea Stadium, right near LaGuardia Airport, a move that would command higher rights fees to their radio broadcasts that brought them to WABC.

In 1965, $400,000 of Werblin's money also bought them a star quarterback, Joe Namath, a risky move given that Namath had already had knee surgery, but a logical move given his howitzer right arm, lightning-quick release, and galvanic presence, his white cleats seeming to light up the ground he tread upon. Namath was an unlikely prototype of sixties nonconformity, having been raised in western Pennsylvania mining country and recruited by Bear Bryant to quarterback the Alabama Crimson Tide, but he soon wore an outlaw scent when he was suspended for half of his junior season for drinking. Namath, with his droopy eyelids, slumped posture, and bulbous nose, was more antiheroic than glamorous in the conventional mold of Bart Starr and Roger Staubach. Werblin's vision for him was as a raised middle finger to the NFL, which also coveted Namath, though the team that drafted him, the St. Louis Cardinals, could not hope to compete with Werblin's contract offer, which was by far a football record.

Cosell took an immediate liking to the cocky young man, seeing him cut from the socio-political-cultural cloth, if not nearly with the same profundity, of Muhammad Ali. Cosell helped brand him as "Joe Willie Namath" and regarded him as an essential flame for a social moth like himself, the Cosell modus being to ingratiate himself with any fresh new face that could keep him relevant by association for years to come. Namath's star power and raw talent were so natural that Cosell saw him as a can't-miss commodity. And Namath, on his part, figured that, as did Ali, he had to play along with Cosell's attentions. Indeed, to him, Cosell was so uncool that he was übercool, a man to joke about but also to humor, for the public relations reward of being favored by a media creature whose voice reached across radio and TV waves.

Thus, he became so friendly that the aging broadcaster, as if vicariously living the swinging bachelor life he never had, was a regular guest at Namath's East Side, much ballyhooed bachelor pad. Once, he was in the living room in a lather about something or other when Namath's roommate, fellow Jet Ray Abruzzese, was jarred out of his sleep in his bedroom by the sound of that familiar fine whine. Thinking it was the TV, he yelled, "Someone shut that damn sound off!" Everyone guffawed, fully aware that if Cosell was live and not on the tube, there was no way to turn the sound off. Namath would have an open line to Cosell; when, in the spring of 1969, he was given an ultimatum to sell his East Side bar Bachelors III, the first reporter he told that he would prematurely retire instead was Cosell— who was also the first he told, a month later, that he would sell his interest in the place after all, and was right next to him at both announcements.

Namath's public paeans to Cosell came slyly, such as when he told

*Sports Illustrated*'s Dan Jenkins in 1966, "Look man, I live and let live. I like everybody. I don't care what a man is as long as he treats me right. He can be a gambler, a hustler, someone everybody else thinks is obnoxious, I don't care so long as he's straight with me and our dealings are fair. I like Cassius Clay, Bill Hartack, Doug Sanders and Hornung, all the controversial guys. They're too much. They're colorful, man . . . But I like everybody. Why, I even like Howard Cosell."[20]

AS HEAD of sports programming for WABC Radio, Cosell had originally hired as the Jets' broadcast team Merle Harmon and the former quarterback Otto Graham. When Graham was hired as the coach of the NFL's Washington Redskins in 1966, Cosell replaced him with none other than Dick Young. Frosty as their relationship was, he once again showed how big he could be, hiring Young and then keeping a distance from him, confining his presence on the broadcasts to hosting the pregame show. But not everyone was convinced he was so altruistic; the theory arose that he had actually hired Young so that he could take pleasure in firing him, an inevitability that occurred after the 1967 season when Young was replaced by a former Jet lineman, Sam DeLuca, with whom Cosell had become tight.

Some suspected that Cosell may have believed Young was damaging the product by writing with less than affection for Namath, who, mocking Cosell, he derisively would call "Joe Willie White Shoes"—though Cosell himself was hardly a blind booster of the team, raking the aging, roly-poly coach Weeb Ewbank over the coals just as he had Casey Stengel, calling Ewbank "passé." Whatever led him to pull Young's plug, the firing was "the talk of the news room," says Phil Pepe. "It was like: uh-oh, clear the decks, World War Three has just started."[21]

Young's firing seemed to escalate their never-ending schoolyard brawl. Rarely would a week go by without a brickbat in a Young column about what he began to call "Howie the Shill," the point of which was to impugn Cosell's integrity by implying that he would attack sports not carried by ABC, mainly baseball but also the NFL, yet constantly pimp anything, trash-sport or otherwise, that appeared on *Wide World of*

*Sports*. Cosell would never fail to notice. He had long ago concluded that Young, as he told people, was the "worst excuse for a human being I've ever met." He also believed that the silver-haired writer was something like Javert, ever stalking his Jean Valjean.

Still, Cosell kept moving upward. *Sports Illustrated*, in its March 13, 1967 issue, featured a saucy profile by Myron Cope, titled "Would You Let This Man Interview You?" It was mainly a valentine to the subject's ego, the lead paragraph letting Cosell have his run-on sentences about the TV business being "the roughest, toughest, cruelest jungle in the world," his heroic endurance ("It may be that my greatest accomplishment was my mere survival"), and his classic name-dropping ("*I'm* the guy . . . who gets to Lombardi. *I'm* the guy . . . who gets letters from Pancho Gonzalez! *I'm* the guy . . . Champagne Tony Lema visited the very day he got back from the British Open, one week before his tragic death").

These self-congratulatory paeans were uttered, as Cope wrote, while he was "fondling martinis" at the Warwick Hotel. But the flattery ran thick, too, for example: "His interviews with Muhammad Ali are the Hope Diamond in ABC's 'Wide World of Sports,' television's most successful sports series." Cope also revealed the rather startling fact that at the time Cosell was earning $175,000 a year from ABC. Cope allowed him to get away with spinning the end of his Mets gig with the canard "We [the station] didn't want to be identified with a loser," and conscript a term originally used by Red Smith when he declared, famously thereafter, that "I'm in the toy department, sports!" and modestly concluded, "I have been an electronic first, and I don't mean that egotistically. Yes, when you get right down to it, I am a hero." Even Young had to give him his due, allowing in the piece that "he asks better questions than the other radio and TV interviewers, but he hokes up his questions so that actually they sound better than they are."

COSELL, AND pro football, had come a long way since he had incorrectly surmised in 1959 that the NFL would never grow enough to afford giving players a pension. As for himself, he had become too big for his role producing Jets broadcasts on WABC, and would give it up in 1968.

By then, he had become a lead voice pimping the AFL in the war between the leagues, reporting with relish its primal challenges of the NFL's old boy network, such as by raiding the latter's teams and squirreling away some top-flight college talent. He was a reliable media courtier for Al Davis, the scamp from the old neighborhood who gave up coaching the Oakland Raiders to become part owner of the team, then gave up that to become AFL commissioner.

Cosell, in effect, had taken sides with Davis against the NFL, whose entrenched status was perfectly represented by the smoothly patrician Pete Rozelle, and Cosell was a valuable ally for the upstart AFL in forcing a merger of the two leagues. What's more, he and Davis, who went back to running the Raiders, would continue to be thorns in Rozelle's side. At Rozelle's press conference announcing the armistice, Cosell conspicuously sat in the first row of the press section as Rozelle took questions on a sofa flanked by Dallas Cowboys general manager Tex Schramm and Kansas City Chiefs owner Lamar Hunt, the real brokers of the deal. The vibe was meant to be collegial, happiness all around, but Cosell bore in like a migraine. Coming off like the lawyer for the younger league, he asked if the AFL had forced the merger by secretly making huge offers to NFL stars. "You know that it's true," he impudently told Rozelle.

"No, I do not know that it's true," Rozelle replied, trying not to look miffed.

"I know that it's true," Cosell volleyed. He then addressed it to Hunt, who equivocated, prompting him to thunder, "You mean you're negotiating for your league without knowing what your league is doing?"

"I've tried to answer your question," the mild-mannered Hunt replied, adding contritely, "I don't mean to be abrupt."

"It's not a question of being abrupt, Lamar. It's a question of being evasive at a time when the American people are entitled to know the truth!"[22]

The merger wouldn't go into effect until 1970, but it immediately mandated a championship game between the league winners, which would not officially be called the Super Bowl until the '69 game. When the inaugural game was played, simulcast by NBC and CBS, Cosell was three thousand miles away, in Pound Ridge, filing *Speaking of Sports* spots throughout the day. At halftime, with the spunky Chiefs trailing only 14–10, Cosell waxed rapturous:

> The whole country has been served notice that the American Football League is very, very far from a minor league. The Packers may win but they are scared, and so are the supercilious owners who run the National Football League along with Pete Rozelle, the commissioner . . . I picked Green Bay by seventeen points. I think I may have been a fool.
>
> Time will tell.[23]

Of course, this impetuosity was ill advised, since the Pack ran the Chiefs off the field and won 35–10. Yet the next day, he simply flipped like a coin, now heaping scorn on the *AFL* owners.

> The headline question this morning is a question for the American Football League: What price membership? AFL owners were in heaven at halftime. However, a football game has 60 minutes in it, which some owners don't really know, naive as they are. And at 4:45 P.M. the owners were nowhere to be found. They were getting their excuses ready.
>
> Lombardi said the Chiefs don't compare with the top teams in the NFL. I wonder how many of you really want to see Boston playing Unitas in Baltimore, Houston playing Meredith down in Dallas with Bob Hayes . . . [The AFL owners] *don't* belong, and they're paying $20 million-plus for the privilege . . . The naive men of the AFL are beset by doubt and terror today.[24]

Having made the safe prediction, even with his shilling for the AFL, he could preen to Myron Cope: "Just what I predicted! Just what I predicted on the air, right down to naming Willie Wood! I said, 'The hero, the guy who will break the game open, will be Willie Wood,'" who had run a key interception back for a touchdown. He also turned on a dime, criticizing the new league so heavily that a radio station in an AFL city axed Cosell's syndicated radio shows, notifying him that "You have destroyed the image of our city," before reversing field a few weeks later.[25]

He may not have even known how shamelessly he was trying to make himself foolproof; nor did he care. There was already an art and a science to being Howard Cosell, geared to the moment, to immediate gratification, an instant rendering of the gospel according to Cosell. Clearly, that meant he would be speaking out of both sides of his mouth, sometimes within minutes. And on *that* skill, no one could come close to him.

MUHAMMAD ALI, meanwhile, was marking time as a storm began to build around him. As he signed to make his next title defense, in the Astrodome against WBA champ Ernie Terrell on February 6, 1967, which would finally allow him to officially unify the heavyweight crown, his bravado in the eye of the burgeoning storm seemed metaphoric of the fissures within American culture. One could, in Ali, almost feel the parboil of near-daily convulsions like antiwar marches and race riots in Watts, and hear it in a new kind of music that seemed to take a cue from Timothy Leary's exhortation to "tune in, turn on, and drop out"; that year, the Beatles' wondrous *Sergeant Pepper's Lonely Hearts Club Band* came out, aurally and intellectually soldering images both loud and subliminal of protest and pot, angst and acid. Though Ali was more cool jazz than hard rock, nowhere did the cultural divide seem more stark than in the Astrodome ring.

Before the fight, Terrell's mouthing off about Ali and the draft and his relish in calling him Cassius Clay unleashed an ugly Ali. Tarring Terrell as an "Uncle Tom," he vowed, "I'm gonna give him a whupping and a spanking and a humiliation . . . I want to torture him. A clean knockout is too good for him." He made good on the threat, making his old sparring mate pay for every minute he let him stand, taunting with a ghoulish grin, "What's my name, Uncle Tom?" as he tore into Terrell, fracturing a bone under his eye early on and rendering him helpless for most of the fifteen painful rounds.

The mass outrage in the old-world press about this "barbarous display of cruelty," as Tex Maule called it, was headed by Jimmy Cannon, who wrote of it as "a kind of lynching"—though no one could recall Cannon ever railing against *actual* lynchings. He went on: "This, the Black Muslims claim, is one of their ministers. What kind of clergyman is he? . . . [He] had a good time beating up another Negro. This was fun, like chasing them with dogs and knocking them down with streams of water. [Ali] is a vicious propagandist for a spiteful mob that works the religious underworld."[26]

And, just as he had after the Liston rematch and the Patterson mismatch, Cosell could not take issue with the prevailing opinion. Vaulting as usual into the ring after it was over, he was met by an Ali he barely recognized. When he asked him about the nastiness of the fight, Ali "turned on me with a meanness I hadn't seen before," he would recall.

"I'm sick and tired of talking to you and taking your stuff," Ali barked at him, then escalated into an incoherent rant at the media that left Cosell speechless—perhaps his greatest achievement of the night.

However, the next morning at a press conference, Ali seemed to know he had behaved in a way that would be antithetical to his immediate future—when he would need all of the goodwill he could count on. Seeing Cosell, he strode toward him.

"I was really bad last night, wasn't I?" he said.

"You sure as hell were," Cosell told him. "You made an ass out of yourself."

"Well, when I go into the press conference I'll make up for it."[27]

And he was indeed apologetic, specifically so to Terrell, whom he graciously complimented despite the latter's claim that Ali had intentionally thumbed him in the eye, effectively blinding him. Ali then came to New York for the *Wide World of Sports* fight postmortem, facing Cosell's stone-faced wrath and questions about the thumbing issue, which he denied, needlessly, given that the tape of the fight showed no such thing. Cosell kept boring in. Why, he asked, had Ali revived the "What's my name?" taunts? Calmly, Ali answered, "My blood was hot. I'm a warrior, I'm a fighter. It's kinda hard to hold me down when I get hot." There was, Cosell noted, "cruelty in your eyes, malice in your voice." Still evenly, Ali said, "I'm out to be cruel, that's what the boxing game is about," adding that the ref could have chosen to terminate the fight at any time.

At that, Cosell was aware Ali had him checkmated. Turning away from somber matters, he gave him a pass, lightening the tone by remarking, somewhat oddly, "You are not a stupid boy." Knowing a setup line when he heard one, Ali smashed the batting-practice pitch out of the park. "Thank you, Howard," he said. "You know, you're not as dumb as you look." However, Ali was not quite ready to drop a grievance he had come in with, that Cosell's intense criticism of him meant he had lost his nerve and caved in to the media hordes. Continuing directly, he told him, "If you defended me like you usually do, you will catch criticism, too."

Cosell blinked, caught off guard. "I've never defended you," he said, quickly adding, "And I have never gone against you. The test of a man's courage is not necessarily his willingness to support you. Do you understand that?"

"Well, I'm trying to [understand], but your words are so large . . . I don't understand the meaning of the big words you're talkin'."

"Yes, but as I said, you're not a stupid boy."

He then asked who among the heavyweight challengers Ali might fight.

"You," Ali said, without a blink.

"That might come about someday," Cosell said, eye glinting.

For Ali, the sometimes caustic but always affable battle of wits, one of many more to come between them, was an hour well worth his time. A week later, after signing to fight veteran heavyweight Zora Folley in Madison Square Garden on March 22, he showed his gratitude. "I want the people of America to know that Howard Cosell was very fair to me on our *Wide World* show last Saturday," he announced to a crowd of eye-rolling media people.[28]

WITH THIS return to normalcy, there was also a return to goofiness. A silly story was going around that Ali wanted to fight seven-foot two-inch Philadelphia 76ers center Wilt "the Stilt" Chamberlain, and Cosell brought both men into the studio a week before the Folley fight, with hysterical results. Playing instigator, he had each measured for reach— Ali's normally advantageous seventy-nine-inch span was dwarfed by Wilt's ninety-two inches—and dutifully let Ali pepper Chamberlain with bon mots. Near the end, gazing up at the big fellow, he said, "And cut that beard off, because I'm not fighting billy goats." Then, to Cosell, who was doubled over in laughter, "This is belittling to me, a world champ [fighting] a basketball player. You getting this man in trouble." Of course, that match, such as it would have been, never came to pass, much to everyone's relief, especially Wilt. But for one last, brief moment, there was still comic relief to be had in watching Muhammad Ali and Howard Cosell.[29]

The Folley fight was bathed in a maudlin pall, it coming only a fort-night after a Selective Service appeal board upheld Ali's 1-A classifica-tion, eight days after he was ordered to report for induction on April 28 in Houston. As the pincers closed in on him, he stepped into the Garden ring—the first heavyweight title fight there in sixteen years—and with crisp dispatch and a merciful lack of cruelty knocked the outclassed Fol-ley out in the seventh round. There were no snubs or recriminations in the ring afterward, only a laying on of hands about Ali. Folley, seeming more like a fan than an opponent, aggrandized him as indeed the great-est of all time. "He could write the book on boxing," Folley enthused, "and anyone that fights him should be made to read it first."[30]

Ali's mood was humble and fatalistic, resigned to facing up to what might befall him if he refused induction, including the very real possibil-ity of jail time. Implicit was that this would be his last fight for a while, perhaps a long while. Implicit, too, was the broad, long-term implication—for him, for Cosell, for the role of sports in society and how sports were to be covered—in his remarks over the coming days. "I've left the sports pages," he would say. "I've gone onto the front pages . . . I've got no jails, no power, no government, but six hundred million Muslims are giving me strength. Why can't I worship as I want to in America? All I want is justice. Will I have to get that from history?"[31]

Suddenly, it wasn't about boxing anymore.


FOR COSELL, calling these freeze-frames of an Ali reaching critical mass as indeed the greatest champ of 'em all was highly rewarding, but he felt he could perform that part of his craft better. On April 17, 1967, ABC carried middleweight champ Emile Griffith's title defense against

Nino Benvenuti in Madison Square Garden, with Cosell at the mike. Perhaps less than confident he was prepared enough, that afternoon he had invited Jerry Izenberg to lunch at Manuche's restaurant and asked a favor of the writer, whose expertise was boxing.

"Howard didn't know anything about the fighters and wanted me to pass him notes during the fight," Izenberg recalls of the strange request. "He'd pay me five hundred dollars out of his own pocket, but nobody was to know about it. So late in the fight, I gave him a note that Nino was setting Emile up for a left hook. And Howard goes, 'Fans, watch for a left hook from Nino.' Sure enough, Nino landed a huge left hook, and afterward Howard is the hero. He's telling everyone, 'Did I call that left hook or what?' He even said it to *me*. I looked at him and said, "Yeah, you called it, Howard—I wrote it and you called it.'"[32]

For Izenberg, the task of making Cosell look brilliant would continue, earning Cosell further goodwill at the network. When Cosell produced two more superb documentaries, he hired Izenberg again to write them. The first spilled from Cosell's fascination with—and to hear him tell it, contributory role in—the NFL-AFL merger, and his fawning over Sonny Werblin. Called *Pro Football's Shotgun Marriage: Sonny, Money and Merger*, it ran over the entire ABC network at 10 P.M. on January 5, 1967. Then in the fall came his last, his putatively best and most ambitious work, *Grambling College: 100 Yards to Glory*, about the small black college in Alabama that under coach Eddie Robinson had bred more pro players per capita than any Big Ten or Southeastern Conference football factory, a story that Izenberg broke in the white press with a story in *True* magazine.

Credited as writer and coproducer for both projects, Izenberg recalls working on a skimpy $13,000 budget for each, and says he earned it putting up with Cosell, recalling overheated and barely comprehensible demands in endless calls from New York. He would say, "I want this picture to be the long hot summer of Grambling," though it was already late September. Another demand was to see on film streets without sidewalks with puddles gathering in the gutters. Exasperated, Izenberg told him, "Howard, you want water? Okay, I'll piss in the gutter. Just get off the phone and we'll talk when I get back."

Izenberg, working with Collie Nicholson, the only black marine war correspondent in World War II, felt like he was in boot camp but brought home a superb piece of film verité, including being among angry demonstrators who briefly took over the student union. But he was thrown for a loop when Cosell told him it stank and needed heavy revision. Incredibly, for all his sensitivity for schmaltzy family narratives, and sympathies to race issues, his reaction to a poverty-stricken mother of a Grambling star struggling to find words for her beloved son was to scream, "Get that illiterate woman out of my show!"

Not willing to do even a little revision, Izenberg humored Cosell, agreeing to hole up with the film editor, whom he told, "If you change one frame of this movie I'll kill you." For three days, they sent out for pizza and entertained women, on ABC's dime, but never touched the film. Then he bade Cosell to give it a look. When he did, amusingly in retrospect, he pronounced, "It's magnificent! That's television! Now you see how a pro works." Izenberg could barely stifle laughter, seeing how easy it was to cater to Cosell's ego. And if Cosell's reaction was a lot like the way the ABC brass took bows for his shows after panning them in advance, it was an irony he missed because like them he would admit to no hypocrisy, or that he had any shortcomings.

From experience, Izenberg says: "Howard was the best television reporter in history. He was not a good maker of documentaries. But he was absolutely fantastic at getting the shows on the air. Howard always had to walk a very thin tightrope because of the network people, the three-piece suits. I had no conception of that. I didn't answer to them. In fact, when we showed the rushes of the merger show to the network honchos, one of them was complaining, saying things like 'This train doesn't stop at Scarsdale,' whatever the hell that meant. I was livid, because I saw what that was about. I told him, 'Let me be honest here. You're really bothered because there are three black guys in this scene. How 'bout I find a Swede for you?' "

It was the sort of cheeky remark one might have expected from Cosell. But he was furious at Izenberg, and tried to give him a stern look to stifle him. When the network men, reeling from Izenberg's remark, were about to walk out, Cosell shouted, "Wait a minute! Wait a minute!"

then said, "He's fired." He then put his arm around him and walked him out of the screening room. Later, he took the writer back—mighty big of him considering Izenberg was the backbone of the show—but told him, "Don't you ever do that to me again!"

"I said, "What I did to *you*!? You didn't stand up for me!'" the writer relates. "You just could never get him to see logic like that when his reputation was on the line. It was all about him. But I'll tell you something. That scene stayed in. And not a single frame of any show we did was ever taken out. Howard fought for it all, all or nothing. I just wished he would have done that for me and Collie, when he thought it was our work, not his. But Howard was unable to see anyone else in the media on equal ground. And that's why I told him, 'Howard, we can be acquaintances from now on, but don't ever ask me to make another show with you again.'

"And we never did. In fact, we never were particularly close after that."[33]

ON APRIL 28, 1967, life stopped being a hoot for the Ali-Cosell two-wheeler. At 8 A.M. on that historic morning in Houston, Ali made his entrance into the army examining station in the Federal Building on San Jacinto Street, and with twenty-five other inductees underwent physical exams. At 1:05 P.M., they were brought into a ceremony room and instructed to "take one step forward as your name and service are called, and such step will constitute your induction into the Armed Forces." When the name "Cassius Marcellus Clay" was called, he did not budge. He was advised that refusal to accept induction was a felony punishable by five years' imprisonment and a $5,000 fine, and his name again called; again he would not take the step. In accordance with routine, he was asked to sign a written statement. In his own hand, he wrote: "I refuse to be inducted into the armed forces of the United States because I claim to be exempt as a minister of the religion of Islam."

A large crowd had gathered outside the building, some of them protestors carrying signs like DRAFT BEER, NOT ALI, some gawkers waiting for a glimpse of Ali, the rest media. Cosell, of course, was among them, shielded from the wet weather by a raincoat and a fedora on his head. Significantly, he had been assigned to cover the story not only for ABC Sports but ABC News; for the latter, he was working with correspondent John Scali on a special called *The Champ: Count Me Out*. The connection to the network news division was a major milestone for a sports reporter, and a no-brainer given that Cosell had advantages in his encyclopedic knowledge of the legal issues involved and also, perhaps more critically, the trust he had with and the access he had to Ali.

The night before, in fact, he had been the only media delegate to be allowed into Ali's room at the Hotel America. Finding him in bed staring at the TV, sheets tucked under his chin, he asked him, "What are you going to do, Champ? You going to refuse to take the step?"

A taciturn Ali responded, "Can't tell you a thing. I'm under orders not to talk to nobody. I only let you into the room because it's you. But I can't talk."

Cosell tried to press him, presumptuously suggesting that Ali call Herbert Muhammad for permission. "Okay, let's see what the boss says," Ali relented, dialing the phone. When Muhammad answered, he told him, "Howard's here."

Just to get that far proved how favored Cosell was in the inner circle; in the past, Herbert had often come to his aid in easing restrictions put on Ali. However, Ali's expressions indicated that Herbert was not wont to ease this restriction. Brazenly, Cosell grabbed the phone out of Ali's hands. "Herbert, I think—," he began to say before the manager interrupted, "Absolutely not, not a single word. It's Elijah's dictates, and that's it."

Cosell left without the scoop he wanted but with the impression that Ali was remarkably serene and prepared to face whatever would befall him. "During all of these days, and all of the years of turmoil that followed," he wrote later in *Cosell*, "I never observed any single evidence of weakness or loss of faith on his part."[34]

What he didn't add, nor need to, was that he was every bit as resolute defending him, which was perhaps just as perilous.

# 8

## A MORAL IMPERATIVE

O N THAT historic day in Houston, where the media had descended with a dizzying intensity, Cosell was among the media mob milling about on San Jacinto outside the Federal Building, waiting for Ali to arrive for the induction that never was. After the fighter drove up, Cosell followed him up the stairs, asking the same question he had the night before.

Ali, as he had after the Liston rematch, heard the nasal whine behind him and found time for a grin. "Howard Cosell," he said, "why don't *you* take the step?"

"I did," Cosell said, keeping it light, "in nineteen-forty-two."[1]

Hours later, he was one of a handful of reporters permitted to observe the drama in the ceremony room when the most famous athlete in the world refused to wear the uniform of his country. After Ali had signed his written statement claiming conscientious objector status and left the building, a free man for now, pending the government's next move, Cosell was naturally on his back again, asking to accompany him to his hotel with a film crew, where Cosell would read the statement with Ali by his side.

"You'll get me in terrible trouble," Ali said, no doubt meaning Elijah Muhammad more than the government.

But Cosell talked him into it, bypassing Herbert Muhammad, and got his scoop, though it hardly shook up the world. After Cosell read the statement, Ali said nothing. "Is there anything else you want to say at this time?" Cosell prodded him.

"No."

"You're satisfied that this is a fair representation of your position?"

"Yes."

After the cameras stopped rolling, Ali had one thing to say.

"I may have talked too much."

"If you did, Muhammad," Cosell joshed him, "it will be one helluva scoop."[2]

Cosell flew back to New York to do the special, and his reporting was again impeccable, relating the story without embellishment. Even before judgment day, like a law clerk, he was researching the legal precedents of conscientious objector cases, which Ali's lawyers had indicated would be their defense. Then, over the ensuing days, one state commission after another took unilateral disciplinary action against Ali, stripping him of his title. Watching these dominoes fall, Cosell became nearly apoplectic, offended as a former lawyer and a current friend of the man whose rights were being trampled in a rush to judgment.

In the press, with few exceptions, the villain was solely Ali, in tones that had grown shrill and tired—for example, Milton Gross's assessment that "Clay seems to have gone past the borders of faith. He has reached the boundaries of fanaticism."[3] For Cosell, it was a simple issue, though one that could not be explained simply. Choosing his words carefully, he began to piece together and perfect a defense of Ali that had nothing to do with his religion or opposition to the war; instead, it was rooted entirely in the United States Constitution. As this rap went, certain elements were constant, including a useful stooge—Edwin Dooley, the New York State boxing commissioner, whom he mercilessly demonized as an autocrat and a "boob," as he would call him, a political hack doing the bidding of men of dishonor.

Even a decade later, he still had it down, such as this inspired recitation on *The Tomorrow Show*:

> You know what law and order is? It's a government of laws, and it begins with a judicial process. These fools didn't even know that the man had been deprived of two constitutional guarantees! Due process under the Fifth Amendment and equal protection under the Fourteenth Amendment. There had been no charges, no grand jury arraignment, no trial, no conviction, no appeal to the first court or the Supreme Court.
>
> Strip one American citizen of those rights and you strip all of them.
>
> That's what happened in these United States. At the same time, that New York State boxing commission was licensing to fight convicted deserters of the military. How can you ask a man to accept such unconscionable action? How did the overwhelming majority of American sportswriters, knowing nothing of the law but saying they're great Americans, support it? How can my colleagues in broadcasting support it? But they did.
>
> I did not. I'm so proud of that, you'll never know.[4]

Bits and pieces of this peroration made their way into his shows and *Wide World of Sports* segments. And when they did, the art and craft of sports journalism took giant strides.

THE OTHER shoe dropped on May 8, 1967, when Ali was indicted for draft evasion by a federal grand jury in Houston; then, on June 20, he was convicted of refusing induction into the armed forces and sentenced to five years in prison. Released on $5,000 bond, he was prohibited from leaving the country while he appealed the conviction. There would be no more jaunts abroad to fight British bleeders and awkward Germans, with ABC cameras and Howard Cosell in tow. While Ali's lawyers worked the legal system, his fight was to present himself as a sincere man of faith and integrity on public speaking tours. For the rest of the decade, he would never lace up a glove or step in a ring.

For Cosell, taking up the cudgels meant he was wading into waters that were treacherous, given that his point of view was going to be based entirely on constitutional grounds and delicate legal nuances far beyond the ken of almost every other sports journalist who would be heard from about the case. At a time when emotional patriotic fervor and "silent majority" fear dominated the Middle America that would carry Richard Nixon into the presidency the following year, a dry recitation of legal jargon about this or that constitutional-amendment right being denied a pampered prizefighter would hardly seem to play in Peoria, or anywhere.

Cosell knew well that he was the voice and face of the network on this story, and if that was undeniably gratifying—and something he had long awaited—it meant that he was the one who was taking a risky symbolic step of his own. What he could not have known was how crucial his step forward would be in charting the future—his, Ali's, and that of the still-evolving animal that was sports journalism. But, for sure, he was no longer working in the toy department.

At ABC, controversy was always desirable, but not necessarily the kind that might lead to viewers switching channels, and again it was up to Roone Arledge to calm flutters about Cosell among network people, *big* people, one being Chairman of the Board Leonard Goldenson. It was no small task, but Arledge saw something he called "other-worldly" in Cosell, something even suggesting a karmic scale. "Even at his most controversial moments, when any audience he addressed was sure to include a preponderance of Cosell haters," Arledge wrote in *Roone*, "he always at the end got a standing O. Amazing man."

It would have taken as much nerve for Arledge *not* to back up Cosell in the way Cosell backed up Ali, something Arledge later said he "admired." Speaking of Cosell, he acknowledged, "There was no career boost in remaining loyal to Ali . . . But Howard wouldn't be moved; as he saw it . . . injustice had been done and that was that."[5]

To another, newer ABC Sports hand, Don Ohlmeyer, who had arrived after graduating from Notre Dame and been put to work as a factotum in the department, that was much too modest of Arledge. "Had Roone not believed deeply in Howard, there would not have been anyone on American television who would have taken a principled—and correct, in legal terms—position on one of the most egregious cases ever of a man being deprived of his rights. Think about that. Ali would have gone dark on the screen. Roone kept the lights turned on. But it was Howard who was out front, his behind on the line. I think that made him see it as a moral imperative."

Ohlmeyer, who would one day be tasked with running the NBC TV network, and has seen several generations of people who made a difference to his medium and whom he personally held in high esteem, adds: "Howard didn't just have answers—he had the *right* answers. In a sense, everything he had done up to that day in Houston had prepared him for what he was about to do."[6]

To have heard Cosell tell it, it was he, not Arledge, who had won over Goldenson, a man he always insisted was a major fan of his work. He would throw Goldenson's name around like an anvil, as an unerringly loyal benefactor, whenever he locked horns with anyone around ABC Sports. What he apparently didn't know was that the chairman regularly considered cutting him loose, only to be talked out of it by Arledge. The irony was that even though he had won over Tom Moore, that did him no good since Moore was canned in 1968, replaced as network president by Elton Rule. What's more, Cosell had made no strides with Ted Shaker, the balky head of the affiliates, who never believed he was anything but a clown on the air, serious issues aside. It also helped Cosell that, while Shaker had wanted to kill the Grambling documentary, the show won the Golden Eagle Award, the highest honor for network journalism.

Shaker would be pushed to the limit in March 1968 when Cosell walked a picket line in front of the ABC studios in support of a strike by the TV engineers' union, NABET. For Cosell, the strike posed a thorny dilemma. While he was best known as an on-air performer, and his union, AFTRA, had voted to honor the picket line, he was also management, as executive producer of the radio network. Cosell tried to have it both ways; because he could conduct his radio shows from home, he wouldn't need to cross the picket line. AFTRA, however, still regarded him as a scab, and the union fined him $17,500, a sizable and possible record chunk of change that reflected his top-end salary, $500 more than Chris Schenkel, though he and the other fined talent appealed, and never would pay a cent. But Shaker was livid, and told an associate, "Get rid of Cosell! I never wanted him on the air anyway."[7] However, someone in a high place, perhaps even Goldenson, stopped it from happening.

Still, the proposition that someone, anyone, or *everyone* was out to get him never would leave Cosell's mind, even when he was undeniably the network's most neon-lit name. For now, though, he had the comfort of acceptance, the weight of justice, and the salve of ratings. And, of course, he had Muhammad Ali and a moral imperative. "I took an unpopular stand," he once told *Playboy*'s Lawrence Linderman. "Many people were offended by the idea that a boxing champion would declare himself to be a conscientious objector. But that was a matter for the courts to decide. My support of Ali had to do only with the fact that his championship and his right to earn a living had been unfairly taken from him . . . I was right to back Muhammad, but it cost me."

But just what it cost him was open to question, given his now sky-high visibility. When asked by Linderman if there was a financial toll to the Ali crusade, he said, "Not at all, but it caused me major enmity in many areas of this nation," citing "thousands upon thousands of letters [that] were written to my company," many of which demanded ABC "get that nigger-loving Jew bastard off the air" and made threats on his life.[8] This was a serious matter, causing ABC to hire bodyguards for Cosell and his family. Cosell, trying to keep his sanity, would joke that he had more muscle around him than Muhammad Ali did in his exile.

"It's true; Howard took the brunt of public revulsion about Ali," says Jerry Izenberg. "That doesn't mean he was doing what a lot of us weren't. I was defending Ali right from the start. I was there before Howard got into it. I didn't mind that Howard said, 'I was alone, and I did this, I did that . . . ,' because I believed in the *principle*, and he was getting the principle attention much more than I was. That was more important, I felt, than who was getting the credit. But I guarantee you that I got more death threats than he did."

He adds: "Howard stood for a lot of good things. The problem was, Howard milked a good thing too much. Somebody once took an ad out about Howard, that he should be off the air. Howard lived on that ad for a month. He loved being the living martyr."[9]

Overtly and implicitly, the stakes for Cosell and his network could not have been higher. And neither, as it turned out, could the ratings. That connection was hardly coincidental. In *Supertube*, Ron Powers theorized that Cosell had a "primal hunger to belong, a hunger that attached itself to [the] charismatic Ali" but was aimed straight at the heart of "the *inside* of sport, and celebrity, and ruling-class power . . . It was like nothing so much as the hunger of television itself." That, Powers concluded, "may have been Howard Cosell's ultimate secret. He *was* the medium, personified."[10] And in 1967, maybe only he and Roone Arledge knew it.

IN THE course of defending Ali, he would deliver speeches before college audiences, something Ali did to earn some money but which Cosell did to enlighten the academic community—correctly perceiving that it was the young demographic that could leverage influence in the court of public opinion. That was when Arledge noted that Cosell "wielded his voice like a musical instrument, now speaking so softly people had to lean forward to listen, now rising in decibels and conviction with an almost evangelical fervor," and his total recall of minutiae that was "just spookily *there*" at his fingertips when needed.[11]

The voice that so irritated his contemporaries was on the way up now, claiming more and more turf for himself, every inch of it with presumption. On a visit to Ali's hotel room in the late sixties, Cosell and Arledge stepped off the elevator to find themselves surrounded by a phalanx of Black Muslim bodyguards, at which, Arledge recalled, "my pulse began to pitter-pat." The two white guys stood there being stared at, nobody saying anything. Finally, Cosell spoke up.

"All right," he bellowed, going into his act, "everybody who isn't white, get out!"

Remembered Arledge, "Again, [there was] a split second of dead silence. But then they got it—all at once the Muslims collapsed in hysterics."[12]

For the generation that came of age in the sixties, Cosell was indeed one of their own. His voice was clearly one of reason and enlightenment as the soul-wrenching locus of events in the late sixties played out, with Ali's seemingly impossible crusade a legal issue wrapped inside a greater moral imperative. In the maelstrom of the new culture, the lords and heralds of sports were—just as Cosell had foretold—playing a losing game trying to hold back the ugly world outside the stadium gates. At UCLA, even steely, ultraconservative John Wooden couldn't keep the best center in the land, Bill Walton, from demonstrating against the war, and getting himself arrested. The wind had to be shifting if bad-boy Joe Namath and straight-arrow Tom Seaver of the now suddenly competitive Mets—itself a sign of changing times—were on record challenging the war.

Ali's boxing exile was just one convulsion that spring of 1968, and seemingly a minor one beside the horrific assassinations, just three months apart, of Martin Luther King Jr. in April and Senator Robert Kennedy in June. Cosell was on the air hours after Kennedy's murder, and following his eulogy of Bobby Kennedy on his *Speaking of Sports* show, a steady string of listeners called in to complain.

"Don't tell me how to live," said one, "just give us the scores, that's what you're paid for."

Sadly, as if mourning the end of enlightened society, he recalled, "I began to wonder if that 'fan' kind of thinking is one of the things that makes us so prone to assassination . . . in this country. Maybe there is such an absence of intellect and sensitivity in the United States today that only violence is understandable and acceptable."[13]

Cosell at the time thought he might be sacked from ABC Radio. His longtime patron there, Robert Pauley, caught in one of those periodic corporate bloodletting rituals as ABC and IT&T planned to merge, was fired along with almost the entire radio upper staff—one of whom, the president of the owned stations division, went home and suffered a fatal heart attack. Pauley would move on to become involved with satellite TV news and later the National Black Network radio chain. Cosell, however, was on safe ground, insulated by his new TV éclat.

As immersed in corporate politics and power games as everyone in the broadcast arc was, Cosell was on safe ground. In an era that simmered with anger and grief for a country that was imploding, there was a premium on announcers who could make sense of it all with fact, with pluck and dash, and cast a spell over an audience. A look around the media landscape seemed to indicate that there was only one man who could do that, and pull in the numbers.

"Howard was exactly what we all needed at the time," says Don Ohl-meyer. "The country was going to hell and yet sportswriters had nothing to say about it. They all thought they could just ride it out. But America changed in '68. Sports changed, because there were athletes directly affected by war and the draft. Sons were coming home in body bags. You couldn't separate sports and society anymore—which was Howard's message all along. We talked about the implications of all this at ABC. Roone was very up front about it. The issues needed to be addressed. And who better to do that than Howard?"[14] Thus, the outcome of the Ali case would be critical, with a just resolution as important for him as for Ali if he was to entrench the Howard Cosell brand.

COSELL'S SUDDENLY profound yet entertaining persona was on high-level display that year for the first time on an Olympics broadcast, the Summer Games in Mexico City. For Arledge, getting them was an obses-sion, his master plan being to "own" the Olympics and cast it in his net-work's image, and ABC had to break the bank for the privilege—for the formerly bargain-basement quadrennial Games, ABC's desperation drove the price into the stratosphere: $2 million for the Winter Games in Grenoble, France, and $5 million for Mexico City. At Grenoble, there was to be extended satellite coverage of a sports event, and America was mesmerized by the princesslike story line of figure skater Peggy Fleming and the breakneck bravura of downhill skiing.

The Summer Games of the Nineteenth Olympiad, in the high alti-tude south of the border, were held in October. They neared as a post-script to the long, hot, and cruel summer of '68, following the assassinations and the convulsive Democratic National Convention in Chicago, and with their own trail of potential trouble. Early in 1968, civil rights activist Professor Harry Edwards of San Jose State put forth a manifesto of rights for black athletics with demands for more black

coaches, the restoration of Muhammad Ali's title, the barring of South
Africa and Rhodesia from the Games, and the termination of Avery
Brundage's reign as IOC head. Edwards had even enlisted Dr. Martin
Luther King to the cause, and as autumn approached, Edwards's threats
that black athletes would boycott the Games endured right up until the
opening ceremonies.

None of these demands were met—in fact, the movement was a total
failure—and political and social storm clouds hung heavily over Mexico
City; ten days before the events began, government *policía* reacted to
student unrest in the Tlatelolco section by gunning down forty-four people. Cosell, naturally, wanted in on this opportunity to report on the
chaos, reflecting his belief that sports reportage could only exist with the
larger world as a backdrop. His withering criticism of Brundage seemed
prophetic, and he now blasted Brundage for the IOC's cold indifference
to the Tlatelolco massacre. Cosell also wanted in on the most elaborate
televised sports event in history, forty-four hours in all, covered by over
fifty cameras and a production crew of more than three hundred.

Cosell's assignment, logically, was to call the boxing events, but he
was also given wide latitude to interview athletes at will, mostly at the
Estadio Olímpico Universitario, where he would float around the track
waiting to pounce on gold medal winners—a chore given him with the
full knowledge that the Olympic governing body had prohibited any
interviews at the venue of each event, and would post guards everywhere, including on the infield of the stadium.

Thus, a paunchy, fifty-year-old man would put on a nifty athletic
performance himself, lying in wait before almost comically breaking
through the guards to chase twenty-year-old athletes around the track,
microphone in hand. He was nearly collared and ejected from the stadium several times, and admitted he should have been, "for making a
farce of the scene."[15] Still, his dogged pursuit landed the two most
memorable interviews of the year—one that is still cited frequently by
sports and cultural historians as an act few Americans alive then will
ever forget.

The afternoon of October 18 began promisingly enough. Tommie
Smith and John Carlos, finishing one-three in the 200-meter finals—

with Smith setting a world record, 19.83 seconds, that would last eleven years. The two sprinters then mounted the podium to have their medals draped around their necks. In an undying freeze frame of history, the two black Americans removed their shoes, put a black glove on one hand, and, as the national anthem reverberated through the stadium, thrust their glove-covered fists into the thin night air. When the anthem ended, they picked up their gear and strode toward an exit. One could almost literally hear a pin drop; the crowd, not knowing what to make of the display, buzzed quietly about it. Some booed. In the ABC control room, overseeing every aspect of his network's coverage, Arledge knew exactly what was happening.

"Get in there!" he shouted into his headset when the anthem began, whereupon his cameramen in the stadium zoomed in for tight shots of the demonstration. "This is Black Power!"[16]

Only a hundred feet away, Cosell knew it, too; something viscerally stunning had happened before his eyes, the two runners' salutes doing what a thousand raised voices or snarled threats could not have. Without a word, Avery Brundage's pretensions of amateur sports as an impregnable bastion removed from the crises of the larger world were shattered, and in the longer view, television sports had changed forever.

THE ABC crew had wondered how it would cover such eruptions. Although the IOC doled out the broadcast rights to the Olympics with the understanding that coverage be strictly upbeat, Arledge had his own agenda; for all the money ABC invested, he resolved to take the sports division to new heights, on a par with the news division.

Such marching orders seemed to channel Cosell's inherent operating philosophy. When Smith and Carlos came off the stand, he tried every con and move he could on the guards to get close to the pair, cursing them and himself when he couldn't make it through. He retreated under the stands, trying to find them, but both had been ordered out of the Olympic Village by the IOC, soon to be officially banned from athletic competition. As the mystery heightened about their whereabouts, talk of the incident dominated the air on ABC.

But talk was not good enough. At around 1 A.M., Arledge put a call through to Cosell's room at the seedy Del Angel Hotel—where Arledge had consigned all the announcers and their staffs, insisting it would keep them hungry for the tasks at hand (the brass, Arledge included, was never hungry at the opulent El Presidente Hotel)—to tell him to do all he could to find and interview them. But Cosell wasn't there. As Don Ohlmeyer, by then a producer-director, remembers, "Howard never came back to his room that night. He was on the scent all night and all morning. He stayed in the truck, calling everyone he knew who might have a connection with Smith and Carlos. Nobody ever worked as hard as Howard did over those hours. And those of us who saw him working the phones didn't want to leave, either. Howard was after the single biggest interview in the history of television sports. We had to see if he could do it."[17]

Finally, early the next morning, bone tired but still hungry, Cosell got his break. He had left a message for Hayes Jones, the former gold medal sprinter who was doing announcing work for ABC during the Games. Now Jones returned the call and told Cosell that Carlos's whereabouts were unknown, but Smith had checked into the Diplomat Hotel. Cosell jumped into an ABC van and at 8 A.M. was in the lobby of the hotel. Told at the desk that Smith was not taking calls, he nonetheless kept trying his room on a house phone, over and over, until ultimately Smith's wife picked up and told him the same thing. But clearly the connection to Ali paid off. "I had never met her or Tommie," he recalled in *Cosell*, "but she knew of me. I finally induced her to let me come up to the room."

For a long while, it was a redux of Ali's hotel room stonewall in Houston; Smith refused to be interviewed, saying he had been treated unfairly by the media because of his stated support of Edwards's protest. "You'd think I committed murder," he said. Cosell did not reflexively agree in order to suck up. As with his blunt reproach to Sonny Liston, he told Smith he was wrong to keep silent and that "I think you should state what you did, and why. Then at least some people might understand." At that, Smith's wife agreed, melting her husband's resistance. Ten minutes later, Smith followed Cosell into the van and they drove back to the ABC studio for the interview, scooping every reporter in the world.

It would be a brief interview, taking barely more time than the race

Smith had run, but when the lights went on, the entire ABC Sports contingent had crowded into the hallway outside, staring through the glass. Arledge stood hard by where Cosell sat with Smith, while in the control room Jim Spence communicated to Cosell through his earpiece.

"Tell me, Tommie," a somber Cosell began, "what did you mean symbolically by the bowed head, the shoeless feet, the outstretched fist?"

Smith, quietly but determinedly, said, "The right glove that I wore on my right hand signified the power within black America. The left glove my teammate John Carlos wore on his left hand made an arc with my right hand and his left hand also to signify black unity. The scarf that was worn around my neck signified blackness. John Carlos and me wore socks, black socks without shoes, to also signify our poverty in racist America. The totality of our effort was the regaining of black dignity. This was our platform, and John and I used this moment to take a stand. We were embracing those who had no other platform but the streets. My silent gestures were designed to speak volumes."

Spence then fed Cosell a simple, direct question, which he repeated to Smith. "Are you proud to be an American?"

Smith answered just as simply and directly. "I am proud," he said, "to be a black American."[18]

It ended right there, as did Smith's and Carlos's careers; both quickly vanished, suspended from the Olympic team and blacklisted from competition. While they got a lot of street cred from their gesture, neither ran again. Smith played pro football as a wide receiver for two games with the Cincinnati Bengals in 1969, then taught second grade in San Jose, California, before becoming assistant athletic director at Oberlin College, and later taught sociology at Santa Monica College. Carlos—who emerged from the shadows the day of Smith's interview, jumping out of a car to tell Cosell, "We're grateful for your fair treatment"—tried in vain to make it in pro football as a wide receiver with the Philadelphia Eagles and later, with stunning irony, if not absolution, worked with the U.S. Olympic Committee, helping organize the 1984 Olympics in Los Angeles.

However, Smith and Carlos ensured that ABC, and Howard Cosell, would have a lingering place in the sun. The interview—perhaps the sparest one he ever did—was picked up by newspapers and TV stations worldwide, and for Cosell this marked the apogee of his career as a "sports journalist." He earned even more bragging rights when he reported on American athletes' support for the banned black sprinters and allegations of under-the-table payments from a sneaker company to members of the U.S. track team. Yet Cosell was not done. He would also elude the guards to come right up to Lee Evans, who had won the 400-meter race, to ask him if he would emulate Smith and Carlos on the stand—indeed, Jim McKay had teased the race by saying, "What will he do on the victory stand if he wins? Howard Cosell is at trackside to find out." When Evans won, and Cosell put it to him, Evans was torn. "I really don't know," he said. As if seeking compromise, Evans and his medal-winning teammates donned Black Panther–like berets when the anthem was played, but were unbowed, and gloveless, and merrily waved to the crowd. The IOC let it go unpunished.

In the glare of the center ring, Cosell seemed on fire. As the Olympics played on, the ratings climbed sky-high. The thin, dry air spurred numerous records and thrilling performances, none more so than the electrifying decathlon victory of Bill Toomey, a schoolteacher neighbor of his in New Canaan, Connecticut, whom Cosell had become so close with during the Games that for days they seemed inseparable. Just before the climactic event of the decathlon, the 1,500-meter run, Cosell came into the athletes' rest room and found Toomey lying on the floor, exhausted. "I gave him no chance," Cosell would say.[19]

But then, as rain began to fall and a chill cloaked the night, Toomey miraculously—it seemed to many divinely—began running hard, then harder, pulling away on the final lap. As he neared the finish line, Jim McKay, announcing the race, warbled, "Bill Toomey, running in the footsteps of Jim Thorpe and Rafer Johnson and Bob Mathias . . . running in the cold and dark of Mexico City . . . wins the decathlon!" Toomey's grueling victory, achieved under so much physical duress, provided a distinct counterpoint to the stormy saga of Smith and Carlos. Cosell, watching on the infield, recalled later, "I couldn't believe that at my age I could be so touched by an athletic victory. At 48 [sic] there I was cheering like a damned kid." In his radio spots, he would say that Toomey had displayed the "magnificence of the human spirit."[20]

Cosell still had the boxing to call, and did so in form, openly questioning decisions that seemed to rip off American fighters like Al Jones and Al Robinson, the latter of whom was disqualified for head-butting though replays showed no such infraction. As *Washington Post* TV critic Laurence Laurent wrote of that fight, "Cosell drily admonished the viewers to judge for themselves, but left no doubt as to where he stood." The cause célèbre, however, centered around another rising boxer, nineteen-year-old heavyweight George Foreman. Before the Games, Cosell had touted the big, raw Texan. Foreman didn't disappoint, rampaging his way to the gold medal, destroying an older, proven Russian fighter in the second round—but even then, as Cosell called the bout he was calling attention to Foreman's habit of punching himself out. After the decision, Foreman toted a small American flag around the ring, which some assumed was meant as a riposte to his "Black Power" brethren. Cosell, of course, asked him if that were so. "I just do my own thing," Foreman said, "and make sure of one thing. I'm no Uncle Tom."[21]

Those manic two weeks of unpredictable drama, kept on an even keel by Arledge, Cosell, and the rest of the ABC team, all but wrote the template of Olympic coverage. These were no mere sports events. Even Avery Brundage realized that, and he was prepared to live with ABC catering to controversy, as long as its reporters did it with an even hand. He would see to it that ABC would retain rights to the next two Summer Olympics, though he had no idea, nor did Cosell, how ill a wind would intrude on them at the next installment, in 1972 in Munich.

IF COSELL'S performance in Mexico City was regarded as masterful by most, he was still panned by the usual suspects in the press, some of whom believed he somehow disgraced his country by giving Tommie Smith his say. But that was now distinctly a minority opinion. What's more, he was now the object of affection of the upper crust of the writing game, the literati set within which Cosell always swore he belonged. Mostly, this was another by-product of the Ali association, given that, as the writer Garry Wills has noted, "by the end of the sixties, Ali was the intellectual's catnip." Indeed, according to *The Guinness Book of World*

*Records*, Muhammad Ali would become the most written-about human being who has ever lived, surpassing Lincoln, Christ, and Napoleon. Certainly, Ali was sweet meat for the sixties' intelligentsia, comprised of lofty names like Norman Mailer, A. J. Liebling, Tom Wolfe, George Plimpton, Murray Kempton, Roger Kahn, Garry Wills, and Joyce Carol Oates— and now Cosell.[22]

With his dilettante instincts, Cosell was a natural fit with this coterie of earthy, elegant writers steeped in wine, chateaubriand, and liberal doggerel. Yet Cosell was loath to wear a liberal intelligentsia sign around his neck. Thus he never would qualify as one of those dreaded intellectuals tarred by Richard Nixon's hatchet-wielding vice president Spiro Agnew as an "effete corps of impudent snobs who characterize themselves as intellectuals" and "nattering nabobs of negativism." What's more, his place in that coterie was never as pronounced as some assume, the natural, and mutual, wariness between print and TV media being a distinct barrier. Still, Cosell could get mileage out of this intellectual aesthetic, and was only too happy to sprinkle these people into his name-dropping stew.

Nor was the intelligentsia loath to conscript his name. In 1969, on the cover of *Esquire*'s November issue, twelve angry men of distinction in nice suits stood in a boxing ring, left hands on their hips, pointing accusing index fingers toward the camera, under the words "We believe this: Muhammad Ali deserves the right to defend his title." The diverse lot included Plimpton, Truman Capote, Budd Schulberg, antiwar Alaska senator Ernest Gruening, actors James Earl Jones and Theodore Bikel, director Sidney Lumet, artist Roy Lichtenstein, boxer José Torres—and Howard Cosell.

As well, the liberal lion Pete Hamill, who did maintain a friendship with him through the years, helped solidify Cosell's intellectual credibility. Called onto Tom Snyder's *The Late Late Show* after Cosell's death in 1995, Hamill waxed nostalgic:

I met Howard [at the Olympics] in Mexico City. We met, as befitted Howard, in the bar of the press section of one of the events, and he said, to me [in a Cosellian whine], "Pete Hamill, the only goy from

Brooklyn who never chased me down Eastern Parkway." At the time, I thought of him as an announcer of some kind. I didn't realize he was a phenomenon. Then, a couple days later, Tommie Smith and John Carlos did their Black Power demonstration and when it was over the great mob of us [media people] were all waiting, pencils poised, pads in hands. Smith and Carlos came off the stand, went right past all of us, maybe hundreds of us, and straight to Howard Cosell. I knew the world had changed, that the print guys were left in the dust and Howard was triumphant.[23]

The part about what Smith and Carlos did right after their demonstration, of course, never happened. But because the last part about Cosell becoming triumphant was true, this was easy to believe. Cosellian legends thus would fuse into the literary argosy, as if they *must* have happened, or at the very least *should* have happened.

COSELL COULD now enjoy being regaled in the national press, in brief but sententious profiles of him in *Newsweek* and *Time* only weeks apart over the summer of 1968. In these, he was a rare breed, biting the hand that fed him by, for instance, calling on ABC to "apply journalism to the last bastion of provincial TV sports coverage, NCAA football," positing that "that pious body will move to another network, which will be glad to get the business and which will regale the NCAA as God's gift to Americanism, sportsmanship and all the platitudinous rest."[24]

Clearly, such pontification was not appreciated at ABC, but it was the price they'd have to pay for Cosell's rising star. At the time, indeed, he was just warming up. This sort of dyspeptic criticism of sports would eventually fill hundreds of book pages. And with his irresistibility, no one was going to stop him. Or even register much of a complaint if he was just a tad deceitful. Before Super Bowl III, he swore on his radio show that Joe Namath would make the earth move and beat the eighteen-point-favorite Baltimore Colts. Then he went on TV and predicted the *Colts* would prevail. It was not the last time he'd play both ends. If, as *Newsweek* titled its Cosell article, "Sports Is Life," it was also show biz.

And Cosell may have been the only one who *didn't* take Cosell seriously, at least not all the time.

He did regard himself as so outsized that he was conceded the right to play *Howard Cosell*, the object of which could seem to be as unnerving as one could get. After all, he had the right to mock-insult Muhammad Ali. To be fair, he had long practiced the art of the put-down; it was part of the Cosell experience, even at NYU Law School. Now it was his very calling card, with put-ons that could insult people who didn't know him. Introduced to an attractive woman with her husband in tow, he would purr something like "You're a girl of rare and great beauty, my dear; it must thoroughly break your heart to know that you've so obviously married beneath yourself."

If it was funny at all, it was because it came with the foghorn delivery, and the oleaginous ego that pushed it onto his tongue. Always, it was discomfiting, but because no one would ever tell him to his face what they thought of it, and him, in private, he had license to perform this routine, and he did, regularly, in office corridors, in restaurants—even at *weddings*. Terry Jastrow, a raw-boned Texan who joined ABC Sports as a producer in the early seventies—and later a movie and theater producer—invited Cosell to his wedding in 1978, when he married actress Anne Archer. "I think Howard had already imbibed a few clear libations," he recalled, "and just when the minister said, 'And now you may kiss the bride,' Howard's voice came booming from the back of the room: 'Young man, you lay one hand on that lovely young lady and I'll break your arm.'"[25]

Jastrow told the story as those of its kind most often were told publicly, as a semipaean to the Cosellian jive, nothing if not innocuous. He, like the other men in Cosell's line of fire, was expected to be aggrandized by his attention to their women. Jim Spence, who had more power at ABC Sports than anyone but Arledge, watched the routine escalate— along with the "libations"—for two decades. He too stood by, a good audience, as the remarks became forward and at times genuinely tasteless. "For as long as you live," he quoted Cosell oozing to one woman he had cornered, "every time you are in his embrace, you will think of me."

Whenever he acted out like this, Spence said, Cosell "threw back his head and laughed that familiar laugh, the one that sounds curiously sinister and forced . . . At this point, the ritual called for everybody to laugh. This was part of Howard's shtick and everybody was supposed to know it and accept it."[26] And Spence did. As a fellow staple in the ABC Sports silo, he would need to ignore what his gut told him was wrong, even unconscionable, because the offender was Howard Cosell.

Gradually, though, the laughter would die. That would happen when Cosell became not a man or a sportscaster as much as an effigy. For now, he was just coming into his own as a sports journalist of distinction. Thus, while he earned his indemnity, the prime cause of his later dysfunction— his drinking—was ignored. Cosell off the air always had a martini at the ready; his lunch and dinner tabs were ballooned by round after round of them, and his cramped office had a refrigerator in which he kept pitchers of premixed martinis. Cigar in one hand, glass in the other, feet up on his desk, wig ajar on his head, he would regale visitors to the office for hours, with spiraling incoherence. But this was a Cosell he would permit no one to see at public functions. And because, on the air, he was straight as an arrow, or at least could will away the effects of mass quantities of gin and vermouth, it was not an issue.

Few put two and two together when, in the face of enormous pressure because of the Ali cause, he also became extremely cutting. Cruelty, in fact, was always his least admirable quality—one writer would note that he was "almost sadistic in embarrassing people with his 'put-ons,'" another that he was "an intellectual bully"—but one he would wield as a cudgel against his own insecurity, to convince himself as much as others that he was so worthy of envy and swagger, and riches. To Don Ohlmeyer, all those excesses in ego and behavior were straight from Psych 101. "Howard," he says, "was one of the most insecure people I ever met in my life. He was unbelievably insecure. And that bravado was a classic psychological overcompensation for it."[27]

# 9

## A STYGIAN BURDEN

B Y THE late 1960s, Cosell was becoming the Brahmin he had always wanted to be. Turning fifty, he no longer was the domesticated dad of that 1964 newspaper article that now seemed so long ago. Nor had his daughters matured without complication, most notably finding their religious identities. Because of Cosell's gnawing ambivalence about religion, and Emmy's own hands-off approach to the subject, Jill and Hilary had been left rudderless about their faith, something that Emmy would come to regret. With unusual frankness, she almost seemed to blame her husband, telling *Cosmopolitan* in 1979, "Howard thinks religion is a woman's work. He was never even bar-mitzvahed. What he didn't want to do, the little prince, he didn't *have* to do. We didn't bring up our daughters to be religious, either, for which they now both condemn us."

Jill was eventually baptized at twenty-one by a Methodist minister, and according to Emmy, "Hilary says she can't believe in anything and that it's all my fault for never giving her a reason to. Children want to belong; I guess that's the important thing. I guess ours grew up feeling left out."[1]

In 1968, Jill married the son of *Life* magazine sportswriter Tim

Cohane, Peter Cohane, who would work his way up from salesman to national sales manager for a shirt company. One year later, Cosell became a grandfather when Jill gave birth to a son named Justin, and three years later came a second grandson, Jared, both of whom would be baptized Methodists. Hilary, meanwhile, gravitated to Judaism, with scant help from her father; indeed, far unlike him, she leaped into if not the faith then at least the political and geographic entity that exemplifies it.

Hilary, eschewing the picket-fence family life of her sister, went to a posh East Side prep school. That left her parents alone in a big country home, which only made their mutual interdependence stronger; rarely did he go anywhere now, no matter the event or its venue, without Emmy as a personal buffer and confidante as his world became more rarefied and, given the death threats, constricted. Almost suffocating in his fame, he began to feel too isolated in Pound Ridge and wanted to partake of the high-voltage rhythm of the city. Before the decade was out, they would be splitting their time between Pound Ridge and a newly rented twenty-seventh-floor penthouse apartment with a sweeping view of the city, in a building aptly called the Imperial House at 150 East 69th Street, then a prime "silk stocking" neighborhood on the Upper East Side. They happily decorated the place with fine art and antiques. By the midseventies, they'd put the house up for sale and lived exclusively in town.

Cosell had now, in effect, typecast himself out of the lower classes of the sportscasting realm. He had become too big for not-quite-important events, and he was relied on by ABC to score the momentous interview. That meant he had been effectively, and ironically, boxed in again, though on a far more elevated level. He was on the scene at major championships, whether the Grand Prix, the Kentucky Derby, or the Penn Relays, but not used in quotidian proceedings such as ABC's Sunday afternoon NBA games—not that his antennae weren't tuned to that league's subterranean doings, having scooped everyone in 1968 in reporting that Wilt Chamberlain would jump the Philadelphia 76ers for the Los Angeles Lakers.

But not until 1970 did he lend his star to the roundball league, and then only for Game 7 of the finals, as a third wheel with the broadcast team of Chris Schenkel and Jack Twyman as Chamberlain's Lakers and the New York Knicks vied for a title long overdue for either team. Not that he was too much the dandy to do his job. Following the Knicks' dramatic victory keyed by gimpy-legged Willis Reed's entrance bare minutes before the opening tip-off, Cosell reveled as champagne was poured over his head by Dave DeBusschere and Bill Bradley, who hoped to dislodge his toupee. This was a ritual he had experienced in the locker rooms of the victorious Jets and Mets only months earlier, but seen only on local TV. But, even dripping Moët before the entire nation, when he interviewed Knicks guard Dick Barnett he couldn't help but bring up rumors that Barnett might be traded. Barnett blinked. He then denied he was going anywhere, such a question being about the last thing he expected to be asked on a night his team won it all.[2]

Of course, the Cosell sine qua non—and, by extension, that of ABC Sports—was still boxing. As wedded as Cosell and ABC were to Muhammad Ali, his enforced exile from the ring could not keep him off the air. He would drop by *Wide World of Sports* periodically to discuss with Cosell the course of his legal challenge to the government. Roone Arledge also hired him to do color commentary for a 1970 U.S.-Soviet amateur boxing tournament in Las Vegas—an enormously brave decision for many reasons; one, the tournament was sponsored by the ultraconservative AAU; two, as Arledge would recall, "ABC's upper reaches were inclined to cave in to pressure from Washington," a situation they again faced when the FCC was bombarded by irate mail; and worse yet, the State Department also registered disapproval, having become "somehow convinced that detente itself would be compromised" if Ali spouted off about America. But Arledge stood firm, eliciting from Ali, who jumped at the offer because his legal bills had drained him, a promise not to talk politics.

"Maybe I had some Cosell in me," Arledge wrote. "I stuck by my guns and so did my bosses, and the State Department, I suppose, found someone else to harass."[3]

That day, wearing a tuxedo ABC rented for him, an earnest Ali sat at ringside and, as Cosell said, "did his thing, taking special note of the U.S. heavyweight Ron Lyle," wryly adding, "The cause of democracy did not seem noticeably to suffer."[4]

Cosell stuck close by Ali during those years of exile, keeping the act alive in lean times when he could, albeit with a sort of wistful quality. Once, when he had garnered Ali for *Wide World*, the pair did some mandatory kibitzing. Stepping on risky turf—for anyone but him—Cosell began by twitting Ali that he had gone into exile because he "didn't have the courage to fight Joe Frazier, Jimmy Ellis, and Jerry Quarry." Ali did a slow boil, remembering how the act was supposed to go, then parried, "Every college I go to, everybody asks me about Howard Cosell, and my answer is: We just don't get along. I mean, you just talk a lot of stuff that doesn't make sense . . . Do you really think these homemade champions can beat me? That's the kind of appreciation I get from you, from you comin' all over the world. If I hadn't been fightin' you wouldn't have gotten to see the world."

After several minutes of mock insults, Cosell said, "All right, you son of a gun, you've had enough fun with me. You know that the one guy who has maintained that there is one heavyweight champion of the world, it's Howard Cosell, and I have said repeatedly that you could beat all of these guys . . ."

"You're right," Ali countered. "But you make all of these cracks. You just said I had a lot of trouble with these boys and me gettin' out of boxing in time to duck Frazier and this and that."

Then a curveball, with Cosell again encroaching on delicate territory for anyone else, saying, "You don't look as broke as you're supposed to be."

"What you mean broke?" Ali demanded.

"Everybody says you're broke, you got no money, you gave it all to Elijah Muhammad."

"No, how could I give it all to Elijah Muhammad? The American government took ninety percent of all of my money before I got it."

"The fact of the matter is," Cosell told him, turning sentimental, "the thing you've missed the most are the steady vocal sparring sessions that we enjoyed on *Wide World of Sports*."

"Well, we had a lot of fun."

"We've missed it."

"Well, things may be better soon."[5]

AS ALI toured campuses, Cosell served as a kind of conduit for potentially exciting news. Once, when Ali gave a lecture in a college outside Dallas, he went to a local TV studio to tell Cosell on a long-distance hookup with *Wide World* that Texas was about to grant him a license to fight. But it was not to be; and promises made by promoters in other states that led him to believe he'd be back in the ring proved empty—they came close in California, until Governor Ronald Reagan vowed: "That draft dodger will never fight in my state, period." The constant letdowns took a toll. They worsened when the Black Muslims suspended him for speaking about his plans without Elijah Muhammad's approval. He retreated into a shell that even Cosell couldn't draw him from. Whenever he tried, Ali would tell him, "Can't talk to you no more, not without Elijah's permission."[6]

Although an equally dour Cosell regarded any attempt by boxing to crown a champion in Ali's enforced exile to be illegitimate, life had to go on in the sport and at the network. When ABC signed onto a World Boxing Association eight-man heavyweight tournament culling the top contenders, he would announce it. This only seemed to prove, as Dick Young delighted in pointing out, that he was a shill for his network no different from the writers and announcers Cosell censured for sucking up to teams and leagues.

Being hoist upon his own petard would become a growing problem for him as his duties at ABC branched out further. He would indeed call the WBA tournament, with a decided unease, and a certain cynicism, a quality viewers had come to expect from him anyway. He would not sugarcoat the fact that the tournament was undercut from the start when the number-one contender, Joe Frazier, the Philadelphia brawler known as "Smokin' Joe," opted not to participate. Instead, Frazier, who had won the 1964 Olympic gold medal, fought Buster Mathis, who had once beaten Frazier as an amateur, for the New York State heavyweight championship in the new Madison Square Garden, knocking Mathis out in round eleven.

ABC had to make do with Jimmy Ellis, the slick former Ali sparring partner who had won eight fights in a row, as the main attraction. After he stopped Leotis Martin and Oscar Bonavena, Ellis defeated Jerry Quarry to win the WBA crown, one that almost nobody believed he would have if Ali was around. Cosell's own skepticism of Ellis was clearly displayed in his first defense, a fifteen-round decision over Floyd Patterson that September in Stockholm that Cosell strenuously disagreed with, venturing on the air that Floyd had won.

Worse, Ellis was himself inactive, for seventeen months, due to injury, opening the door to Frazier, who also beat Quarry to earn a unification bout with Ellis on February 16, 1970, at the Garden. It was the first big fight of the new decade, and in round four, when Frazier began to pour it on, so did Cosell, the narrative sounding like this: "Frazier's giving it to him . . . giving it to him. A right there. A left that missed. Another right that connected . . . DOWN GOES ELLIS! DOWN GOES ELLIS! He is beaten. Jimmy Ellis is going to try to get up. He is worn to a frazzle. He is a game, game young man. He is up . . . Frazier again with the left. Ellis standing there . . . OH! A tremendous left hook! The fight may be over . . . Ellis with tremendous coverage is up and the fight continues. A tremendous display of courage by Jimmy Ellis!"[7]

It was possible to feel winded just listening to Cosell's call, the lyricism of which was fueled more by genuine emotion than perfect grammar. He was, to be sure, at his peak as a boxing announcer, delivering far more impact and drama than the restrained enthusiasm of Don Dunphy, whom he had replaced on the blow-by-blow A-list. Thus it seemed something of a letdown when Angelo Dundee threw the towel in from Ellis's corner before the fifth round began, conceding Frazier the victory. In fact, the "Down goes . . ." refrain was not only this fight's earmark but one that was so persevered in Cosell's mind and the pit of his gut—and came to him from so natural a reflex—that it would be stored within his memory bank, to stream free again, and even more memorably so.

WITH ALI in exile, his appeal of his conviction making its way through the courts inch by inch, the ascendance of Frazier seemed profound enough to signal the Ali era might well be over for good. Indeed, the

*Ring*, boxing's hoary magazine/bible, which had continued to recognize Ali as champ, finally broke off and acknowledged Smokin' Joe. What's more, George Foreman was rising fast toward what was prophesied by his camp and the press, Cosell included, as an eventual collision course with Frazier. His pro debut came in June 1969 against journeyman Don Waldheim at Madison Square Garden, a minor event that ABC saw fit to televise, with Cosell at the mike. Set up for an easy win, Foreman scored a knockout in three rounds, but Cosell spared him no scrutiny, following up on his prescient Mexico City observation that Foreman had a tendency to punch himself out in early flurries, leaving himself sucking air, even within three rounds. Afterward, in the ring, he told the gleeful, childlike wunderkind that he had been "tentative," wasn't "sticking his opponent," and was "tight." Watching the replay, Foreman merrily disagreed: "Man, I'm tough. Lord have mercy."[8]

Foreman became a whirlwind, fighting every two weeks through the year, stealing some of Frazier's thunder, as Ali had with Sonny Liston, when he fought on the Frazier-Ellis undercard. That bout, too, was broadcast by ABC and called by Cosell, with Foreman winning a tougher than expected ten-round decision against Argentinian Gregorio Peralta. But all of these merging story lines seemed to come to a sudden halt when another rumor of an Ali comeback fight gained traction. In Georgia, black politicians pulled enough strings—and enough money from promoters, including Bob Arum—and greased enough palms for a match against Jerry Quarry to be scheduled in Atlanta on October 26, despite the howls of the segregationist governor, Lester Maddox, who declared the twenty-sixth a "Day of Mourning." Tuning up, Ali fought three opponents in an eight-round exhibition in September.

As fate and timing would have it, late in September came a favorable court ruling that further eased his way back. Acting on the very same angle Cosell had long pushed, Ali's lawyers had filed suit in New York, presenting a list of ninety men who'd been licensed to fight in the state despite convictions for all sorts of crimes, including military desertion. District Judge Walter Mansfield concurred. After years of vying for the moral and legal high ground in courts of law and the court of public opinion, the decision was a simple matter of fact, announced by a clerk not with fanfare but as dryly as one of Cosell's old summaries in the *NYU Law Review*. Still, even though the decision was narrow, limited to Ali being able to fight pending final dispensation of his case, no one knew more than the erstwhile editor of that review how seismic it was. In a few sentences, Mansfield had dealt the U.S. government a monumental defeat, and shown it the future, by separating what seemed propitious and "safe" from what was constitutional. Decades, even centuries, of hypocrisy and bromides about a democracy that applied only selectively, to certain Americans, perished under Mansfield's pen.

As Angelo Dundee recalls of that momentous day, "Howard knew about it I think before I did. I think he knew before anyone except Muhammad and the lawyers who were in the courtroom. Howard had sources all over, not just in boxing or sports but in the courts. I always considered Howard to be instrumental to those court rulings, because what he said about the case was what the lawyers put in their papers. I thought, and I still do, that we owed a lot to Howard."[9]

THE LONG-TERM course of boxing was reset when Ali climbed into the ring after three and a half years in exile, to his credit not against a cream-puff but Quarry, a leatherneck who had given Joe Frazier hell the year before, when cuts forced the ref to stop what the *Ring* magazine named as the fight of the year. Indeed, on that night in Atlanta many in a crowd of star-studded and beautiful idolaters in the Municipal Auditorium—as well as among his followers worldwide—feared he might be too rusty to beat Quarry, who may have been the only one in the house not there to see an Ali coronation, and on this day was the hope of white Middle America.

With so much at stake on either side of the racial and political divide, Ali, sensing the stakes at hand—and mindful that people of color world-wide had never deserted him—ventured that "I'm not just fightin' one man. I'm fightin' a lot of men." He went on to say that if he lost, "so many millions of faces throughout the world will be sad; they'll feel like they've been defeated." Thus, as he construed it, "I'm fightin' for my freedom."[10]

Cosell would be calling the fight on a delayed basis for *Wide World of Sports*. For a time, it appeared as if he would be handling the closed-circuit broadcast as well, until he made a money demand that the producer of the closed-circuit show, corporate attorney Robert Kassel, told him was "ridiculous."

"You'll pay that, kid, or you won't have anybody," Cosell snarled at Kassel with laughable egomania.[11] In fact, though Kassel says Cosell implied that Ali would only fight if he did the call, Kassel heard no such plea, and he gave the job to the former football star Tom Harmon, who, astonishingly, called Ali "Clay" most of the time, clearly to the discomfort of the equally odd choice for a color analyst, comedian Bill Cosby.

Cosell described the fight as "a victory for truth and order" and "a return to games" rather than polemics; for the black bourgeoisie in their furs and diamonds, he would later recall, "it was like Van Gogh discovering the vineyards. They came to rejoice. The king was back. Long live the king."[12] It certainly seemed to be an apt theme early on when Ali, his old quicksilver guise suddenly reappearing, landed some good combinations and opened a cut under Quarry's left eye that became a gusher, leading the ref to stop the match after round three, upon which an incredulous Quarry stomped around the ring.

Amid the euphoria in the house, Cosell was more tempered. Ali, he said, had looked anything but a champion. "The old hand and foot speed seemed diminished," he said, adding that "few conjectured about what might have happened had Quarry not been cut."[13] It was a postmortem Ali had no trouble accepting. In fact, on the *Wide World* coverage of the fight, Ali, in a split-screen phone hookup, was contrite, agreeing that he profited from Quarry's bum luck and that it was not a fair test of where he stood as a fighter. He also promised Quarry another fight, a promise he would keep.

But the king was indeed back, if not with the crown that now sat on Joe Frazier's head, and comfortably. Playing a game of one-upmanship, Frazier in his next defense on November 18 razed light-heavyweight champ Bob Foster in two rounds, making the notion of a match with Ali seem to make. sense to no one except Ali, who continued stalking him, dusting off the old material he'd used with Liston. Now it was Frazier who was "too ugly to be champ," who "can't talk," who was unfit to share the same ring with him. But if Ali won few points for originality as a phoenix rising, he clearly had more than a few miles left on him—several more of which were logged a bare three weeks later on December 7 when he took on another beautiful bum, Argentinian Oscar Bonavena, in the prime-time venue of Madison Square Garden, New York being still the only state to officially reinstate his license (the Quarry bout having been a one-off deal).

While Bonavena had, like Quarry, given a hard time to better fighters— putting Frazier down twice in a split-decision loss in 1966, then taking him fifteen brutal rounds in a 1968 defeat—he was also, like Quarry, a reliably dependable stepping-stone. His style was naturally compared to that of his countryman Louis Firpo, "the Wild Bull of the Pampas," who in 1923, in a similar mismatch, knocked Jack Dempsey through the ropes and out of the ring in the first round, before the champ climbed back in and knocked Firpo down seven times, then out in the second round. As if seeing a red sash, the slack-jawed, cinder-block-like Bonavena would charge headlong toward his opponent, sometimes landing a big punch, more often running right into one, though not once had he ever been knocked out. Despite Ali pitching him as a dangerous threat, helping sell out the Garden, Cosell bought none of it; from the start he mocked Bonavena as "Ringo," hung on him for his post-Beatles shag hairdo, and reduced him to insignificance as an "alley brawler."

Fight night saw Ali enter the ring not in his usual white trunks but red ones, an outfit complemented by matching red shoes with tassels. The new look did nothing to ease Cosell's doubts, but after the bell rang, suddenly Bonavena wasn't such a joke. Unable to capitalize on "Ringo's" laughably inaccurate swings, Ali seemed to age by the round. Calling the fight live on ABC, a perplexed Cosell remarked early on, "Oddly, I don't see Ali circling with the steadiness and swiftness to the left that's his usual landmark." By the late rounds, it had become something of an Ali requiem, with Cosell attributing to Bonavena a "physical confidence that must be apparent to Ali." For the viewers, he tried to pump up the ennui as "just an astonishing fight . . . not a classical fight in the sense of fistic greatness but astonishing in the trend of events." Few in the restless house saw it that way, their booing directed at Ali, leading Cosell to say that "the crowd has really turned on him." Not waiting for the end of the bout, he concluded, "What everybody will have to assess is what the years have taken from him . . . There is no speed, no movement left."

But no sooner was that observation out of his mouth than Ali finally found his way to Bonavena's jaw with a bolt of lightning with his off hand, crumpling the Beatle wannabe to the canvas. Switching gears, as was his wont, on a dime, Cosell rasped, "That left floored him! It came from nowhere!" and as a suddenly animated ex-champ moved in for the kill, gloves upraised, tassels flying, and "acting like the old Ali," he decked Bonavena twice more, the last hit ending the fight at the two-minute mark of the fifteenth round.

The stagnant previous rounds notwithstanding, it was 1965 all over again for Ali and Cosell both, with the latter dusting off an old standard and bellowing, "I'm going up to ring center!" He intended to grill Ali about his lack of training and élan, but before he could, Ali grabbed the microphone and preened, "I have done what Joe Frazier couldn't do. I have knocked out Oscar Bonavena." Even Cosell could not poke a hole in that verity, and an Ali-Frazier engagement was already being sold to the public before he signed off that night. Interviewing Frazier's manager, Yancey Durham, Cosell unearthed his usual scoop, getting Durham to say, "I hope we can get together in February."[14]

And so it was. But even as that appointment of two fighters so opposite in style and personality neared, Cosell had seemingly grown bigger than the event itself. His transformation from broadcaster to superstar had become evident that autumn, not through boxing but a sport he had never announced in real time. It happened when Roone Arledge, the paterfamilias of ABC if not TV sports itself, had brought to fruition one of the most far-fetched dreams anyone in football had ever had: broadcasting a pro Game of the Week not on Sunday but on a "school night," Monday night. And because in ABC's purview it was envisioned as a marriage of sports and pop culture, Arledge knew it could not possibly have succeeded without Howard Cosell.

MONDAY NIGHT football did not originate with Roone Arledge. It had been played periodically since the 1930s, and televising it was first floated by NFL commissioner Pete Rozelle as a new wrinkle in the league schedule as the 1966 merger went into effect and new rivalries would be opening up worthy of prime-time coverage. Three such experimental games were actually played on consecutive weeks in October 1969, two broadcast by CBS, one by NBC, neither with any ratings success.

ABC, too, had considered night football, when Tom Moore proposed licensing an NFL game in place of the fading Friday night fights. The network, however, was in a bind because of its relationship with the imperious NCAA, which was adamantly opposed to its TV partner carrying *any* pro game, day or night; Arledge agreed to the injunction in writing, only to breach it two years later, though the NCAA had assumed it meant in perpetuity.

Arledge never thought he'd have to reverse field until the summer of 1969 when Rozelle was trying to sell CBS and NBC on Monday night football and, unable to get them to come aboard, agreed after much groveling to hear out Arledge's pitch for ABC. It made sense, since unlike the other two networks, ABC had anemic prime-time ratings, and Leonard Goldenson, for one, was all for Monday night football—which would be ABC's first foray into live pro football coverage. But Goldenson's second-in-command, Elton Rule, was skittish. Rozelle then went to Sports Network, owned by the reclusive billionaire Howard Hughes—a brilliant ploy trading on the fact that, as Arledge said, "our affiliates were the least loyal in the land," and perhaps a hundred might defect to a low-level syndicated network each Monday.[15]

That brought Rule around, and within days ABC had forked over $25.5 million to the NFL. Only then did Arledge sheepishly tell NCAA President Walter Byers that the network's ban on pro football was inoperative. Byers sputtered about a double-cross, but was mollified by a pledge not to promote NFL games on NCAA games—the NCAA *would* be promoted on NFL games—or to utilize the lead NCAA game announcer, Chris Schenkel, on Monday nights.

Arledge had no trouble agreeing to the last. He had given a lot of thought to how the network would make a success out of a property most TV people thought was a sure loser. To Roone, the key was winning over women to a male pastime, a pipe dream then that he envisioned would help transform the sport and the medium. That meant the Monday game would need to be more than a game; it would need to be "a prime-time event," irrespective of which teams were playing. He figured ABC's now-proven exemplar of sports as high drama gave him a leg up. He wanted a new kind of broadcast paradigm, not a play-by-play man and an ex-jock color man spouting dry, conventional clichés. "Was there any law?" he would recall, "that said games had to be announced as though they were being played in a cathedral?"[16]

That rap was grossly unfair to great announcers like the lead men at NBC and CBS, respectively, Curt Gowdy and Ray Scott. Arledge and Cosell both would, in fact, criticize in particular the tersely mesmerizing Scott, who'd become synonymous with the Lombardi Packers' reign, as a bogeyman to defend the manic and circuslike ABC framework—made such, of course, by the prime bogeyman of the other networks. Yet it wasn't Cosell who was Arledge's first choice for what he wanted to be the real grabber of ABC's pro football coverage—the radical notion of a *three*-man booth, the alchemy of those three voices driving made-for-TV story lines. That choice was Frank Gifford, a longtime crony of both Arledge and Cosell, who was under contract calling games for CBS and would not be free until a year later.

Arledge was prepared to go elsewhere for a temporary play-by-play man. But he still came to Gifford for advice and consent about filling out the *MNF* booth, the first occupant of which he hired solely on Gifford's recommendation—Don Meredith, who at thirty-two had just retired after nine seasons as the Dallas Cowboys' quarterback. Meredith, who was working as a fledgling stockbroker, had done no broadcasting and had little interest in doing so, a critical distinction between him and those Cosell loved to target as the biggest problem in TV sports—the "jockocracy," the swelling population of ex-athletes with scant experience in the TV booth but a major yen to pocket network coin to gain it.

Indeed, Arledge perceived Meredith's lack of polish as a plus given that, as Gifford touted him, he was a rake, a rugged, good-looking Texan who had won a lot of games, lost the big ones—the biggest being the heartbreaking, last-second defeat to the Packers in the 1967 "Ice Bowl" NFL title game—and was said to possess homespun wit and wisdom. Arledge told Gifford to have Meredith call ABC, and Meredith tried four times to contact Arledge, who had become notorious for not returning calls. Only when Arledge got wind that Meredith was pitching himself to CBS did he set up a lunch meeting at Toots Shor's. Meredith was still fuming.

"The only reason I came," he hissed, "is to tell you to your face what a horse's ass you are."[17]

Arledge, who lived in a universe of sycophants, was disarmed, if not charmed. He then extended the offer. He scribbled on a napkin a salary he thought appropriate for the *MNF* gig: $20,000. Meredith, not batting a lash, said that was what CBS offered him. That day, he walked out of Shor's with a one-day-a-week job for fourteen weeks that would pay him thirty grand. Arledge walked out knowing he had a talented con man on the payroll, hardly the redneck *Hee Haw* tintype Meredith portrayed himself to be—not, as he liked to say, "Jeff and Hazel's baby boy from Mount Vernon, Texas," but a rather canny, sensitive fellow who understood he was hired to humanize, sometimes satirize, the ritual of football for a mass audience, and only incidentally to inform it of the intricacies and strategies of the game going on.

The proverbial taste that would be left in viewers' mouths—the third man in the booth, Arledge's ace in the hole—required some hard swallowing before Roone hired him. To be sure, Cosell was to Arledge the perfect surface for Meredith to bounce his prattle off of. But there was, too, undeniably, a downside to consider. As Don Ohlmeyer notes, "Remember the context. What was Howard known for then? His defending Ali and giving Tommie Smith a say when everyone else wanted to crucify him. So to much of the country Howard was that 'nigger-loving Jew.' No matter how good he was calling fights and reporting on issues in sports, his reputation among the general public was controversial, at best. And among the press, he was just despised.

"Roone knew, we all did, that Howard would ultimately get the job. Roone was committed to him. But it weighed on everybody that this was not boxing, it wasn't track and field. It was network prime-time TV. It was a whole new dimension for us. It was make or break. You had to be extremely mindful of who would be watching in America. There was so much money at stake, so much of ABC's future was built around this program. In that light, Meredith was an easy call; Howard was not."[18]

As he did before the Mexico City Olympics, Arledge, still not entirely sure, held off officially asking Cosell to join the crew. Not completely irrelevant to Arledge, either, was that Cosell had no experience calling football games live, and had nothing in his résumé that met the burden of a football color man—though again, Arledge wanted to play against type so as to attract an audience of females and casual football fans. For a time he felt out opinion about Cosell, perhaps believing negative feedback would give him a reason to go against his instincts. He asked both Gifford and Rozelle what they thought of Cosell being in the booth.

"Not much," answered Gifford, whose long friendship with Cosell had soured when he became an announcer, primarily because when Cosell would sneer at "pretty boy" football broadcasters he assumed that meant him. When Arledge said the concept would be to make Cosell a kind of on-air "columnist," Gifford laughed and said, "You're kidding, right?"[19]

Rozelle was a little harder to read. He had come to know Cosell well and had dined with him and Emmy several times, but he'd had his run-ins with him as well, although who hadn't? He asked Arledge with a giggle, "Cosell? Why don't you just dig up Attila the Hun?" While Rozelle had no say in picking the announcers, that he had no real objection to Cosell was a hurdle cleared. Indeed, Rozelle believed Arledge was merely trying to get everyone accustomed to the reality of Cosell being part of the show—and as Cosell told it, the omnipotent commissioner could not have been more thrilled. After he interviewed Rozelle on his local TV sports report, the two men repaired to Tavern on the Green, the glitzy Central Park extravaganza of a restaurant, for cocktails. "This," Cosell would recall, "was when Pete said that he hoped I would do the color commentary on the games. I was frankly surprised, because . . . I did not fit his mold, nor the traditional NFL mold," in which, Cosell believed, "every telecast sounded like every other."[20]

But Rozelle apparently was ready for a new approach—very new. Cosell, too, was ready, and had been for weeks, having convinced himself that the gig was his divine right, and in fact was already his. Arledge, though, had avoided all his calls, far more strenuously than he did the other calls he always ducked. In fact, Cosell's insecurities were such that he had taken to ringing him up at all hours with constant complaints, leading Arledge to hire an answering service to expressly screen the calls Cosell made to his home. In his own good time, Arledge at last did lunch with Cosell at Jimmy Weston's restaurant. He didn't tell him why, but Cosell knew, and when they sat down and Arledge said, "There's something I need to talk to you about," he was ready with more parodic amour propre, the riff now going, "From the desperation of your tone, the bon vivant who is Roone Pinckney Arledge is beseeching me to rescue the trifle he's devised for Monday evenings. Am I not correct?"

"As always, Howard," Arledge assented, by rote.

When they got down to details, Cosell was well aware that his contract stipulated that his hefty salary was all-inclusive, irrespective of how many events he did.

"And you expect me to shoulder this Stygian burden without additional compensation," he said, using a mythological reference that somehow befitted how he saw himself, though the underworld river Styx seemed not the ideal metaphor for what he seemed to envision about the rigors that lay ahead; rather, it was more like the "burden" of a Sisyphean boulder.

"Yes, Howard, I do," Arledge replied.

It took not two seconds for Cosell to say, "I accept."[21]

And so—in health and in sickness—the NFL had Howard Cosell, and vice versa. For better or worse, although just which it would be no one could know. But a wild ride was in store, such that when he looked back only two years later in *Cosell*, he would write that *Monday Night Football* had made him "the recipient of the biggest publicity wave (good and bad) any sportscaster has ever received."[22] If anything, that was actually, for once, an *understatement*.


WITH MEREDITH and Cosell in the bag, Arledge needed a pleasing cipher as a play-by-play man, as a placeholder for Gifford. He first queried Curt Gowdy, who had two years left on his NBC contract and said no, as did the golden-throated voice of the L.A. Dodgers, Vin Scully, who when asked if he could work with Cosell replied, "He's a roomful all by himself." Arledge therefore promoted from within, hiring Keith Jackson, the big, affable guy who had ironically been on the rise doing college football.

With Arledge having put in an inordinate amount of time and work filling his three-man booth, then parading the chosen ones before the national media in a massive publicity campaign in the rollout of the program, he achieved his prime goal: to generate more attention and curiosity about the announcing team than about the actual upcoming schedule. The angle was always the byplay, and horseplay, between Cosell and Meredith, the sort of thing no one had ever cared much about on a sports broadcast. Arledge, of course, wanted to re-create the chemistry that worked so well for Cosell and Ali, with the tall, homespun Texan now the pinprick to deflate the hot-air balloon.

Cosell was not averse to recreating the old formula, but with a most intriguing twist—rather than playing foil for an angry black man, he would do so for a carefree "redneck," or at least a man playing to that stereotype. It meant that, from a political bent, the act was defanged. Cosell was still the so-called New York Jew, but the black component was stripped away. This was a buddy act contrived to be folksy, not rooted to anything societally meaningful beyond the sharp stereotypes. The problem at the start was that Meredith couldn't find any kind of conversational groove. When the new crew assembled at a Lions-Chiefs exhibition game in Detroit for a nontelevised rehearsal, Arledge blew his top at how shabby the production was. He spared no one, strafing Cosell and Meredith—whom Cosell would describe as "painfully ill at ease"—for their lack of cohesion, and the latter for a rash of clichés and generic football swill. Meredith took it so hard he ripped out his earpiece and yelled, "Fuck this," then rose from his chair, told the crew, "I'm not qualified for this," and announced he was going to quit and go home to Texas. He repeated that the next day in New York at a staff production meeting, saying, "Ah'll just leave."[23]

Cosell, who was personally fond of Meredith and was one of the few who knew that he was going through a terrible personal travail— his young daughter, born blind and retarded, was about to be institutionalized—caught him later, his bags packed, after Meredith had left the Warwick Hotel and was trying to hail a cab to the airport. They went back inside to the hotel bar, where Cosell told Meredith he was about to make the biggest mistake of his life. Projecting how their coaction would play out, he said Meredith, without even trying, would be a national folk hero for it. "Middle America will love you. Southern America will love you. And there are at least forty sportswriters in this country who can't wait to get at me . . . You'll wear the white hat, I'll wear the black hat."[24] Clearly, Cosell knew himself, as well as his critics did.

According to how Cosell would recall this colloquy, Meredith, liking what he heard, lifted his drink and said, "I'm with you, coach." Thereby saving the impending glory of *Monday Night Football* and ABC's hoped-for bacon. Many around the network, hearing the tale, scoffed that Cosell alone could have turned Meredith back to his appointed task. "I'm sure Howard had something to do with it," says Don Ohlmeyer today, "but the truth is, we had all made clear to Don at the start that he would bounce off Howard and be the good guy. Don just had to sort it all out, make a commitment once the show took flight. I think he would have come back from Texas to do it in any case. He wouldn't have cottoned to the idea of being a quitter."[25]

Cosell, meanwhile, had a broader vision than that of a caricatured man in a black hat. He was sure he would shake up the world of sports journalism. "With the intelligent viewers, I'll destroy the parrots in the cages who have been providing us with their fatigued litany for years," he said in one interview.[26] To be sure, it was screamingly obvious who the "big cheese" of *Monday Night Football* would be. In *Sports Illustrated* a week before the show would debut with a Jets-Browns game in Cleveland, Robert Creamer wrote in his "Scorecard" column:

> Keith Jackson, who will do the play-by-play on ABC's Monday night telecasts of NFL games, was asked how he expected to get along with the outspoken Howard Cosell, who will do the color commentary. Jackson diplomatically praised Cosell, pointed out that Cosell's job was more difficult than his own play-by-play responsibility and added, "He will not be the dominant personality on the telecast."

> And all we can think to say is: Wanna bet?[27]

COSELL WAS already prickly as the *MNF* premiere approached. The week before, the cast and crew had done a warm-up broadcast of a Giant-Steelers preseason game in Pittsburgh. As a gimmick, the Giants' loquacious quarterback Fran Tarkenton was persuaded to wear a microphone during the game, which outraged the old-guard sportswriters as a breach of in-game etiquette. Cosell had nothing to do with the idea, but because he had been the one who mainly spoke with Tarkenton—and because he was Howard Cosell—he took the heat for it, sparking a demand by Dick Young and several other New York scribes that they be allowed to sit on the sideline benches during games.

Already, he was the cause célèbre, and he was chided in print for his commentary—with Young, his perennial nemesis, writing that he had tried to belittle Meredith in order to "make himself bigger than the event." And because he had dubbed Meredith on air as "the Cowboy" or "Dandy Don"—a bit of classic Cosell, who had a nickname for most everyone—some believed he was being condescending. Of course, this was the role he was supposed to be playing, but Cosell—who would, by plan, introduce Meredith on the first show with a comical montage of the latter's on-field mistakes such as fumbles, missed handoffs, and being sacked—was so wary of not offending the oversensitive Meredith that he purposely explained to him that he was simply trying to be folksy and collegial, and that the montage was meant in fun and would make him a sympathetic figure right off the bat. As if it were a prenup agreement, Meredith signed off on it.

During the week before that first game, concerned that Meredith knew too little of the Jets, Cosell took him to the team's practices, and both stayed in Joe Namath's bachelor pad. But the game was a potential pitfall for Cosell, too, since it revived old suppositions in the press that he was too close to Namath and the team to objectively report on them. Yet in truth the opposite may have been the case, since he had soured on the team ever since Sonny Werblin was bought out by Jets management before the 1968 championship season. Despite the fact that Werblin remained on the board of the team, Cosell had ever since maintained, speciously, that Werblin had been "fired," and he seemed to be carrying a grudge against the new owner, oilman Leon Hess.

Whether Cosell would be able to find room in the telecast to vent about the Jets or anything else was problematic for him. He was a man with much to say, but openly doubted he would have the freedom to utter anything but inane banter. It genuinely worried him, though he would not let on. In fact, he tried to act, unconvincingly, as if the impending broadcast meant little to him in the grand scape of his duties. Before the two men had flown to Cleveland, Cosell had invited Arledge, who lived in Bedford Hills not far from Pound Ridge, to share a limousine ride home, but only after they stopped at the Warwick bar for some drinks to take with them. Then, as they rode, elbows bent every mile, Cosell sniffed, "I suppose that in a strange way it matters to you whether this succeeds or not." Arledge wouldn't even try to play the same game. "Yes, Howard, it does," he told him, sternly. "And it better damn well matter to you."[28]

Cosell was the first voice and face the nation heard and saw when the Jets-Browns game came on the air—for many around the country, the first time they had really focused on the face behind the voice, which was now jowly and pale, with swollen bags under eyes that seemed glazed. The voice itself was shaky, that of a man nervous enough for the hand holding his microphone to tremble and his words to quaver, prompting Dick Young to mercilessly write that "the brash, superior announcer [came] off like a bundle of frayed nerves." In a flat monotone, Cosell intoned, "It is a hot, sultry, almost windless night here at Municipal Stadium in Cleveland, Ohio, where the Browns will play host to the New York Jets. Good evening, everyone, I'm Howard Cosell, and welcome to ABC's Monday night prime-time National Football League television series."[29]

Cleveland was indeed warm and humid that night of September 21, 1970, but the air hung especially heavy with expectation in the television booth and in the trailer parked outside the stadium. In that airless tube, Chet Forte, who was given extraordinary sway as coordinating producer/director, sat before monitors for nine cameras, as did, in a separate truck, the replay producer and director, Dennis Lewin and Lou Volpicelli, respectively. All of them would need to communicate not just with the cameramen but Cosell and Meredith, to coordinate the flow of dialogue around each live shot and each replay.

It was a hellacious task all around, with so many cameras and so many voices to keep smoothly on track, which would be even more nerve-wracking with Arledge hovering over the directors' shoulders barking orders or haunting the crowded booth. It's a wonder anyone was able to focus on his job that night without his head imploding—not least of all Cosell, who had made himself the fulcrum of the entire production. But he did shake off his early vapors to carry out his personal agenda, treating the Jets with disdain and pumping up the Browns, whose quarterback Bill Nelsen, he insisted, had knees just as bad as Namath's but didn't get the publicity Namath did because he didn't play in New York. His enthusiasm and swagger frothing, he worked, and overworked, the obvious story line: that the Jets were racking up massive yardage, 454 in all, but getting nowhere fast. "The Jets are outstatisticking them, but the Browns don't make mistakes" was his analysis at halftime.

Such banalities were inevitable when things ran at a breakneck pace. So was his habit of stepping on Keith Jackson's game calls. The game would be decided by two huge plays, both of which were punctuated by Cosell bellowing an overly loud and almost juvenile "OOOHHH!" atop Jackson, the first time when Homer Jones ran back a kickoff ninety-four yards, the second when linebacker Billy Andrews intercepted Namath and scored the clinching touchdown in the Browns' 31–21 victory. And yet, in an early barometer of how overwrought viewers of this series would be, he came away from the game as the heavy in *Cleveland*, for noting that the Browns' All-Pro halfback Leroy Kelly "has not been a compelling factor in this game," though he hastened to add, "But make no mistake about it, he will have his days of glory, such are his talents."

By this he was being more than evenhanded—at the time he said that, Kelly had just forty-four yards, and in fact would end up with sixty-two—but the first part of the statement seemed to be all Cleveland heard; the newspapers fixated on it the next day, slamming Cosell for the heresy about the hometown icon and somehow construing from it that Cosell had venerated *Namath*. Amazingly, this was also an argument made by some of the New York press. Other, less chauvinistic writers

simply slapped him for generic reasons, such as that he was a "master of
the verbal cheap shot," a dispenser of "retching prattle," and showed a
"towering ignorance of football."

Cosell surely had to suck up a hard dose of reality with that opening
game—the new reality of TV combined with a new order of sports coverage. Anything he said was liable to be taken as a grave insult by *somebody*. But the greater perspective was that if there was bound to be
criticism—and wasn't there always when he was on the air?—it was simply by dint of the unprecedented size of the audience for these football
games. When the numbers came in days after the first game, it became
clear how exponentially magnified every single word of his would be.
ABC, in fact, hit the jackpot, racking up a 35 share, meaning that more
than one out of every three televisions in the country was tuned to the
game, about the same as the entrenched CBS sitcom lineup and better
than an NBC movie with Liz Taylor and Richard Burton that had been
aimed purposely at a female audience. No one believed this would be a
fluke; the message was that *Monday Night Football* was a powerhouse.

Cosell was absolutely right when he told Meredith about who would
wear the white and black hats, though the caricature of each man had
congealed a lot more quickly than he had believed it would. Immediately,
he now had to resign himself to the added reality that he had to be on top
of the game just to make up for Meredith's vacuousness, though it was
"Dandy Don" who came off indeed as the more sympathetic, perhaps for
the very reason that he seemed massively *un*prepared.

In fact, Meredith had hit a jackpot of his own with a throwaway line
that had not a thing to do with football. When Browns receiver Fair
Hooker caught a pass, he turned impish, saying what everyone else had
to be thinking. "Isn't Fair Hooker a great name?" Jackson could only
rejoin, "I'll take a pass on that one." Cosell, for perhaps one of the few
times in his life, said nothing. In the vacuum of studied silence, Meredith
finished the thought: "Fair Hooker—I haven't met one yet." It was sly,
cheeky, and knowing, even daring for the provincial hamlet of sports.
And it was all that was needed for a star to be born, a boom to begin, and
a network to rest smug in knowing it had already earned back the money
it spent on him and on *Monday Night Football*.

Cosell himself was not overly amused or impressed with Meredith's work. Once, after he asked Meredith to explain what pass interference was, Dandy Don fumbled around for the right words, then—to Cosell's disbelief—gave up and said, "I don't know for sure what it is, but it's a no-no." He even believed Meredith had shown him up a couple of times, such as when, plumbing a cliché, Cosell noted with an air of great authority that unless the Jets could get the ball, Namath couldn't score. Meredith waited, considered that profound observation, then deadpanned, "You've got a point there, Howard." Still, the audience "got" that Meredith was there not to enlighten but entertain, and that gave him a lot of latitude. Even when he was caustic, he charmed America. In his pique, Cosell couldn't realize that his persona, too, had worked, merely by the overheated reaction. When the chemistry between them became, almost despite them, ingrained in the American culture, he would remark that he felt as if he were living in a world created by Lewis Carroll.

Already, it was abundantly clear that, no matter how little they thought of each other, Howard needed Don, Don needed Howard. For a while, that was a rush. But just until the thrill was gone and they could only detest each other.

WIDELY PUMMELED in the press—Young's very biased judgment was that Cosell "doesn't seem cut out for this type of thing"—with jealousy no doubt a prime influence for that, all the *MNF* announcers were being dissected on a cellular level.[30] This was clear proof positive that Arledge had achieved what he had planned for. While the announcing dynamic was not what gained *MNF* the huge ratings for the opener, it was what would keep bringing eyes and ears back for lesser attractions on the field. And the byplay between Cosell and Meredith grew more breezy and offhandedly piquant, and at times testy, as they became more comfortable with each other, not that Cosell would ever respect Meredith's work, or be comfortable with Dandy Don the folk hero. For now, there was the shared sense of satisfaction and wonder that they were rising to heights of public awareness neither could have anticipated. But for both of these oversensitive men, that would not be good enough.

Naturally, Cosell needed to be coddled for his own work. Right from the start, any number of ABC staffers on the show would serve as his shoulders to cry on whenever a write-up in a newspaper—virtually *any* newspaper—would critique him or the show. Dennis Lewin was a regular sounding board. "I'd get calls from Howard at ten o'clock on Tuesday morning saying something like 'Did you see what the *Elmira News* said about us?' I'd say, 'The *Elmira News*?! Who cares?'" Lewin recalls. But *Cosell* cared, needlessly, his numerous protestations to the contrary about the "insipid little rats" of the press corps notwithstanding. And not being able to laugh off such opprobrium, no matter how trivial, Lewin surmises, "wore him down in the end, if you want to know the truth."[31] Eventually, Lewin, Forte, Volpicelli, associate producer Jim "Doc" Feeney, anyone Cosell could cry to, had to field calls like that and soothe his fragile ego—everyone but Arledge, who preempted him with his phone screening.

A more serious repercussion than the reaction of the sportswriters was the volume of mail that came in eviscerating him. As Cosell would say with gaping understatement, "Only a minimal amount of it . . . favored me."[32] Amazingly, it was even more hate-filled than the mail that came in whenever he interviewed Ali. As Arledge recalled, there were sacks and sacks of it. "Not letters that began, 'In my opinion,' but 'We, the undersigned,' and ended with three hundred names . . . [I]n Howard Cosell, they'd found the man they loved to hate."

Arledge loved the fact that one football telecast had sparked this tumult. Asked by sportswriters if he was worried about the controversy entirely beyond the white lines, he quoted himself, "*Worried?* That's exactly what I'm looking for."[33]

He took pains to succor Cosell, telling him that ABC Sports executives had graded him "very favorable" in their review of the Jets-Browns game tape. However, what Cosell did not know was how close he actually became to being fired, the fans' execration having far more impact among the sponsors and, thus, the ABC brass. When it reached Leonard Goldenson, Arledge knew he had a problem on his hands. Cosell, of course, had for years sworn that the flinty ABC chairman was his biggest ally, a claim the brass always snickered at. Yet in *Cosell*, he unwittingly weakened that assumption when he noted that Goldenson had in fact joined in the chorus of contempt ABC officials had for him, relating that the boss had regularly called Elton Rule to ask him, "What about Howard? What are you going to do about him?"

"Nothing," he insisted was Rule's response. "Howard works for Arledge."[34]

That was entirely correct. Goldenson *did* take a backseat to Arledge in dealing with Cosell. Still, it was kept from Cosell that Goldenson was hardly defending him. At the time that Cosell's floppy ears were burning from the negative reaction, no less than Henry Ford, the owner of the automobile company that was the show's biggest sponsor, told Arledge, "I listened to that gab [between Cosell and Meredith] and I couldn't concentrate on the football. Take that guy Cosell off." Goldenson, in turn, asked Arledge, "Shouldn't we reconsider this Cosell thing?"[35]

Cosell was hanging by a thin reed. As angst-ridden as he always was, the man was nothing if not proud. And so Arledge had to somehow stunt Cosell's prying antennae. "Disclosing what Ford had said might make him quit," Arledge said. "It certainly wouldn't improve his performance."[36]

Caught between all these pincers, Arledge could only, as if this in itself were a game of football, play for time. "Give me four weeks, Leonard," he implored the chairman.[37] Goldenson did, thereby turning, in the end, four weeks into fourteen years.

# 10

---

# "THAT SON OF A BITCH
IS DRUNK!"

For the second episode of *MNF*, a Chiefs-Colts game, Cosell breezed into Baltimore with his gut in a knot because of the criticism from the previous Monday. Luckily, one of his closest cronies among the sports upper crust was Colts general manager Don Klosterman, who met him at the airport and squired him about town, providing salve to a bruised ego. Dining at the Chesapeake restaurant, he gave a few impromptu interviews with the local press. Later, the great Colts halfback Lenny Moore came over and threw his arms around him, braying loudly, "This man is the greatest broadcaster in the world!"

"Lenny," Cosell, in character, replied, "you're exactly right."[1]

Even so, the flak and rumors that ABC, despite the extraordinary ratings, might take him off the show were wearing on him. "I could feel myself crashing," he would recall. "Some of my friends thought I was in trouble. I didn't need to be told this. I could read it in their faces." Emmy, true to form, bucked him up, saying, "Don't let anyone know that it bothers you," which for him was easier said than done.[2]

Arledge, wanting to take some pressure off, told him it might help if he "held back" a tad rather than going too "Cosellian." When the game hit the air, it began with an interview of the rapidly aging Colt quarterback Johnny Unitas. Almost as if foreseeing that send-up in *Mad* magazine two years later, Cosell waded right in, asking Unitas if he could "still throw the long ball." Though Johnny U took no offense, the town's sportswriters blistered him for mortally insulting the deity that Unitas was in Baltimore.

He simply could not buy a break. While he did admit later to holding back some during the game, he didn't get through the first quarter before he found more trouble. It came when the Chiefs' slippery running back Mike Garrett hobbled off the field. "Dandy," he said, "there's little Mike on the sidelines . . ." As he went on, the TV audience could hear Garrett over an open sideline microphone asking teammates, "Wonder what Cosell is sayin' tonight?" Laughing at the remark, which was like nectar to him, Cosell laughed. "Tough little cookie," he mused. "He'll be back." It was, like the Leroy Kelly line, harmless. But Arledge, a bit too censorious for sure, and under immense pressure of his own, reacted badly. "There you go, Howard," he barked into Cosell's earpiece. "That's the very kind of thing that's going to get you in trouble because they're looking to sock you. What if he doesn't come back?"[3]

Cosell could hardly believe it. Now his own boss was abusing him for a picayune comment. In a fit of self-absorbed vanity and pique, he said nothing by way of defense—and, in fact, almost nothing the rest of the game. When Jackson or Meredith threw it to him, dead air would ensue. Spitefully, he would only recite a few scattered statistics. His boothmates looked at each other quizzically, not knowing what to do. Arledge tried cajoling him, gently and then firmly, to no avail.

As it turned out, Arledge was right about the Garrett comment; he never did return, and the triviality of Cosell getting it wrong, as well as his "disrespectful" Unitas interview, became the latest tirade in the press against the briny broadcaster. Watching it play out during the next week, Cosell came to another of his momentous life decisions, or so he thought. On the Sunday night before the third game of the season, a Bears-Lions tilt, Cosell was drinking his dinner at a Detroit restaurant with Jackson and Meredith when he told them, "I'm not coming back," meaning for the second season of *Monday Night Football*.

As if that weren't ominous enough, a sloshed Jackson, who knew nothing of Arledge's commitment to Frank Gifford, chimed in that *he* too would cut out, feeling that Arledge, whose only directive to him was to say as little as possible, had no commitment to him—an inkling that would prove remarkably prescient. Meredith, however, had no similar beefs. Few and far between were negative reviews of him, and he was coming to enjoy the scent of fame. "The ol' Cowboy, he's coming back," he said. "I got nothing better to do that pays me so much."[4]

Arledge was at wit's end. The series was thriving in the ratings, yet the Cosell problem was keeping him from enjoying it. Cosell seemed to be having a nervous breakdown. On the afternoon of the sixth game, between the Rams and Vikings in Minnesota, he accosted Pete Rozelle's top aide, Don Weiss, screaming in his face about how the NFL did not appreciate what he was doing for it. Moments later, he was screaming at Arledge his latest threat to quit. Cosell himself would admit that his conduct that day was disgraceful—"I behaved badly, boyishly, monosyllabically all day, with Forte, with Dandy, with Keith, with all of them."[5]

Roone was so sick of him that when Cosell confronted him, he was prepared to call his bluff. "Howard," he told him, "this may be the most important game we have yet done . . . And you've got everybody unnerved, everybody, the way you're acting."

Cosell, feigning contrition, mumbled, "Yes, sir, yes, whatever you want."

Arledge cut to the heart of the matter, going on, "If you want to quit after this game—fine. If you want to talk it over tomorrow—fine. But give us all a break and do your thing tonight."[6]

It was gentle, but rebuking—and as Cosell would later write, "I knew he was right." Arledge had been what he wasn't—an adult, and smarter and far more professional. Perhaps it was then that he realized it was Roone and Roone alone who was going to the mat for him. Arledge learned something from that interlude, too—dealing with Cosell head-on would unfailingly make him back down.

When Rozelle was told by Don Weiss about the press box incident, he kept his famous calm. Not wanting to lose Cosell as an asset, he took the extraordinary step of dropping by the Cosells' apartment, unannounced, during the following week—"for a cocktail," as Cosell remembered.

"Howard," he told Emmy, "is taking this thing much too seriously." He then counseled him to "just have fun" with the Monday night games. When Rozelle had his drink and was out the door, Emmy dispensed her usual wisdom. "He certainly does oversimplify," she told him, "but, basically, he's right."[7]

Cosell for the next few weeks was still a bit circumspect and unsteady; acting on a suggestion by Elton Rule himself, he refrained from using the sobriquet "Dandy Don," which Rule believed was patronizing to Meredith. But then, realizing how silly it was not to accentuate what had become a signature of the show, he broke the "Rule" and went back to the "Dandy Don" exchanges; when he and Meredith filmed a commercial for Gillette razor blades, he improvised the last line about himself—"Just another pretty face, Danderoo."

By now, Arledge's four-week deadline to deal with the Cosell situation had passed. However, as it turned out, the point was moot because Henry Ford, predictably, had become convinced that no changes were needed, certainly not with ratings that were going through the roof every Monday night. Arledge breathed a deep sigh of relief when he picked up a call from Leonard Goldenson, who related some news. "Leonard, I want to apologize," he quoted Ford as telling him. "I like the patter between Cosell and Meredith. I want to withdraw my objections."[8]

By then as well, Cosell, perhaps hearing of this from his own sources, had brightened in his mood. He backed off his vow to quit the show—for now. And, having worked with Meredith for almost half a season, he too had come to appreciate, take pride in, even revel in the chemistry they had clearly struck, though with a continuing animus about Meredith's almost gleefully lax approach to game preparation. He now began looking forward to each Monday game. Just as millions of Americans looked forward to what he would have to say.

COSELL'S ALMOST complete co-opting of everything that mattered to the public about *Monday Night Football* came as no surprise to Lou Volpicelli, who had seen him rise from an unsure producer of documentaries. "When I worked with Howard on his documentaries," Volpicelli says, "he used to be so insecure that he would be hesitant to ask me to do something, because I had a lot more experience. He would wait to see that I was in the building and then call my wife at home, so she would tell me what he wanted to do. And he was the producer! But now I get to see him on *Monday Night Football* and he couldn't wait to order me around—[in an exaggerated, staccato voice] 'Vol-pi-cel-li! Make sure you're rol-ling!' But he'd give me that wink, you know, like he was playing with me. I loved the guy. I was in awe of him, to tell you the truth."

The folksy director, today pushing ninety, knew Cosell as few did; the two of them were close enough for Cosell to affectionately call him "guinea" or "wop," no matter who was in earshot. "I would take it as a sign that he felt comfortable enough with me to do that," says Volpicelli, though he admits it would sound a lot less affectionate when Cosell drank too much, which he now almost always did. The two men also were gin rummy partners, and usually cleaned out other players around the table back at the hotel during downtimes. Those players more and more included Forte, who often challenged whoever he could to a rummy or poker match, displaying the first signs of a nagging gambling addiction that was only stoked by the fact that Cosell always seemed to beat him. But then, as Volpicelli adds, Cosell knew how to bluff. "All that about the threats to quit the show, I never believed it. He was just playing another hand."

The trouble was, in playing it, Cosell's ego could not accept anything but praise. As Volpicelli adds, "When nobody patted him on the back, I think that really hurt him. To tell you the truth, it may have affected his mental health."[9]

More so, perhaps, because of what Cosell perceived to be at the core of any criticism of him. That unpleasant reality was addressed by Jim Spence, Arledge's right-hand man at ABC Sports. "To be boldly frank," Spence said, "a lot of Americans looked at him, not a handsome man, and listened to that grating voice, and perceived in both demeanor and tone a haughty manner, and decided he was first and foremost a Jewish guy from New York who supported blacks." Cosell recalled in his memoirs that Chet Forte had told him of the avalanche of mail, so much of it against him. "More than half of it," Forte said, "doesn't even relate to the telecast. It's about you and Muhammad Ali." Wrote Cosell: "I knew instinctively what he meant. It was a pattern with which I was painfully familiar: 'Get that nigger-loving Jew bastard off the air. Football is an *American* game.'"[10]

To Cosell's shock, *MNF* caused a more visceral reaction to him than even his alliance with Muhammad Ali. It didn't matter that the black component was missing. A good many of those letters came from people who made up the bedrock of the show's male audience—white, southern men. Racism was hardly a vestige of the distant past in 1970, nor is it even now. To them, stoked already by Cosell's ethnic background and his affinity for Ali, it was almost *necessary* to hate him. And use Meredith for cover, knowing nothing of his decidedly nonredneck nature. If boxing had made him a national cause célèbre, the football audience was far larger and angrier. It was one thing for self-appointed American patriots to hold him in contempt; but that was nothing compared with the populace that held the game of *football* sacred. Never did Cosell anticipate the breadth of the hatred he now was living with. But live with it he'd have to. After all, they would have to live with *him*, no matter how much they said they couldn't. In fact, as he now knew, they simply couldn't wait for him to come on that screen every Monday night.

HALFWAY THROUGH its inaugural season, the underlying context of *MNF* was already ingrained: It was as if a narcotic had become mass-consumed, a creature comfort for some, maddening for others. Even a seemingly innocuous matter such as the halftime interlude, when Cosell ad-libbed commentary over filmed highlights of select Sunday games— for many, the only chance to view such league-wide game action in an era before endless replays became common on ESPN—touched off over-heated reaction from fans who became incensed if their favorite team wasn't included in the package. The nasty mail about *that* led Cosell to pointedly state by way of prelude that the highlights were "chosen by the producers," not by himself. In any case, it now seemed that, as Arledge would crow, "the show is bigger than the game."

The proof was that the inevitable blowout games didn't depress the numbers much for ABC. The third hour would be about as strong as the first. This was solely attributed to the Cosell-Meredith byplay, which in circumstances like those would often become an extended needling session between them. Sometimes Meredith would forget the game completely to delve into a personal anecdote apropos of nothing. During a Raiders wipeout of the Washington Redskins in Oakland on October 19, a long touchdown pass by quarterback Daryle Lamonica made it 14–0 in the first quarter, a harbinger of the 34–20 rout to come.

"Well, our good friend Lamonica really knows how to capitalize on an opportunity, Dandy," Cosell offered.

"That's right, Ha'hrd," volleyed Meredith in his best affected hayseed accent, adding, "Speaking of Daryle, that reminds me of a funny story." Whereupon he wove a tale about going on a hunting trip to Africa with Lamonica for ABC's Sunday anthology *The American Sportsman*, though Lamonica had nothing to do with the story as it evolved, which was about how Meredith contracted "amoebic dysentery" and the unpleasant effects it created. Cosell and Jackson, much as with Fair Hooker, knew not what to say, leading Meredith to end the silence by saying, "Well, I guess it doesn't sound as funny as it was."[11]

Meredith's monkeyshines, including his off-key warbling of the Willie Nelson song "The Party's Over" whenever a team would put a game out of reach, captivated millions of people. And, tied as he was to Cosell, they had become something of an "item" in the media; for the most part, one couldn't be mentioned without reference to the other. As with any other high-visibility couple, tabloid-style rumination followed about how they actually detested each other.

One panting newspaper dispatch would even claim that Cosell and Meredith actually had a fistfight under the stands in Milwaukee during a Colts-Packers game on November 9, notwithstanding that such a fracas would be preposterous, and perhaps as fatal for Cosell as squaring off against Muhammad Ali. In point of truth, Cosell would need to relate, they "never had a single quarrel or a single disagreement," and "each accepted the other, knowing each had his own place in the telecast. It worked like a charm."[12]

Indeed, a story the papers missed was that Cosell once again had to rescue the hypersensitive Meredith from quitting after he had become incensed when Chet Forte, in his normal gruff manner, criticized his work, upon which Meredith confided to Cosell, "I'm getting out of this thing." With another crisis at hand, Cosell appealed to his "asshole buddy," as he playfully called Forte, to go easy with Meredith, that he was more sensitive than anyone knew.

In fact, Meredith never really put in the kind of work required to discourse on football matters. His mistakes were a bane. During a Cincinnati Bengals–Pittsburgh Steelers matchup, a night on which Cosell later recalled, "Dandy had a massive disinterest in the game," Steeler linebacker Chuck Allen made a nice tackle, prompting Cosell to set up Meredith by saying, "Well, Dandy, our old friend Fifty-eight made the play on that one." Meredith, who had not a clue who Allen was, checked his roster sheet for No. 58—except he absent-mindedly checked the wrong team and began extolling "our old buddy Al Beauchamp"—who played for the Bengals. Forte, who was under pressure that night with Arledge away on other business, nearly swallowed his lit cigarette. Apoplectic, he yelled through his microphone to Cosell, "That fucker has the wrong player on the wrong team!" then to Meredith, "Listen, you stupid son of a bitch, you had the wrong guy on the wrong team. Don't say a word until Howard asks you a direct question!"[13] Meredith must have been a pacifist to keep from wringing Forte's neck after the sign-off that night. But the flak he was getting from above was grating on him.

On a deeper level, Cosell was surely peeved not at Meredith but *about* him. If the two of them were in this thing together, he couldn't help but believe that he was doing all the work, setting Meredith up for a one-liner, covering up for his faux pas, guiding the broadcast along on his sensibilities and instincts. As Lou Volpicelli notes, "Howard was making room for Don. Remember, he had never worked with anyone else, not in all those Ali fights. Howard was a jack of all trades, announcer, analyst, reporter, everything."[14] Now he had to hold his tongue and let Meredith utter things that were stupendously dumb, even save him from embarrassment, whereas when Cosell threatened to quit Meredith was solely concerned about himself. And yet here was Cosell being raked over the coals in the press and by the public, yet seemingly unwilling to strike back.

One of the few in that select coterie, the cerebral *New York Times* book critic John Leonard, issued the challenge in the November 13, 1970, issue of *Life,* imploring: "Will the real Howard Cosell please stand up? Or at least speak up?" Cosell, who he wrote "has always predicted, criticized and probed," was on *Monday Night Football* "uncharacteristically bland," and "right now Don Meredith is stealing the show out from under him. If Cosell is the last angry man, Meredith is insouciant youth, with a Southern drawl and a bracing lack of seriousness."[15]

These judgments congealed in the back of Cosell's brain. He had to keep them there as a good soldier, something he considered himself to be beyond argument. Ratings and achievement aside, he later moaned about that first season of *MNF* being a roller coaster ride, up one day, depressed the next. In the future, things would magnify to the point that the voices and faces in the booth of *Monday Night Football*—for all intents and purposes the *real* players on the show—would seem to their audience to be buoyant and carefree. In truth, they'd be about the sourest people under the sun.

THE MOST telling aspect of that frenetic first season of *Monday Night Football* was that it would be recalled beyond its general success primarily for two games on consecutive Mondays—neither show for the game itself. One was the Cowboys–St. Louis Cardinals game in Dallas on November 16. At the time, the game was crucial. The surprising Cards came in with a 6–2 record, a game ahead of the NFC East-leading, perennial powerhouse Cowboys, and had beaten them in St. Louis earlier. Now the Cowboys were poised to get even in the snakepit of the Cotton Bowl, where they almost never lost, but were run off the field. As it was the first time Meredith would call a game by his old team, that became the hook of the show. And when he reacted with increasing pique to Cowboy miscues, and lamented at one point, "There's not much tackling going on down there, boys," Cosell only turned up the heat, egging him on.

"I wish the viewers could see Don Meredith right now," he said. "He's upset, gritting his teeth. It may make a better picture than the game."[16]

At the half, it was 17–0 and the rabid crowd was chanting, "We want Meredith!" That led Forte to focus on crowd shots waving to the booth at a forlorn, genuinely depressed Dandy Don. "I'm not going down there, not on a night like this," he said sadly. It was priceless television. And when Meredith announced that he'd had some great stories to tell, "but I can't tell funny stories when something like this is going on," Arledge, back on the scene in the truck, could have burst in joy. He would be even more ecstatic when the ratings came in and showed that a blowout game had lost none of its numbers as the night went on, and even beat a Johnny Carson special on NBC. Not even a near catastrophe in the booth— precipitated when Cosell dropped a lit cigarette that ignited some papers on the floor, setting Keith Jackson's pants on fire—could disturb the rhythm of a show that had comfortably settled into a winning groove.

Could it get any better?

It took all of a week to find out. During that interim, Cosell was criticized for the usual inane reasons. This time, for evincing Meredith's meltdown on the air, proving that he really did loathe Dandy Don, who took a good deal of heat himself, a rare occurrence, for letting his emotions run wild. Cosell even heard from Pete Rozelle about the broadcast, with the commissioner having found the clowning in the booth disrespectful of Tom Landry, who was a demigod in Dallas. Though Cosell had said nothing disparaging of Landry, Rozelle was irked. "You really killed Landry," he accused.[17]

This round of caviling was one that Cosell could laugh off easily enough, as could Meredith, who admitted he got carried away. And in the end, Landry would laugh, too, all the way to the Super Bowl, after the Cardinals crumpled like a cheap seersucker suit, leaving the door open for the Cowboys to march through with a late-season winning rampage. Cosell, meanwhile, would quickly move on to his mortification— providing the gruesome but highly entertaining answer to what could possibly happen next.

The next game, between the New York Giants and Philadelphia Eagles on November 23, fell on a frigid night on the now frozen tundra of ancient Franklin Field. "I'll tell you how cold it was," says Dennis Lewin. "Keith and I that afternoon went to a store near our hotel so that he could buy a topcoat to wear during the game." Cosell came to the park early that Monday to tape the highlight package, feeling, as he later said, "queasy." He sat shivering for two hours in an open press box after the electricity, and the heat, in the stadium went out. He and Lewin then taped the highlight package, finishing up at around six thirty, at which time they went to a pregame party hosted by Eagles owner Leonard Tose, another bigwig whose name Cosell dropped regularly.

How much, or how little, he insulated himself with alcohol would be a matter of speculation a few hours later. Lewin, who was with him at the party until he had to go to the truck an hour later, says that "up to that point, around seven thirty, he had not had a drop to drink the whole time." But Cosell stayed at the fete, and Lewin adds, "What happened after that, I've only heard from Keith and Meredith and others that Howard had been drinking." Jackson would indeed later confirm that Cosell had consumed "vodka, straight up," and not one glass. "Howard," he noted, "could tote a lot."[18]

Yet he still did his work, taping some interviews back down on the freezing field. Cosell, in his trench coat and hat, stayed out in the cold even longer to trade insults with the crowd, "because they always ragged him wherever he went and he loved going back at them," says Volpicelli. "He was down there a long time, and I would imagine he had to have some antifreeze in him, if you know what I mean."[19]

Cosell eventually climbed the rickety steps back up to the press box, the wind cutting through him. When he reached the booth, Keith Jackson could see that he was stewed. And that was *before* the game. *During* it, an accommodating Tose had an attendant deliver two large buckets to the booth, one with a bottle of Courvoisier, the other a premixed jug of vodka martinis. Hardly by coincidence, Cosell was upbeat in the first half, playfully attributing to Meredith observations that came as news to the latter—"I don't remember saying that," a baffled Meredith said after one such remark, "but if you say I did, well, I'll stick to it." Cosell would later say that Arledge told him the first quarter of the game "was our best job of the year." But then, in the second quarter, there was a weird 180-degree turn. Suddenly, Cosell began to stumble over his words, then slur them. He left sentences hanging in the air. As he would relive it, "I began to sink," suffering from "a loss of balance," feeling "uncommonly light-headed," and "having trouble articulating."

Arledge, in the truck, grew uneasy. "What the hell is the matter with Howard?" he said to Forte. "Goddamn it, he's really fucked up."

Cosell's rummy-playing stooge knew what was the matter. "That son of a bitch is drunk!" he growled. "Take him off the air."

Because Arledge had invited several newspaper reporters to watch the game from the truck, he hoped none of them heard the remark "Jesus Christ, shut up!" he breathed in Forte's ear, then ordered, "Leave him on." He hoped Cosell would get himself together and nip any speculation of public drunkenness. In truth, this was really all anyone could do; that was the price for Cosell having become too big to fail, a rise accompanied by a conditioned reflex to look the other way about his heavy drinking. If this was a consequence of that excess, it wasn't only his fault—they were all in it together, and more so when his speech kept deteriorating.[20]

He did make it through the half without major embarrassment, and during the intermission Arledge, thinking the crisis was over, simply urged him to tank up on black coffee; This Cosell did, as the prerecorded halftime highlight package was played. When it ended, he had to go back on the air, live. Standing beside Meredith, an arm around his shoulder, in his other hand a trembling microphone, he began, now famously: "Half-time . . . Franklin Field . . . ," then, trying to somehow make his mouth pronounce the city they were in, it came out as a slow motion sound, something like *Ful-a-dul-fia*. As Meredith bit his lip, clearly amused, he went on, slurring each syllable, "Halftime score . . . 13–9 Giants . . . Tough game . . . Don Meredith, key points . . ."[21]

By now it was obvious something was wrong with him. In New York, Emmy, who had decided not to accompany him on this trip, was watching on TV. She too was an enabler of his drinking habits, ever the dutiful wife. But she was so alarmed by what she saw that she called Jim Spence at his home. "Howard doesn't sound right," she said. Spence, who also was watching, agreed. He subsequently called the truck and got through to Forte. "Is Howard okay?" he asked.

"Jim," the producer told him, "Howard's had too much to drink."[22]

In the B truck, Lou Volpicelli, on *Ful-a-dul-fia*, yelled through his microphone at Forte to cut away. But the show went on. "And let's face it," he recalls now, possibly reflecting what Arledge was thinking, "it wasn't bad for the ratings. It was like a traffic accident you can't look away from."[23] That included millions of people at home.

After Cosell cued a commercial, Arledge had seen enough. He wasn't going to let him back on the air again that night. And that wasn't even the worst of it. Cosell, seated in the booth waiting for the second half, now became ashen. His eyes began to roll backward, then he jerked forward, his head nearly crashing into the table in front of him. A groan came from his throat, followed by a stream of vomit that covered the floor, some speckling the brand-new cowboy boots Meredith had bought that afternoon.

In Arledge's retelling of the incident, he had by then informed Cosell that he was to leave the stadium—and Baltimore. "I put him in a limo for New York, told him to go home and sleep it off, and in the morning, I had a statement put out that Howard had suffered an adverse reaction to flu medication." However, that is a highly abridged version. In actuality, Cosell, helped out of the park by a police officer, got in a taxi, hoping to catch a late-night flight home, but when he got to the airport and staggered to the ticket counter he was told that the flight had been discontinued. At that point, he wrote in *Cosell*, "With all the dimness of my mind, I suddenly thought, 'My God, I'm going to die in Philadelphia.' And then, oddly, I thought of W. C. Fields's epitaph."[24]

He could have gone back to his hotel. Instead, thinking he might in fact breathe his last that night, and that "I don't care what happens to me, as long as I'm with Emmy when it happens," he got into another cab. He told the startled driver to take him all the way to New York, no matter the fare, which ran to a then extraordinary ninety-five dollars by the time he reached his apartment at 3:45 A.M. There, Emmy, whom he had phoned before leaving Philadelphia and who was sick with worry, had received calls from people who had seen the telecast, including Don Klosterman and Al Davis. She helped her husband, who was shivering and unable to stand, into bed and mummified him with layers of sheets and blankets—but even a near-death experience, or so he feared, could not keep him from grabbing a microphone and doing his scheduled morning sports report on the radio, bundled to the neck under the covers.

Later that morning, his doctor made a house call and, after the patient passed an electrocardiograph test, determined that he had been felled by an inner ear infection called toxic vertigo, which affects balance and speech. This condition, Cosell would note a year afterward, was so insidious and stubborn that "to this day I have vestiges of it. I will wake up in the morning, on occasion, get out of bed and totally lose my balance, tumbling back into bed."[25] What he did *not* say in any retelling of that night in hell was that he had bent his elbow.

Arledge believed that booze had caused it all, but he had a cover-up going within minutes of Cosell's exit from the booth, passing out to the press the bogus story about Cosell having taken ill and being on medication that caused the speech problem. When the game resumed, Meredith puckishly told the audience, "I'm sure some of you fans are worrying what happened to our friend and cohort Howard Cosell," who he explained "has been sick this week" and as a result had gone to rest up. Standing in the residue of Cosell's vomit, he could barely keep from saying what he *wanted* to say, which as related to his friends went like this: "Yeah, he got sick—all over my boots."[26]

Because the game ended in a thrilling finish, the Eagles upsetting the Giants 23–20, most recitations of the incident were fleeting. Even Dick Young went relatively easy on him. In a grab-bag *Daily News* column a few days later, it was the last item, under the heading "Announcer Stricken Ill During ABC Football Game." Cranking up, Young wrote, "I understand that Howard Cosell vomited in the broadcast booth and had to leave. It absolutely is not true that he was listening to an instant replay of his comments at the time." But then he begged off, adding, "ABC says he had a touch of the flu. Fans tell me he was slurring his words, so I guess the official version is correct because one common symptom of the flu is slurred speech." Young had juicier gossip to bite into, or so he believed, reporting the now-old canard that "rumors persist that all is not sweetness between Don Meredith and Cosell. They were supposed to have had a shouting match, off-mike, two weeks ago, with Meredith telling Cosell what to do with his tiresome patronizing and redundant polysyllables. Dandy Don, for the record, assures me that he and Humble Howard are palsy-walsy."[27]

THE FIRST season of *Monday Night Football* proved to be a ratings monster. It ended with an 18.5 average rating (meaning of all households)—third best among new shows, behind only two other classics-to-be, *The Flip Wilson Show* and *The Mary Tyler Moore Show*. It gained a 31 percent share (all turned-on televisions during its hours on the air). And with it, ABC had finally found its means to equality, and soon supremacy, in the network ratings wars, the brute power of the series such that programming honchos at the other networks quaked before it, CBS, for example, moving the wildly popular *Carol Burnett Show* out of its Monday night time slot rather than cross *MNF*.

To be certain, *MNF* had none of the political baggage of Mexico City—which in the light of the next Olympics would seem almost harmless. But like other classic early seventies diversions like the Mary Tyler Moore and Flip Wilson shows, it helped transfer sixties nihilism into a more meaningful realm based on cultural standards fought for—and won—in the wreckage of the previous decade. Years later, in 1978, *TV Guide* got lots of mileage when it conducted a "reader poll" of the most popular and unpopular TV personalities, with *both* categories going to Cosell; thus, the heroic and the antiheroic could now be one and the same, if the one was pivotal enough. And if the 1970s proved anything about Cosell, it confirmed Jerry Izenberg's observation that "Howard was necessary." To his network, and to his culture.

Not to be overlooked was how greatly ABC profited from the new wave in the NFL, with the merger broadening the already vast expanse of the league's popularity. It was almost as if there were a new game in town. Furthermore, Cosell had a unique standing with both orders, the old and the new. He had covered himself in the rising glory of the AFL— at least when it won—and its tabloid-worthy icons like Al Davis, Joe Namath, and O. J. Simpson, who in 1969 had begun his rookie year with the lowly Buffalo Bills, three thousand miles and light-years from his neon-lit collegiate heroics as a USC All-American. Cosell clearly was daz-

zled by the poised, personable young man and his back story of transcending his delinquent, ghetto upbringing. More and more, Bills games
on *MNF* became a virtual PR exercise by Cosell with his fevered yelping
about "the Juice" being "turned on by the Electric Company," as the
media dubbed the Bills' Clydesdale-like offensive line that had been
drafted to squash people in front of him.

At the same time, Cosell at fifty-two was rooted in the age of the
NFL's historic glory. This was underscored at Vince Lombardi's funeral
at St. Patrick's Cathedral in early September 1970, days before the premiere of *Monday Night Football*, when Cosell wept openly in his pew
beside Giants owner Wellington Mara. As much as he unashamedly
loved Lombardi, who died within months after being diagnosed with
colon cancer, Cosell considered his death to have etched a line of demarcation between what had been and what would be. While he was only
five years younger than Lombardi, he could see far into that future as
few men in football or sportscasting could. That he had left symbolic
footprints in the past, he believed, accurately, marked him as a wizened,
evenhanded justice of the peace as the game faced a younger, more brazen, more materialistic future. And *Monday Night Football* was the avatar of this new sensibility, something that was confirmed by *Sports
Illustrated* in October 1971, when an article by Bud Shrake about not
the game but the show asked, cheekily but not necessarily disapprov-
ingly, in its headline: "What Are They Doing With the Sacred Game of
Football?"

BY NOW, Cosell could with plausibility preen like a star. In the spring of
1970, he had been offered a small but pivotal role in Woody Allen's fourth
self-directed movie, *Bananas*, the casting fully approved by the movie's
producer, none other than Edgar Scherick. The plot relates the saga of
perhaps the best of Allen's cinematic nebbish misfits, Fielding Mellish,
who after the assassination of a banana republic president takes his place
as a puppet for revolutionaries. Cosell, playing himself with perfect serio-
comical earnestness, reports the assassination, rushing over to interview
the dying dictator.

Allen, who had met Cosell in 1968 during the Jerry Quarry–Jimmy Ellis WBA title fight in Oakland, recognized that Cosell's influence on pop culture was such that such a knowing blend of reality and absurdity was precisely the formula that had brought both of them to prominence. Indeed, that Cosell's overheated boxing cadences—"He turns! And down! It's over. It's all over for El Presidente!" he bellows during the scene—were tailor-made for any injection of melodrama, serious or otherwise, was proven at the end of the movie when he narrates the honeymoon night of Mellish and his new wife, crooning, "The action is growing more rigorous, it is swift, rhythmic, coordinated . . . What's that? A cut over Mellish's right eye. The doctor comes in to examine the cut. No, it will not be stopped. I have never seen action like this—That's it! It's over! It's all over! The marriage has been consummated!"

Allen would say at the time that "Cosell was crazy about being in the movie. He's a tremendous ham, a cartoonlike character. He comes across that way on television, too. He's the same way if you're eating dinner with him—he broadcasts the meal." Today, the seventy-five-year-old auteur is even more effusive, reserving for Cosell bouquets better suited to Laurence Olivier. Cosell was, he says, "a pleasure to work with," "completely in command from the second he got off the plane in Puerto Rico," "totally confident. He did his work wonderfully right off the bat. He had a great sense of humor, knew exactly what he was doing with no direction. I found him highly intelligent and hyper-confident."[28]

As Cosell would later note, Allen had given him only one abiding direction for his scenes—"Do your thing." It was, of course, a thing no one else could possibly do. Yet he would recall that when he left Puerto Rico after the shooting, "I had grave misgivings about having done it," thinking he'd made a fool of himself. Then, "a few months later, Woody called me and said, 'Howard, we've rough-cut the movie and the best thing in it is your opening.' When I finally saw the film, I couldn't believe my scenes came over as well as they did."[29]

When the movie was released in the early spring of 1971, to mostly critical raves that invariably referenced his contribution, he had gone even more Hollywood. He had by now enlisted a big-gun agent, Lou Weiss of William Morris, whose client list included Barbara Walters,

Carol Channing, Bill Cosby, Sammy Davis Jr., Buddy Hackett, Alan King, Jack Paar, and Diana Ross. He also had an equally high-powered show business lawyer, Bob Schulman, who landed him appearances on David Frost's talk show in March 1971, then on *The Dean Martin Comedy Hour* in December.

So successful was Cosell that Allen, too, would want him to reprise his performance in future films. His next one, in fact, *Everything You Always Wanted to Know About Sex but Were Afraid to Ask*, from the book by Dr. David Reuben. Cosell, prude that he was—or thought he was—begged off, then gave in when Woody persevered, promising him his role would be tasteful. Then he saw the script and nearly had a coronary, his role being that of, as he once said, "a sex pervert." When he called Allen's producer, Jack Grossberg, to decline, Grossberg told him, "Woody will really be hurt."

"Woody will be hurt," Cosell said, "I'll be destroyed. I have no desire to peremptorily terminate my career."[30]

Quite capable of earning chits like that from the royalty of the entertainment world—indeed, Allen was hardly done with him yet—he had cause to be enamored of himself. Thus, he could barely believe it when, shortly before the premiere of *Bananas*, the decade's biggest sporting event—one that he considered to have come about in no small part due to his work and influence—stamped the sports and cultural landscape and he could only get in as a spectator.

# 11

---

## LISTING TOWARD
## BABYLON

A S HOWARD COSELL would have been the first to argue, the intensely anticipated Ali-Frazier fight, agreed to in December 1970 and set for March 8, 1971, was a victory of sorts for his own ascendance. Outside of the fighter himself, there was no more pivotal a mover and shaker in the Ali argosy than the man in the gray suits with the microphone and an eye for opportunism.

They had been through the wars together, to the extent that Cosell had access and license to provoke Ali as no other man could. In fact, Cosell had been so loyal to Ali during his enforced exile from boxing that he had run afoul of the Madison Square Garden boxing powers. Calling the Frazier-Quarry bout there, he had identified Frazier as the recognized champion in two states, correctly, since at the time Jimmy Ellis held the World Boxing Association title. Of course, New York was one of those two states, and Harry Markson, the Garden's boxing director, was incensed that Cosell wasn't properly deferential to the fading glory of the arena by saying Frazier was implicitly "the" champ.

Cosell would have none of it. He told Markson to take his case to Chet Forte, who produced the ABC broadcast, but if he was ordered to say it Markson's way, he would leave the arena and not come back, an empty threat since he knew Forte would back him up. Nothing more was said about the matter, and Cosell later would claim that Markson sent ABC Sports a letter of apology for the scene he made, which hardly placated Cosell, who knew that if the Garden had its way, he would have been excluded from all fights in the building. But the days when the dying bastion on Thirty-third Street could control such things had receded in the era of corporate network hegemony in sports.

In that evolving atmosphere, Cosell's decision to become indivisible with Ali had returned dividends beyond imagination. When the event to be hyped—needlessly—as "the Fight of the Century" started down the road to pugilistic legend, it was implicit that Cosell would be courted to play a part in what would certainly be the biggest promotion in fight history.

And, in fact, he was much on the mind of the promoters, an odd couple of Hollywood fops, the high-profile one, the dashing multimillionaire sports entrepreneur Jack Kent Cooke, who owned the Los Angeles Lakers and a piece of the Washington Redskins. His partner, and the one who would have to do all the leg work putting the deal together, was talent agent Jerry Perenchio. With a pledge from Cooke to finance $4.5 million, he logged thousands of air miles getting agreements from Ali and Frazier—actually, Frazier held the key, since Ali was in financial straits and so eager to get Smokin' Joe in the ring that he said he'd take whatever was offered, as long as he got the same as Frazier.

The original offer was $1.25 million for each against 35 percent of the gate, but Frazier held out for $2.5 million. That meant the venue that hosted the fight would need to pay the difference, $2.5 million. The Garden, desperate to land the bout, footed it in exchange for the live gate, a real bargain since it would charge a top ticket of $125—unheard of for the times. Cooke and Perenchio, meanwhile, would get every penny of the closed-circuit telecast, which was sure to generate a fortune.

That was where Cosell came in—or was supposed to. Indeed, the Cosell/ABC Sports imprimatur was so strong in the boxing orbit that, at first, the two promoters came east to meet with Roone Arledge about ABC broadcasting the fight in real time, instead of a closed-circuit showing. But Roone was unimpressed with the TV variety-show people Perenchio had who would be in charge of the broadcast. He was, moreover, unwilling to go to his bosses and ask for the kind of money Cooke and Perenchio wanted, which was $600,000, roughly ten times more than the network had ever paid for a fight. Arledge declined, out of hand—though this may well have been the promoters' intention, knowing bigger money was waiting in the closed-circuit realm.

Even so, Cosell was still a very viable choice to handle the closed-circuit broadcast that was subsequently put together. In fact, Perenchio's top production man, Neal Marshall, seeking a strong announcing team, favored him for the assignment. Perenchio, however, who had never met Cosell, was not fond of him, telling people that Cosell talked too much rather than letting the action do the talking. But Perenchio wavered when he heard from the Ali camp urging him to give Cosell the gig. Marshall also kept pushing for Cosell, so often that an exasperated Perenchio snapped, "You want him, *you* pay him!"[1]

In the end, no one would have to pay him—because, in contrast to the Ali-Quarry fight, no one gave him the chance to name, or bluff, his price. And not even Ali could have intervened in a promotion of such magnitude, with so much money on the line. So the job went to the venerable, "safe" Don Dunphy (who, mostly overlooked now, also had a cameo role in *Bananas* that was completely dwarfed by Cosell's performance) and the analyst job to Burt Lancaster, the tough-guy actor—whom Perenchio happened to represent but who had never done a broadcast.

Cosell would try hard, perhaps too hard, to make people believe that being snubbed meant nothing to him. "I'm in my fifties now and I couldn't care less whether I do an event or not," he wrote breezily in his memoirs, saying that "sometimes you prosper by not doing something—you might even be missed" and that "life doesn't begin or end with a telecast of a sports event." Others privy to the machinations of who would be behind the mike remember a quite involved Cosell lobbying hard, even dirty. One, the boxing writer George Kimball, recalled that Cosell and Dunphy were both so desperate for the job that "either would have gladly done it for free. Each monitored the other in the run-up to the fight, fearful that the other might outmaneuver him to gain Perenchio's ear."[2]

Before the decision was made, Dunphy's son, who was an ABC assistant director, was informed by Cosell, "I'm not going to do the Ali-Frazier fight, and neither is your father. They're going to use Andy Williams, Kirk Douglas, and Burt Lancaster."[3] Not by coincidence, all three of those big names were Perenchio clients, and the baldness of that tidbit of misinformation may have had several explanations. One was that Cosell's always-active antennae had picked up on it from someone around the scene. Another was that, with the Burt Lancaster rumor already in the air, he was embellishing it by lumping in two more Perenchio cronies, hoping Dunphy would become so angered that he would pull out. If that was the plan, it went up in smoke when Dunphy, Lancaster, and the former champ, the old "Mongoose" Archie Moore, were officially named as the broadcast team.

As for Cosell, he apparently was not able to laugh off that news. This became obvious to Jerry Perenchio's former stepson, Robin Thaxton, when he ran across Cosell in the lobby of the St. Regis Hotel, where Perenchio and his family were staying, and where Cosell often could be found in the bar. As could Thaxton one night. "He was drunk. He was putting on a performance," he said. "I went upstairs and told Jerry . . . We went downstairs [for dinner, and] Cosell . . . was off to the side talking to somebody. Jerry walked by, nodded his head and said, 'Hello, Mr. Cosell.' Howard didn't say a godamn line. He just walked right out."[4]

Not being the voice of the fight didn't deter Cosell from his function as a reporter. In January, a few weeks before the gloves flew at the Garden, Cosell flew to Miami to catch the Super Bowl between the Dallas Cowboys and the Baltimore Colts, won by the latter by a last-second field goal. By chance, Ali was also training for Frazier at Angelo Dundee's Fifth Street Gym, and Cosell arranged for a visit. He and Emmy were lounging by the pool at their hotel, the elegant Americana in Surfside, when Ali sauntered over to them, screaming, "Where is he? Where's that white fella who gives me so much trouble? Where's Cosell?"

Ali only then found out that his old foil and comedy confrere might not be calling the fight. That, Cosell would say, "set Ali back." Apparently it also sent him to the telephone urging the promoters to do the right thing. It was in vain. But if Ali wanted Cosell in his accustomed spot at

ringside, he also had a bone to pick with him. Seriously, by all appearances, he said he wanted to talk to him about "that football business
you're involved in. And this guy who works with you. What's his name?
Dandy? I think you're making too much of him. You gotta remember that
we're the number-one act in sports."

Could this possibly have been so, that the world's most recognized
figure now felt as if he were playing second fiddle to a Monday night cowboy? If so, Cosell would admit to being "utterly astonished" by the proposition, and that Ali would even have such a trivial thing on his mind
weeks before the fight of his life.

"You're a nut," he told him, his astonishment no doubt amplified by
the fact that, if Ali was to be believed, *Monday Night Football* was even
bigger than anyone thought.

"You gotta do the fight," Ali insisted. "We gotta fix that. It's no
Muhammad Ali fight without Howard Cosell."[5]

It did genuinely bum Ali out that Cosell would not get the nod,
though not even the latter would make a specious claim that it had anything to do with the outcome of the fight. Still, Ali acted like it was his
business to reestablish old, personal ties with Cosell that had become
loosened. That day, he hauled Cosell into his car and drove him on a wild
joyride through the mean streets of the Miami ghetto, to "meet my people." Pulling up to a dirty, dingy pool hall, Ali told the denizens inside,
"Here he is, the white guy who gives me all that trouble on television."

For three hours the two of them, with no Ali bodyguards and no tape
recorder running, did urban Miami. It was, as Cosell told Emmy when he
returned to the hotel, a "strange" encounter, and a sad one, a premonition
that it would be the last time they would ever share such a sentimental
journey in their prime years. Cosell left Miami with the nagging feeling
that Muhammad Ali, the "people's champ," was for all his lackeys a lonely
man trying to find some way to grasp a time and dimension lost to him
now. And that it was not the way to prepare for Joe Frazier's left hook.

ALI TRIED hard to re-create past rituals at the press conferences leading
up to March 8. There was the usual litany of blustery prose and poetry

The onetime labor lawyer walked a picket line outside ABC's Avenue of the Americas offices during a 1967 strike by AFTRA, the TV employees union, along with newscasters Peter Jennings and Murphy Martin. Because Cosell, as a producer, was technically management, some executives wanted him fired, but controversy never stopped Cosell from taking a principled stand. *(Bettmann/Corbis)*

Such were the emotions that Cosell ignited during *Monday Night Football* games that this hostile sign was actually mild by comparison with some others in the stands. Uglier still were the many death threats mailed to Cosell—one of which threatened to set off a bomb in the booth—that led to armed guards being assigned to protect him and his family. *(AP Photo / FK)*

One of the most mocked public figures of his time, Cosell was bedeviled by the lampooning he was given in the newspapers. The most stinging shots came from his biggest critic, *New York Daily News* sports columnist Dick Young, typically accompanied by caricatures such as this 1970 illustration by the paper's cartoonist Bill Gallo skewering Cosell's legendary features and pomposity. *(© New York Daily News, L.P., used with permission)*

Besides Muhammad Ali, Cosell supported other athletes' challenges to sports' long-held practices. He defended Curt Flood, seen here on a January 1970 episode of *Wide World of Sports*, for taking a stand against baseball's reserve clause after refusing to accept a trade from the Cardinals to the Phillies. Flood lost his lawsuit against baseball, but his cause would soon prevail, changing sports forever. *(Bettmann/Corbis)*

The architect of Cosell's rise, Roone Arledge, longtime president of ABC Sports, made a rare public appearance when he was given a cameo role in a January 1975 *Odd Couple* episode, characteristically hovering over Cosell in the booth. But their tenuous relationship eroded after Arledge refused to let Cosell go on the air the night that Israeli athletes were murdered at the 1972 Munich Olympics—a slight Cosell never forgave him for. *(ABC Photo Archives / Getty Images)*

Befitting his exalted status, Cosell, who earned a half-million dollars a year at his peak, lived in splendor until his death in the penthouse of this skyscraper at 150 East 69th Street on Manhattan's tony Upper East Side, appropriately called the Imperial House. (*Courtesy of Michael K. Dorr*)

The most memorable call of Cosell's career, and arguably the most memorable in boxing history—"Down goes Frazier!"—caught all the shock and drama when George Foreman floored Joe Frazier five times in winning the heavyweight championship on January 22, 1973. Three years later, when they met for a belated rematch, Cosell was again a presence, conducting a prefight interview of the combatants. (*AP Photo / Richard Drew*)

Despite Foreman's rise, Cosell maintained an allegiance to Muhammad Ali, though his sour expression in this photo taken on the eve of the fateful 1974 Ali-Foreman "Rumble in the Jungle" may have reflected his view that Ali would be clobbered. When Ali instead regained the title that had been stripped from him, an exuberant Cosell turned poetic on the air, celebrating him as "forever young." *(Bettmann/Corbis)*

The ABC corporate headquarters since 1964, at 1330 Avenue of the Americas in Rockefeller Center, is in no small part the "house that Cosell built." After decades of failure, the network found its voice and brazen image in the irresistible, curmudgeonly sportscaster, finally pulling big ratings. In time, Cosell's liquor-stocked twenty-fourth-floor office was his sanctuary, from which he only rarely emerged. (*Courtesy of the author*)

News Photo by Mitchell Seidel

## Cosell Resigns From Class

Howard Cosell resigned from teaching his NYU class because of "conflicts in his schedule" and an incident in his class on March 30, according to his teaching assistant.

The announcement was made by the assistant in the course "Big Time Sports In Contemporary America," before a class of more than 100 students. The remaining five sessions will be taught by guest lecturers.

On March 30, a student not registered in that course allegedly exhibited "irrational behavior," and disrupted the class, according to Edward Schnell, director of protection services.

—**Daniel Aquilante**

Returning to his alma mater, Cosell in 1977 taught a ten-week course at NYU called "Big-Time Sports in Contemporary America," relishing the opportunity to express his pet peeves about athletes and his industry's alleged complicity in the corruption of sports. However, he seemed to tire of the chore and, as reported by the school newspaper, terminated the course five weeks early. (*New York University Archives, Photographic Collection*)

Cosell eagerly accepted invitations to testify when congressional committees held hearings on the serious issues facing sports. Here, he strikes a typical pose, gesturing for effect, as he makes a point during one such appearance in 1974. So comfortable was he among powerful politicians that he periodically hinted that he would run for the U.S. Senate, but he never did throw his hat into the ring. *(Bettmann/Corbis)*

targeting Frazier as a "gorilla," "ugly," and "dumb," a charade belying the fact that the two men had actually been close, with Frazier having dropped some money in Ali's pocket to help him survive the lean times, and even attending Muslim prayer services at Ali's request. It genuinely hurt Frazier that Ali, a man of upper-class tastes now, painted him as a man who turned his back on his roots, though Frazier still lived in inner-city Philadelphia. Neither, of course, did Ali give him his due as a champ, merely a placeholder. He, not Joe, had a "cause," warning Frazier that "you gettin' yourself in trouble with the brothers."

However, Ali could not get into Frazier's head. Hurt to his core by Ali's betrayals for the sake of discount hype, he only steeled himself further, banging his lethal left hook nearly through the gym bag with more grimness and torque. He was also younger than Ali, in better shape, and willing to take two, three, no matter how many shots to move in for the kill. And kill was what he wanted to do. Ali may have sold the public, but by fight night, almost everyone in the media was picking Frazier to win.

Cosell was among that tide. Indeed, even with Ali's aggrandizements— a line of one of his new poems went "Frazier will catch hell. From the start of the bell. Then we'll jump out. And take on Howard Cosell"— there were too many ominous signs in Ali's casual training and mental state. "I didn't like what I saw," Cosell would say, looking back. "He didn't seem in any sense to be the old Ali. He seemed tired." Consequently, though it stung like a bee for Ali, he predicted that Frazier would win by a knockout, "anywhere from the tenth to the twelfth round."[6] And this time he didn't feel it necessary to make the opposite prediction just in case.

IF EVER there was a sporting event—any event of the era, including presidential inaugurations—at which to be seen, it was the Ali-Frazier fight. Being there, to use the credo Cosell had adopted, was a mark of class, distinction, and privilege, which is why those record-setting top-priced tickets flew from the box office like confetti in the wind; indeed, Cooke and Perenchio could have kicked themselves for not charging *more*, since while they made money from the promotion, their giveaway to corporate friends and other VIP freeloaders (technically, this included Howard Cosell) cut their profit margin severely. All the "beautiful people" were there, of course—some, including Dustin Hoffman and Diana Ross, not able to score good enough tickets, tried sitting at ringside, only to be rousted by Garden guards; Frank Sinatra was able to land there, but only as a photographer for *Life*.

It was, as Cosell suggested in his populist preening, sports' first unapologetically exclusive soiree, excluding polo or yacht races, an opiate not for the masses but for the plutocracy of the well heeled and well connected. In the parlance of the times, more a "happening" than a sporting competition. Twenty-five years later, by way of anniversary commemoration, *Sports Illustrated*'s Bill Nack was still humming the scenery:

> There had never been a night like this one in New York City. By 10:30 P.M. . . . when the two fighters climbed into the ring at Madison Square Garden, Ali in red trunks and Frazier in green-and-gold brocade, there was a feral scent and crackle to the place. The Garden was a giant bell jar into which more than 20,000 people had drifted, having passed through police barricades that rimmed the surrounding streets. They came in orange and mint-green and purple velvet hot pants, in black leather knickers and mink and leopard capes, in cartridge belts and feathered chapeaux and pear-gray fedoras. Some sported hats with nine-inch brims and leaned jauntily on diamond-studded walking sticks. Manhattan listed toward Babylon.[7]

IT BEGAN without flourish, with Ali in the familiar mode of sticking and moving. All through the fight he would find Frazier an easy target, peppering him with his left jab with alarming success, turning Joe's face into "a hideous pulpy mess," as Cosell would say later. But he couldn't really slow Frazier—"that gritty stump of a man," as *SI* called him—from inexorably boring in on him, and after tasting a few flush Frazier lefts, he began a charade.[8] With his aging legs unable to dance him out of trouble, he would lie against the ropes saving his energy—giving away several rounds by not initiating any combat. In this "turtle" defense, his gloves framed his face, his elbows his torso, but he took grievous punishment anyway. Trying to con people otherwise, he would mug with his own battered face, contorting it into a comedy mask, his mouth wide open, his eyes popping, shaking his head "no" or at times chattering through his mouthpiece, "You can't hurt me, Joe," or mouthing "No contest" to press row, though from the tenth round on the crowd began to anticipate a Frazier knockout.

Joe indeed had blood in his eyes. Once, when referee Arthur Mercante tried to separate the two men in a clinch, he spat at him, "Goddamn, fuck, man, keep your hands off me!" In round eleven, he caught Ali with a hook to the cheek that buckled his knees and almost detached his head, but Ali somehow stayed erect, and even exaggeratedly wobbled around the ring trying to flout the punch. He also fought back enough to keep himself in a fight slipping away from him. And, contrary to what he had believed, there was little sentimentality for him in the arena, or in the closed-circuit theaters; smelling blood in the water, spectators turned, from cheering everything Ali did early on to bellowing for a Frazier knockout late. Then, in round fifteen, the moment seemed to come when Frazier exploded from his crouch and his left hand crashed into Ali's jaw with fissionable force. *Bam!* In an eyeblink, he went down on his back, tassels flying as his legs rose perpendicular into the air. As Ferdie Pacheco, who watched in horror from the corner, recalled, "It looked like Ali was out cold. I didn't think he could possibly get up."[9]

Yet, drawing on some hidden reserve in his body and mind, almost as soon as he hit the canvas he was climbing to his feet again, to take a standing eight count. In the long lens of history, that fleeting sequence of pain, humiliation, and immense courage stands as perhaps the apogee of Muhammad Ali's greatness. Even after the thunderous knockdown put an exclamation point on the fight, he gamely hung in until the final bell, though the unanimous decision announced for Frazier was almost an anticlimax. By the time Frazier's hand was raised in victory, many in the press were engraving Ali epitaphs. In *Sports Illustrated*, only days after Mark Kram had posed him as a timeless, ageless artiste, it was pronounced, "Ali gave away much more by his bizarre charades . . . [T]hese acts, designed to steal time, failed in their purpose. Ali's time was past."[10]

One can only salivate imagining how Cosell would have described that knockdown, and its aftermath. Indeed crestfallen that he'd been unable to define and contour the fight in real time, he leapt into doing that ex post facto. At first, Ali had accepted defeat with grace, seeming not altogether crushed. As Cosell and his wife waited outside the Garden for a cab, Ali and his entourage came out. Seeing him standing there, Ali winked at him. For the media, there were no excuses. "I didn't give it away," he said of his pacifist rounds. "Joe earned it." As for what it meant, he was philosophic. "Presidents get assassinated, civil rights leaders get assassinated. The world goes on." He hinted that it might go on without him in a ring. "I had my day," he said.[11]

He came on *Wide World of Sports* a few days later, his jaw swelled to the size of a casaba but otherwise unmarked. He told Cosell, almost touchingly, "I guess I'm not pretty any more." But by then a fresh narrative had emerged, based on *Frazier's* condition. Rather than celebrate victory, his face had been so maimed that he was rushed to a hospital after the fight—as had Ali, to have his jaw X-rayed. When Ferdie Pacheco advised him to stay overnight for observation, he recoiled. "He didn't want anybody saying Joe Frazier had put him in the hospital," Pacheco recalled. But now that was exactly what Ali's retainers were able to say, in reverse. And Ali, appearing alone on *Wide World*, surely looked smug when Cosell asked him about the new spin being pushed by Ali supporters—which Cosell stressed he didn't agree with—that Frazier's confinement proved the decision was a sham, that Ali had really won but was deprived of the belt because of his religion and attitude toward the draft.[12]

Ali didn't take the bait, still sticking to the high road. But the very next day, he was releasing statements pushing just the framework Cosell had adumbrated. Thus he was able to get more mileage out of the old theme that he was "the People's Champion," battling not only other fighters but a never-forgiving establishment. Neither did it hurt that a New York paper erroneously printed a story with the screaming headline "Frazier Near Death." Just days later, Frazier, news of his near death greatly exaggerated, got out of his bed to take belated bows, although with no great desire to get back into the ring—the truth was, Ali *had* damaged him more than the other way around, and he was never quite Smokin'

Joe again. Ali, on the other hand, was rejuvenated by a loss that could be called a victory. As Cosell codified it, "It may have been the greatest fight Ali ever fought"; but for the three and a half years he lost he certainly would have tamed and defused Joe Frazier, and even now had "inflicted untold physical damage" on him.[13] These sentiments would be cadged and heavily repeated almost word for word by Ali.

THERE WOULD, for the sake of mercantile madness, have to be a rematch—the only barrier to it would be lifted when Ali was further rejuvenated by knowing he would not go to jail. That happened three and a half months later, on June 28, when the U.S. Supreme Court, even with its conservative majority of Nixon appointees, ruled 8–0 that his draft-dodging conviction be overturned, based on his religious beliefs. On that landmark day in history, he called Cosell, who recalled that Ali was "quiet, almost humble," and that in the spirit of magnanimity, he cut a break for those who wanted him behind bars. "The people who were against me," he said, "thought they were right."[14]

Cosell was not as charitable. If Ali let go of any bitterness, Cosell's only escalated for the people he had come to loathe for their contempt of the Constitution. Long after Ali had forgotten the name of Edwin Dooley, for one—if he had ever known who the hoary little New York State boxing commissioner was at all—Cosell made him a target in nearly all of his lectures, and most of his books. And as Ali moved on, still brilliant but robbed of his peak skills, Cosell would never fail to remind people of what might have been but for the American apostates who, as he said, "understood law and order only in terms of a policeman with a billy club hitting some bum in the street."[15]

Because a rematch was inevitable, Cosell would later maintain that he was a sure thing this time to call it. He knew this, he said, because Jack Kent Cooke a few days before the fight sought him out and "bluntly told me that he felt Perenchio had screwed up the promotion." Cooke subsequently ended his partnership with Perenchio. In Cosell's rendering, "Jack made a verbal deal with me to do the Ali-Frazier rematch."[16] His was not the only opinion that the "fight of the century" just didn't feel right without his voice. And he would indeed be at ringside for the rematch. But there would be a typically unpredictable series of twists, turns, and complications just down the road that knocked much of the air out of it.


COSELL'S STAR was burning so bright after the first season of *Monday Night Football* that he was not above planting a few minor headlines by dropping hints that he might not be back for the second season. Doing his bidding, *Sports Illustrated* ran an item around the time of the Super Bowl under the title "Goodby, Howard," which read gravely, "It now appears that Howard Cosell will not [be back]," citing a "mutually agreeable separation" and reasons that included Cosell's loathing of all the travel involved; as well, he averred that "I find the format frustrating . . . I have not been able to do my thing."[17]

Most of the ABC Sports herd took these threats for what they were: a pressing need to be told how much the show depended on him. Which they would do, by habit, much like Don Ohlmeyer on those 2 A.M. postgame phone calls. To the surprise of no one, he would be back for more monkeyshines with Meredith. Indeed, the shock was that it was the most solid—and least controversial—sportscaster in the business who was shown the door, confirming the premonitions Keith Jackson had during the inaugural season that he was on borrowed time, and that Arledge was virtually ignoring him as a precursor to doing what he had originally wanted, to hire Frank Gifford once his contract with CBS was up. That came to pass in January 1971, instantly making Jackson expendable.

Of course, Jackson, the pro's pro, had come to Arledge's aid, agreeing to leave his college football duties to try to perform the unenviable task of maintaining decorum and dignity between the Cosell-Meredith palaver, which he did with no complaint. And Cosell was perplexed when Arledge told him he was going to ax Jackson, partly because his long relationship with Gifford had become somewhat prickly of late. Arledge, selling him on the change, remarked that Gifford was "the most popular sportscaster in New York."

"Well, I don't think that's true," Cosell replied.[18]

But while Cosell believed Arledge had a "moral obligation" to Jackson, he went along with the move, and pledged that "I'm not going to have any problems working with Frank." Jackson, who returned to his college football duties, had some bitter observations about the show he had helped establish. Cosell, he said, was "on an ego trip." Meredith was "all bullshit and a mile wide." As for *MNF*, it would be either a "soaring success or a bastion of buffoonery."[19]

A FAR bigger issue for Cosell to absorb that winter was that Meredith, and Meredith alone, garnered an Emmy nomination, as Best Commentator in the Outstanding Achievement in Sports Programming category, which he would win. As much as Cosell had tailored his character on the premise of being disliked, he nonetheless expected his overwhelming presence and effect on ratings to be recognized, and honored, by his industry. Instead, as if to intentionally chide him, the Emmy voters swooned over Meredith. Publicly, Cosell gritted his teeth and toed the party line that the award was putatively rewarding everyone who made *Monday Night Football* possible, Cosell above all others. But not for a day did he believe it, ascribing the contempt for him to a surfeit of left-over anti-Semitism, in the sense that if he had beaten the original purveyors of it, he still had to endure conditioned behavior by their scions. In fact, Cosell was so over the edge in his paranoia about who his enemies were, and why, that only he could have wondered if Meredith, as the anti-Cosell, was a beneficiary of it. At the very least, Don Meredith allegorized for him the superficial star system of the medium, his victory a primer in how to succeed in television without really trying—if your name wasn't Howard Cosell.

Steamed as he was about it, he held his tongue, for now; his references to Meredith's Emmy, such as in the pages of *Cosell*, which came out in the fall of 1973, were fleeting and bromidic—worthy of a crisp, perfunctory huzzah. He would say more in his second book, *Like It Is*, published a year later, writing airily that "as for awards received by my colleagues, they are to be congratulated for having attained them"; as for himself, he counted the awards he had won for the documentaries and more recently Broadcaster of the Year, presented by the International Radio and Television Society, which he proudly noted had previously gone to Walter Cronkite, Chet Huntley, Arthur Godfrey, and Jack Benny. "It is a professional award," he said, not one "based on a popularity poll." He also noted that "Johnny Carson, the best and most durable entertainer in the television business, has never [to that time] won an Emmy . . . The ultimate award for anyone," he concluded, "should therefore lie in his or her own inner satisfaction with what he has done, and the knowledge that he has lived up to the standards he has set for himself."[20]

Even pricklier with time, he told the *New York Times* in 1974: "I never gave a damn about the Emmy . . . The thing's a farce. I don't think televising a football game rates an Emmy." He went on sarcastically, "I've won an award. In the great city of Detroit, they established a new dinner for a new award. The Tell It Like It Is Award, and the first award went to me." Asked by the writer if anyone would get the second such award, he replied, "I don't know, and I don't give a ——."[21]

There was a defensive, sulking tone to such platitudinous porridge. In his roiling rage about nearly everything that had been done to him and everyone that had done it, nothing ever got under his skin quite like the ongoing Emmy snub. Which is why, as Arledge flippantly wrote in *Roone*, the Meredith conquest of the Emmy "made Howard absolutely nuts."[22] In fact, it was actually a quite literal, clinical diagnosis of what *Monday Night Football* had done to Howard Cosell's mind. And there were only thirteen more seasons to come.

COSELL'S ACT never varied much if at all throughout that long tenure on *MNF*. But there was a discernible change of tone and flavor when Frank Gifford entered the booth. Because Gifford was joined at the hip with Meredith, and laid down a more soothing, low-key groove in general—and treated Cosell with a compliant respect that sometimes parted for a verbal pinprick that was not appreciated—his arrival made for a nuanced shift texturally and, significantly only to Cosell, a shift in the axis of power in the booth from two career announcers to two ex-jocks.

For Cosell, who by rote railed at the degradations of the "jockocracy," it would cause much paranoia as time went on. He was now, by the math, the odd man out. Indeed, it took only until the first *preseason* game for Cosell to fret about the implications of Gifford's arrival.

In that game, the August Hall of Fame Game in Canton, Ohio, Gifford—not Cosell—was chosen to interview none other than the president of the United States, based on the fact that Gifford had known Richard Nixon since the 1950s and had publicly endorsed him when he first ran for the White House in 1960. The interview was harmless enough, with Gifford even asking Nixon about rumors he would soon visit China. But Cosell steamed about it being a mutual admiration society. He averred he could have done it better, that he had earned the cachet to get the gig. Not giving it to him, he claimed, was an unearned victory for the jockocracy.

Cosell hardly helped Gifford's frame of mind by pointedly telling the media only days before the season that Gifford was "a tense young man who is aware that he is performing before millions in prime time, something he had never done before."[23] That Gifford, who was catching heat in the media for getting the job only because he was an Arledge crony, didn't take these jibes personally was a tribute to his character. By contrast, Cosell kept on belittling him. During the first *MNF* telecast of the season, a nervous Gifford made several mistakes, one being to misidentify the Minnesota Vikings' starting quarterback. They were greeted by Cosell either rolling his eyes or shaking his head in disgust, which Gifford had to see. But Arledge cut Gifford slack, preferring to let him grow in the very difficult job, and Cosell quickly concluded that the two ex-jocks had aligned against him—a bugbear that would become locked in his mind.

Arledge could only react as he usually did to Cosell's half-cocked accusations—by ignoring him. And Cosell let it drop, though not without branding Gifford with a couple of nicknames that carved his identity as an adjunct to Dandy Don and Humble Howard. One was obvious: "the Giffer," channeling Ronald Reagan in *The Knute Rockne Story* as the doomed running back George Gipp, imploring Notre Dame from his deathbed to "win just one for the Gipper." The other—"Faultless

Frank"—was more ambiguous, on its face a bouquet but perhaps a sardonic private send-up of Gifford's image and a jape at his many errors. Whichever it was, Gifford, who had enjoyed years of lower-visibility Sunday afternoon games wholly dependent on the competition on the field, was learning what Meredith already knew: Simply being in close proximity with Cosell did indeed mean there was less oxygen in the room. Finding his own air was a never-ending pilgrimage.

Although Cosell would use the pages of his first book to cover his resentment of Gifford—a "serious-minded man," he wrote, whose gaffes were merely "wrinkles [that] can be ironed out." He insisted Gifford sympathized with him for the abuse Cosell was getting. But beyond these sops *he* never cut Gifford any slack, ever.[24] "Howard was all over him, belittling every slip," was Arledge's recollection. "Faultless Frank," Cosell would tell Roone, was "an embarrassment." Arledge, in fact, had to move in quickly to stanch the potential bleeding when Cosell scorned Gifford in the press. "I told him to knock it off or I'd run a reel of *his* mistakes," he related. "He complied—for a while, until he began complaining that, with my approval, Frank and Don were conspiring to make him look bad on the air!"

Knowing Cosell as he did, Arledge assumed that none of this had anything to do with football or the quality of the broadcast, and everything to do with envy for what Cosell knew he could never be: "I knew what was eating him. It wasn't Frank's stumbles, it was Frank himself: his ease and self-assurance, his status and connections, his appearance and grace. Everything Howard was not."[25]

Which was why Cosell could brighten when he was able to "get even" with the two jocks. This he did by playfully exploiting their lingering team allegiances, and making it seem like Gifford versus Meredith when the Giants played the Cowboys later in the season. By the end of the telecast, Meredith and Gifford truly had gotten on each other's nerves, to Cosell's delight. That night, too, he was able to skewer Meredith, with some help from Chet Forte. Midway through a rather boring game, won by the Cowboys 20–13, Cosell happily twitted his boothmates—"Well, gentlemen, neither of your respective teams is showing me much tonight." To which Dandy Don retorted, "Well, Howard, at least we do have respective teams."

This, of course, was meant to tar Cosell with his greatest fault, as athletes saw it—that he never played the game, a proposition that usually made him frustrated to have to respond to. But Forte made it easier for him to parry the line, having unearthed that Meredith held the NFL record for most fumbles in a game. Cosell, being fed this fact through his earpiece, squared up and asked Meredith if he knew who held that sorry record. If he did, he wasn't saying. So Cosell promptly revealed the answer. Meredith, a close-up of his face ordered by Forte, looked like he wanted to drop through the floor. "Aw, I didn't do that, did I, Hah'rd?" he asked with a sheepish grin.[26]

It was, of course, another of those indelible, dippy *MNF* moments, which continued apace for so many years. So too would the subterranean rumblings by Cosell, which would lead Meredith and Gifford to become equally paranoid and distrustful of *him*. Games could be great or godawful, but without any great deviation would garner the same high ratings; in fact, the numbers for 1971 were spectacular for a seasonal series. With a 20.8 rating and a 36 share—an increase of three percentage points over 1970—it made the top thirty shows for the first time, coming in at No. 25, with an audience of just under 13 million. In addition, ABC for the first time in its history had the top-rated show, *Marcus Welby, M.D.*, and turned an overall profit. Marching ever upward, ABC was now a serious player.

The conditioned American habit of tuning in to ABC became especially profitable late in the summer of 1972, a time of year when television watching is traditionally at its nadir. That was when the network sent everyone it had—and spent nearly every dollar it had—to broadcast two weeks of the most elaborate sports programming that had ever been produced. Those two weeks would, in fact, break the bank and set the highest possible standard for excellence in TV journalism ever broadcast.

# 12

## MUNICH

ROONE ARLEDGE, keenly aware of how well financially ABC had fared from the 1968 Olympics, began to move in on annexing the television rights to the Twentieth Olympiad in Munich even before the Mexico City Games were over, making a getting-to-know-you call to the West German organizers to express ABC's strong interest in broadcasting its second consecutive Olympics. Arledge trusted that the ABC brand, and the lack of interest from the other two networks, might allow him to collect the rights for $6.5 million, which, while $1.5 million more than the price tag of the Mexico City Games, would have been a bargain.

But then Carl Lindemann, president of NBC Sports, barged into the fray, anteing astounding sums, first $9.5 million, then $11 million. When ABC could only counter with $10 million, Lindemann began to celebrate his victory—only to find out how creative ABC could be in expanding its bottom line. Noodling with the numbers, the network would need to turn itself into a virtual Olympic stage for two weeks, giving over every hour of its prime-time schedule. It would have to up its ad rates to $48,000 per minute, more than the going Super Bowl commercial rate. All told, that would be worth $24 million, which would be the total production and lodging budget; from that, Arledge could safely use $12.5 million for a final offer. As it happened, that would match NBC's final offer. Swallowing hard, Arledge sprung for another million, whereupon Lindemann folded his hand.

For that kind of coin, and all those hours to fill, ABC Sports could not possibly go it alone. Because the network's news and sports divisions had collaborated at the politically charged Mexico City Games, it was agreed that the two sides would pool talent and producers. Accordingly, while Chris Schenkel would be the in-studio host, and Jim McKay again would handle the track and field and gymnastics events, Peter Jennings, an erudite, patrician-sounding Canadian who covered foreign affairs for ABC News, would be a roving reporter.

Not that anyone was expecting Munich to engender much nonsporting news. A threat of a boycott by African and U.S. blacks led the International Olympic Committee to expel Rhodesia from the Games, warding off a potential Mexico City hive of controversy. Cradled by panoramic mountains, Munich was a beacon of worldly culture—home of one of the world's great symphony halls and many of its greatest beer halls, as was obvious during the autumn Oktoberfest. Even the bloodless Avery Brundage didn't seem capable of ruining what was officially dubbed the "Happy Games."

There were worries, all the same, that the echoes of the Third Reich were still too strong to justify bringing the Olympics to Germany. After all, it had been Berlin where the execrable 1936 Olympics had been held, with the blessings of Avery Brundage—recalled by many as a Nazi sympathizer[1]—as a propaganda coup for the "peace-loving" *Führer*, though the propaganda value reaped by the domination of the German team was blunted by the quicksilver American sprinter Jesse Owens, who even as a member of an "inferior" race was able to compete, unlike two Jewish runners.

But the West Germans, intent on erasing those memories, spared nothing, spending $600 million to build the finest facilities the Games had ever seen. And when most of the ABC team arrived, the city was painted in pastel blue and covered with flowers, with stadium security guards in powder blue uniforms. It was, said Jim McKay, "more Hansel and Gretel than Hitler and Goering." For Arledge, it promised to be "the most fun Olympics yet."[2]

For Cosell, however, the ghosts of something only Jews could feel from deep within seemed to be waiting for him on his arrival. Recalling in his memoirs the pomp and circumstance of the opening ceremonies at the Olympiastadion on August 26, he said that when the West and East German teams entered, each squad marching sternly, unsmilingly, "I got a sense of World War II and the days that preceded it—it was almost like seeing Warsaw and Prague again." He went on: "I couldn't shake it. Right then my whole background surfaced in me. I felt intensely Jewish. Suddenly, I knew, I remembered, that Dachau was only 22 miles away." He hyperbolically told of hearing the crackling of Bavarian bullwhips that "echoed in the clear, sunlit August air, under the curved acrylic dome. The sound was unnervingly like gunfire." Even the Olympic torch burning in the basin of the stadium brought to his mind the fires of the Nuremburg rallies. He said that "I was very troubled" and had a "sense of unease."[3]

Characteristically, it took only a few days for controversy to find Cosell. On August 31, the first day of heats in the sprint events, two Americans, Rey Robinson and Eddie Hart, had—beyond comprehension—missed getting to their blocks on time for the 100-meter dash and were out of the competition. Cosell, as usual hanging around on the periphery to pick up on any breaking story, was told that the two runners and their coach, Stan Wright, had been seen in the Village watching on television as the race began. Finding Wright, he asked what happened, and was told, "Howard, I'm to blame, but I can't talk to you now."

Cosell, staying on the story like glue, taped an interview with Robinson, who put the blame directly on Wright. But he wouldn't run the interview until he could get to Wright, who was dodging the press amid a general cover-up by the USOC, which disseminated the folderol that a "traffic jam" had caused the snafu. The committee was even stripping the credentials of newspapermen who tried asking questions. Undeterred, Cosell kept working the committee to allow Wright to speak. An interview was set up for that night, with Wright, a sad-faced, middle-aged man, looking beaten before a word was said. Cosell, taking no pity, bore in on him, his first question relating that Robinson had said Wright was "the culprit"—a word Robinson never used.

"Well, that's a pretty harsh word, Howard," Wright wearily protested, before doing a lot of hemming and hawing about a "misunderstanding of time schedules" that had been given him by unidentified officials. Cosell, in a comment loaded with self-importance, went on, "I feel deeply sorry for you, but we all have to answer to the American public. Why in the world was America the only country to have the wrong information?" Wright could only say something about "those a little higher up on the echelon" and "a breakdown in communications," though he did say, "I'm deeply grieved about it, and will forever, I guess, be sorry on their behalf." Clearly, as if kicking Wright, Cosell asked, "Do you believe that your young men can still have confidence in you as the coach?" Wright, in a whimper, said, "I think so."[4]

Cosell had been overbearing and hectoring. Even when he called Wright "a fine, decent man," it sounded patronizing, but he had unwittingly done Wright a favor. For the first time in the episode, the blundering coach could be seen as a sympathetic figure, browbeaten as he took Cosell's withering heat. Rather than hold poor Wright to account, Americans watching at home, especially many black Americans, reacted viscerally to the inquisition, as did many in the media. Papers at home were calling Cosell things like "Mr. Obnoxious" and demanding his firing. That week, Martin Kane in *Sports Illustrated* derided him on the "Scorecard" page, writing that "the superior job ABC-TV is doing with the Olympic Games" had been "badly marred by Howard Cosell's treatment of Stan Wright."

Kane continued: "Cosell relentlessly badgered the obviously suffering Wright, even though the coach had already accepted responsibility for the incident. The gratuitous 'commentary' that followed the interview was cruel and unnecessary. Cosell seems to think himself a crusading district attorney, and his behavior in the Wright interview brought keenly to mind the gibe of sportswriter Larry Merchant, who once mockingly saluted the pretentious broadcaster for 'making the world of fun and games sound like the Nuremberg Trials.'"[5]

Wright would, months later, threaten to sue Cosell and ABC for defamation of character, but dropped the charges. In his defense, Cosell would point out that "my questions were identical to those asked by the press," and that the same issue of *SI* had elsewhere taken slaps at Wright. "Too often, one suspects," he sniffed, "anger waits not for bad tidings but for the messenger."[6] And if the Olympics were somehow privileged turf for American athletes and their coaches, to Cosell they were fair game.

To this day, Don Ohlmeyer, the coordinating producer of the Olympic telecast, who had egged Cosell on from the control room, looks back without any contrition. "I mean, how do you not get your guys to the starting line on time? You wouldn't do that in a high school track meet. And that was Howard's point. People were moaning and crying, oh, you destroyed Stan Wright. Well, he *should* have destroyed Stan Wright. That was his job."[7]

THROUGH THE first ten days of the "Happy Games," huge crowds thrilled to near-supernal performances, headed by American swimmer Mark Spitz—felicitously, a Jew—who in that time won five individual events and two relays, all in world-record times, the first time anyone had won seven gold medals. As Spitz began to show up on seemingly every magazine cover in the world, his swarthy looks catnip for women of all ages, the engaging seventeen-year-old Russian pixie Olga Korbut— "Little Olga," as a smitten Jim McKay took to regaling her—captured viewers' imaginations by dominating gymnastics until she would miss her mount on the bars three times and lose the all-around finals to teammate Ludmilla Tourischeva. But, as the Stan Wright incident presaged, for Americans the Games were in many ways jinxed.

Cosell, on his usual boxing beat, shoveled the story line of the newest potential heavyweight contender, Duane Bobick, a block of granite from Minnesota who would use the Olympics as a jump-off. Bobick had beaten the favorite at Munich, Cuban Teófilo Stevenson, at the Pan Am Games the year before, in Cuba, no less. Months before, Cosell had broadcast the Olympic Trials at West Point, and Muhammad Ali, doing the analysis, helped stoke the Bobick buildup, predictably calling him "the Great

White Hope," not incidentally seeing him as a profitable opponent down the road. However, Stevenson had annihilated his opponents since then. Bobick, though, believing his publicity, did not lack for confidence. Running across Cosell in the Olympic Village, he waved.

"Hi, Mr. Television," he called out. "I'm glad you're here to see me do it."[8]

AT AROUND six o'clock on the morning of September 5, Cosell was awakened in his room at the München Hotel when an engineer named Harry Curtis came to his door, as he did each morning, to tape Cosell's network radio shows for broadcast throughout the day. As Curtis unpacked his equipment, he asked, almost cursorily, "Did you hear the news?" He then brought Cosell up to speed on news that had broken overnight when most of Munich was asleep. "Arab commandos," he said, "got into the Village, took over the Israeli building, shot some of them dead and are holding the rest hostage." Cosell, in a normal reflex, told Curtis not to joke around about a thing like that. Assured by Curtis he was not kidding, Cosell found himself disoriented, and nearly speechless.[9]

By instinct, he knew to call Roone Arledge, who, having put the previous day's coverage to bed only minutes before the takeover of the building, was also asleep. When his daughter Susie woke him with an urgent call from an ABC Sports staffer doing routine morning chores at broadcast headquarters. "This better be good," Arledge told him. The response was "It's the worst fucking thing you can imagine."[10]

Details at this point were sketchy, but enough to turn anyone ashen. According to the first reports on the AP wire, a band of invaders, wearing hoods, their faces sooty with shoe polish, automatic weapons drawn and grenades hanging from their belts, had scaled a seven-foot fence surrounding the Village at around 4:30 A.M. They entered 31 Connollystrasse, where the Israeli team was quartered—the sort of security breach that many had speculated was not only possible but inevitable, the result of the Germans' refusal to beef up anything beyond minimum security levels so as not to clash with the "Happy Games" motif.

At the door to the Israelis' sleeping room, one of the group began pounding on the door. Sensing something ominous was happening—as Jim McKay would later say, "No Jew needs to be told what a knock on the door in the middle of the night means"—several team coaches began waking up athletes and sending them through windows to get out of the room. A number of them had gotten out by the time the masked mob, one of whom was a woman, burst through the door, whereupon the remaining, unarmed Israelis tried repelling them with their bare hands. In the struggle, Moshe Weinberg, coach of the Israeli wrestling team, and a burly weight lifter named Joseph Romano were shot and killed. The rest, nine in all, were ordered to stand in a circle, back to back, and blindfolded.

A cleaning woman, hearing gunshots on the floor, called authorities. When police arrived, a note was dropped from the window, which demanded the release of 234 Palestinian prisoners being held in West Germany, as well as two leaders of the country's notorious Baader-Meinhof terrorist gang. If the release didn't happen by 9 A.M., the note threatened, hostages would begin to be shot. To prove their point, the mutilated corpse of Moshe Weinberg was dragged onto the balcony that wrapped around the floor and tossed down to the entrance of the building where the police were gathered, landing at their feet.

The pieces soon started to fall into place. In the note, the invaders called themselves members of Black September, a shadowy splinter of Fatah, which was known to the U.S. State Department to be a faction of Yasser Arafat's Palestinian Liberation Organization. In retrospect, this was the first major act of international terrorism, with airplane hijackings, suicidal bomb attacks, kidnappings, and hostage crises not yet common events. Only now did many in the West become aware of the horror of this new and odious form of political guerrilla warfare rooted in the desperation of Arab militants to cripple Israel.

Either slow to anticipate or realizing how gravely serious the situation was, the German police held their positions outside the building while negotiations began between the terrorists and the government. By then, Arledge had already started gearing up for a long day—coming on the air not in the usual prime-time hours but as early as the network could clear time from all of its affiliates. The first person Arledge called was Leonard Goldenson, who was in Munich as well. Arledge dialed his hotel room, waking *him* up with the dire news, and apprised the chairman of what was happening. Goldenson, who was running a high fever, gasped. Then, not asking but demanding, Arledge told him, "I'll need the network." Goldenson replied, "You got it."[11]

Arledge was told he could get on the air at 7 A.M. in New York, or 1 P.M. in Munich. That left him about four hours to coordinate his broadcast, and he put out word to find Jim McKay, whom he wanted to anchor the special coverage. Conceivably, he could have considered another man of high intellect and experience—Howard Cosell. But if he did, it was a quickly forgotten thought. Cosell, after all, had never held down a live broadcast of such gravity. "It had less to do with Howard and more to do with McKay," says Dennis Lewin today. "Jim's sensitivity, being able to handle these situations, his depth, made it an easy call. It wasn't a slap to Howard—which is not to say that Howard didn't take it that way."[12]

When Cosell reached Arledge, he began to say, "Roone, you heard—." Arledge cut him off, barking, "Get over to the Village and hold the fort there. We'll get a camera crew to you." The plan was for him to reconnoiter there with Peter Jennings; the two of them would be the only ABC reporters on the scene, meaning perhaps in the direct line of fire from the windows of the building. The network, however, couldn't pull any strings for them, and they would need to get through police lines on their own. Arledge didn't tell Cosell to try to do it, but to just *do* it. Putting down the phone, Cosell looked at Emmy, just staring. "What the hell do you say at a time like that?" he remembered thinking.[13]

Nevertheless, he had little time to get himself together and to the Village. Once there, he would put to use, on a far more critically urgent level, the skills he had displayed in Mexico City when he outfoxed guards to get into the infield. Now the entrance to the Village was completely blocked off by security. As canny as a character from a Dashiell Hammett cloak-and-dagger tale, he peeled off his yellow ABC blazer and, in shirtsleeves and wearing a pair of Puma sneakers, convinced the guards he was a Puma salesman and strode briskly to Building 31.

It was now 8:30 A.M. and, incongruously, athletes all around the Village were coming and going, unaware of the crisis. Cosell met up with Jennings behind Building 24, where the Italian team was staying, which overlooked Building 31 from fifty yards away. The only way any of them would be able to communicate with the ABC office was with Telefunken walkie-talkies. Cosell settled down on a patch near an underpass that separated the Italian and Burmese buildings and led to Building 31. Jennings, who from his time spent reporting from Beirut was able to provide invaluable background with what he knew of Black September and Fatah, was able to get past guards and camped on the sixth floor of Building 24. When cops made a sweep of the building, he hid in a bathroom until they were gone.

From where Cosell was, he could see what was going on in front of the building, how many plainclothes cops carrying submachine guns were being deployed for the developing siege. Lying on his belly so as not to be spied by police—or through the terrorists' zoom lenses—he would make mental notes, then use his walkie-talkie to relay his information to the ABC headquarters.

Live ABC coverage of the crisis began with McKay sitting in front of a cheerful MUNICH 1972 sign on a beige wall. "This is Building Number 31," he said over a camera shot frozen in ghostly gloom on the bay window of the Israeli headquarters, as it would be for hours after. "At this moment, here eight or nine terrified humans are being held prisoner." When a terrorist poked his head fleetingly out of the window, McKay mused, "A man with a stocking mask on his face. Weird. What's going on inside that head and that mind."[14]

Arledge was careful to adhere to responsible journalistic practice. There were to be no opinions, no emotion, no reporting of unsubstantiated rumors. The only good news McKay could pass along was that the original 9 A.M. deadline had been pushed back, first to noon, then to 5 P.M., at which time the terrorists vowed to begin publicly executing one or two hostages every hour until their demands were met—raising the horrific possibility that ABC's audience in the millions might bear witness to murder on live television. And yet, even with two Israelis dead and the others bound in a room, Avery Brundage refused to suspend the events of the day; he was eighty-one now and these Games would be his grand finale, and nothing would ruin it for him. Cosell called the continuation of the Games "obscene" and railed on his radio shows—amazingly, he recorded them, off the cuff, while staked out in the Village during the crisis—that his network's partners in the broadcast were "the tired old men of the IOC."

As McKay continued his coverage, a monitor in the room carried a volleyball game between Germany and Japan, with a crowd of three thousand German fans as oblivious as Brundage cheering wildly. McKay ignored it. At that moment, German snipers were perched on the roof of an adjacent building, training guns on Building 31, and sports were a long way from McKay's mind. "This is happening now," he said incredulously, "if you can possibly believe that, at the Games of the Twentieth Olympiad."

In the Village, Cosell reported another odd reaction to Jews being in mortal peril. Sightseers were climbing over fences, whereupon they would stand in the open gawking as if they were spectators at a sports match, or else wander around without a care trying to get autographs from athletes. At the ABC building, while he had his eyes trained on the monitor showing that cold gray balcony, Arledge took a call from the head of the network's entertainment division, Marty Starger, who, astonishingly, asked if he'd be available to attend a cocktail reception that night for advertisers. As Arledge would tartly recall, "I conveyed regrets."[15] Clearly, Avery Brundage was not alone in his callous indifference to what was happening in Building 31.

At one point, after ABC had gotten a camera and microphones into the Village, McKay threw it to the shirt-sleeved Cosell for an interview he'd secured with a friend of Moshe Weinberg, who he noticed had an Israeli Olympic team button pinned to his lapel. "What was the last thing he gave you?" Cosell asked. Sadly, saying nothing, the man lifted up his lapel to display the pin. (A week later, he would relate, that same man would ask to be compensated; a disgusted Cosell turned on his heel and walked away.) Meanwhile, McKay kept focusing on that dreaded balcony—"a balcony not too much unlike the one Martin Luther King Jr. walked on and met his death," he said, referring to Reverend King's assassination in Memphis four years before. On the roof of neighboring buildings, he noted men dressed like athletes but carrying bags that obviously contained weapons. And when a terrorist stuck his head out the window, McKay tersely said, "You might wonder, why doesn't a sniper take off that head right now?"

In late afternoon, the number of men with those gym bags had multiplied. "It would appear that some sort of operation is under way very, very, very slowly and delicately," McKay assumed. Cosell confirmed that fact; he now reported that "more cars are pulling up beneath the underpass . . . police are getting out . . . submachine guns and pistols plainly visible." Having seen too many operations like this in Beirut, Jennings chimed in, not optimistic. "I have a strong feeling," he said, "this is going to turn out badly." In fact, no operation was under way. Negotiations were, and as darkness fell over Munich, Cosell, lying on his belly on a slope mere feet from Building 31, had little to do but sort involuntary thoughts streaming through his head that were tied to his own life as a Jew. As he recalled in *Cosell*, "I found myself wanting to scream at the German authorities: 'YOU DIRTY BASTARDS! Where was your security? Did you purposely allow this to happen?,'" even though he knew "I wasn't being rational or really fair."[16]

He was snapped out of his introspection at around eight o'clock by the sudden movement of police exiting the building and beginning to rope off the area. He rose to his feet and asked the man he knew to be the head police official, "What goes on here?"

"A deal," he was told. "A deal has been made. The helicopters will be here. In moments they come."

He dutifully reported it on the air, causing a great air of anticipation that the hostages might be freed. But then . . . nothing happened for over an hour. Then, helicopters indeed came, touching down not in the Village where cameras could have filmed them but rather in an isolated field. Only later would it become known that the gang, realizing their demands were not going to be granted, and with dozens of guns trained on Building 31, switched tactics. Now all they wanted was to get away. Their new demand was that the Germans provide a bus to ferry them— and the hostages, who would be forced to accompany them as human shields—to a helipad, from where they would be lifted to a remote NATO air base just outside Munich. There, a Lufthansa Boeing 727 waited on the tarmac, which would fly them and the hostages to Cairo—or so the German authorities wanted them to believe.

At 9:15 P.M., after over fourteen hours of torturous inertia, they were allowed to leave from the rear of the building, out of sight from all but the police, and piled the hostages into the bus, then into two helicopters. But as the choppers, their red taillights streaking across the night, were en route to the airport, a caravan of police cars and trucks loaded with reporters and camera equipment sped behind the bus. Unbeknownst to them, a trap had been set at the airport. Five snipers, and two police officers dressed as pilots, lay in wait, in bushes and at the edge of the runway, with orders to shoot to kill whenever they could get a terrorist in their sights.

Cosell did not make the trek to the airport. Neither did Jennings, who had in late afternoon gone to the ABC studio. Cosell, finally free to move about, was told to come to the studio as well, so he could prerecord background segments for the fight between Duane Bobick and Teófilo Stevenson, which would take place the next day, to be won by Stevenson with a third-round technical knockout. Exhausted and in no mood for such mundane matters, Cosell at first told Arledge he would do no work on any subject other than the crisis, but eventually gave in. As if on automatic pilot, Cosell managed to switch his brain into sports mode.

That chore done, he had none of Arledge's reluctance to attend Marty Starger's cocktail party. He almost certainly had a few, or many, drinks. Then, at 11:31 P.M., German time, came a startling bulletin on the Reuters wire saying that "ALL ISRAELI HOSTAGES HAVE BEEN FREED, ALL TERRORISTS KILLED." McKay tentatively reported it, carefully refraining from any premature celebration pending confirmation. He brought on a West German government spokesman who, with the caveat "As far as we can now see," eagerly claimed that the rescue operation at the airport had been "perfect," adding brightly that the entire affair "will be forgotten after a few weeks." But Arledge and McKay weren't ready to declare the crisis at an end—though many in Munich had gone to sleep thinking there had been a happy ending. And, sure enough, a few minutes later, AP sent a very different report over its wire. The good news was that three of the terrorists were said to have been killed and another had committed suicide, but the others had escaped on foot.

Nothing was said about the fate of the hostages, who had sat helpless and blindfolded in the bus the whole time. Retracting the earlier bulletin, McKay added, "We are afraid that the information given out so far is too optimistic." Now the mood in the studio, and throughout the world, turned dark. Few who were watching would forget that sense of foreboding. With still no further word, McKay began to moderate a panel discussion. At that point, Chris Schenkel, the nominal studio host of ABC's Olympic coverage, about whom Arledge had completely forgotten, approached Roone and asked him meekly, "Is there room for me?" Arledge, feeling guilty about how he had slighted Schenkel, put him on the panel, where he mainly held a microphone being passed around among McKay, ABC News' Bonn correspondent Lou Cioffi, and Jennings—whose ominous premonition about how things would end was seeming more prophetic by the minute.

As the discussion ensued, Cosell wandered over from the party, tired of waiting around and doing nothing, his boiling point near. As Arledge would later recall, he "burst in on all of us," presumably meaning the studio nerve center where Arledge, coordinating director Don Ohlmeyer, Lewin, and coordinating producer Geoff Mason were huddled around the board, and began bellowing, "I want to go on! I've got to be on this story! Put me on, Arledge— I'm the only one who can tell it!"

He had, as Arledge suspected, been drinking again—"four silver bullets, maybe five," Arledge would estimate in retrospect, referring to Cosell's own metaphor for his units of alcoholic consumption. He was right in Roone's face, showering him with saliva, screaming, "Dirty bastards! They already killed six million of us. What's a few more?"

"No, Howard!" Arledge said he screamed back. "We're in the middle of it. There's no place for you."

"C'mon!" Cosell persisted. "Put me on the air!"

"No, Howard. Trust me. You'll be the first to thank me in the morning."[17]

Indeed, putting him on the air at that point seemed a very bad idea. He was quite possibly drunk, surely overwrought, close to unstable, in no way the cool, crisply articulate, and collected Cosell who had covered Muhammad Ali's court case and Curt Flood's legal challenge of baseball's reserve clause, which perniciously bound players to their teams in perpetuity. He had recently testified before Congress on the issue, mesmerizing the politicians with lawyerly arguments about yet another abridgement of an athlete's constitutional rights. But now he wasn't a wise, lawyerly protagonist; he was an addled, increasingly mercurial man ready to boil over. Arledge was right; he *wasn't* needed. And if Roone did consider it, could *Ful-a-dul-fia* be far from his mind?

Perhaps it is revealing that this unpleasant scene was nowhere to be found in *Cosell*, nor ever to be mentioned by him in interviews. Certainly, any way he could have spun it wouldn't have made him look good. But he would neither forget nor forgive. Partly because of the way Arledge took to talking about the incident, with shockingly little tact and respect for arguably his network's top asset, although he waited until after Cosell's death before making it public, writing in *Roone* that "I'd just saved his ass—it would have been a disaster if he'd gone on the air—but years later, he still brought the subject up, with enormous resentment toward me for having deprived him of his moment."[18]

Today, Lewin insists, "I don't remember that at all. It might have happened, I don't know, but it wasn't a big deal at the time." Ohlmeyer does remember, and says he agreed with Arledge's decision. "Howard was too close to what was going on. To my knowledge, Howard was not drunk. It ran deeper than that. Howard wanted to be in on that moment of horror. As a Jew, it was the biggest story of his life, it affected him on a very, very deep level—and that was why he *couldn't* be. But Howard could never understand that. And it's why I don't think Howard ever forgave Roone for keeping him off the air that morning."[19]

Lou Volpicelli has the same recollection as Ohlmeyer, except that when asked if Cosell was drunk he says, "I dare say that could have been a part of it."[20]

The root cause of the outburst, however, had little to do with alcohol. Jerry Izenberg says of Munich, "It ate him up. Because he could do nothing about it. And it ate him up that he wasn't the focal point when it all happened. But thank God Arledge did the right thing. McKay's performance is a classic. Howard could not have done what McKay did."[21]

Dealing with a Cosell tantrum, sober or otherwise, was surely the last thing Arledge needed. As things were unfolding, and more, grimmer details about the battle at the airport came in, a chillingly somber McKay intoned, "The latest word we get from the airport is that, quote, all hell is breaking loose out there, that there is still shooting going on, that there are reports of a burning helicopter." Over the next two hours, unconfirmed reports had it that all the Israelis had been killed in the raid. Arledge refused to let McKay mention them, even as unverified.

Then, at around 4:30 A.M., twenty-four hours from the start of this nightmare, Marvin Bader, the network's vice president in charge of Olympic planning, who had made it to the airport, cornered a German Olympics official he knew who'd come from a meeting with government authorities. The ABC broadcast was facing a hard deadline—at 5 A.M., 11 P.M. back home, the local late evening news shows would take over the airwaves. Desperate for news, Bader demanded to know what was happening. The official first said he couldn't talk. Bader kept pressing. Then, his eyes filling up with tears, the official broke. "They're all dead, Marvin," he said.

"Who?" Bader asked.

"The Israelis."[22]

He relayed the news to McKay, who related in his memoir that Arledge considered that official word and said McKay should report it as such. Arledge, in his, maintained otherwise, that he waited until official word came from Olympic headquarters, minutes later on the Reuters wire. Whichever it was, McKay now had to confirm the worst of news to a worldwide audience, the ABC coverage having been picked up by dozens of countries, swelling the audience to what Arledge estimated to be perhaps a billion people. Interrupting the conversation that was in progress, McKay began to speak, fatigue in his voice further slowing his words to a crawl:

"Gentlemen, we have the official word from the airport. [Pause] When I was a kid, my father used to say, our greatest hopes and our worst fears are seldom realized. Our worst fears have been realized tonight. They've now said that there were eleven hostages. Two were killed in their rooms this morning—yesterday morning. Nine were killed at the airport tonight. [With a sorrowful shake of the head] They're all gone."

His voice never rose above a hush, his eyes stared, fighting tears. There were no dramatic pauses or rhetorical flourishes, no betrayal of any personal emotion. In its simple tug at the heart and mind, it was, and still is, along with Walter Cronkite choking back tears to announce John F. Kennedy's death in Dallas, arguably the saddest, most heartbreaking and profound thirty seconds of television ever broadcast. No one else could likely have done it anywhere near as well, or affectingly, except perhaps in the opinion of one man. Howard Cosell didn't thank Roone Arledge the next morning.

AFTER ARLEDGE had refused to put him on the air, Cosell had sat, forlornly, in the studio, saying nothing. Watching McKay report the final ghastly outcome on a monitor, it felt as if a part of him had died along with the Israelis. Numbly, he returned to his hotel room. Emmy was asleep, having gone to bed after the first reports of a successful end to the crisis. He awoke her, and when he told her what had really happened, she cried. He tried to sleep, but the phone kept relentlessly ringing, with calls from friends and even strangers from the States who somehow were able to get through to his room.

He was used to that by now. Erich Segal, the *Love Story* author, who was in Munich as a track and field commentator, spent time with Cosell and noticed this odd phenomenon. Weeks later, in a *New York Times Magazine* story Segal wrote about the Games, he noted, "For all the criticism Cosell gets, people believe in him. All during the Olympics, he's the one who got the steady flow of calls from America. 'Tell us what's really happening,' they would ask him."[23] Contrary to his public image, he would usually speak at length with the callers, even the ones he didn't know, considering it a relief to converse with Americans rather than Germans.

Now, he no longer even wanted to look any Germans in the face, clearly blaming their country for allowing the atrocity to happen. He would later say that in the hours after the massacre, "I just wanted to get home. I didn't want to stay in Germany. I didn't ever want to go back [there]."[24]

By the time the sun dared come up over Munich on September 6, the awful and grim details of the catastrophe were known. In the pitched battle at the airport, four of the terrorists had indeed gone down, but when snipers missed one who had gone into the plane, he ran back to the bus and exploded a grenade, killing all eleven Israelis. The three surviving terrorists were captured—though not for long. On October 29, the German government, fearing more terrorist attacks in the country, agreed to release the trio in exchange for a hijacked Lufthansa jet. To many, it was an outrage as perfidious as the crime itself. (Unable to prevent it, Israel's prime minister, Golda Meir, would approve plans for the elite Israeli security force, the Mossad, to hunt down all those responsible for the murders. Eventually more than a dozen Palestinians were assassinated, including two of the three released terrorists; the third eluded the dragnet and today still remains in hiding.)

The memorial service went on a few hours later, yet Brundage wouldn't hear of suspending the rest of the Games. Rather, he agreed to a day of mourning—beginning, retroactively, at 4 P.M. the previous day, so that the Games could resume at the same time that day. Worse, the erstwhile Nazi sympathizer seemed less disturbed by the tragedy than that the victims had the audacity to mar his showcase. When he took to the platform in the basin of the huge tureen of the stadium, ringed by flags of every nation at half-mast, the dead were mentioned only when he noted that "the Games of the Twentieth Olympiad have been subjected to two savage attacks. We lost the Rhodesian battle against naked political blackmail." Then, with a bathetic reference to "a handful of terrorists" not being permitted to "destroy" the Games, he vaingloriously declared, "The Games must go on."

Many in the packed stadium gasped and some hooted, offended that the booting of an all-white team sanctioned by an apartheid South African government could be held equal to, or a greater crime than, innocent athletes being slain while blindfolded in a bus. Several black athletes, outraged by the false equivalency, were so angered they got up and walked out. Cosell, who had decided not to leave Munich, as such an act would violate all of his professional ethics, attended the memorial with Emmy, becoming more and more inflamed. On his radio shows that day, he again lit into Brundage, reprising an old Cosell chestnut when he said, "There was a time for Avery Brundage—that of William of Orange," the sovereign Dutch prince who invaded and became king of England in 1689, proclaiming the divine right of kings. Brundage, Cosell went on, was merely interested in minimizing the damage from the stark reality that, as he put it in *Cosell*, "once again Jews had been killed" in Germany.[25]

These were brutal comments, but if they got back to Brundage, as in Mexico City he had no recourse but to suffer indignity from the network he expected to glorify him. The millions of dollars ABC paid for the Games, and the unheard-of ratings it racked up during the competition—in each of its three weeks on the air, forty-nine of the fifty top-rated prime-time half-four segments were the Olympics—were not to be tampered with, even by Brundage. That went for Cosell's license to pontificate.

Cosell, who would write, "For me, the Olympics died with the Israelis. But not my job," would stay in Germany until the end of the Games on September 11, the rest of the events bringing no relief, neither for him nor any other American.[26] The U.S. team, as in a daze, suffered unforeseen stumbles, literally so when the great long-distance runner Jim Ryun was beaten by Kenya's Kip Keino in the 1,500-meter run after being tripped and falling to the track. Worse, the basketball team infamously lost the gold when in a comedy of errors the referees gave the Russians *three* chances to score a last-second basket—a decision that stood even after Cosell elicited an admission from the scorekeeper who when asked who really won answered, "The United States of America."

For all who had spent the late summer in Munich, the bitter aftertaste would never fade. Says Don Ohlmeyer, "It was just devastating to me. Right after we confirmed the deaths of the Israelis, I couldn't go on anymore, I had to get out of there. I went back to the hotel and went straight to the bar and got drunk. And I'll tell you, when I turned on the

television on 9/11 and saw those planes go through those towers, all I
could think of was Munich. It was the same feeling. It's inside you. It
sickens you. And if it had that effect on me, I can only imagine what
effect it had on Howard."[27]

THOSE HARROWING and traumatic events at the Twentieth Olympiad
affected Cosell to the core. Munich, he said, was "the worst time of my
life . . . so grotesque, so remote from the spirit of the Games, as though it
had happened on some other planet." When he left, he said he felt
"unclean" and "undignified."[28] But there was, he believed, a chance for
redemption on a personal level, if he could somehow force himself to
figure out just who he was as a Jew.

In the immediate aftermath, he believed the horror of the Israeli
massacre would bring him closer to his neglected Judaic roots. Yet this
would turn out be more public cant than reality. Cosell would give gener-
ously to Judaic charities, fund-raising heavily for Jerusalem's Hebrew
University, of which he became a trustee and an honorary fellow; years
later, after Emmy's death, the school named a recreation center in his
and her honor. But while his daughter Hilary would make her admission
about being a "raving Zionist," her father never would commit to being
even a casual Zionist; although Israel's wars against its Arab neighbors
would be a matter of pride to him, he was uncomfortable when Israel
began building settlements in Palestine, even if it made him a pariah
among "celebrity" Jews. Adventurism, as he saw it, turned his stomach,
and could not be justified in the name of self-defense. What's more, he
and Emmy had little enthusiasm for making pilgrimages to Israel. In
1979, Emmy admitted, "I was so relieved when we didn't have to go to
Jerusalem for the dedication of a soccer stadium they were going to name
for Howard. I'd rather watch my grandsons play soccer."[29]

"A hybrid character," Cosell called himself in his memoirs, in a fleeting attempt to explain his standing as a Jew, a man who had married
outside of his religion and had a daughter who had converted to her husband's Christianity.[30] And this hybrid would not find himself any closer to
any meaningful religious study of or commitment to Judaism, or for that

matter to the synagogue in his Upper East Side neighborhood that he called his congregation but that saw little of him. A man of his time, wary of American anti-Semitism, he seems not to have ever resolved the ambivalence he had about whether he *should* boast his Judaism as a part of his identity, despite the fact that so many Americans saw him as the ultimate, parodic Jew.

Dennis Lewin, who soldiered with him for three decades in places like Munich, says, "I never saw any signs of Howard practicing religion. The only time it ever came up, it was very weird and very uncomfortable for me. We were in Cleveland for a Monday night game once and some reporter asked me about why people pick on Howard. I said it was because he wasn't your typical kind of announcer. I said that he was a Jewish lawyer from New York. I didn't mean anything negative by it. I'm Jewish myself. It was just a fact. But Howard called me and said, 'I don't know why you brought up that I was Jewish. You're bringing up bigotry.'

"Howard was just so sensitive about being Jewish, and so conflicted about it on so many levels. He was deeply affected by what happened in Munich, yet he didn't want me mentioning that he was Jewish. He never sorted it out, what he wanted to be."[31]

Maury Allen, the longtime *New York Post* scribe with whom Cosell shared some very private thoughts, has an example similar to Lewin's. "We were at the airport one time waiting for the same plane to L.A. And in the airport there was an announcement, 'Calling Howard Cohen, calling Howard Cohen.' And he knew it was meant for him. And Howard, when he heard it, didn't move. He wouldn't accept the call, didn't say anything about it. So we get on the plane and fly seven hours to L.A., and we get off and as soon as he walks into the terminal he hears this same announcement again, 'Calling Howard Cohen, calling Howard Cohen.'

"Whoever it was, he was on the plane and it was his plan to get Howard on both ends of the country, by doing something he knew would get his goat. Because the Howard Cohen thing really irritated him. It wasn't that he didn't want people to know of his background, that he was a Jew, because Howard never denied that and spoke openly of it. He said in interviews that his real name was Cohen. But it was something that irritated him when others brought it up."[32]

Because of the ethnic implication of his forgone surname, Cosell seemed to bridle about the *way* people would say it. And yet, contrary to how he usually reacted to any zinger, he generally refused to tackle what were clearly anti-Semitic barbs. Part of the reason why may have been a carryover from his early days in the industry, and perhaps even further back in time, when Jews—such as his parents—were conditioned *not* to mention their Judaism. Interestingly, he did mention an instance similar to the one witnessed by Allen, in his second book, *Like It Is,* published in 1974, but only as it related to the gauntlet he often ran in public. He was at a benefit in San Diego for sickle-cell anemia when two teenagers way-laid him in the lobby, with one sticking a piece of paper in his face and demanding, "Sign here, and sign your real name, Howie Cohen." He recalled that, ironically, "the lad looked Jewish, and he was implying that I was ashamed of being Jewish," though it also struck him that it could have been a jab at him for going out on a limb calling Ali by his adopted name. He said he assailed the teenager, "You despicable brat, I'll not sign. If your parents heard what you just said to me, your father would . . . slap you in the face. I can't do it."[33]

His real point in telling the story was the upshot: Weeks later, the kid had gotten himself a lawyer and sued for $100,000, claiming Cosell had slapped him. Wrote Cosell: "Fear for your physical safety is not necessar-ily as troublesome as fear of what somebody you never saw in your life can do to you in the way of harassment." If it was in any way redolent of anti-Semitism, he reserved his thoughts. In this light, it becomes clearer why, if he did have any original intent to reclaim the religious implica-tions of his birthright, he was doomed from the start. That was some-thing he would keep on hold—to the effect that, as Dennis Lewin muses, "I don't even know if Howard understood who Howard was. He would have told you he knew, but at the end of the day, he didn't. Maybe he didn't want to know."[34]

That being so, Cosell's unstinting desire to be a latter-day delegate of "Our Crowd" had far more to do with economics and status than reli-gion. He had reached the point where he was the most famous Jew in broadcasting, if not entertainment. Yet what it meant to him was never clear. "Howard didn't embrace Judaism, but he used it," ventures Jerry

Izenberg. "If Hilary is a raving Zionist, Howard was simply raving. Zionism had nothing to do with it. There were many, many times that Howard talked about anti-Semitism, and he would accuse many people of it. But I always got the feeling he was doing that because he felt he had to, like he was getting points for it. He would just throw it into a conversation, gratuitously."[35]

As Cosell reached his professional zenith, he didn't seem to mind that his cultural being was now woven into the Middle American fabric that defined his country. He had never anticipated earlier, given the anti-Semitic tenor of the nation, that he would ever fit in, so his acceptance, albeit limited, became a triumph of a sort. There were even times when he would exclaim, in vast wonderment and a kind of real pride, "They're making me out to be another Jesus Christ, Superstar!"[36]

THE HORROR of Munich did no less than make the ABC network major. Arledge and his crew would win *twenty-nine* Emmys for its Olympic coverage, topped off by Outstanding Achievement in Sports Programming, with Arledge—as he had four years before—winning for executive producer and McKay for best commentator. For Roone, that made *thirteen* Emmys on his mantel, en route to what would be twenty-five; and for McKay three, having already won two of the four he would garner as host of *Wide World of Sports*. McKay also was given the prestigious George Polk Award for excellence in journalism, winning for television reporting—a rarity for anyone in the sports orbit—putting him in the company of such other Polk winners that year as the *Washington Post*'s Bob Woodward and Carl Bernstein for reporting on the Watergate scandal and *The New Yorker*'s Frances FitzGerald for her groundbreaking Vietnam reporting. That many of these honors came as the result of the continuing coverage of the crisis allowed Arledge to crow that it was ABC Sports and *not* ABC News that was being so honored, a circumstance that would have enormous impact for Arledge before long. Cosell, meanwhile, was still waiting for his first major award, of any kind.

The same production core had scant time to ponder Munich. As soon as they returned, the fall had to go on, meaning a dive right back

into the *Monday Night Football* end of the pool. The show began its
third season in late September, ABC having renewed its contract with
the NFL by shelling out $72 million, almost thrice the $25.5 million
price tag of 1970, which would be easily earned back with sixty-second
commercial time selling for $100,000. Cosell was still numb, and his
resentment for Arledge only came to add to the moments when he felt
unloved by his own network—whose "ass" he believed *he* had saved. It
did not take long before the undercurrent of stress, dissatisfaction, and
discontentment was once again being felt by all three men in the booth.
For "Faultless" Frank Gifford, there would be more unease, and defer-
ence to Cosell even when Cosell blew hot air and not real football
information. Terrified to make a mistake, or get on Cosell's wrong side,
he was frequently hollow and uptight, earning him brickbats in the
media; one columnist dubbed him "a walking mannequin"—a phrase
Cosell would become particularly fond of, and requisition for himself.
In public he was still solicitous of Gifford, but in private he hated Gifford's mistakes, and became convinced the producers' failure to hold
Gifford to account for them constituted special treatment, the kind
never accorded him.

At the obligatory Monday afternoon luncheons at which the ABC
crew would do a meet and greet with guests from the local ABC affiliate,
businessmen, city politicians, and the like, Cosell would perform surgical
sarcasm; draping an arm around Gifford's shoulder, he would bray,
"Ladies, this man is a Greek God. A Greek God, I tell you!" before finishing off with a rude, sexual remark that would embarrass everyone, not
least of all Gifford, who would bite his lip hard and try to laugh.

Arledge was able to avoid the soap opera going on in the booth, now
that he had decided he no longer needed to be regularly on the scene
each Monday night. That left Ohlmeyer, who for the 1972 season was
elevated to coproducer with Dennis Lewin, as primary holder of Cosell's
hand, a chore he handled with compassion. "I always heard Howard out,
it wasn't just humoring him. I really loved Howard, and I could see what
he was going through. Howard was very, very sensitive to rejection. He
couldn't handle it, and bravado was his cover. That was easy to see. But
what people didn't realize about him was that Howard had a great sense

of humor, which made him a lot of fun to be with—except if he didn't take something that was said about him as a joke. Then he would try to eviscerate you, and very nastily, and then he would stop being funny."[37]

The surprise for Ohlmeyer was that this phobia was not exclusive to Cosell, only the most conspicuous in him. "After the second game of the [1972] season, Meredith said he was going to quit because Howard was making him look bad, so I had to smooth things with him. Then the next week, *Howard* was gonna quit because he felt Roone was catering to *Don*. And Frank at various times thought those two were trying to make *him* look bad. It just got to be . . . it was ongoing, never ending. I always felt that we basically needed a psychiatrist's couch that we could put somebody different on each week."

Or, perhaps, put them in a kindergarten. "Look, most people in entertainment are that way—they all act like children. Nobody I've known in the business—including myself—had an emotional age above fifteen. We are not normal people. Success can be here one day and gone the next, and it's a hell of a long way down. Howard, as big as he became, never felt he was safe, and that feeling was infectious to those around him. And the kind of life Howard and I lived then was so unnatural, you *couldn't* be a normal person. I used to travel two hundred thousand miles a year. But at least when I got into a town, I wasn't constantly mobbed, harassed, and put under the microscope like Howard was. He was the lightning rod, he took the brunt of it all. You really had to understand that to understand why he felt he was treated unfairly."[38]

In this respect, it seemed to Cosell that he was "taking one for the team," leaving Meredith and Gifford to enjoy a serene journey. For his part, Gifford explained that his role was that of "a traffic cop, to move everything along," but in reality "I was a resident psychiatrist. On any given night, almost anything could affect the mood of the two guys I worked with . . . Their unpredictability made them terrific. But I never knew which Don or Howard was going to show up," either the "wildly gregarious" Cosell or the "sulking" Cosell. Sometimes, when he ignored some babble or other so he could keep his eyes on the field, Cosell, seemingly aware that Gifford wasn't listening, would ask, "Isn't that right, Giffer?" leaving him with not a clue what Cosell had just said. "On some nights," Gifford said, "I walked out of that booth feeling like a survivor of Omaha Beach."[39]

What even they didn't fully appreciate was the innate chemistry they had. "You had three distinct voices and three distinct points of view," Ohlmeyer says. "Frank thought everything about the NFL was terrific. Don thought the players were great and the owners were pirates. And Howard thought the whole thing was a sham. And when you added to that the underlying tension between them, that's what made it a trip."[40] To appreciate that was to accept that Cosell's ego was the glue that held the entire mélange together. It was, for Ohlmeyer, a learning curve that required living with some typical Cosell conceits.

The same could be said for an America that had come to appreciate and even crave him. If the 1960s birthed Cosell, the 1970s entrenched him, especially post-Munich, when the medium of television clearly matured into something more than a vehicle for escapist entertainment. Watching the tube was serious business, soon to intimately chart the downfall of a president. While Richard Nixon would win a landslide reelection that November, the stain of Watergate would before long be TV fare in itself, with daily televised congressional hearings that produced incredible revelations about the depraved conduct within the White House that led all the way to the Oval Office. It was the kind of must-see TV that Cosell deemed worthy of the medium he believed, rightly, he had dragged into seriousness.

Indeed, he and Richard Nixon, two products of 1950s America and similar in many ways, were each metaphoric and symptomatic of the culture they helped define. Nixon, a paranoid man given to anti-Semitic remarks, was hurtling toward his end, constricted in an era of TV's prying eye. Cosell, a paranoid man only five years younger, harboring unresolved issues about the anti-Semitism he had experienced, was hurtling to even greater heights, broadening the reach of the medium that brought Nixon down. Politics and religion had nothing to do with this divergence; timing did. For the old Brooklyn lawyer, his time had come.

# 13

## A BIG PROPERTY

To the general public, which simply assumed it must be grand fun to be a part of the *MNF* cast, periodic gossip about Cosell being at odds with Meredith, or Gifford, or both, was the sort of inane showbiz piffle that qualified the show as entertainment, helping to keep its popularity self-sustaining. Now, in season three, things were on such a steady track and rolling so smoothly that Roone Arledge felt comfortable in his decision not to attend many of the games and play mother hen. Though he was still billed as executive producer, which would allow him to keep harvesting Emmys, it was now the job of Don Ohlmeyer, Dennis Lewin, and Chet Forte to deal with all aspects of the broadcast—and the bigger challenge of dealing with all aspects of the ego circus in the booth.

Yet never did the show disappoint on the air. As much as Cosell recoiled at such things, Meredith's generally lame one-liners, his crooning, and his "alter ego" guise, Harley Smydlapp, sent viewers into beatitude. For public consumption, Cosell would issue the usual perky, if not quite sincere, self-deprecation—he was, he said, "the thorn between the two roses." But once in a while, the jaw would unclench and he'd bare sharp fangs, reiterating his earlier plaint in *Sports Illustrated* that "this is starting to be boring, and I think I may get out of this intellectual thimble and not do any more TV sports except the Olympics, which I find very exciting."[1]

As prominent as he had become, Cosell seemingly needed to convince *himself* he was doing more than buffoonery. Indeed, sensitive to criticism as he was, he knew that some regarded his work on *Monday Night Football* as an exercise in vanity. One who did, Jerry Izenberg, says the show "changed him, who he was, what he was. The caricature was always part of all that, but now he *became* the caricature. Howard had stopped going to a lot of sports events. *Monday Night Football* was his life. I always thought he was good in that role. I understand about showbiz. But it got to the point where he just tried too hard to be the caricature, and all the rest fell away."[2]

Cutting himself slack, Cosell would tell people that having to engage in mindless banter on *Monday Night Football* was throwing him off his game. He had to wonder if others were still noticing his tough-edged commentary. Just in case, he had developed a peculiar ritual, for a man of his status. He'd head right home after each game, ensuring that he would be able to be in the lobby of the ABC corporate offices on the Avenue of the Americas at eight o'clock in the morning. That way, he could accost some high network executive or another coming through the revolving doors, strike up a conversation, and at some point query the suit about how he had done on the telecast the night before. It was a scene he, easily the most famous sports personality in the nation, carried out with such regularity that—like those New York Giants who rode the rails into the city back in the early sixties—the executives would try mightily to avoid him. Many would come in later on Tuesday mornings, if at all. Their happiest days were Monday mornings, when Cosell would be out of town.

Unfortunately, no matter how much praise he could elicit—foolish indeed would have been an ABC employee who didn't say how great he'd been—criticism always arose from a wide variety of sources. As much as *MNF* had been a gift to the NFL, more than one team owner was making his discontent known to ABC about things Cosell said, the most critical being the Cleveland Browns' Art Modell, chairman of the NFL's television committee, who had been essential in creating the program and was rewarded by being given the inaugural game. Modell hinted that he might perhaps keep the Browns off the show rather than put up with a Cosell fusillade against his team.

Those threats never would be carried out by any owner, no surprise since home teams collected far more TV revenue for an *MNF* game than they did for a Sunday afternoon one. But they too were a marker that the owners had come to realize how all-pervasive the reach of *MNF* was, and that now, unlike in the past, they had no say in controlling the content of how their games were covered; these men were, if anything, more hypersensitive to slights, usually imagined ones, than their teams' fans were. And in *Monday Night Football*, something *always* seemed to pique *somebody*. It was the new paradigm of television sports.

This was where Gifford provided another prophylaxis, to the network. The Giffer, Arledge would tell any such recalcitrant owner, would bring the scale back into delicate balance, by challenging Cosell with his understated guile and charm. Just watch. They did, and whether or not Gifford ever really took issue with anything Cosell said—and one can count on one hand the times he actually did—soon the threats were quieted. It just *seemed* that Gifford, who could always get Meredith to agree with *him*, was putting Cosell down. Not surprisingly, this was something that Cosell began to think was really happening. It did not augur well for the relationship.

And so the beat, if not the paranoia, went on, and on, as the *Monday Night Football* matrix became chiseled into the culture, its "watercooler" fodder arising from spontaneous combustion. During an October 1972 game when the Oakland Raiders were headed for a 34–0 thumping of the Houston Oilers, and fans emptied from the Astrodome stands during the final quarter, the cameras found a wonderful shot: an Oilers fan, seemingly alone in his section, fast asleep. "A vivid picturization of the excitement attendant upon this game," Cosell threw in, fracturing the language as only he could. Good enough, but when Chet Forte kept the camera trained on the man, he awoke and realized he was being watched. He indignantly stuck up his middle finger. Instantly, Meredith had a better punch line—"He thinks they're number one in the nation!"[3]

Cosell's tête-à-tête in the previous season with controversial Vice

President Spiro Agnew—who within the year was headed toward his own fall, preceding his boss out of office when he would resign on October 10, 1973, after being charged with accepting $100,000 in graft—was another example of the disappearing meridian between televised sports and news. But just as important for Cosell was that after Gifford's frat-boy interview with Richard Nixon in 1971, he could balance the scales and do his own brown-nosing of a high-level politician; thus, he lassoed the veep before a November game in Baltimore, horning in as Agnew was being shown about the locker room by Colts owner Carroll Rosenbloom. Testing the veep's sense of humor, he facetiously asked, to Rosenbloom's horror, "Tell me, sir, what is your position on Jewish ownership?" Knowing the game Cosell was playing, Agnew played it straight. With a twinkle in the eye, he replied, "There's no statute that bans them, Howard." Cosell, not through, went on, loudly enough for the whole room to overhear, "Then your conclusion, Mr. Vice-President, is that this team is saddled with too many blacks?" Agnew didn't flinch. "I didn't put it *that* way, Howard," he said. "What I said was that an intelligent re-examination of the quota is in order."[4]

Actually, Meredith had been braver, and funnier, with his dry wit. Introduced to Agnew, he said to him, "Well, hello, Mr. Vice-President. I luv ya, but I didn't vote for ya. But here's someone who luvs ya and probably did, Frank Gifford." And, referencing a current, short-lived fad, Spiro Agnew wristwatches, he quipped when Cosell threw it to him, "I hope y'all noticed that the vice-president was wearing a Howard Cosell wristwatch."[5]

With the overlap between sports and pop culture unmistakable, it did not take long for ABC to use its home-field advantage to begin cross-promotion of its prime-time schedule, arranging with the entertainment division to parade network stars through the booth, pretending to be football fans but there to make small talk to pimp their shows. This free in-house publicity did a great deal to spark ABC's surge in the ratings, and its shedding of the "third network" slur it had endured for two decades.

Having seen him make guest shots on other networks' shows, ABC honchos had to wonder why Cosell wasn't doing so on his own company's turf. Soon, he was, clad in his ABC sports jacket, playing himself on the sitcom version of Neil Simon's magnificent play *The Odd Couple*, which despite the considerable talent and chemistry of Tony Randall and Jack Klugman was barely afloat in the ratings. While he couldn't do much about the ratings, he left his mark elsewhere—twice, in the September 1972 episode "Big Mouth" and the January 1975 episode "Your Mother Wears Army Boots"—the latter with a cameo by Roone Arledge.

These stints were more than memorable; scripted to be the foil of Klugman's schlubby Oscar Madison, his brilliantly hammy and pretentious self-portraits were a splendid mirror of the real-life chasm between Cosell and Dick Young, albeit with warm and fuzzy endings that would never come about in real life. Randall, who had known Cosell when they had both lived in Peter Cooper Village, would recall that while he never had encountered acting that bad, he never enjoyed acting with anyone as much. In microcosm, that abstraction could explain the unlikely success of Howard Cosell.


THE SAD decline of Jackie Robinson made him realize how paltry his beefing about *MNF* was. Robinson had walked his last mile in pain. At only fifty-three, he was debilitated by severe diabetes and heart disease. Nearly blind and painfully stooped, he was in terrible shape, hair completely white. At the same time, he had lost his oldest son, Jackie Jr., who had been wounded in Vietnam but then fell into serious drug addiction. He had turned his life around, becoming a drug counselor, but was killed in a car accident in June 1971. Cosell was there when Jackie buried him.

Robinson had had his own travails as an elder statesman. A man of contradictions, he was more conservative politically than many in the civil rights movement expected him to be, having emerged as a "Rockefeller Republican" in New York, where the governor, Nelson Rockefeller, helped land him a high visibility job as vice president at Chock full o'Nuts. He also endorsed Richard Nixon against John Kennedy in 1960 and backed the Vietnam War, and to many young blacks he was an anachronism, though he had founded the first black-owned bank in Harlem. And never did he give an inch crusading for the cause of integration that had made him a saint. Before the second game of the 1972 World Series in Cincinnati, barely able to walk but smiling broadly, he threw out the ceremonial first pitch and was presented with a plaque in honor of the twenty-fifth anniversary of the year he made the big leagues; his eyes still burning with the same intensity, he strode to the microphone and in a clear voice said, "I'm going to be tremendously more pleased and more proud when I look at that third base coaching line one day and see a black face managing in baseball." Only nine days later, his voice and massive heart were stilled by a fatal heart attack in his home in Stamford, Connecticut, the one that Cosell had urged him to move to.

Robinson seemed to be about the only human besides Emmy who could instantly command Cosell's attention. Back in the midsixties, through his lobbying, Robinson was given the job of analyst on ABC's Monday night baseball series. Lou Volpicelli was the director, and he, play-by-play man Chris Schenkel, Robinson, and Cosell, the pregame host, shared first-class accommodations on plane rides to the games.

"It could become very uncomfortable with Howard," he says, "because he would have two or three martinis and get bombed, then he'd pick the most attractive stewardess and a typical conversation would ensue—'Lovely lady, as I feast my eyes on your beautiful bosom, I noticed you looked at me with desire, but I have to save myself for Emmy.' Chris would squirm in his seat, completely embarrassed. So we developed a code. Whenever Howard would have a few and do that, Chris would say, 'Lou, it's time.' And I would tell Jackie to go ask Howard a baseball question. Because whenever Jackie said anything to him, Howard would drop what he was doing and talk baseball with Jackie. And the stewardess would mouth to Chris and me, 'Thank you.' "[6]

Cosell then rarely went a week without speaking with Robinson. He was in Washington, D.C., when Robinson died, on his way to giving a dinner speech. Throwing out his script, he instead spoke off the cuff for an hour about Robinson, relating the near-life-changing experience of first meeting him and how only months before, at Gil Hodges's funeral, as he had watched Jackie enter the church, he saw him as his mind's eye always would, as the daring young man "swinging around first in that wide turn, tantalizing the outfielder." His voice quavering, he closed,

"There is only one word to describe Jackie Robinson and that is 'uncon-querable.'" Just days later, after the funeral at New York's majestic River-side Church overlooking the Hudson River, and after a long, sad procession to a cemetery in Brooklyn, he and Don Ohlmeyer produced a half-hour documentary for the local New York ABC affiliate. Ohlmeyer recalls it in a blur, with Cosell virtually doing it all off the cuff, narrating clips and conducting interviews with some of the surviving Brooklyn Dodgers. When it was done, deeply affected, Ohlmeyer had to tell him, "Howard, that was incredible." There was no response. Looking closer, he saw that Cosell was quietly sobbing.[7]

Cosell became progressively more bitter about baseball for inching ahead on Robinson's legacy, refraining from hiring blacks in management and as field managers. In *Cosell*, which was in production when Jackie died, he groused: "What did baseball do for Jackie Robinson? I'll tell you. It tortured him, tormented him. What he had to live with was the great-est debasement of a proud human being in my lifetime."[8]

But if the end of Jackie Robinson's life was a primer in how transitory fame really is, and how permanent pain can be even for the greatest of men, the lesson would fade as soon as Cosell's next assignment. There would be yet another round of self-absorbed self-torture, over the slight-est, often most nonsensical of matters. At those times, the serenity Rob-inson found on his deathbed was enough to make Howard Cosell feel envious, not to mention that, at this stage of his own life, he understood that while he had made more of himself than he ever could have dreamed, he could never be Jackie Robinson.

WHEN NOT on the road for a game or TV shoot, Cosell was basically a hermit, stewing in his own neuroses. He chose mainly to hole up in his small office on the twenty-fourth floor of ABC's glassine corporate head-quarters on "TV Row," at 1330 Avenue of the Americas, where the mar-tinis and highballs flowed like water as he played gin rummy with regular cronies, including Chet Forte and Lou Volpicelli, the latter of whom recalls that "Howard would bum every cigarette I had—that's why I haven't smoked one since 1971."[9] Other than for football games or boxing matches, he would leave the building usually only to hop a limo to Café des Artistes, next door to ABC's West Side studio, where he would invariably find a celebrity of some sort to down martinis with and hold court at the bar before making his way through a back-door entrance to the studio for his local radio and TV sports shows.

Whenever his legs would hit the street, large crowds would inevitably envelop him. "It was an incredible sight," says Frank Deford. "I don't think I ever was with him when we were walking on the street, even for literally thirty seconds, that people wouldn't just grow around him, even if only to say, 'Hey, Howard!' or 'Howard, tell it like it is!' It would be a cross-section of humanity. Construction workers, businessmen, housewives, kids, cabdrivers yelling out their windows. And never, ever did I hear anyone say something nasty to him. That could be the definition of a star. He turned people's heads. He was bigger than life. And Howard really began to believe that it meant he was beloved. Well, he was, as a famous person. That's the nature of fame. But many of those same people would still go home, turn on the TV, and curse him out. He had won people over, but not with anything you could call love."[10]

Not surprisingly, Cosell's most contented moments came on the semiregular occasions when he was invited to testify before one or another congressional panel investigating some issue or other related to sports, such as baseball's reserve clause, the NFL's antitrust exemption status, and a proposed commission to regulate abuses heaped upon athletes by sports leagues and Olympic officials. In 1972 and 1973 alone, he appeared twice at Senate Commerce Committee hearings in favor of an omnibus bill to create a National Sports Commission to oversee amateur and pro sports, and for a similar bill before the House Special Committee on Education and Labor. In this he was a useful prop, a high-visibility name who could drum up a few headlines and snippets of film on the news about these issues. The old labor lawyer, when paged for one of these dates, would come running. He would saunter through the halls of the Capitol with an accruing mob of press and tourists in his train, then perform a one-man theater piece in stentorian soliloquies about the arrogance of baseball's owners led by their latest marionette, Bowie Kuhn.

A lawyer who lived near him up in Connecticut, Kuhn was a jumbo-sized, bland man who had become one of his favorite pincushions, by serving the interests of baseball's "carpetbagging" owners and for his timidity in failing to put men who had labored in the Negro Leagues into the Hall of Fame. For such perceived lack of courage, Cosell heaped scorn on Kuhn, branding him as "stiff and aloof, a man who took himself terribly seriously," "not a forceful personality" nor "a particularly shrewd man," and "absorbed with personal publicity," and saying that "while he is ceremonial, he has little impact"—the exact opposite, in Cosell's eyes, of "Alvin 'Pete' Rozelle," with whom pro football's success was, he said, "inextricably interwoven."[11]

Through all these battles with the sports establishment, he could testify in great moral dudgeon. He would wallow in the attention of a captive audience, blissfully unconcerned that those congressional hearings were mere dog and pony shows. Because while they did create a seed of fear among sports leagues, nothing materially changed in the sports labor structure until a whole new strategy evolved, with some important help from Cosell's microphone. For example, there was the case of Curt Flood, with whom Cosell for a time was nearly as fixated as he had been with Muhammad Ali, and for the same reasons. For Cosell, any cause engendered by a black athlete came full circle back to Jackie Robinson. It was reflexive. Though the reserve clause was an equal-opportunity headlock, affecting ballplayers of all hues, that Flood was black seemed to lend it an element of added shame; his crusade was a progressive step toward the civil freedom and protection implied by Robinson's arrival but deflected ever since by the baseball ruling class—full freedom, not just that given as a concession to public pressure.

No one had seriously challenged the reserve clause until Flood, the speedy veteran outfielder who after he was traded by the St. Louis Cardinals to the lowly Philadelphia Phillies in 1969 refused to report, his opinion that the Phillies management was blatantly racist. Cosell took to the air on his radio shows and to the lectern at his dinner and college lectures to mount rigorous, highly eloquent arguments in defense of Flood, whom he encouraged to file a $1 million lawsuit against baseball—Kuhn by name—seeking to invalidate the reserve clause, which Flood likened to slavery, though he carried the metaphor too far when he called himself a "well-paid slave," finding scant sympathy from the public or an already hostile media that had been bred and conditioned as baseball yes-men.

Flood made it all the way to the U.S. Supreme Court, losing his case in 1972 by a 5–3 vote that upheld the antitrust exemption, and with it the reserve clause. Legal scholars—Cosell among them—were rightly outraged by the ruling, pointing out that Justice Harry Blackmun's majority opinion all but admitted that antitrust exemptions were tenuous, that baseball was indeed interstate commerce for purposes of the act and the exemption was an "anomaly." Cosell reviled the ruling as "egregious" and "an embarrassment to the court," and pronounced himself "very much disturbed" by it.[12] In this he had a real effect on the unexpected fallout from the decision, which with its shaky legal and logical reasoning further galvanized and sharpened the focus of the players' union under the tenacious leadership of the pugnacious former labor lawyer Marvin Miller.

Smartly circumnavigating the courts and the congressional hearing rooms, Miller worked the labor law back road. Soon, by the midseventies, more players would dare to claim free agency rather than play for their teams, and would be able to take their cases to binding arbitration. That would be when players' unions in other sports began to make the same strides as their baseball brethren, antitrust exemptions notwithstanding. So if Cosell's high-profile meanderings into brightly lit congressional hearing rooms weren't pivotal, or even very helpful in changing the world according to his precepts, they were surely pivotal and helpful to *him,* in that the overheated reaction he would get, the way he could hold court in the cafeteria of the Capitol building, regaling congressmen, proved to be a much needed relief from his chores having to be a burlesque comic, foil and straight man for Dandy Don and Muhammad Ali. Here, he was, finally, a *serious* person. And that was just enough to submerge his insecurities—at least until the next Monday night game.

Says Lou Volpicelli, "It wasn't just that when he entered a room he wanted every head to turn; he wanted every head to turn and every ear to listen. There was one thing Howard couldn't take, and that was being ignored. And he never was, no matter where he was."[13]

There would be endless teases by him over the next decade about

running for the Senate. Addressing the graduating class at Annapolis in
May 1974, he told the midshipmen that 1976 might be the year he
declared his candidacy for the seat held by New York senator James
Buckley. "There are not 10 people in the United States better qualified to
run for the Senate than Howard Cosell," he characteristically added.
And, to the *New York Times*, "Watching the Watergate hearings, I felt
like screaming out, 'Let me question these guys.' I watched Watergate
drag out and drag out, saw the Congress languishing, afraid to take a
position that seemed to me obvious and necessary with regard to the
President. I just decided I wanted to be in the Senate."[14]

Showing he knew how *that* game was played, he said he had "talked
with a number of important people in the Democratic party" and one
gubernatorial candidate in the state had "already offered me his organization." Summing up, he seemed to try out a campaign theme: "In this
age of Watergate, I might be exactly right for the voters." And yet, when
push came to shove, when filing deadlines loomed, "might" remained the
operative word. He would put it off, again and again, well into the *next*
decade, to the point where only he didn't take his vows to run as a running gag.

THERE CAN be no overestimating how unique, and even unprecedented, Cosell's fame was by the middle of the 1970s. He had done no
less than make himself a one-man industry by turning scabrousness into
an endearment.

His guest shots also kept galloping apace. That year, beside *The Odd
Couple*, he made the scene on the molto hip, if a bit dated, *Rowan and
Martin's Laugh-In* in December, and sat on Johnny Carson's hallowed
couch no fewer than five times between January and June. The next year,
he would do *The Sonny and Cher Comedy Hour*—coming away complaining loudly about how rude and unimpressed with him Cher was. Yet
as oversized as he had become, his resentments were still petty, and he
could not help but vent about them, as he did in *Cosell*.

By doing so, of course, he was aware that he was opening the door for
greater abuse from the media, especially in their reviews of the work.

And indeed, while there were some raves—The *Chicago Tribune Book World* enthused that it "comes on fang first" and was "as entertaining as its subject" with "not a dull page in it," and the *Cleveland Plain Dealer* called it "pure, unrelenting Cosell from cover to cover"—the sporting press generally took it apart. The sharpest blade was dropped by *Sports Illustrated's* Jonathan Yardley, for whom it was "390 interminable pages" of "bluster and bathos" that did "little more than massage the author's elephantine ego . . . Much of Cosell's notoriety rests on his penchant for sesquipedalian oratory. Transferred to the printed page, its grammatical deficiencies become embarrassingly evident . . . His prose, like his television commentary, butchers the English language, a delicate instrument that deserves better."[15]

In truth, the book was nowhere near so embarrassing; if anything, Cosell's lawyerly language narcotized pages that could have, in fact, used some good egotistical bombast, yet, tellingly, it was reviewed unfavorably when compared with Jim McKay's memoir released at around the same time. That Cosell could never win a popularity contest with the now-sainted McKay was, as he believed, patently unfair, since it further tainted any sense of objectivity about his work. Around that time, Gary Deeb, the acerbic television critic of the *Chicago Tribune*, outdoing even Dick Young in anti-Cosell bile, labeled him a "pimp" and a "prostitute." Hilary, who after graduating from Manhattan's exclusive Bedford Prep School was now living in Evanston, Illinois, just outside the Windy City, while attending Northwestern University, was so upset—rightly—that when she told her father, he threatened to sue for defamation.[16]

At the same time, he did not drop the grudge he had against the media in general, which was only growing worse. In a 1974 article about him in the *New York Times Magazine*, he let his frustration show, admitting, "I've been very hurt by writers, and I know I'll be hurt again. Christ, all I've done in my life is try to bring a little journalism to sports broadcasting."[17] His best recourse, he reckoned, was to hoist the press on its own petard, using the very platform offered by them in the mad rush for headline-grabbing interviews with him. When he agreed to a long *Playboy* interview in May 1972, "the fustian oracle of sports," as the magazine dubbed him, was appropriately fustian, windily allowing that "I really believe I'm the best [sportscaster], for I have sought to bring to the American people a sense of the athlete as a human being and not as a piece of cereal-box mythology."[18]

MOST STRIKING about Cosell's tirades were that in the process he had to reduce himself just by mentioning people whose arc he had long since eclipsed. Dennis Lewin could never figure out why Cosell was so fixated on what was being written about him. "When he'd tell me that some paper from a hick town had ripped him, I'd always say, 'Howard, who cares?' But he did. He'd say he didn't, but he did. And Howard really was to blame for a lot of it. It was a double-edged sword, because Howard was not shy about going after people in the press. He'd fight back, and it became an ongoing war, a vicious cycle."[19]

Always, the most obvious example of this dynamic was his contretemps with Dick Young. But he would even fall out during this time with Red Smith, his old confrere and dinner mate. By the midseventies, the eloquent, elegant dean of the press box had become to Cosell a dinosaur, his delicate prose all but obsolescent, his loathing of Muhammad Ali near corrosive.

Smith at the same time had come to pity Cosell, regarding him as a man being eaten alive by his insecurities, at the expense of the talent and depth he rarely displayed now. Smith was with his daughter at a restaurant one night when he saw Cosell at a table, dining by himself—a sight that was becoming more common all the time. When Cosell came over to their table, Smith's daughter muttered, "Oh, no," under her breath. Smith then engaged him in a few minutes of idle chatter. According to Ira Berkow's affectionate biography of Smith, when Cosell left, Smith told his daughter, "Don't be too hard on Howard. It's no fun to eat dinner alone."[20]

In print, his pity turned to hostility. Smith increasingly dug at Cosell. Interviewed by Chicago sportswriter Jerome Holtzman for his now classic 1974 book about the brotherhood, No Cheering in the Press Box, Smith said, "I'm not a psychologist, but I do know, for example, that a fellow like Howard Cosell is the braggart that he is because of a massive insecurity. He has to be told every couple minutes how great he is because he's so insecure. And if you don't tell him, he tells you. He can't help this." As always, Smith was preternaturally wise and perceptive, but at the same time he would also drop mocking barbs into his columns about Cosell, à la Dick Young. "Cosell doesn't broadcast sports," one went, "he broadcasts Cosell," adding at another time, "It doesn't surprise me to see Howard pre-empt God. But I still believe God does the creating and not ABC."[21]

Smith's remarks in the Holtzman book burned his former friend. Not long after the quotes came out, he had it out with Smith on a plane ride. Smith, who himself admitted privately that his pseudo-analysis of Cosell's psyche was "gossipy" and that seeing it in print was "a little embarrassing," recalled that Cosell sat himself down next to him and brought up the quotes. In his recollection, Cosell wound up *agreeing* with the analysis, telling him, "You're probably right," to which Smith said, "I think I am right."[22]

In Cosell's hindsight, it was just the reverse. "In effect," he would say, "Red was apologizing," and insisted that he was big enough to tell Smith, "It's not necessary, Red. You have every right to say what you like about me. I have the same right to say what I think about you." Whoever said what, when they got to Las Vegas, they found they were both staying at Caesars Palace, and in adjoining rooms. As Cosell told it, Smith came by his room for drinks and hoisted a toast: "Here's to Jerry Holtzman!"[23]

But things never were good between them again, and soon Cosell was delivering his own rabbit punches. In 1980, he would even lump Smith in with his worst enemy, confronting a writer for a sports magazine, Robert Friedman, with a tirade that went: "You call yourself a sportswriter? Aren't you ashamed to be in the same profession with the likes of Dick Young and Red Smith?" According to Friedman, "He pronounced these names with all the venom normally reserved for mass murderers or incompetent referees."[24] Cosell openly criticized Smith for being "locked inside the sports establishment," something he felt was proven when in 1979 Smith was one of the few American writers who would travel to South Africa for a heavyweight fight, at a time when the boycott of the segregationist government in Johannesburg was in full force.

For Cosell that was another great moral issue. In Baltimore at the time to cover the World Series, he was at the bar of his hotel with a clutch of reporters when he began to tear into Smith. Incredulous about an interview Smith had given on NBC, he bellowed that the writer "saw no evidence of censorship [in South Africa]. I couldn't believe my ears!" He concluded—fallaciously—that Smith was "on the take" from the promoter of the bout, Bob Arum, whom Cosell vilified as "the apostle of apartheid." That did it for Smith. While he continued to chide him with a velvet glove—"I find it possible to tune him out"—he was more pointed in 1981 on a CBS *60 Minutes* show where he was being profiled. When asked about Cosell by Morley Safer, he puckishly answered: "I've tried very hard to like Howard—and I've failed."[25] It has endured as one of the great Cosell aphorisms.

In a sign of the attrition in Cosell's own generation, Smith died in 1982 at age seventy-six. Others were about to, and even near their deaths the great reporters could not resist swiping at Cosell. Jimmy Cannon, for example, was near the end of the line in 1973, soon to die at age sixty-four, and had not grown any fonder of Cosell. Indeed, his most famous shot at Cosell—"This is a guy who changed his name, put on a toupee, and tried to convince the world he tells it like it is"—was also the most mean-spirited, Cannon apparently not aware that Cosell had reclaimed his immigrant grandfather's heritage. For Cosell, the implication to the contrary was a wound that silently bled as many repeated the line ad infinitum.

According to legend, Cannon also had a conversation on a plane with Cosell, who harangued him the entire ride about how Cannon and his cohorts had made his life miserable. As the plane was landing, Cosell was said to have eased off a bit, telling Cannon, "But we shouldn't be fighting, Jimmy. After all, there's really just a handful of us that really care about the important things in sports. Isn't that right, just a handful of us?" Cannon looked him in the eye. "That's right, Howard," he said, "except that there's one fewer than you think."[26]

COSELL COULD take some cold comfort that the old-guard sportswriting fraternity was withering, and that younger writers who were gradually replacing them were more kindly disposed, or at least neutral about him. The new guard, which included Tony Kornheiser, Peter Gammons, and the hard-living, ill-fated Lewis Grizzard, had as many problems with their forebears as he did. Another, Joe Marshall, was hired by *Sports Illustrated* on the basis of his master's thesis at Columbia University's Graduate School of Journalism—the subject of which was Howard Cosell, who readily agreed to be interviewed for it. (In 1971, the paper was bought by and run as an article in *Esquire.*)

Concurrently, Dick Young was becoming slightly unwrapped, the root cause being the omniscient influence TV now had on sports, a new world order that, to him, wore Cosell's face. When television cameras were allowed into the dugout in the seventies, Young wanted the writers to go on strike unless baseball would let a writer sit in the dugout as well; no one took him up on it. But not far behind in derangement was Cosell, who seriously advised Phil Pepe that he should quit the *Daily News* rather than work for Young. "Howard would always tell me, 'Little Philly, how can you work for a man like that?' He wanted me to take a stand. I said, 'Howard, I'd be glad to. Will you take care of my family?' That sort of thing never occurred to him."[27]

EVEN THOUGH Cosell was roundly attacked by sportswriters, he was alternately pursued and feared by other networks. After the Munich Olympics, he was scheduled to go on *The Tonight Show,* but was dropped since it was so close to the start of a new *Monday Night Football* season. "You're getting too much publicity," Carson's producer told him, and NBC "[didn't] want to add to it."[28] Taking the injunction in stride, he said, he called Carson's late-night rival Dick Cavett and went on that show instead. But what Cosell could never fully comprehend was his own fatal inability to keep even allies from turning into enemies. For one, he wound up at odds with the writer he hired to ghostwrite *Cosell.* His first choice for the job was Gay Talese, the *Esquire* essayist whose profiles of an elusive Frank Sinatra and a sad and lonely Joe DiMaggio, among others, practically created the "gonzo" journalism of the era. But Talese, who had recently written the best seller *Honor Thy Father,* begged off— perhaps having heard of other writers who had regretted getting close to Howard Cosell.

Talese instead recommended David Halberstam, whose Vietnam reportage for the *New York Times* had won him a Pulitzer Prize and who was finishing up his future best-selling Vietnam proscription *The Best and the Brightest*. Halberstam was receptive to the Cosell book, mainly because it would pay six figures. However, when they met at Talese's house, they took an immediate disliking to each other. "The kindest word I can use to describe Howard on that night is overbearing," Halberstam would later recall. "He knew everyone. He not only knew them, they were dear friends," and "he had the inside story on everything. No one else managed to talk. Howard dominated because he *had* to dominate; it seemed to mean so much to him. That night, it was exhausting to be with him."[29]

Halberstam during the night asked him about Jim Bouton, the ex-Yankee pitcher and author of the irreverent tell-all baseball classic *Ball Four*, who had just landed a job on New York television as a sportscaster. Cosell, not kindly, said, "Jimmy is, I am afraid . . . a *small* property," using industry terminology that nonetheless left Halberstam offended, never having heard a journalist—or any man outside of a raging bigot—ever call another a "property." He asked pointedly, "Howard, are you a property, too?"

"Yes," he replied icily. "But I'm a big one."

Halberstam thought he was indeed a big one, though "property" would not have been the word he used. As he remembered, "The next day, independent of each other, Howard and I both called Talese to tell him that collaboration on a book was not a good idea."

Cosell finally hired Mickey Herskowitz, a sportswriter of note for the *Houston Chronicle*. Herskowitz did little on the manuscript that Cosell would accept; most every sentence was rewritten, with Cosell getting some in-house assistance from Frank Gifford's stat man on *Monday Night Football*, a new young ABC Sports staffer named Terry O'Neil, who helped him with the editing. This led Herskowitz to wonder just why he was there, the only seeming reason being for Cosell to boast that he could buy, then ignore, a sportswriter.

In 1979, Cosell recalled that "I'd never written a book before, but I sat at the typewriter and went through hell and did it. My apparent collaborator, Mickey Herskowitz, just made suggestions." Even so, if he was not big enough to give the writer a coauthor byline on the cover, he added a one-line sop on the title page reading: "With the editorial assistance of Mickey Herskowitz." That, however, may have been a sweetener, since Herskowitz had signed to ghostwrite two books for him, an agreement Cosell broke when he began work on the follow-up, *Like It Is*, without him. Rather than hold him to the contract, Herskowitz let it slide, grateful for his brush with the Cosell legacy, still wondering what he had done to earn it and acknowledging that Cosell "has a mind that's out there where the meter doesn't register, and his standards are so far above the average person's that when the book was finished, he had each *page* put under a plastic cover, as if he was submitting it to a museum."[30]

Whatever Cosell's eccentricities, his eponymous book sold over two hundred thousand copies in hardcover, was a best seller for six months, and earned him over $300,000 just that year alone. *Like It Is*, meanwhile, followed in 1974, sans a coauthor credit; instead, there was a brief but intriguing dedication to his salesman-turned-executive son-in-law. It read: "I would like to acknowledge the assistance of Peter Cohane, without whose efforts, patience and help this book could not possibly have been written." Thus did Cohane serve a purpose, that of allowing Cosell to boast that no sportswriter, or any other writer but himself, was involved in the book. When it too became a best seller, his point was made and he could log another victory for the gifted one—at least in his own mind, the only place where a scoreboard for such things existed.

COSELL'S IMPULSES during the 1970s were governed by his pathological inability to let slide others' contrary opinions, or even their innocent mistakes, as if by flogging them he had dibs on being the ultimate judge of human behavior. All it really did was bring him scorn. Wearing the same ABC blazer as Cosell guaranteed other broadcasters little if any loyalty from him. One, the *Wide World of Sports* car-racing analyst Chris Economaki, has no fond memories of Cosell, recalling him for "an enormous and monumental ego," and saying that he "may have been the most pompous man I've ever met."[31]

For years, Economaki bore the scar of being ridiculed by him for a long-forgotten mistake Economaki made in an interview with Cale Yarborough. Though he could hardly believe a man with no more than a middling grasp of automobile racing could be so censorious, Cosell, he said, "never let me forget that." A while later, Economaki was at an ABC Christmas party. Seeing Cosell there, Economaki's wife asked to be introduced. He complied. "Howard," he told him, "for some inexplicable reason my wife wants to meet you." Economaki, with great pride, beams, "It pissed him off to no end. He really took it personally."

Cosell's legendary insecurity clearly played a role in the resentment and suspicion he had for fellow broadcasters, and especially his fellow ABC broadcasters. Never convinced that he was on safe ground, always seeing conspiracies behind every door—seeming, on a smaller scale, much like Richard Nixon, whose resignation in August 1974 was the ultimate price to pay for such paranoia, and a cautionary tale for Cosell if only he could see the parallel—it was as if he hoped that badmouthing cohorts behind their backs would cause doubt about them that would tip the scales more his way. This was clear from the endless backbiting of Don Meredith and Frank Gifford. But Lou Volpicelli, often the receptacle of such trash talk, witnessed Cosell's similar troubles with Jim McKay and Chris Schenkel, who not incidentally were ABC's top sports anchors.

"They had perfectly good professional relationships with Howard," says Volpicelli, "but neither Jim nor Chris was ever comfortable with Howard. And those two were the nicest guys in the world." Even for them, Cosell didn't make it easy to like him. They, like all ABC Sports stars, knew he was sniping at them behind their backs. Thus, the best thing to do was to steer clear of him, lest they give him ammunition to use against them. Besides which, Volpicelli notes, "they were so different than Howard, there was no common ground. Chris was from Indiana, he never 'got' Howard, and there was no love lost there. You could see that on those plane rides with Jackie Robinson in the sixties. And Jim, he was a very classy man, a poet, everything Howard wasn't. So Howard really had just two people besides Emmy that he could be friends with, Chet Forte and me."[32]

One perhaps telling footnote to Cosell's tepid relationship with McKay, the man who had outshone him in Munich, is that in the latter's 1998 autobiography, *The Real McKay*, there was not a single mention of the name of Howard Cosell, who had died but three years before. This raises the question of whether McKay was slyly exacting payback for some unpleasant moments between them in a way that *really* would have gotten to Cosell: by making him conspicuously disappear from an important memoir about the world of sports that Cosell knew perhaps too well. If so, it proved that Cosell could still haunt the sports world, even without being here or being mentioned.

# 14

## "DOWN GOES FRAY-ZHUH! DOWN GOES FRAY-ZHUH! DOWN GOES FRAY-ZHUH!"

THE SOCIETAL evolution of the early 1970s was emphatic. As if with a common imperative to distance the previous decade—punctuated metaphorically by a peaceful Woodstock and a violent Altamont—few seemed interested in marches or grand political designs. And while there would be fresh episodes in which bullets were fired at presidents, this was a time when most Americans wanted simply to take a few deep breaths in uncluttered peace.

There was no more vivid example of this retrenchment than Muhammad Ali, whose battles with the government and affiliation with the Black Muslims paled before the greater drama of his quixotic comeback to the ring. To many of his old enemies, Ali was now almost teddy-bear-like, an eminently sympathetic and compelling figure, and more so because of his heroic defeat at the hands of Joe Frazier.

The inescapable conclusion from their work in the ring since was that both men left a lot—perhaps too much—in Madison Square Garden on that storied night. In the interim, both men had taken their lumps, big ones. Ali, fighting frequently, won three more bouts in 1971, six in 1972. All were carried by *Wide World of Sports* with Cosell at the mike, and though none of these fights was especially memorable, they did prove that Ali was now mortal, particularly one in which the light-heavyweight champ Bob Foster cut him over the eye. Ali marched on, his twelve-round technical knockout of Jimmy Ellis in Houston on July 26, 1971, technically making him a champ again, of the lower-tier NABF.

That was followed by a bout four months later, also in the Astrodome, against the once-feared, now-porcine Buster Mathis. Having seen that both fighters were grossly out of condition, Cosell ventured that the fight should not have been licensed. Calling the fight for a delayed broadcast on *Wide World*, he derided both fighters for being woefully out of shape. When Mathis, who provided comic relief by reacting to Ali's now gauche "shuffle" with a pathetic, blubber-bouncing version of his own, finally went down in round twelve, Cosell scorned the entire affair as a sham, saying "the highest standards of professionalism had not been observed by Ali."[1] On the ABC replay of the bout, Mathis was ridiculed by over-dubbed songs like "Help Me Make It Through the Night."

Cosell again took Ali to task for lowering himself, and Ali, who took a beating in the media for it, seemed to agree. He expressed no anger at ABC or Cosell for chaffing him, saying that *"Wide World of Sports* has been very good to me," adding obligatorily, "I'm gonna whup Cosell." Mathis, though, became the next Cosell target to threaten a lawsuit for libel, calling him "a cruel man," although he never went through with it.[2] Ali went on picking off whatever fighter wanted a piece of him while waiting for a rematch with Frazier, the heavyweight field being so thin that both Jerry Quarry and Floyd Patterson came back for a second helping of defeat.

That the thirty-seven-year-old Patterson was clearly inviting another terrible beating revived for Cosell residual feelings of pity for the inscrutable Patterson. Neither did it help that the fight, in late September 1972 at Madison Square Garden, came so soon after the Munich Olympics, since Cosell remained maudlin and testy. Even more so than the Mathis fight, this one, he opined, should not have been sanctioned. When Ali questioned Cosell's sentiment, the latter replied that he didn't want to see Patterson get hurt.

Ali promised he wouldn't, going on to say he only took the fight to aid Floyd, who he revealed was broke. Cosell was floored by that revelation, since he had believed that Patterson, unlike most fighters, had wisely looked after his money. Checking out Ali's assertion, he learned that the IRS had indeed taken almost all of Patterson's funds to pay his back taxes. Floyd took his licking, the fight being called as a technical knockout when the referee stopped it after the sixth round because of a cut over Floyd's eye. In fact, he would never again step into a ring, but that payday would help him survive, and in the future he would resurrect himself as chairman of the New York State Athletic Commission.

Cosell's coda about Patterson was less than wholly sympathetic. When he had interviewed Floyd after the fight, the battered fighter wanly said he would be open to another rematch "if the public will buy it." As Cosell would write, "That speaks for itself."[3]

THE NEXT fight of note, one that would alter the axis of the sport, was one that Joe Frazier believed would be a quick and easy payday for *him*, his opponent the rising but raw George Foreman in Kingston, Jamaica. Smokin' Joe had fought sparingly since the painful victory over Ali, and he considered Foreman a tune-up for the eventual rematch, as did most of the media corps, though not Cosell, who was ever more becoming a Foreman retainer, shamelessly so. On his radio shows he predicted Foreman would knock Frazier out, early, though the champ was a four-to-one betting favorite. When Cosell encountered Red Smith days before the fight, Smith thought Foreman might make it seven rounds before his demise. He asked what Cosell thought. "I think Foreman may kill him," he said. "Literally, may kill him."[4] Smith wondered if Cosell was feeling well.

In truth, Frazier's manager, Yancey Durham, had wanted to steer clear of the bigger, younger Foreman, and was concerned that Frazier took the fight only to make Ali pay for all the guff he had been giving Joe about the battering he had taken. As Cosell sized up Frazier, he was essentially as uncomplicated as his pulverizing left hook, but was more hurt than he let on by reigning as champ in a shadow, for which he blamed Ali, who had convinced a good many people that he was the real champ.

That might explain why Frazier made Ali wait while he took on Fore-man, a decision Cosell believed was folly. He threw all of his credibility behind Big George, gold-dusting him as "the American Dream." On the eve of the fight, held on January 22, 1973, there were only a few in Jamaica who gave Foreman a chance, but that did not deter Cosell, parading about his hotel in his Bermuda shorts, from telling everyone within earshot that the world was going to be shocked when Foreman knocked out Frazier in two rounds.

The significance of the Jamaican venue was nearly as great as that of the fight itself. It was chosen only for one reason: the infusion of money the island country's backers put up, provided by a small elite of million-aire capitalist businessmen in nonwhite, non-Anglo provinces in the vir-tual "banana republic." Although Jamaica had declared its independence in 1962, the ruling government still catered to a small coterie of native businessmen. One of the most privileged, Lucien Chen, owned a race-track and promoted boxing matches on the island, and when he guaran-teed $300,000, 42 percent of it for Frazier, 20 percent for Foreman, Jamaica had its first title fight.

Cosell would recall Kingston as a seething tinderbox, as "poverty-stricken, as ghetto-like a city as I have ever seen." He noted that "at sun-down the atmosphere is sick with an uneasy feeling" and "there is enormous tension between black and white . . . One rarely sees a white out alone at night."[5] The corrupt government, unlike the West Germans during the Olympics, put on not a happy face but a scowl and a gun belt to keep order. Hordes of club-wielding soldiers ringed the fighters' train-ing camps and the arena, arresting scores of natives who got too close as they strained for a look at Frazier or Foreman. Meanwhile, deep-pocketed American whites were treated like visiting royalty, while black high rollers were eyed suspiciously.

The entire milieu, Cosell opined, was "a whole new and utterly illogi-cal scene for a heavyweight championship fight," into which "came two black fighters and a horde of white sportswriters and tourists." Having been frozen out of the closed-circuit broadcast of Ali-Frazier, he wouldn't wait for another call that would not come. Preemptively, he removed himself because the promoters, astonishingly, were using aging actress-comedienne Pearl Bailey as a celebrity "analyst." The truth was, the blow-by-blow slot had been given from the start to Don Dunphy.

Cosell covered the fight on tape for *Wide World of Sports*, so indelibly that few even would be aware there *was* a call of the fight that wasn't his. This was a Howard Cosell in clover, one whose premonitions of an earth-shattering Foreman victory seemed to swell a preternatural conviction that he was the chosen herald of an apocalypse. He came to ringside at Kingston's National Stadium that night in a tux and with a strut, so pumped and full of anticipation that his hands shook uncontrollably. But his voice was clear as a mission bell. Angelo Dundee, who also believed Foreman would win, was at his side as a technical aide, but as always Cosell was working alone.

When the bell rang, the stunning consequences of Frazier's ill-advised decision were quickly revealed. Two minutes in, when Foreman first clocked Frazier with a stiff right hand, the tone was set. In another few seconds, Foreman would change boxing history, and so would Cosell. Rising to his feet, the microphone shaking violently in front of his mouth, he seemed possessed, his voice straining and gushing in cracking, metronomic time to the frantic images being stitched together by Chet Forte on America's television screens. The coup de grace, for him if not quite yet for Foreman, came when Frazier hit the canvas for the first time midway through round one. Instantly, Cosell bellowed, full-throated, "DOWN GOES FRAZIER! DOWN GOES FRAZIER! DOWN GOES FRAZIER!"

Frazier got up and continued, but not for long. As Cosell, with some self-serving hindsight, reported, "We have a minute left in this first round, and already this fight is proving out what some have expected. Oh! That left is getting in there, underneath . . . Frazier is dazed, he is getting hit again and again and again, the same head that was hit so often by Muhammad Ali!" Frazier went down again, got up, then returned to the mat for a third time, though he somehow survived the round. Then, in round two, Foreman was all over him again, sending him down once, then twice more, prompting Cosell to blare, "Frazier is down for the fifth time in this fight! . . . It's target practice for George Foreman—," then, finally, characteristically, "It is over! It is over! It is over in the second round. George Foreman is the heavyweight champion of the world!"[6]

By now, the walls of the stadium were shaking as the thirty-six thousand spectators were screaming, jubilant that Frazier—whom the natives resented for having beaten Ali—had suffered something akin to murder (indeed, Foreman had yelled to Yancey Durham after the last knockdown, "Stop it or I'm gonna kill him"). Cosell, scrambling into the ring as usual, spoke of "bedlam" reminiscent of the scene in Miami when Cassius Clay beat Sonny Liston. He then got to Foreman, whose first uttering as champion of the world was to say, "Thanks a million for your support. I'd like to credit this championship to Howard Cosell and people of that nature for going out and saying a lot of good things about me . . . So thanks a lot, Howard."

If Foreman could bask in the afterglow, so could Cosell. When most of America tuned in to *Wide World of Sports* the next Sunday for the replay, what would burrow into the pop culture was that trembling intonation of "DOWN GOES FRAZIER!"—which, in Cosell's nasal register, sounded like "DOWN GOES FRAY-ZHUH!" Almost four decades on, it is as classic a call as there has ever been in boxing. As Jerry Izenberg says, "Howard could rise to moments like that. When he stopped thinking of himself—if he didn't have to think about being Howard Cosell—he was a great reporter. Very few people can do what he did, paint a picture that can take you there. That moment happened so quickly, so shockingly. Joe Frazier had never been down. What else do you need to say—'*Down goes Frazier! Down goes Frazier! Down goes Frazier!*' But how many people would be able to do it that simply and say it all? With simplicity and emotion. Not once, not twice, but three times, because any less would be too thin and four times would be shtick.

"When Howard was in situations like that, when he had no time to think, when it was all instinct, he was the absolute best. I wish you would quote me on that."[7]


IN RETROSPECT, "Down goes Frazier" reset the boxing clock. Cosell was far from through, just as Ali wasn't. There were to be fabled moments left for each—far more profound ones for Ali—yet even now the portents were there that they were fighting an upstream current. Indeed, for Ali, a dual dim-out with Frazier seemed nothing but inevitable, and a return to the championship unlikely, as Foreman was in no particular hurry to defend his new belt; other than exhibitions, he would only fight twice over the next twenty-one months. Not only had Frazier's misstep wiped out the corpulent payday awaiting him and Ali for their rematch, Foreman seemed to portend a new era for boxing, in which its old lions were fading out.

Ali, in fact, would prove the point on March 31, 1973, in a fight he called a "tune-up," when he stepped into the ring against former Frazier sparring partner Ken Norton in San Diego and came out dazed, his face lopsided. Though it was not known during the fight, the muscle-bound Norton broke his jaw early on, turning Ali tame, though he not only went the full twelve rounds but won one judge over in the split-decision defeat. Cosell, calling the Saturday afternoon bout live on *Wide World of Sports*, had considered the match a "farce," believing the unorthodox, light-hitting Norton was "tailor-made" for Ali. But, as the fight went on and a listless Ali barely lifted a glove as Norton pummeled him, he found himself breathlessly ventilating as he had in Jamaica, swelling the air with verbal images of Ali being "battered all over the ring by Ken Norton!" In midfight, Joe Frazier, who sat ringside, leaned over toward Cosell and snickered, "Maybe they'll talk now about how much *I* took out of *him*," even as he was seeing his second big payday with Ali swirl down the drain.

When Cosell got to Norton in the ring, the victor wanted to know, "What do you say now?"

"Like most of the country," Cosell admitted, "I was wrong."

Somehow, when Ali had his say, he found it within him to twit Cosell, mumbling through his dislodged jaw, "Cosell, you're always wrong."[8]

To Cosell, that reflexive riff made it all sadder, and made him wonder if Ali was relieved, even if subconsciously, that he had lost, and that he could now retire in peace, which Cosell openly wished he would. Moreover, he saw the fight in shades of something far beyond it, the end of 1960s idealism. Recounting his thoughts at the time years later to Ali biographer Thomas Hauser, he said, "So many of Ali's fights had incredible symbolism, and here [was] Ken Norton, a former Marine, in the ring against the draft-dodger in San Diego, a conservative naval town. Richard Nixon had just been reelected with a huge mandate. Construction workers were marching through the streets supporting the war in Vietnam, which showed no sign of winding down."[9]

Of course, Ali did go back in the ring, insisting the loss was "a sign from God" to get more serious. To Cosell, that was not unlike his crony Frank Sinatra croaking out his nostalgic songs in concert. Neither did many along press row see Ali as anything but a hanger-on. Jimmy Cannon, for example, would be able to enjoy writing that Ali "has a big name and not much to defend it with . . . No one appreciated being a winner more than Muhammad Ali. He is a loser now, and they match old losers with young winners."[10]

Even so, with Ali having made fond memories and a farewell glimpse of him more marketable than anything the titular champion was doing, an Ali-Frazier rematch made economic sense, as a kind of elimination bout for the right to challenge Foreman. Understandably, both aging former champs were eager to get it on.

The match was set for January 28, 1974, at Madison Square Garden. Billed as "Super Fight II," it was a considerable stretch. In fact, the two men settled for a guarantee of $850,000 and 32.5 percent of the proceeds, the same terms as the first fight. And for a long while, ticket sales lagged, prompting both men to dust off their old bellicose shtick—which for Frazier was still real. Provoked by Ali's mocking insults, he revived the "Clay" taunts, in turn leading Ali to derrick him as "ignorant," which always touched a raw nerve with Joe.

As usual, Cosell had a part in the hype. Almost as prominent as the fight itself was the crazed melee that broke out in the ABC studio five days before the event. On that Saturday, Cosell would air a tape of their first fight in full for the first time on television. Ali and Frazier were asked to come to the set and offer their comments. Ali quickly consented, but Eddie Futch, who had become Frazier's manager after the recent death of Yancey Durham, held off, anticipating that Ali would turn it into a freak show with insults of his fighter. As Cosell recalled, "I gave my word that I would not allow that to happen," and that he would "cut Ali off at the first sign of a personal diatribe. And of course, my word was good enough for Joe."

When the two men arrived, Ali in a three-piece suit, Frazier in a tan leisure outfit, Dennis Lewin, the producer, sat them with Frazier in the middle flanked by Cosell and Ali, so as to have them in a tight two-shot. The discussion began polite and relaxed, with both men sharing some laughs. Ali jabbed Cosell, saying, "What are you agitatin' about? You always agitatin'." Then, suddenly, it was *Joe* who began "agitatin'." Ali was in midsentence explaining how he'd been hit by low blows "ninety times" in the fight when Frazier interjected, "That's when he went into the hospital, Howard. Remember?" It was a weird thing to say, given the years Ali had submitted Frazier's extended hospital stay as "proof" of who really won; indeed, Futch had stipulated that the subject be off-limits, which was why Ali responded, "Don't talk about the hospital, you're bringing up the hospital, I ain't gonna say nothin' about the hospital." Apparently thinking he'd touched a nerve, a smug Frazier persisted, "You don't wanna mention it?"

Ali, louder now, went on, "I went in the hospital for ten minutes. You went for a month." Frazier insisted, "I was resting. In and out." Ali countered, "That's embarrassing. I wasn't even gonna bring up the hospital. That shows how dumb you are." With the fuse now lit, Cosell tried to redirect their attention to the tape, but Frazier, no longer smiling, tossed off his earpiece, stood, and glowered over Ali, who for a split second seemed afraid. Looking up, he could only say, "Sit down, Joe."

As Cosell looked on helplessly, unable to do anything but stare, a foreboding figure in a long overcoat—it was Ali's brother, Rahaman—appeared, verbally challenging Frazier. Eddie Futch then rushed over and grabbed Frazier's arm, which Joe angrily yanked away. Ali at this point knew *he* would have to be the one to defuse a very tense situation. He may have actually saved his own life by not waiting to be attacked. Rather, he quickly shot to his feet, shouting comically, "Sit down—quick, Joe!" as he reached around Frazier's neck. Bull-like, Frazier wrapped his arms around Ali's middle and hurled him to the floor, whereupon they rolled around, half holding, half wrestling, as people from both camps streamed onto the set, mostly watching in shock as the melee gathered steam.

There was a strangely surreal, slow-motion quality to it, as everyone tried to determine if they were players in a staged farce or if it was an actual street fight on the studio floor. Cosell, still seeming stunned, began by trying to play it down. "Well, we're having a scene, as you can see," he began, unsteadily adding, "It's hard to tell whether it's clowning or for real . . . This kind of thing has been going on all along in terms of promotion of the fight." Then, progressively worried that Ali might get seriously hurt, his voice rose. "And this time it seems to be for real. Because Joe Frazier is really angry . . . It's a bad and an ugly scene."

After being pulled from Ali, Frazier stormed off the set, with Ali yelling at him, "You be on time!" Futch screamed not at Ali but at *Cosell*, blaming him for seating the fighters elbow to elbow. Cosell himself appeared to be feeling guilty and was overly sympathetic to Frazier, repeating several times that Joe was set off by Ali calling him ignorant, while never pointing out that Frazier had instigated the episode. Swiveling in his chair toward Frazier as he stalked out, Cosell tried to assuage his hurt feelings, weakly calling to him, "I'm sorry, Joe." Frazier, however, wasn't sorry. He told Futch in the limo outside, "Did you see how wide that nigger's eyes opened up? Now I really got him scared." ABC could not have been sorry, either. Immediately, interest in the upcoming bout spiked as debate sparked about whether the floor fight—for which Ali and Frazier were fined $5,000 each by the state athletic commission—was real or contrived. Dick Young, predictably, swore the latter was true, enraging Cosell.[11]

In truth, Ali *was* scared, but was smarter than Frazier on fight night. Having learned much from the first fight, Ali grabbed, held, and tied up Frazier. He fought only in spurts, peppering Frazier with enough head shots to rack up points. With Frazier stymied and waiting to uncork his left hook, long stretches went by with very little transpiring. Cosell, calling the fight on tape for *Wide World*, seemed close to yawning. "There's a realization among everybody that this is a bout between two past champions that is lacking much of the excitement of the previous fight," he noted. Ali, he said, was "raining blows upon Fraser's head" but "quite clearly without power," while Frazier "has shown nothing of what he showed in the first fight." In the end, Ali could crow; this time his was the glove raised in victory after twelve close rounds.[12]

Given the chance to modify his earlier harsh judgment that Ali was through when the paperback edition of *Cosell* came out a few months after the fight, he still had only limited praise for him. Super Fight II, he wrote, clearly proved that Ali was still the juice of the boxing game—the worldwide gate was over $8 million, the closed-circuit telecast seen by around a *billion* people, and the fighters would reel in nearly $3.5 million each—but Cosell still was not convinced Ali had another championship in him. "I remain convinced," he wrote, "that Ali will never touch George Foreman, vocally or otherwise," adding, "For the sake of all that he is, I hope that the ending is one of dignity."[13]

THE VICTORY enabled Ali to apply his "people's champion" argument, and update yet again the tired old racial slurs begun with Sonny Liston, with Foreman this time the receptacle. Such a match offered him the chance to be rewarded on a baronial scale. He intended to create a spectacle more lucrative than anything ever seen in the sport—if not in *sports*. Established promoters such as Bob Arum, Teddy Brenner at the Garden, Jack Kent Cooke, and Jerry Perenchio had to pass on the promotion, with no chance of getting it financed. That left the door open to a postmodern boxing hybrid of Nicely-Nicely Johnson and Super Fly named, aptly, Don King. A small-time promoter from Cleveland, King had ingratiated himself with Frazier, coming to Jamaica though having no part in the fight. When Frazier went down, King was one of the first into the ring to greet Foreman, embracing him and shrieking, "George, I told you so!" As King would cackle, "I came with the champion, and I left with the champion." Few knew who King was, but with his Falstaffian dimensions, finger-in-a-light-socket Afro, and trendy jive garb, he caught the eye of Hank Schwartz, president of Video Techniques, an electronics and satellite technology firm instrumental in closed-circuit broadcasts, which produced the theater telecast that night. Liking King's chutzpah, Schwartz made him his vice president.

The grimy details of King's past—he had killed two men as a street hoodlum in Cleveland, the first time getting off on grounds of self-defense, the second serving four years in prison, being sprung in 1971—were not necessarily debits in the age of up-the-establishment black movie icons. In fact, nothing prepared him better for the diabolical jungle that turned millionaires into maggots, screwing each other over to gain favor with fighters, than his prison experience. "I had to learn how to meditate in a room full of violent men . . . ," he once explained. "What a sight in the urinals. Prisoners sucking guards . . . Guards going down on prisoners. One man taking another's ass. Hell, man, you got to get your head in order. I read Karl Marx, a cold motherfucker. I learned a lot from him."[14]

Garrulous and obnoxious, covered in diamonds, with an earsplitting laugh and a tendency to mangle the language, he was an instant celebrity, his crackling battle cry of salvation "Only in America!" obscuring the character traits of a "slimy, reptilian motherfucker" who "would kill his own mother for a dollar"—a glowing testimonial that, a decade later, would come from heavyweight champion Mike Tyson, whose promoter at the time happened to be Don King.[15] Turning his sights on Ali, he read back to him the Black Muslim tenet of blacks coming to the aid of blacks, which he said *required* a black promoter for this fight. Heaping attention on the media, he made ample time for boxing columnists, literati dilettantes like Norman Mailer, who regarded King as a "genius," and, most importantly, the preeminent figure in TV sports.

Indeed, Cosell took a real liking to King, his opinion no doubt influenced by his eagerness to do the blow-by-blow for the closed-circuit telecast, which would be seen by even more eyes than had watched Ali-Frazier II. King was moving toward a position alongside Ali and Cosell as the most entertaining blowhards in sports. And so despite the fact that Ali's manager, Herbert Muhammad, detested King, Ali allowed him the chance to prove he could back up his boast of making possible a $10 million fight. Amazingly, King did.

His most effective quality was doggedness. He would journey far and wide for most of 1974, trying to re-create the Jamaica model of melding black government leaders and white money to bankroll a big fight—in this case, a *big* fight, as both Ali and Foreman were holding out for no less than $5 million each. Ultimately, King found what he wanted in a place few had heard of, Republic of Zaire, the former Belgian Congo, led by General Mobutu Sese Seko, who had seized power in the mid-1960s, forcing out European colonialists, his anti-Communist pose drawing the covert backing of the United States. As president, Mobutu put into place an African nationalism program that included annexing the country's lucrative copper and cobalt reserves and ordering the renaming of all its cities—the former capital of Leopoldville, now Kinshasa, would be the venue of the Ali-Foreman fight.

In 1974, Mobutu was supreme in his power, sitting on a personal fortune of $4 billion he had embezzled from foreign aid that never reached his citizens. Thus he could easily foot the $10 million King hit him up for, a small price to pay for showcasing his glittering rule. And King was only too happy to parrot propaganda about Zaire being "a fortress against imperialism and a spearhead for the liberation of the African continent." Certainly Ali and Foreman bought into the timely fable, or at least pretended they did in justifying taking their $5 million.

The fight, christened with political incorrectness "the Rumble in the Jungle," was made for September 25, at 3 A.M. so Americans could view it on closed-circuit—which, as a confidant of King, Cosell believed would surely include him, as blow-by-blow announcer. Perhaps not by coincidence, Cosell had nothing to say about the utter hypocrisy and blind greed of African American fighters and an African American promoter tacitly endorsing a murderous black dictatorship in the heart of Africa. Clearly, the indignant observations that he had leveled in Jamaica were now forgotten.

FROM THE early 1970s on, Cosell was a ubiquitous presence on the tube. Many of his appearances seemed at best tenuously connected to sports. The September 20, 1973, Billie Jean King–Bobby Riggs "Battle of the Sexes" tennis match, for example, was a slice of crass commercial cheese that he could dish up with little effort, and even call a sporting event. This was the second such tennis gender clash to hit the air, four months after the fifty-five-year-old Riggs—an admitted "male chauvinist pig" who wanted to "show those women who was boss"—had defeated the world's best distaff player, Margaret Court, on Mother's Day, to big ratings on CBS. But, in an ironic twist given his past hostility to Cosell, the promoter of the tennis match, Jerry Perenchio, who sold Riggs-King as a prime-time program, preferred that ABC cover it and that Cosell be the host.

The enormously popular Billie Jean King took Riggs's challenge, on the pretext of avenging Court and striking a blow for "women's lib" but not incidentally to generate publicity for her new pro World Team Tennis League. Her presence convinced Roone Arledge to pay for the match, and he agreed to exploit the women's rights cause, as well as to hype it as a winner-take-all match. Booked into the massive Houston Astrodome, a setting more accustomed to a championship fight, with a hundred-dollar top ticket, it featured free-flowing booze and celebrities, leading Cosell to look back on the event as "extraordinary, almost bizarre."[16]

King was carried onto the court before a screaming crowd of thirty-two thousand by four beefy men in football uniforms, Riggs in a chariot drawn by nubile females, both to the breathless commentary of Cosell. King's three-set blowout of the wheezing Riggs entrenched a new idiom into the sports broadcasting landscape—"trash sports," a trend that ABC would soon be investing heavily in. Soon to follow was a *Wide World of Sports* broadcast of motorcycle daredevil Evel Knievel's jumping over increasing stacks of cars, buses, and trucks, an event also covered by Cosell.

Such assignments—as opposed to purer, but low-level, sporting events not in his ken—were accepted with the only objectives being ratings and profits. Though he would advance the dubious proposition that the women's rights cause was served by the King-Riggs match, it was the latest ongoing proof that his game now was showbiz. To be sure, he kept his journalistic blade sharp as well, such as on a half-hour show he was given on Sunday afternoon, *The Howard Cosell Sports Magazine*, and he rarely deviated from serious matters hosting his Sunday evening radio show, *Speaking of Everything*, assembling panels that included athletes, actors, journalists, and politicians. Still, Cosell's main occupation, or rather preoccupation, was increasingly that of an entertainer, whose vanity was such that his second book, *Like It Is*, was mainly an extended, narcissistic Q&A session with Cosell answering questions asked by . . . himself.

He also decided his image necessitated a cosmetic fine-tuning that would make him seem younger and hipper. Repairing to the salon of Dean Martin's hairstylist, he had a new wig fitted, with a lower "hairline" to match his now long sideburns. Even if the result was not identifiable as any sort of human growth—and no less a target of shtick from Muhammad Ali, who would say Cosell "was a phony and that thing on your head is the tail of a pony"—Cosell showed it off on the TV variety show circuit. Within a few months, he was once again on *The Flip Wilson Show* and three Dean Martin *Celebrity Roast* episodes, easily exchanging good-natured insults with Hollywood dinosaurs and larding praise upon the guests of honor—no less than Bette Davis, Hugh Hefner, and Johnny Carson—as if he had known them forever.

Cosell seemed particularly well suited to those roasts, given that his first reflex always was the good-natured (or not) insult. Return fire from a big star was a high compliment and, as he saw it, a privilege he allowed them. These wonderfully savage rituals had begun in New York, at the Friars Club, the all-male showbiz fraternity where he was a member. When the Friars roasted him in the midsixties, Milton Berle asked, "Why are we honoring this man tonight? Did we run out of human beings?" No one laughed harder than Cosell, though his favorite jape was when Carson took to calling him "a legend in his own mind."

In Hollywood-speak, such ragging only meant that he belonged in that high-toned crowd, and indeed when he felt like name-dropping now, he could choose from virtually anybody, no matter how celestial. Even his elderly mother, hearing his stories of celebrities and seeing how much of one her son had become, took him up on his offer to take her away from the decaying boulevard of Eastern Parkway and pay for her to live in a posh New York hotel near the bright lights of Broadway. Here was where Nellie Cohen would live out her life.

In 1973, when Woody Allen's next movie, *Sleeper*, was released, Cosell was seen and heard in a *Wide World of Sports* blazer, prattling away on a tape being shown on a monitor, as a twenty-second-century historian explains to Woody's time-traveling nebbish Miles Monroe what his theory is about this strange prehistoric mutant creature. "We weren't sure at first what to make of this," he says, "but we developed a theory:

we feel that when people committed great crimes against the state, they were forced to watch this."

Miles thinks, then says: "Yes. That's exactly what it was."

Once, Cosell had pretensions of being a star; now he was, and then some. Thus what Dick Young only superficially put his finger on whenever he called Cosell a "shill" went much deeper. In the early eighties, David Halberstam, notwithstanding his personal loathing for him, trenchantly filled in the broader context of Cosell's fatally conflicted roles, writing: "If during the Sixties, the great story for a serious sports journalist was race, in the Seventies, it was more and more what television and its concurrent big money had done to sports. But Howard was part of that very issue; he had ridden to the top on the prime instrument corrupting college athletics, a television network. Instead of the probing journalist, he now became the classic modern telecelebrity."[17]

With network self-interest suffocating games to a degree never before seen, *Monday Night Football* was the main protagonist in leaving sports journalism all but dead. Cosell eagerly complied with that new paradigm, raising the question of whether it was even possible that he could be a sports journalist while performing his duties as a full-time celebrity. With each passing week, it seemed, he was proving he couldn't.

"What happened to Howard," says Jerry Izenberg, "was that he got tired of fighting, of being out there on a limb. *Monday Night Football* was his life now, and it made him soft. He would put up a front about all the things he really should be doing. He used to tell me, 'What I really should be doing is reporting from Vietnam.' And I'd say, 'Howard, you're right. I want you to go to Vietnam, get down in the mud, and get the real story.' He'd say, 'Well, if I didn't have a family . . .' He wanted to do everything, and in his mind he would have if only there wasn't that *something* in the way."[18]

THE CALL to hire him as the blow-by-blow man of the Ali-Frazier fight never came—the job was given to "Colonel" Bob Sheridan, with British TV talk show host David Frost as analyst. Ironically, only a few months earlier, Ali and Cosell had shared a harrowing few moments that might have sealed the perfect metaphorical ending for both. They were on the same flight leaving Caracas, Venezuela, where Cosell had gone to broadcast, and Ali to observe, the Foreman-Norton heavyweight title fight on March 26, 1974. On takeoff, the pilot aborted and the Boeing 727 skidded down the runway. As the passengers, who also included Joe Louis, feared that the plane would plunge off the runway and into the Caribbean Ocean, Cosell squeezed Emmy's hand hard and thought of the family he would be leaving behind. The plane came to a stop mere feet from the water's edge, and as it taxied back to the terminal, Ali, who was remarkably jaunty for a man who hated flying, looked for Cosell's face.

"Howard," he called out to him, "I saved you again. Allah and me. If I wasn't on this plane you'd be in the ocean."[19]

Yet only months later, in a September 1974 *New York Times Magazine* article about Cosell, there were some very curious quotes by a heavily introspective Ali that made it seem plausible he had soured on the man he had "saved." While he praised Cosell for having "courage to defend me during those three-and-a-half years," he continued, "People say that if I had lost in the Supreme Court, Howard would have been in terrible trouble. Not really. He's going to have his job if I stopped tomorrow. He'd have lost one of his good interviews." Worse, he insisted, "No, I don't feel he's a friend of mine." He expounded, almost evangelic:

> However loyal a person may be, however wise, however intellectual, however spiritual, if this person has not yet learned the nature and character of friendship, then he hasn't learned anything . . . Real friendship means regard, deep regard for the pleasures and displeasures of his friend, making sure that no words shall hurt his friend, making sure that no accidents shall harm him, not the slightest shade of coldness shall fall upon his hearth. So, we can't consider Howard Cosell a friend.[20]

Cosell was hurt when the author of the piece, Robert Daley, read the quotes to him. "You mean Ali wouldn't say I was his friend?" he asked Daley. "But he must have said something else about me, didn't he? He must have said he respected me or something, didn't he?" As Daley wrote of that moment, "Cosell is hurt. There is no doubt about it."[21]

There were clues that a falling-out was in progress. Cosell had publicly written off Ali's ability to rule boxing again, and Ali had seen him transfer his affinities—and setup one-liners—from him to Don Meredith. "He's a tricky man," Ali said. "One day he'll defend you, he'll talk up for you, then he'll turn right around and ask you something that, if you don't answer it right, you're in trouble . . . To me, [Cosell is] just another man who's good in his field, and I don't understand what the rage is over him, the special writeups and the banquets."[22]

Of course, Ali could have said much the same thing about Cosell back in the 1960s, since the suddenly confrontational question was part of their shtick. But now it was clear that whatever relationship they would carry on would be business, not personal. The same playfully manic interviews would continue, the same burlesque with Ali reaching for Cosell's toupee and imitating his nasal whine; but gone were the breakneck car rides with Ali through "mean" inner-city streets, the heart-to-heart confessionals. For each, the sole reason for the act was mutually rewarding hype. There was a good deal more profit to gain from it. But, silently, he bore the sting of Ali's public reproof. And though he believed that Ali was still a partner, he came to realize that Emmy had been right when she had told him about Ali, "As long as you know him, you'll never really know him."[23]

FOR ALL of the heady sermonizing by its principals about "the Rumble in the Jungle," it would prove to be a royal pain. Members of the media moaned about the long trip to Africa. The eminent *Los Angeles Times* sports columnist Jim Murray—who petulantly called Zaire "the Congo" just as many of his brethren had once persisted in calling Ali "Clay"—quipped, "I guess the top of Mount Everest was busy." Even Ali, once he landed in Zaire, grew homesick fast, telling his aide, photographer Howard Bingham, "I'd give anything to be training in the United States. They got ice cream there, and pretty girls and miniskirts."[24]

Making it worse, Foreman was cut by a sparring partner, pushing back the fight until October 30. During the maddening delay, Ali suggested canceling the bout and fighting Frazier instead in Los Angeles or Houston, until the Zaire government, protecting its investment, warned the fighters not to try to go home. Ali kept up his now-weary quinine and poetry about Foreman—who was now "a big mummy" and a "big old bully," whom he would dispose of with a new punch, the "Ghetto Whopper," so named because "it's thrown in the ghetto at three in the morning." On the thirtieth, they finally entered the ring.

The champ was a three-to-one betting favorite, Cosell now being in the majority with his prediction of an early Foreman knockout, with Ali facing the same possibility that Frazier had in Jamaica of being a homicide victim. Once more Cosell's *Wide World* call of a fight played days later would serve as most Americans' chronicle of a major event. For most of the early-morning bout, a cranky Cosell would mainly hector Ali for taking his pacifist strategy against Joe Frazier to a seemingly absurd level. Early on, he began leaning against the ropes—which had been loosened not, as some would suggest, by Angelo Dundee preparing for the strategy but by the oppressive African heat. Ali kept his elbows firmly at his sides, his forearms and gloves up in front of his face in a kind of tortoise shell pose. Once, between rounds, Ali's corner man Drew "Bundini" Brown went to tighten the ropes. "No, don't!" Ali shouted to him. "Leave 'em alone!"

Cosell, like everyone else, was puzzled about Ali's behavior. Hearing Dundee angrily yelling at his fighter, "Get back on your toes, move!" he began to carve the trope that "heavy damage" was being done by Foreman's punches to Ali's midsection, too much for Ali to be able to endure. Cosell noted that Ali was weathering some deathly shots and tiring Foreman out. But how could Ali win, he asked, if he was spending his time against the ropes, not fighting, giving away points and rounds?

In truth, Cosell and almost everyone but Ali missed what was really going on. Ali *was* fighting, effectively nailing Foreman with hard jabs and combinations, winning three of the first four rounds, while reverting to the ropes to wear him down and sap his confidence. In Ali's thinking, he said later, it was *Foreman* who was "trapped," not him, unable to adjust to anything other than attacking. By round six, Foreman was so exhausted that his punches were soft, his legs immobile, his hands down, his chin an inviting target. Rebounding off the ropes two rounds later, Ali caught him flush on that chin with a stiff right hand, sending Foreman into a spastic spin, arms spread wide like a condor, tumbling to the canvas. On his back, stunned and looking up with glazed eyes, he tried rising but was counted out. This provided yet another opportunity for Cosell to wail, "It's over!" as Ali strutted across the ring, gloves thrust above his head. He was then engulfed in the usual mob of aides and leeches, forcing Ali to himself fall to the canvas, intentionally, to be able to gasp some thin air.[25]

Cosell would not have to brave the mob this time, spared by an intense thunderstorm that erupted, as if on cue, moments after the fight ended, causing the satellite feed to go out. As scores of local fans celebrated in the rain, Ali was given a police escort to his dressing room and then driven through delirious crowds to the private compound where he was staying. He would leave Zaire, blessedly, the next day. Cosell would get him for the *Wide World* tape-delay broadcast. Perhaps as damage control for having—at least in Ali's mind—dumped him for Foreman, Cosell now nearly fell all over him in adoration. And if he was still not Ali's "friend" by the latter's definition, it was clear the working relationship had not been totally breached. Six months later, before Ali's second defense of his renewed title, against Ron Lyle in Las Vegas, he favored Cosell by christening for him during another interview the strategic ploy he had unveiled in Zaire. Applying an old rubric used long ago by Joe Louis to the present, he said, "I have a new style, Howard. I want to announce here now the new style about laying on the ropes sometimes, let the man punch hisself out. It is called the Rope-a-Dope."

"The Rope-a-Dope?" repeated Cosell.

"The Rope-a-Dope."

"Obviously," Cosell said, easing back into the old-time hijinks, "the champion enters tonight's fray shaken, with a full loss of confidence."

"Shaken?" Ali retorted, contorting his face to put on an angry look.

"Good luck."

"You be there."

"We will be."

"And after the man ring the bell, I'm gonna jump on the rope and sock Cosell."[26]

As with any repartee they now indulged in, there was a whiff of nostalgia. This was, to be certain, not the Ali of 1964; he was markedly less political, lighter-hearted, comfortable in the mainstream. The change had come around February 1975 with the death of the intractable Elijah Muhammad, after which Ali began to speak of finding "a new phase" in his Islamic faith. Guided now by Elijah's seventh son, Wallace Muhammad, who ascended to Supreme Minister of the Nation of Islam, Ali converted to the less militant Sunni Islam.

But neither was Cosell still cut from the exact same cloth as before. While his new wig and old brio may have belied it, he was pushing sixty. He had become more soft-boiled than hard. Ali had a priceless riff for that, too. Whenever Cosell would press him about his advancing age, remarking that he was "not the man he used to be," Ali's inevitable response would be, "Howard Cosell, let's ask your wife if *you're* the man you used to be." Yet the both of them, alone and as a pair, could still make news and influence the culture they had so heavily influenced. The Rope-a-Dope, for instance, went straight into the vernacular of sports and pop culture, a rubric without which the Rumble in the Jungle cannot be spoken of. It was a marker of the times that had been shaped—or reshaped—by forces of nature that carried Richard Nixon out of the White House and Muhammad Ali back into the realm of "the Greatest," as the first man to regain the heavyweight championship of the world.

And not by coincidence, the expression was coined with Howard Cosell in the room as a catalyst. He, too, was part of the new times, like Ali playing the game differently but stubbornly refusing to let the earth move without him being there.

# 15

## "THINGS BEGAN TO TURN SOUR"

COMMONLY RANKED in the early 1970s among the top twenty prime-time network shows each season, the unprecedented success that was *Monday Night Football* helped swell ABC Sports' revenues to $120 million, more than that of CBS and NBC Sports combined. It was a sum that made the network's investment in *MNF* a real bargain. By no means limited to broadcasters, the caravan of celebrities kept on passing through the booth, ranging from Burt Reynolds, Senator Ted Kennedy, Secretary of State Henry Kissinger, and figure skater Dorothy Hamill to singer John Denver, all of whom were interviewed, and comfortably, by Cosell. California governor Ronald Reagan and ex-Beatle John Lennon appeared during the *same game*, a November 1973 clash at Candlestick Park between the San Francisco 49ers and the Green Bay Packers. As the halftime break approached, in a scene out of *The Twilight Zone*, the right-wing icon governor stood at the back of the booth making small talk with the left-wing icon singer of "Give Peace a Chance," Reagan with his arm draped around Lennon's shoulder.

Given a choice of whom to interview, Cosell opted for the bigger name—"the Beatle," as he put it—leaving Frank Gifford, logically, to chat up Reagan. Seeking to appeal to the Woodstock Generation, Cosell introduced "a most familiar figure and face . . . of the original Beatles, Mr. John Lennon," who expressed wonder at the big crowd, calling the game "an amazing event that makes rock concerts look like tea parties," but who couldn't understand "why half the team is off and half the team is on." Then came the obligatory question of whether the Beatles would ever reunite. Coyly, Lennon said, "You never know, you never know, it's always in the wind." When Cosell, ever in the know, countered with "You did just spend the weekend with Ringo [Starr]," Lennon said he indeed had. He had promised Ringo that he'd mention his new album but not his own—slyly adding, "which is out now, too." Ending an affable minute and a half, Cosell said it was time to "join the Giffer."

"Okay, Giffer," parodied Lennon, "over to Giffer."[1]

Clearly, the *MNF* booth was the place to be, and, not insignificantly for the local ABC affiliates, the place where the TV was tuned in when the jazzy *MNF* theme came on. According to anecdotal evidence, business in restaurants across the country was off by some 25 percent each Monday night—though not those that held the anti-Cosell brick-through-a-television promotions. There was, at the same time, no diminution to Cosell's essential, ornamental hyperbole. Describing a certain Buffalo Bills running back, he gabbled that O. J. Simpson—who by the early seventies was already a part-time hand with ABC Sports during the off-season—was a man with "an uncanny instinct for sensing when to make the move, when to make the cut. He can kill you with a head fake, he can kill you with the swiftness of his legs and the ability to be in a direction at any single second. He also kills you with his variation of speed."[2]

His give-and-take with Don Meredith and Frank Gifford was still after three years a matter of great fascination to the public and the media. Articles were written even now endlessly dissecting the chemistry and the personal interrelationships, with each man making sure to laud the others. In that 1974 *New York Times Magazine* piece about Cosell, Dandy Don was far more charitable than Muhammad Ali. "I really do like Howard," he said. "I truly enjoy Howard. He can be a lot of fun, and terribly entertaining, and occasionally even informative." He told of a gracious Cosell congratulating him for winning the Emmy Award, adding, "I won the Emmy, but if we have a star in that package, the star was Howard."

Meredith did concede, "To say that Howard never offended me, never hurt my feelings, would be wrong," citing as an example the time when Cosell said on air that Meredith despised Tom Landry. "I'd rather speak for myself on something that personal," he said, as soft a rebuke as he could have managed, and then vouched for Cosell as a compatriot. "If some drunk at the bar rips me . . . Howard is the first one to jump right down their throat. In a way, there [is] a father image that Howard has toward me, and I appreciate it," though Cosell's own habitual inebriation made the statement at least obliquely ironic.[3]

No such allowances were made for him among the vast population of virulent Cosell haters. His mail was even more malevolent, and it came to discomfort his daughter Hilary more than it did him. While her sister, Jill, and Peter Cohane were raising their four children in Connecticut, Hilary was maturing into a passionate liberal activist herself. She more than anyone else in the family had become a committed dissenter about the Vietnam War, not an easy stance for Cosell, the old major and American Legion post commander. Often as emotional and socially concerned as her father, she was, in a filial way, most likely to uphold her father's honor, and she bridled at the fans who made sport of insulting him. Every Monday would be torture for the impressionable daughter.

"Those *Monday Night Football* crowds, some of them, in some cities, were animals," she said. "I'd watch those games just to make sure some lunatic wasn't there with an Uzi or an AK-47 shooting up the booth. I wanted to make sure my father got through those four-plus hours."[4]

Gifford, too, was always startled by such reactions. "I never saw anyone take such a hammering; it was almost a lynch-mob mentality," he said. "I'd look out at a stadium and see signs and banners proclaiming everything from WILL ROGERS NEVER MET HOWARD COSELL to HOWARD IS A HEM-MORHOID [sic]—and those were the printable ones."[5] Among the unprintable ones were vile comments like HOWARD IS ABC'S DEEP THROAT—HE SUCKS, while others included a crude likeness of his face and a penis stuck in his mouth, a crude substitution for his signature El Producto. Dennis Lewin maintains that the latter variety was actually rare, and far outnumbered by the positive ones he could show on the air, some, such as the Will Rogers one, quite cleverly poking fun at the usual target. But, he clarifies, "I can only talk about what I saw during my years as producer. What happened after that, I don't know because I wasn't there for that. It could have been worse, though, because people became more and more hostile to Howard as the years went on. Things began to turn sour."[6] As they did, so did the signs. A particularly sickening one, not shown on the air, had a Star of David sitting atop the Satanic numbers 666.

As it turned out, Hilary's fears were well founded. Days before the seventh game of the 1973 season schedule, between the Kansas City Chiefs and Buffalo Bills at the latter's new home, Rich Stadium, a postcard arrived at the park that read: "Howard Cosell—the MOUTH—why don't you drop dead. There's a bomb in Rich Stadium. It will blow you up at 10:00 Monday."[7] When he and Emmy got to the stadium, they both were put under the protection of FBI agents. As it happened, he was to be filmed that night by a crew from NFL Films, preparing a sixty-minute documentary called *Howard Cosell at Large*, which may explain why Cosell remained so stoic that night, as opposed to everyone else in the booth.

Meredith, for example, drank a quart of straight vodka from the bottle during the game to calm his nerves, unconcerned that reporters down the way in the press box could see him, making Don Ohlmeyer, the new producer, want to wring his neck. According to Marc Gunther and Bill Carter in their book *Monday Night Mayhem*, even one of the FBI men assigned to Emmy asked her, "Does he do that all the time?"[8] But at least her husband, in contrast to that storied night in Philadelphia, was not imbibing, not with the NFL Films camera on him. Here he was the image of John Wayne. During the game a firecracker exploded near the booth. As people ducked for cover, including Meredith and Gifford, he bravely stood erect and tall, keeping his gaze on the field. As Ohlmeyer recalls, "At halftime our entire crew decided they needed to go take a leak all at the same time and cleared out. But Howard refused to leave the booth. Nothing was gonna drive him out, even a goddamn bomb."[9]

Fortunately, nothing else exploded, and soon afterward the FBI tracked down an unemployed steelworker from Pittsburgh who had sent the poison pen letter. When he was tried in 1977, Cosell's testimony helped convict him of mailing a threatening communication, though he was given only a suspended sentence and placed on a one-year probation. By then, another letter had been sent to Denver's *Rocky Mountain News*, calling him "the Loud Mouth" and vowing to blow him up, possibly with a bomb placed under his car. No one was ever arrested. There would be at least three other threats taken seriously. In 1979, a letter came to the Brown County sheriff's office in Green Bay, inscribed: "If Howard Cosell comes to Green Bay on October 1 [for a Monday night Packers-Patriots game] I'm going to kill him. And your sheriff's department can't stop me." The FBI contacted Cosell, and again he was given protection at the game. Again, no one was ever charged.

In 1982, a prison inmate in Deer Lodge, Montana, wrote to Cosell, in deranged fashion, "You will now die because of your government lies . . . I will be out in October and will be there to get you and all ABC government liars," which may have made him feel, at least, like a senator. Federal officials declined to prosecute, believing that the suspect, who also sent threatening letters to Supreme Court Chief Justice Warren Burger and officials of Pan American and Lufthansa airlines, wrote them in an attempt to be moved from a state to a federal facility. Then, in 1986, Cosell was sent a rambling letter and ninety-minute tape from someone in Milwaukee demanding $42 million from him and other prominent figures including President Ronald Reagan, warning that if he didn't get it, "tens of millions of people will be killed." Authorities investigated a former mental patient, but once again no charges were brought.[10]

Clearly, there was something in Cosell's outsized ego and personality that struck a raw nerve, for some psychologically unbalanced people far too deeply. Cosell himself recognized this, turning his amusement about the signs and chants to despondency. After one game in 1973, he was with ABC Sports assistant Dick Buffinton in his hotel room. As Cosell nursed a vodka, he said, "Buffer, I don't know how I can continue to do this. These people are vicious."[11]

Because Cosell reveled in the crowds that he attracted on the street, the very real danger that someone in the crowd could be dangerous posed a conundrum for him. Once, he and an ABC Sports director, Lou Aceti, were having drinks in a hotel bar with Woody Allen, Warren

Beatty, and Julie Christie—the sort of A-list celebrities whose company he craved. Not aware of the irony, he asked Allen how he could stand the hordes who congregated around him. "These people never stop bothering you," Cosell said. "I can't take it. I never get a minute of peace." Aceti could hardly believe his ears, and let Cosell have it. "You sit in that fucking lobby, where they can see you, you ever think of that?" Aceti asked him. "In a yellow coat that looks like a fucking canary? And you tell me that you don't want to be noticed? The day you're not noticed is the day you'll be very unhappy. The day nobody says, 'Hey, Cosell, you asshole,' you'll be very unhappy."[12]

Cosell had no comeback. Why he sought out attention, even abuse, from people he despised remained an essential conundrum, yet the answer surely lay in the constant reassurance he needed. Nor did he seem overly upset that he was escorted into and out of the booth on Monday nights by armed guards. The threat to him meant less than the validation the guards provided that he was bigger than the game. And yet, to others the more sobering reality of these escalating threats was a symptom of a changing mood around the show itself. "That's really when the fun peaked, '73, '74," says Dennis Lewin. "I know that by the time I came back to the show in 1977, very little about it was fun anymore."[13]

FOR DON MEREDITH, the fun was already gone by 1973. As was apparent by his open boozing in the booth at Rich Stadium, he seemed unconcerned about making ABC look bad. Another time, his first words before a Denver Broncos–Oakland Raiders game were "We're in the Mile High City and I sure am," making Ohlmeyer almost faint. On another occasion, he mirthfully called Richard Nixon by his notorious nickname, "Tricky Dick," for which the network forced him to apologize on air the following Monday. Some nights, he would disagree with whatever Cosell said, just for the sake of disagreement, either because he truly disagreed or as a way to juice up the broadcast. At a production meeting during the season, Meredith said, "I'm all talked out. I've got nothing more to say about football, the games aren't that interesting."[14]

Cosell commiserated with him. "I understood exactly how he felt," he would write in *Like It Is*, citing the "sameness" and "redundancy" that "amounts to a stereotype in professional football." He and Meredith, he said, were much alike, sharing the philosophy that "there is more to life than that down there."[15] But while he was bound to the network by history and loyalty, Meredith possessed a freedom of movement. And the changes in his attitude were a "tell" that he was halfway out the ABC door, for various reasons.

Cosell also believed that Meredith had come to detest his redneck image and was disappointed by his failure to become a superstar. Mostly, Cosell surmised, Meredith resented having to play second banana to him. To be sure, there wasn't enough room in the *MNF* booth for two egos each with an overglorified sense of self-importance, but only one could go. And by late in the season, Meredith had hired big-time Hollywood agent Ed Hookstratten, who had a close relationship with NBC— for which Meredith had acted in an episode of the cop series *Police Story*. That proved to be an effective entrée to that network, especially when ABC rejected a pilot dreamed up by Meredith that would have made him and Cosell unlikely stars in an *Odd Couple*–like sitcom, with Meredith a "white-suited and invincible cowboy" and Cosell a black-clad "'hanging judge' . . . paunchy of body but acute of tongue."[16]

Even though Meredith's ABC contract was up after the 1973 season, Arledge assumed he would be back. It was Cosell who informed Roone that Dandy Don was all but gone, having heard that news at the NFL owners' meeting in Miami in late February 1974. "Once more," Arledge would recall, "I thought Howard was an alarmist." To prove it, Arledge called Meredith in L.A., where he was filming another *Police Story*, and asked him if the rumor was true. Sheepishly, Meredith told him, "I don't know what to tell you, Roone." Knowing what that meant, Arledge would later say, "I felt as if I'd been kicked in the head."[17]

The eventual postseason announcement that Dandy Don had defected to NBC was almost anticlimactic, but for Meredith the package deal was fit for his ego. It provided for him to appear not only on occasional Sunday football games but also in TV pilots and movies, as well as on regular shows and as a substitute host for Johnny Carson on *The Tonight Show*. Given that NBC was treating him as a bona fide star, the

$400,000 a year he got—which Arledge had matched—seemed irrele-vant. Tellingly, he demanded in his NBC contract that he was never to be called "Dandy Don," by anyone there, on or off the air, *ever.*

Cosell's contemporaneous reaction to Meredith's flight was a simple declaration that "emotionally, he had to go," but what he did not seem to say was that he thought Meredith's angst resulted from his jealousy of Cosell. Years later, when he felt he could skewer Meredith liberally, he tore into him for being anything but the bumpkin he came off as, citing an alleged "behavior pattern that I call 'Texas Cruel.' There's a mean streak within him . . . He groused and grumbled, snapped at people, and he could be contrary in the extreme. On those occasions, he was hardly the lovable ol' cowboy with the homespun view of the world. Not in the least."[18]

Cosell was, by his own shading, heroic for enduring a litany of such abuse directed at him by Meredith, even if this abuse was not obvious to most outside the Cosell family. That Meredith was so vexed by his situa-tion at ABC was a wonder to Cosell, who recalled, "At first I thought, How do you like that? He had won an Emmy. I didn't. He had received raves form the press. I was pilloried day in and day out. Well, I figured, that's the way it is with jocks. How shallow can they get?"[19]

Meredith had only encomiums for Cosell, but behind the scenes he shed few tears about leaving the ABC booth. Terry O'Neil, the young ABC Sports staffer who had helped edit *Cosell,* recalled asking Meredith if he had ever read it. "Read it?" asked Dandy Don contemptuously. "I had to *live* it. Why would I want to read it?"[20]

ON THE other hand, few at ABC—not least of all Cosell—mourned Meredith's departure. They considered it a vindication that after NBC Sports president Carl Lindemann had made some snide public indict-ments of the *MNF* booth, he had gone out and pilfered Dandy Don. As Cosell put it, *Monday Night Football* was no less than a "social institu-tion," and even though he believed that was implicitly traceable to him, not Meredith, he admitted that the series was immune to even his own loss. Still, the rumpled man who boasted "I never played the game" was undeniably the nucleus of the most popular football broadcast of all time. Because, also undeniably, he was himself a social institution, even as the self-parody seemed to assume a larger role.

Jerry Izenberg says, "I thought he was good at what he did, but I thought he tried too hard after a while. For Howard, the hardest thing to do was reaching a level in showbiz where you really are the best and people expect you to get better. And I give him credit for it, because Howard did that, at least while he cared about what he was doing. He had to, because *Monday Night Football* was really the Howard Cosell Show." The draw of which, as Larry Merchant adds, was "to find out what Howard was going to say next."[21]

Cosell was right about the institution *MNF* had become. Not even a monumental screwup in replacing Meredith would disturb ratings, or the anticipation of what Howard Cosell might be saying next. When Arledge began considering replacements, he interviewed O. J. Simpson and Joe Namath, though only Simpson was prepared to quit the game to take the job. But in the end Arledge could not have chosen a more inappropriate candidate, Fred "the Hammer" Williamson, a former defensive back with the Oakland Raiders and Kansas City Chiefs. Williamson was a handsome man with a blinding smile who worked off the Muhammad Ali blueprint, striking peacock poses and freely dispensing praise of himself. He had some success as an actor on TV and in a few of the early-seventies "blaxpolition" movies such as *The Legend of Nigger Charley*, but was known mainly for trash-mouthing the Green Bay Packers before the Chiefs' Super Bowl loss, only to be knocked cold during the game—a metaphorical moment for a poseur.

Cosell tried in vain to sell Arledge on a *second* nonjock, pitching one of his trophy cronies, Burt Reynolds, who had been a football star at Florida State, but he played the good soldier when Williamson was hired, with a six-figure contract that, à la Meredith, included acting work on ABC TV programs. Cosell, Arledge, Roone's assistant Dick Ebersol, and Don Ohlmeyer found him irresistible, though why wasn't clear. When Cosell told him, "You won't be the star with me there," Williamson flashed his smile and replied, "I'll be the sex symbol. They won't know Gifford is there." During an early-summer promotion tour, Williamson was decked out in gold chains in the shape of a penis and testicles. When asked how he would prepare for the games, he said he would "swim a lot in my pool, . . . brush up on my dancing, dress real pretty, and show up."[22]

Williamson did seem capable of some sly humor, telling the press he would bring some "color" to the show. But most everything he said and did provoked stunned, embarrassed silence. Cosell likely imagined Williamson as an update of Ali, but the Hammer had none of the latter's impish humor. His one-dimensional egotism, in fact, challenged Cosell's view of the black man as oppressed but heroic and dignified. The Hammer was none of that. In his debut, an August preseason game, he wore gold chains (fortunately, not the penis and testicles variety) and a shirt open to reveal his bare chest—having seditiously told Arledge before the game, "I wear your ABC yellow jacket. I ain't wearing no fucking tie."[23]

However, Cosell did his best to succor him, bringing him on as a man who was "already a movie star," taking a sly slap at Meredith. In *Like It Is*, he spent an entire chapter pimping Williamson. The chapter was titled "Say Hello to the Hammer." However, by the time the book came out, timed to the opening of the season, *MNF* had already said good-bye to the Hammer, who had been a disaster in three preseason telecasts. Throwing out harsh, uninformed judgments of players he barely knew in between billing himself a "star," he tried to update the Meredith role not by twitting Cosell but humiliating him, pointlessly taking issue with whatever he said. Once, he laced into Cosell as "an old cripple," after which Cosell stopped trying to feed him lines, then stopped talking to him altogether. That's when Arledge knew how badly he had messed up.

"No matter how much you didn't want Howard to control things," he would say, "as a practical matter, if Howard wasn't going to get along with the person [in the booth], it's not going to work."[24]

With reviews of Williamson in the press uniformly and brutally negative, Arledge could wait no longer than three weeks before making a move. Within a few days, he had paid off Williamson's contract and hired another candidate whom he had considered, Alex Karras. Cosell had a long history with him, both having come a long way since Karras was the "big, heavy pudding-faced kid" on Cosell's early radio show, revealing how his mother threw him out of the house and told him to "be a man."

After his college career at Iowa, Karras played a dozen seasons for the Detroit Lions, not counting the 1963 season when he and the Packers' Paul Hornung were suspended by Pete Rozelle for betting on games, the lingering memory of which had led Arledge to hold off on him originally, thinking it might offend some NFL owners. Karras had also done some acting, starring in the TV movie *The 500 Pound Jerk* in 1973—which also featured a Cosell cameo—and appearing in Mel Brooks's *Blazing Saddles* as Mongo, the brainless, lovable cowboy bad guy. His niche was as a big lug with a wry and ready quip, and unlike Williamson, he had a sense of timing and self-deprecation.

Karras fit in nicely, turning in one of the best lines in the history of *Monday Night Football* when a close-up shot appeared of an Oakland Raiders defensive lineman, helmet off, steam rising from his shaved head. "That's Otis Sistrunk," Karras said. "He's from the University of Mars," an inspired bit of observational humor that played off Sistrunk's appearance. But Karras's arrival was simply a matter of rearranging deck chairs on ABC's *Queen Mary*, as the good ship rumbled on, copping even bigger ratings, sponsor dollars, and crazed Cosell haters.

And yet, preen as Cosell would about how bulletproof the series was, Dandy Don had left a parting shot that went straight to his heart when *Meredith* earned another Emmy nomination in 1974 for Outstanding Achievement in Sports Programming. Though Meredith didn't win, it was yet another affront to Cosell that the second banana was doing something that he couldn't—make industry people not only appreciate him, and pay him, but *like* him. But he had plans that he suspected might change all that.


EVEN IN the comfortable niche of self-parody, he could still cut to the heart of the matter as if with a scythe. That he could cause a major stir with any given observation, even those meant without provocation, demanded that his journalistic instincts remain acute. His Sunday afternoon magazine show seemed to redirect and recenter him. On one, he journeyed to Oberlin College, where Tommie Smith had moved far from his Mexico City Black Power demonstration to become, in semiobscurity, the school's athletic director. Catching up with him, Cosell asked, "Have you grown less militant?"

"What does militant mean?" Smith wondered, trying to play it safe by being nebulous. But Cosell wouldn't let him squirm off the hook.

"Don't spar with me," he shot back testily. "We're not going back to 1968, Tommie. A militant is a guy who speaks out in protest, whether by a physical symbol or vocally with a truculent effect or tone of voice against the existing establishment's procedures. Now with that premise, have you changed?"

"I am a militant," Smith said.[25]

Nor would he be left out of the latest chic causes. In 1975, he would lend his considerable name to the movement to pass the Equal Rights Amendment, which had passed both houses of Congress in 1971–72 but had stalled four states shy of the thirty-eight needed for ratification. In the October issue of none other than Gloria Steinem's *Ms.* magazine, a publication that marshaled the feminist viewpoint, came his plea. Having already pitched for Title IX, the 1972 law that prohibited dispensing any federal funds and scholarships to colleges that practiced gender bias, he proclaimed, "It's long since past time in this country that women were treated coequally with men." He blasted opponents of the amendment, who he noted were principally women, as "truly not part of a contemporary society" who were "engaged in a self-destruct wish" and took their stand "out of ignorance." He concluded, "But they can't win. Their time is past. Their arguments are absurd [and] synthetic."[26] However, this was one fight he lost; the ERA would eventually die aborning.

THE PROFESSIONAL freedom that Don Meredith enjoyed was simply not possible for Cosell. He was boxed in at ABC. Though he would breezily float the notion that he could defect to NBC or CBS, no one took him seriously, nor did he honestly expect anyone to. If on a surface level he was using it as a bargaining chip, more pressing was his need to always be told how much he was wanted and needed at ABC. He was bonded, lock, stock, and toupee, to Roone Arledge and Leonard Goldenson. His gratitude to them knew no end, yet the obvious truth was that only they could tolerate him or his brand of self-serving reporting. Having been born at ABC, as if caught in Vulcan's mythological net, he would die at ABC.

Cosell had certainly cultivated capital and credibility for the network as the face and voice of Roone Arledge's sports dynasty. The problem was, he could detect little gratitude. Indeed, few around the shop would come out and say what Chet Forte did to a reporter in the late seventies, vis-à-vis *Monday Night Football*, that "it's not a damn football game. It's a show. That's what those guys [Gifford and Meredith] never understood. They never appreciated what Howard did."[27] His only recourse was to make it impossible *not* to appreciate what he did. To do that, sports wasn't enough. He wanted more.

It would serve him well that his pursuit of fame had left him with a first-name familiarity with the biggest names in show business, whom he could seemingly summon at his whim. Indeed, Cosell could effortlessly merge his sports and crass showbiz sensibilities. In 1974, Frank Sinatra had specifically requested that Cosell be a part of a live ABC special on which the aging singer gave a "comeback" concert at Madison Square Garden, billed as "The Main Event." Sinatra wanted the show to approximate the vibe of a championship fight, and Cosell presented an introductory rap in mock-fight prose, observing that the "celebrities are here in profusion."

As it happened, Roone Arledge, making new strides of his own, coproduced the Sinatra special, opening the door for a wild idea by ABC's president of entertainment, Fred Pierce, who at the time was more interested in keeping Arledge mollified than he was Cosell, as Roone's ABC contract was due to expire in 1976 and he could have written his own ticket out the ABC door. Looking to gift Arledge with another project, Pierce threw out his idea during dinner with Arledge—"Hey, maybe Cosell could become the next Ed Sullivan!" Cosell, of course, readily agreed, believing himself to be the ideal Sullivan doppelgänger, though he would admit that not everyone in the ABC executive suite agreed. The new head of programming, Fred Silverman, who had just been lured away from CBS to oversee the ABC prime-time lineup, hated it, and predicted the show would last four weeks, coincidentally the same time frame Arledge had requested for Cosell to prove himself on *Monday Night Football*.

Contrary to Cosell's starry-eyed optimism, the core problems with such a project were obvious. For one, the hoary variety show format had grown geriatric since Sullivan had gone off the air in 1971. While Cosell and Arledge wanted wholesome "family" fare, TV programmers were adapting to a new sensibility of adult, boundary-pushing content; indeed, they were blaming the soon-to-be-discarded "Family Hour"—8 to 10 P.M.—for the erosion in their overall ratings. But then Cosell and Arledge were products of the sixties, the swaggering, boozy Frank-Dean-Sammy "Rat Pack" model of cool the standard, though Cosell's need to be among each generation's cultural "in" crowd made him seek out new icons; one of his latest finds was a struggling stand-up comic from Long Beach, New York, Billy Crystal, whom he sponsored for membership in the Friars Club after seeing him do a dead-on imitation of Muhammad Ali— and Howard Cosell.

As Dennis Lewin remembers, "It must have been 1973–74. We were in Miami for a *Monday Night Football* game and I came down to the pool, and there was Howard sitting with this kid he introduced as Billy Crystal. I didn't know who he was, it was way before Crystal became famous, and they were already close. Howard would bring Billy Crystal into town with him and Emmy. He loved to show off that he had a sort of protégé, that he was keeping up with the times."[28] Thus, receptive to the smirky, snarky seventies' irreverence, he began putting together TV's first repertory troupe of young sketch comics to appear weekly on the show—to the consternation of Arledge, who wanted to more closely follow the Sullivan model of big, shiny stars interspersed with jugglers, animal acts, and talking mice. From the start, there was a cleft, and it would only widen.

IMPLICIT IN everyone's thinking was that the series could somehow transfer the bankable alchemy of *Monday Night Football* to a variety show. To be sure, Cosell's effect could be mesmerizing. And so Arledge got a heady time slot, 8 P.M., just as Sullivan had, though on Saturday, not Sunday, a critical difference inasmuch as Saturday night generally drew the smallest audience of the week. The show—*Saturday Night Live with Howard Cosell*—had a commitment for eighteen weeks and a venue that underscored its mission: the old Ed Sullivan Theater on Broadway and Fifty-second Street, which ABC paid a pretty price to refurbish with the finest lighting and acoustic equipment.

Cosell and Arledge rented space on the tenth floor of the Rolex Building on Fifth Avenue and began hiring their staff. The first to come aboard was comic Alan King as creative consultant, with King's partner in his production company, Rupert Hitzig, named as nominal producer, though Arledge, as executive producer, would call every shot. The director was Don Mischer, who had guided *In Concert*, ABC's hip Friday late-night concert series. Mischer also had gotten an offer from an NBC variety show with the near-identical title of *Saturday Night*, which had gotten an eight-week commitment and an 11:30 P.M. slot. That venture was the brainchild of Dick Ebersol, the former Arledge lieutenant who had been enticed by NBC president Herb Schlosser to develop for NBC a trendy ninety-minute, late-night variety-cum-comedy show. Because Cosell's show was further along, would hit the air first, and paid more, Mischer signed on with him.

Soon the pieces fell into place. Walter Kempley and David Axelrod, who had respectively written for Johnny Carson and Dean Martin, would head up the writing staff, which also included a favored Cosell sportswriter, the *New York Times*'s Robert Lipsyte. A pair of young comics for Cosell's brave new idea were imported from the stage of Chicago's famed Second City improv company—Bill Murray and his brother Brian Doyle-Murray—and the all-the-rage *National Lampoon* radio shows, Christopher Guest. The troupe was billed with self-conscious cheek as "the Ready for Primetime Players." Early on, they showed what their concept of au courant comedy was, rehearsing a skit written by Guest in which Chinese stand-up comics told bad jokes through an interpreter. Cosell loved it. Stone-faced, Arledge didn't. "You really think that's funny?" he asked Cosell.

"It's hysterical . . . These kids are terrific."

"You're wrong, Howard. They're not right for the show, and I don't think they'll ever make it in television."[29]

Cosell, who would allow himself to be overruled by Arledge on all other matters, insisted that the "kids" stay in the show. Still, it wasn't any of them but Cosell himself who would make or break the enterprise. And the signs were not good. Standing stage center before test audiences, he was neither a dinner party raconteur nor a pompous gasbag, but a stiff and uncomfortable amateur knowing not what to do or say. Arledge constantly ran him through his paces, trying somehow to loosen him up, prompting Cosell to bridle at Arledge for messing with his "natural" personality. Hyping the show in the press, he told *People*, "You know what's going to make this show? Me—the born superstar. They didn't give me looks, but they gave me an absolute monopoly on brains and talent."[30] But as the premiere crept closer, such bluster proved hollow. The *People* writer noted that he seemed "serious and, yes, apprehensive." He had reason to be.

For weeks, Cosell believed that, having bonded so well with John Lennon, he could prevail on him to make good on his "you never know" plaint about reuniting the Beatles. Lennon had indeed enjoyed his guest shot on *Monday Night Football*, later sending Cosell and Frank Gifford a complete collection of Beatles albums, autographed by him. Then, when Cosell had aired the pie-in-the-sky scenario of reuniting the Beatles on the debut of his show, John sent him a letter saying that "for personal reasons I must decline any commitments until next year" but that "the equally weird and wonderful monsieur Ringo Starr might well be available for your variety show," and concluding, "I wish you all the best, I'm sure it's going to be a big hit!" He signed, "yer old pal, what's his name?"[31] Somehow, Cosell read this not as a slammed door but an opened one; instead of pursuing Ringo, he persisted in believing Lennon would be receptive to the symmetry of the band performing on the same stage where they made their American debut in 1964.

Still pushing, Cosell prevailed on WABC Radio general manager Rick Sklar, who was close to John, to arrange a lunch date with John at the "21" Club. There, Cosell typically acted as if he and the rock star, whom he had met once, for five minutes, were the closest of friends. "John!" he crowed, cigar in one hand, martini in the other, "I want you guys on my show!"

"What do you mean 'you guys'?" Lennon asked, not cheerily.

"You, George, Paul, and Ringo."

Lennon looked confused. It was well known that things were still dicey between him and Paul McCartney, as they had been ever since the Beatles' messy breakup. The legal tangles around a Beatles reunion were prohibitive—something one might have expected the old lawyer to know, that is, if he knew anything about the group's history. After a long, uncomfortable pause, Lennon said, "I don't know. After what's gone down, I don't know. I thought you wanted me."

"Of course I do," Cosell replied brightly, "but let's be realistic. This is bigger than both of us."

At that point Rupert Hitzig, whom Cosell had brought along, suggested that the Fab Four could be reunited as a pure TV production, via a four-way split screen. That way, they need not even be in the same city, or country.

Lennon gave it some thought. "What would the people expect? We might leave them disappointed. It's better to let them have their memories, have them remember us as we were," he said.[32]

Cosell still wouldn't ease off, going on about "restaging the most electrifying moment in American television." Lennon by now was becoming irritated; finally, he let on that if the Beatles ever got back together, it would have to be for a huge closed-circuit production, worldwide, with top ticket prices and a tour and concurrent album. As Cosell would later admit, "A reunion on network television didn't make much sense to him. He was right." That day, Lennon couldn't get away fast enough, with no more of a commitment to Cosell than a diffident comment that he might perhaps be back at some time for a *Monday Night Football* halftime interview. (Cosell's postscript to the interlude was to claim he had been at least passively responsible for John's reconciliation with Yoko Ono, from whom he had been separated; this because John had left "21" earlier than he had expected to, and when he then went off to an art gallery, she happened to be there. "He brought us back together, Howard did," he claimed Lennon had told Sklar.)[33]

Rebuffed, Cosell had to set his sights a lot lower, settling on another rock act causing a stir mostly in Europe, the Bay City Rollers, a bubblegum band from Edinburgh, Scotland, who dressed in plaid suits and were a favorite of the teeny-bopper set in England, drawing fatuous praise by some as "the next Beatles." They also happened to have a

No. 1–bound hit on the American charts called "Saturday Night," which consisted mainly of the title being chanted over and over. To Cosell, it was perfect, a near-exact replication of Sullivan and the Beatles, with him breaking the "next big thing," channeling Beatlemania into "Roller-mania" before millions of rapt viewers. It was, of course, a fantasia; more-over, it was too late in the game to arrange for the lads to replicate the Beatles by flying them in for their U.S. debut on the Sullivan stage. All Arledge could do was send Don Ohlmeyer across the pond to produce a Rollers concert in London, at 1 A.M. there, that would be carried live by satellite.

ABC devoted a large advertising budget to the show. In the days before its premiere, half-page ads with Cosell's craggy face ran in every major newspaper screaming, "Live Variety! Spectacular! Unconventional! Unpredictable!" All that was certain, however, was that it was, in fact, live. When the curtain went up on September 20, Cosell lumbered out in a tux, more nervous than ever. Breaking the seal, he excitedly introduced the Rollers to an apathetic America as "the next Beatles"—though with a residual journalistic reflex he did hedge that the band was "reputed" to be that, and it "remained to be seen" if it was deserved, a distinction he would later stress by way of self-defense. On cue, the tartan-tufted young men went into "Saturday Night" and the rest of their set, eliciting over-wrought squeals and other raucous behavior by teenage girls, some of whom stormed the stage and bowled over the lead singer.

He then fired his other putative big guns. The volatile tennis champ Jimmy Connors ambled onto the stage to sing, if it could be called that, a number titled "Super Girl, You Turn Me On," accompanied on piano by its composer, onetime teen idol Paul Anka—a performance Cosell gar-nished as "a great magical moment in musical history," an ad lib that confirmed why he had not trusted himself to say the right things and ordered cue cards, almost obscenely for a man who prided himself on not needing a script. But that only robbed him of his best quality— spontaneity, and the prospect that he might say something incendiary.

The pace was surely frenetic. With barely an eyeblink in between, there came a live performance by the Eagles, the hugely popular rock band, and rock thrush Linda Ronstadt from a sold-out concert in San

Diego. Alex Karras added either a comedic or cheesy touch, "playing" onstage with them wearing a long wig. This was followed by a song by British diva Shirley Bassey; the cast of the Broadway musical *The Wiz* singing "Ease on down the Road"; a monologue by crusty comic Redd Foxx; walk-ons by John Wayne and Frank Sinatra—who gushed to Cosell with an unwittingly accurate malaprop, "This show will be a millstone on American TV"; a Las Vegas remote featuring the lion-taming act Sigfried and Roy; and a remote interview with Muhammad Ali and Joe Frazier just days before their October 1 rubber match in the Philippines dubbed "the Thrilla in Manila."

Finally, after what seemed like a dizzying month of Saturdays, he said good night, happy for perhaps the first time in his life to see the red light of the camera go off so he could breathe again.

STILL, WITH it all, he was intoxicated in a way no martini could approximate, buoyant in his delight in how the premiere went. The overnight ratings were quite good, stoked by mass curiosity, though the reviews were scathing. The *Times's* television critic, John J. O'Connor, was unimpressed with Cosell's sudden reformation, which O'Connor defined as "the Horrible Howard monster [that] is now being marketed as the Cozy Cosell doll."[34] The most common reaction was that if the variety show format wasn't dead before, Cosell had certainly laid it to rest. Passing off such quinine as an extension of the lockstep jealousy and pack journalism mentality that pervaded the media when it came to him, he pushed on admirably, given that throughout the fall he would need to be ready for *Monday Night Football* as soon as the lights went dark on *Saturday Night*.

Besides this there was the climactic Ali-Frazier fight to call, which he did on a tape-delay broadcast for *Wide World of Sports*, laying down his narration in a studio as he watched a satellite feed from Manila in real time. The call was a typically gritty, lyrical exposition that rose and fell in rhythm with the pace of a battle royal between two fighters who knew each other's every move—as did he. Describing the match as a "swiftly paced, exciting fight typical of the past two fights between the two," he grew pessimistic about Ali in the tenth round, noting that he was "slow-footed . . . eyes swollen . . . dead tired," as Frazier moved in "steady and relentless" but "unable to land the big punch." But it was Ali who turned the tide by slicing open cuts over both of Frazier's eyes, one of which scabbed over completely. After round thirteen, as the camera zoomed in on the gruesome sight of a bloodied Frazier spitting into a bucket, Cosell said, "Watch the blood come out of the mouth . . . yew." In the fourteenth, Ali, he said, was "working over" Frazier, who staggered back to his corner.

"Eddie Futch leaning over his fighter," Cosell narrated as Frazier slumped on his stool. "Look at Frazier's eyes. Frazier saying 'No—I can't see! I can't see!' That's what he told Eddie Futch. Futch over him—Futch doesn't want the fight to go on!" Ali, who was so spent he had barely made it back to *his* stool, now was on his feet, wearily raising a glove in the air. "He realizes that Frazier will not come out!" Cosell added. "Muhammad Ali is still the heavyweight champion of the world! Frazier, an indomitable warrior, could not make it for the fifteenth round! What a fight!"[35]

The brutality Ali experienced—"the closest thing to dyin' that I know of," he said after the fight—paled perhaps in comparison with the walking death that the staff of *Saturday Night Live* was experiencing. As Don Mischer put it, the show was "a turbulent roller coaster ride," making him rue the day he had turned down the other *Saturday Night*, which by contrast registered as an immediate hit.[36] Dick Ebersol and his producer, Lorne Michaels, had plumbed the same rootstock of Second City/ *National Lampoon* performers for a troupe of their own—named, in riposte to the Cosell band, "the *Not* Ready for Primetime Players." The show was driven by the budding brilliance of John Belushi, Chevy Chase, Dan Aykroyd, and Gilda Radner, who while they backed up a guest host on each program were the ones who captured millions of viewers, establishing new pop culture norms every week. Their confreres at the aboriginal *Saturday Night*, meanwhile, were being buried in a blizzard of lame, anachronistic glitz two and a half hours earlier in prime time.

Yet neither Cosell nor Arledge believed there was anything wrong with their product. Although Cosell had told *People*, "Roone and I don't want to make horse's asses out of ourselves," and had insisted that the show would not compromise his integrity, he ignored all evidence that this was in fact happening. Worse, he also believed he was "running a variety show like a news operation," a contention that surely would have made the crowd at ABC News shudder.[37]


IN THE END, however, Cosell fell victim to his own enormous need to be accepted by the showbiz community. His over-reverence for his guest stars, combined with a belief that Middle America would not tolerate a variety show host who was too abrasive or too arrogant, proved to be his downfall. Accordingly, "the prolix pundit of the press box," as one report dubbed him, was a terse, tense, vanilla-sprayed sycophant, with little nerve or stomach to be himself, either in jest or to express some opinion he thought important. He was not there, he reasoned, to scold anyone. Not even when he was victim of the worst showbiz sin of all. That happened when a segment with Evel Knievel ran long and the next performers, the female soul trio Labelle, they of "Lady Marmalade" fame, was told that their second number would have to be cut. Piqued, their lead singer, Patti LaBelle, refused to have them perform at all, and they walked off in a huff. Arledge—who had vainly tried to change her mind—was so irate he urged Cosell to air the dirty laundry live onstage in explaining the group's absence, and attack Patti LaBelle by name for it, something that Arledge knew would generate helpful headlines and restore Cosell's pugnacious image. Instead, he meekly begged off, telling Arledge he was afraid they'd be sued.

This only proved that there was no chance for a "nice guy" Howard Cosell to flourish. Worse, it might have a residual effect on his regular sports work, eating at his attack-dog persona. As if a chain reaction, everything he did now seemed to make matters worse. Arguably the nadir came when he sang a duet with ABC news anchor Barbara Walters, "Anything You Can Do, I Can Do Better," though one thing neither could do was sing a note on key. It was catching; the high-paid writers and talented comedy troupe seemed to anticipate their early demise, doing bits that left audiences yawning. Alan King, who could perform no surgery that would work, later pinpointed the crux of the problem—Cosell, he said, "made Ed Sullivan look like Buster Keaton."[38]

Calling the whole thing "a detour from rationality," Arledge, with glorious understatement, would say that it "did not work out so well," but absolved himself by invoking the death of the variety format—"You could have Elizabeth Taylor doing a striptease and it wouldn't get a fifteen share." Its cancellation, he said, was "a relief." Without ever coming to Cosell's defense, he readily put the mess behind him and concerned himself with the impending 1976 Winter and Summer Olympics, before moving to his next spot on the corporate ladder, the presidency of ABC News *and* ABC Sports in 1977. So too did Cosell move on, bitter taste in his mouth, insisting that Arledge had "quit on me" and that the press was "relentless" in its attacks, though he did admit that "I don't think the public was ready to accept me, a sportscaster, as the host of a variety show, regardless of how well known I had become." He also allowed that "I was equally at fault" with Arledge, who would never go even that far. As Cosell told it, he could have hindered Arledge's rise to the news division, but didn't, when Fred Pierce asked him if he thought Arledge was a "genius or a hoax." He answered by saying he wouldn't discuss it, though this was hardly a glowing recommendation.[39]

If there was a consolation to the *Saturday Night* debacle, it was that he was able to brag that he had birthed the careers of Murray, Doyle-Murray, Guest, and Crystal, who also appeared on several of the episodes, when they found a home on the hit *Saturday Night Live*—which was free to append the word "Live" when the Cosell entry went under. But, clearly, he was of the opinion that Arledge had done him wrong, then stolen away unscathed while Cosell would have to bear the blame and be the butt of endless jokes about it. Cosell would not try to hide the rift. The show, he said, "caused a split in our friendship," and "that's my biggest single regret" about the entire affair.[40]

ARLEDGE, OF COURSE, still had plans for him. Why not? Cosell still was the franchise at ABC Sports, and he needed to be spared further embarrassment. Thus, Arledge would never use him at the Winter Olympics, for example, using a classic one-liner—that America could never get used to seeing Cosell in ski pants—to avoid saying that his uncompromising style was a poor fit for exotic sports like the bobsled and luge. But Cosell was on his usual beat when the Summer Olympics commenced in Montreal in 1976, saving his most effusive calls for Sugar Ray Leonard, who won all six of his fights by unanimous decision and the light-welterweight gold medal as the breakout star of the U.S. team. But here too Arledge had to save Cosell from embarrassment. Calling a middleweight bout on a tape-delay broadcast, he kept identifying a Polish fighter as Romanian. Arledge caught the error, and while he would admit to being tantalized by the critical reaction—"Oh, the chops licking," he said[41]—if he put the tape on the air, he ordered a new announce track to replace the original on the tape, which a sheepish Cosell did in an empty arena to re-create the acoustics, so perfectly in pitch that no one at home knew the difference.

By midsummer of 1976, as well, Arledge had made sure Cosell would be seen and heard when ABC paid $50 million in a four-year deal to revive *Monday Night Baseball* that season. This was a major coup for Arledge because even though Monday night baseball was a ratings graveyard, the baseball barons reciprocated by permitting ABC to crack NBC's monopoly on postseason games. NBC, which paid $42.8 million to continue its Saturday Game of the Week over this period, would now alternate with ABC coverage of the two league championship series and the World Series; NBC would have the World Series in odd-numbered years, ABC in even-numbered years, giving ABC that bauble for the first time in 1977. Arledge was so giddy about the deal that years later when he recalled it in his memoirs he somehow made NBC disappear, along with reality, writing that "ABC Sports moved closer to *über alles* status with the pilfering of Major League Baseball [from NBC]" for $92 million.[42]

He did not, however, exaggerate how mightily he had to fight to get Cosell on the broadcast package. It couldn't have been a tougher sell considering how Cosell had lacerated the sport as a "medieval pastime" and its "sportsmen" owners as "carpetbaggers," though he saved most of his invective for commissioner Bowie Kuhn, who fought to preserve a dying orthodoxy. He continued these diatribes even after the fall of the autocratic reserve clause. That happened when pitchers Andy Messersmith and Dave McNally, who had not signed a contract with their teams during the previous season, unilaterally declared themselves free agents. On

December 23, 1975, they were vindicated when federal labor relations arbitrator Peter Seitz ruled that they were indeed free to sign with the highest bidders, nullifying for good the reserve clause. (The ruling was upheld on appeal, and in 1976 the owners and players signed a new collective bargaining agreement allowing players with six years' experience to become free agents.)

Hardly nullified was the mutual loathing between Cosell and Kuhn. How Kuhn felt about Cosell was evident when Arledge informed him that Cosell would be on the ABC coverage, news that Arledge said "sent the normally sweet-tempered Bowie into paroxysms. Over his dead body, he vowed. Never in a million years. Wasn't going to happen—and if I tried to make it happen, he'd give baseball back to NBC that afternoon." But Kuhn was a less than gifted dissembler, and an even worse bluffer. Arledge knew that ABC's money was in the bank. He also knew Cosell, inside out, and how to manipulate him. "Go out to lunch with Howard. Underneath it all, you'll see he's really a fan," he said he suggested to Kuhn. "Bowie didn't believe a word of it. But what I said was true. Offer Howard national television time, he'd have good words for Pick Up sticks." In the end, he said, "Howard emerged from lunch proclaiming Bowie his new best friend," having told Kuhn that baseball was "a game that I have loved since childhood."[43]

Here again Arledge fuddled the facts. Cosell actually had no part in the baseball package almost until the very end of the season. For the previous six months, the three-man baseball booth Arledge had assembled— the laconic veteran Pittsburgh Pirates play-by-play man Bob Prince, an eager young Washington TV sportscaster named Warner Wolf, and the former catcher-cum-comedian Bob Uecker, he of the deadpan ad lib— failed to generate any chemistry. Dennis Lewin, the producer, remembers them in one word—"awful." That posed a problem as the high-visibility American League Championship Series loomed, which became more highly visible when the resurrected New York Yankees won their division and would play for their first pennant in twelve years, against the gritty Kansas City Royals, in a series that would climax at the newly refurbished Yankee Stadium. For Arledge, that Cosell had never broadcast a baseball game before was a mere blip, given that he knew the game back and forth and was a natural for such a top-shelf event; and his hostility toward the sport could only add a dimension of incipient melodrama.

Cosell recalled that he was "stunned" by the call to arms, coming as it did "out of the blue." But not as stunned as Kuhn, who reeled when Arledge told him about the change. It was then that the meeting Arledge described took place, mandatorily at the "21" Club. There, Kuhn treated Arledge and Cosell to a harangue. Looking Cosell in the eye, he foamed, "I can't imagine you'd be the right man for the job. It's wrong for the package, wrong for ABC, wrong for baseball, and certainly wrong for you." Given his turn, Cosell defended his baseball critiques as "a matter of principle" and professed that his love of the game was unadulterated, then accused Kuhn of attempting to "put shills" on the broadcast, "and that should not be tolerated." Sticking his cigar in his mouth, he then got up, with John Lennon as his exemplar, and headed out, leaving Kuhn to settle it with Arledge. Kuhn, he recalled, was "taken aback," but he was also "impressed with my candor." Hours later, Kuhn assented.[44]

Cosell would supplant Warner Wolf, who was shuffled off to work on the National League Championship Series between the Cincinnati Reds and Philadelphia Phillies, in a new team with play-by-play man Al Michaels and guest analyst Tom Seaver, the erudite Mets pitcher. For the American League series, Arledge dismissed Prince and brought in his old reliable, Keith Jackson, and as analyst the brash slugger Reggie Jackson, who would sign a gargantuan free agent deal with the Yankees over the winter. But it would be Cosell who would be the center of gravity. Easing into a game he loved to hate, he re-created the *MNF* tone and texture, even if too many of his anecdotes and perspectives, geared to days when he was young and the Dodgers were in Brooklyn, were seriously démodé. Somehow he fit neatly into the creases between the two Jacksons, setting the tone and texture, doing so not as a boor but a "catalyst," noted William Leggett in *Sports Illustrated*.[45]

But this was, after all, Cosell. In Kansas City for the first two games, he played to Middle America sensibilities; but when the series shifted for the final three games, Leggett would observe, "show biz really took over," baseball grist moving over for "interviews with baseball luminaries Frank Sinatra, Bruce Jenner and Hammerin' Henry Kissinger." Back in celebrity-sniffing mode, Cosell grandly welcomed the latter, insisting that the secretary of state had attended the Yankees' home opener at their refurbished stadium. When Kissinger said he had not been there, Cosell nearly argued with him that he *was*. By now, he was, comfortably and immodestly, the only voice in the booth that mattered. Baseball, *and* Bowie Kuhn, were in his hip pocket.

At times, the two Jacksons would all but evaporate; often when a big play occurred, he would step on Keith Jackson's call to inject a stabbing "Oh!" or "What a play!" Dennis Lewin, in the director's seat, was quite familiar with that habit, recalling today that "in 1962, when Jim Beatty ran the first indoor four-minute mile, we had it on *Wide World of Sports*, and when Beatty got to the finish line Howard stepped all over Jim McKay's call."[46]

There was no chance he would be silent when the series was decided, in molto dramatic fashion, in the deciding fifth game. In the bottom of the ninth, the score tied 6–6, burly Yankee first baseman Chris Chambliss got good wood on a high fastball thrown by Mark Littell. As the ball streaked into the night air and the Yankee Stadium crowd roared, Keith Jackson reported, with prudent caution, "There's a high drive deep to right-center field"—when Cosell barged in, barking, "That's *gone!*" The problem was, it wasn't, not yet. In fact, as Jackson picked up his call, the ball descended on a trajectory that might not clear the right-field fence, where Hal McRae leaped high in the air for it. Jackson, needing to wait, drew out his words, crooning, "It . . . is . . ." When McRae slumped against the wall, empty-handed, he finally could cry "gone!" As Chambliss tried somehow to find his way through a horde of delirious fans who stormed the field, Cosell interrupted again, bellowing, "Chris Chambliss has won the American League pennant for the New York Yankees! A thrilling, dramatic game . . . What a way for the American League season to end!"[47]

There wasn't much Jackson, or anyone, could do at moments like that. Such was the price of making room for Howard Cosell, whose presence in the ABC baseball booth would be sporadic but always held in abeyance by the network for big-ticket events—none bigger for ABC than the 1977 World Series. By then, he and Bowie Kuhn had made a dramatic turnaround and had indeed become fast friends. It was Kuhn, in fact, who initiated the rapprochement, inviting the Cosells to dinner with him and his wife in a ritzy Westhampton Beach eatery. Emmy didn't mince words when they got there. "I don't know why we're here," she told Kuhn. "You don't like us, and we're not particularly fond of you." Kuhn explained that while he hadn't appreciated her husband's positions about the game, "I've always found him an interesting man, and I enjoy his company."[48]

The evening went well, and soon they were neighbors on that chic strip of beach, when the Cosells purchased a tony summer waterfront home in Westhampton from New England Patriots owner Billy Sullivan—with whom Cosell had been closer with than any other owner. The irony was that he was becoming comfortable broadcasting a sport that had so irked him for so long but was now something of a sanctuary. Meanwhile, the two sports that brought him to prominence—boxing and football—became more and more discomfiting.

Indeed, Cosell would yearn to get away from big-time sports altogether, and was pleased when the network gave him another shot at a prime-time entertainment show. Taped in late summer, it was an hour-long special that had been spun off from an ABC Sports weekend anthology show called *The Superstars*, which pitted real athletes in quaint competitions like relay races, tug-of-war, obstacle course, golf, bowling, and tennis. Given the earnestly flippant name *Battle of the Network Stars*, it substituted a conveyor belt of TV actors and actresses in outrageously translucent T-shirts playing for their networks, filmed on the lush beaches of Malibu.

The show made its debut on November 13, 1976, a Saturday night that would be kinder to Cosell this time around. The ratings were good enough to stoke a second show in May 1977. Thereafter, ABC, which at last won the network rating war in 1977, would keep renewing the show, running fresh episodes twice yearly through 1984, another in 1985, another in 1988, with Cosell anchoring all save the last two. Whatever else *Battle* was, it came for him as a form of blessed relief, given the sleepless nights caused by his regular workload. Indeed, if the success of this trash-sport show was yet another reminder that Howard Cosell was still coming through loud and clear, for various reasons it was becoming obvious that the signal was getting weaker.

## PART THREE

# Turn Out the Lights

## (1976–1995)

# 16

---

## AN UNHOLY MESS

B Y THE mid to late seventies, sports, like much of the rest of society, were no longer a paleontological preserve, governed by long and unbudging conventions. Now, with a peanut farmer named Carter in the White House, metaphorical walls were coming down all over, including those around the quaint "gentleman's club" of owners who guarded profitable, monopolistic fiefdoms.

Cosell's rise to prominence was in part due to his taking on this power structure, but now the causes had mainly been won. The reserve clause was gone; the first African American manager was hired—not Jackie Robinson, as Cosell had desired, but another eminently worthy Robinson named Frank, so employed by the Cleveland Indians in 1975; women's athletics had begun to get equal financial footing. At the same time, salaries in every sport were mushrooming, bartered by sports agents fulfilling the early promise of Cosell's original incarnation and generating endless player-management strife. The power of the ubiquitous tube reached a new level when Atlanta Braves owner Ted Turner took his team's games national on his own cable TV network, presaging future lucrative pay networks owned solely by individual teams.

That Cosell could have declared *Monday Night Football* an "institution" after three years was in itself confirmation that there were now entirely new borders to confront. And Cosell was better equipped by intellect to grasp what was happening—having predicted so much of it—than, say, Dick Young, whose age and crimped worldview had rendered him a dinosaur. What's more, television was now the main source of sports information, something Cosell had of course divined, and in large part helped codify. Cosell was unarguably on top of the evolving issues. But he was also beginning to feel like he too was a dinosaur, stuck as he was in a bog, his regular duties, aside from his *Speaking of Everything* radio show and the occasional break for baseball or *Battle of the Network Stars*, offering scant relief from a growing malaise.

Nearing his sixtieth year, he still thought of himself as visionary, the ultimate apostate. If he needed convincing, there were his old foils to angry up his blood. The biggest, Dick Young, was just as odious as ever. In 1975, when labor negotiator Peter Seitz killed baseball's reserve clause, giving birth to the new reality of free agency, Young wrote that "Peter Seitz reminds me of a terrorist, a little man to whom nothing very important has happened in his lifetime, who suddenly decides to create some excitement by tossing a bomb into things."[1]

In the winter of 1976, when Cosell was calling a series of amateur boxing matches between the United States and Cuba in Havana, he even landed an interview with Fidel Castro, his first live interview on American television. The session was highly intriguing, with Castro speaking of his young days as a semipro baseball player and his enduring love for the American game. Cosell was furious when ordered to cut short the interview so that the network could switch to its coverage of the Winter Olympics—the decision that of an ABC producer named Ned Steckel, who, Cosell said, "lived his professional life in a thimble" and "thought that speed skating was more significant than an interview with a world leader." Cosell later said that even the U.S. State Department had objected to Castro's being "yanked off the air" and had contacted Arledge about it. But the worst of it was reading Young in the next day's *Daily News* savaging him for being soft on the Communist dictator, his crime being that he referred to Castro as "El Comandante." It's easy to imagine

Cosell stalking around the office, brandishing the *News* and screaming in disbelief, "Now I'm a Communist!"[2]

Jim Spence, the longtime ABC Sports vice president, would by rote nod his head when Cosell went into a tirade about Young. "Did you see this trash?" he recalled one wild-eyed Cosell rant. "Have you seen this piece of shit? Do you know what this son of a bitch wrote about me today? Do you *know*? *Do you*? These attacks on me simply have to stop. My network must do something about this man. He's a *madman*!" For Spence, as for those in the other suites, "there was no point in trying to calm Howard down. You had to let him go until he ran down," which normally meant hearing him blister Young as "the most despicable man in America!" and declare that "he dedicated his life to destroying me."[3]

It was once said that the idea of hell for both men was a place where Young turned on the television set and found that every channel was ABC and where Cosell found the only paper was the *Daily News*. Yet Cosell and Young were alike in more ways than they thought, especially when it came to their generational intolerance about new societal norms such as drug use and pornography. Cosell, the old American Legion commander and inveterate prude—notwithstanding the crass liberties he took when in the company of women—had never been quite comfy about certain mutinous aspects of the "happening" generation he swore he fit into. Yet despite his abhorrence of this new permissive age, he would never admit to being too old to be the ultimate voice of sport, any sport.

To be sure, he was still secure in the aging realm of boxing, as long as Muhammad Ali still owned the sport, which he did by successfully defending his title four times in 1976, with Cosell a vital part of that profitable franchise. However, there were now some chinks in that wall. While he enjoyed narrating the fledgling pro fights of Sugar Ray Leonard, whose flashy moves, engaging personality, and use of Angelo Dundee as trainer made him seem like an Ali redux, he grew tired of covering Ali fights that were now no more than charades in which the aging champ would fight only enough to beat his opponents and pocket a big check. And though Ali could elevate his game for a big-ticket match, such as a third clash with Ken Norton, at Yankee Stadium in September, ABC no longer held a monopoly. NBC, moving in, would break it when it landed a live showing of Ali's September 1977 bout against Earnie Shavers at Madison Square Garden.

Cosell and Ali now seemed like ships passing in the night. They were no longer much interested in doing the old elbow-poking shtick that reeked of times past. Cosell at times seemed to resent that ABC would send him out on the Ali trail, even when it was a road to nowhere. In 1975, for example, ABC carried a cheesy exhibition by the now-vanquished George Foreman, in which he would box five lower-rung opponents, one after the other. Sent to Toronto to cover the affair, with Ali hired to provide ringside commentary, Cosell was aghast as Foreman, seemingly losing his mind at the sight of Ali, attacked several fighters and their corner men after the bell. The sorry spectacle, he said on the air, was "a zany non-advertisement for boxing," a "charade," and "depressing."

The astute Robert Lipsyte would cite this dim episode in *SportsWorld* as an example of why "Cosell is a genuine superstar" who "is the only broadcaster in America who can be the promoter, the reporter, and the critic of an event packaged and merchandised by his own network." Still, he added, "ABC produced a bomb, and Cosell absolved them of responsibility by turning around and blaming [Foreman], the nature of boxing, and the appetite of the public. Cosell is the franchise. He may also be the most valuable property in American sports."[4] Lipsyte's loyalty to Cosell was clear, yet he may not have realized that he was in fact reinforcing the charge Cosell hated the most, that he was a "shill" who would shield his network at all costs. And that would become even more evident, to an embarrassing degree, two years later.

By then, Cosell had returned to his outspoken criticism of and doubt about the man he had pronounced finished before he rose to reclaim the title. After a somnolent Ali needed the full fifteen rounds to defeat a nobody named Alfredo Evangelista in May 1977, Cosell called it "one of the worst fights ever fought." He commented that Ali was "shot," and took to task the World Boxing Council for manipulating its rankings in exchange for a "licensing fee" to place Evangelista in its rankings of the top ten contenders. This calumny had been a central rant on his college lecture tours, when he would judge his own network harshly, though only in general terms, for coughing up big fees for the rights to "phony title fights and egregious mismatches," challenging all the networks to "use some other independent source for ranking fighters." Doing so, he said, "could be a start toward cleaning up the sport."[5]

Thus, some months before, he and nearly everyone else at ABC Sports had been content that they were doing just that, with a new slice of boxing programming that would steer clear of all the boxing alphabet-soup sodalities, but that would—ominously—take its cues from Don King, hardly the oracle of a new, pristine boxing landscape. King, in fact, had become a virtual Adam's rib of the WBC, in antagonistic polarity with Bob Arum, who was equally intertwined with the World Boxing Association. Despite this, in the fall of 1976 King came to ABC Sports peddling an elimination tournament in various weight classes to run ten consecutive weekends.

The ABC Sports brass did hold King to a few conditions. Each bout would feature fighters with rankings certified by the venerable boxing "bible," the *Ring* magazine, and judges would be selected by James Farley, the chairman of the New York State Athletic Commission. Spence, charmed or conned, but mostly in fear that King would go to CBS or NBC with the project, told Arledge he believed that it was "a very well-thought-out plan." Arledge then signed off on a $1.5 million payment to King for the tournament, though he later would cover his back by dumping it all on Spence—and, not far behind, Cosell. Both of them, he recalled later, were "hot" for the proposal, and he particularly ostracized Cosell by quoting him as saying the tournament was "a dream come true for many faceless, hardworking fighters who toiled in backwater arenas for a couple hundred bucks and the use of a locker."[6]

Like everyone else who stepped into this potential sewer, Cosell would retrospectively plead ignorance about his role. He would claim, contradictorily, that "I was a minor principal in the story," though the thought of him *ever* being minor in any broadcast he did was preposterous.[7] By the time the U.S. Boxing Championships premiered on Sunday, January 16, 1977, the only ABC Sports staffer who wasn't sanguine about it was an aggressive thirty-two-year-old associate producer for the tournament,

Alex Wallau, who quickly discerned with minimal effort that not a one of King's fighters was ranked by *Ring* as a top-ten contender. Not atypical was that an undefeated contender who refused to sign with King had been excluded—Marvin Hagler, the future light-heavyweight champ.

So tipped off by Wallau, Spence had told him to file a full report, but the tournament would not be delayed, with undefeated heavyweight Larry Holmes defeating unknown Tom Prater. In fact, Cosell tried to undermine Wallau, portraying him as an arriviste seeking to build himself up by taking down the tournament. When Wallau turned in his report, with ample evidence that the tournament was rife with fraud, the ABC brass did nothing, perhaps loath to be lumped in by King with his detractors, whom he accused of trying to "fry this coon"—a charge seconded by Muhammad Ali, who said, "There's only one thing wrong. They got a spook running the tournament."[8]

For Arledge, it was good enough that Cosell had asked Angelo Dundee if the fighters' rankings were legitimate, and Dundee said they were—without admitting he had a financial stake in several of those fighters. Not incidentally, early ratings for the tournament were excellent. However, the scandal refused to go away, and the tournament began to sink. On February 13, heavyweight Scott LeDoux battered his opponent Johnny Boudreaux, but the latter, a Don King protégé, was declared the winner. As Cosell was interviewing Boudreaux outside the ropes, LeDoux hovered above them on the lip of the ring, shrieking, "Fix!" and "You tell it like it is, Howard! You tell the truth!" Boudreaux spat out a remark about LeDoux's mother, whereupon LeDoux tried to kick him in the face. In the melee, Boudreaux's leg somehow got caught in Cosell's headset, sweeping off his toupee, which fell onto the floor under the swarm of bodies. Reaching instinctively to cover his bald pate, Cosell picked up the rug and stuck it right back on, so quickly that no one watching knew he'd been "naked" for a split second. ABC soon cut away for the start of its high-rated *American Sportsman* anthology series, but Arledge, in the truck, ordered Chet Forte, who was producing, to get the network back so Cosell could interview LeDoux, who proceeded to label the tournament a farce and a fraud. Cosell could only nod helplessly.[9]

He wasn't quite ready to agree. In April, the *CBS Evening News* ran a scathing segment about it by Dan Rather. After watching it, Cosell sniffed, "Dan Rather gave Roone Arledge and ABC a sick, cheap shot. It was totally distorted. He used interviews two months old, out of context. It was a sickening thing to see Rather do. If Rather ever faced me head-to-head, it would be his last hurrah." But if Arledge had been circumspect about taking the tournament off the air, the flak he took in the press made him flinch—none more so than a *Sports Illustrated* piece that speculated Arledge might have "muffed his chances of becoming president of ABC News because of the brouhaha." Only days before the semifinal, Arledge fell on his sword, suspending the cursed tournament, arguably his nadir as ABC Sports chief.[10]

Of course, Cosell too had been an obvious target of derision. As he said later, "As ABC's most visible on-air personality, I took a lot of the heat. One sportswriter went so far as to call me 'the architect of a boxing scandal.'" Looking back, he admitted there had been "gross improprieties," that "King and his cronies had played fast and loose with ABC, and somehow I got caught in the middle." In light of his unqualified support of the tournament, he could not have been more unctuous or hypocritical when he retroactively decried that it had been an "unholy mess," bulging with "favoritism, kickbacks, falsified records, and rigged ratings," and lamented that "corruption was all around." Almost laughably, he praised ABC as heroic, because the network had "initiated its own investigation into the sordid affair and took the tournament off the air." But that did not prevent him from laying the blame for the entire fiasco on Spence. Notwithstanding his own ennui about Wallau's warnings, he was soon overheard by an ABC colleague saying of Spence, "The guy makes $100,000 a year and doesn't read his memos? Fuck him.' "[11]

DESPITE THE ethical issues involved in the boxing scandal—not that he would ever admit to having any—Cosell regarded himself the highest moral authority in sports and sports broadcasting, nearly alone holding back the reprobates at the gate. This was evident when he escaped to the cloisters of academia, extending his sport-and-society lectures into a full curriculum, giving seminars at Yale in 1977 and his alma mater NYU in

1978, under the course title "Big-Time Sports in Contemporary America." As the prospectus read, the course took "a hard look at the contradiction . . . between sports as an American ideal . . . and the exploitation and manipulation of this ideal by vested interests, including Mr. Cosell's own, the broadcasting industry." Guest lecturers would include Pete Rozelle, Roone Arledge, the Knicks' scholarly Bill Bradley, and Yankees general manager Gabe Paul. Both semesters, the classroom was filled with eager students, whom he told, "The first thing I want you to do is stop clapping. I did not come here as a national celebrity to tell you sports stories."

Indeed, he gratuitously vilified some superstar athletes whom he had fawned over in the past. During the NYU course, he called Mickey Mantle, whose excesses he had once coddled, a "drunk and a whoremonger." His former ABC boothmate Reggie Jackson was "sometimes the biggest pain in the ass in the world." Of George Allen, who had quit the Washington Redskins to return to coaching the L.A. Rams, "He'll destroy that team." More familiarly, the sporting press was "insidiously corrupt," and broadcast journalism "at least openly corrupt." However, after only a few weeks at NYU, he seemed to want out, claiming scheduling conflicts. Then, after he said he'd stay on, his class was disrupted by a student exhibiting "irrational behavior," according to school security. Shaken, Cosell resigned from the course a month early.[12]

Such querulousness was becoming typical, no matter where he was. Once haughty but never overly unpleasant, his inner spring was now wound too tightly to allow his playful wit or natural affability to surface. An ABC Sports publicity man at the time, Tom Mackin, recalls that during the 1976 Olympics in Montreal, his own young daughters were thrilled at the prospect of meeting Cosell. Seeing him at the network's headquarters, the two girls ran over to him and squealed, "We're Tom Mackin's daughters." Cosell looked down his cigar at them with disdain. "So what," he responded.

"My girls were crushed," Mackin says. "I never forgave Cosell for that."[13]

Mackin was also with Cosell when he traveled to the Missouri University School of Journalism to give a lecture. He recalls him unnerving people the entire time. Once, when a student asked him about the Ku Klux Klan organizing a local chapter, Mackin says, Cosell looked indifferent and declared, "I don't care if they kill the Jews, but I want the niggers left alone." Another time, he was asked, "How do you like being disliked?" He stared down the kid and told him, "You are the dumbest white man I ever met."[14] In the past, of course, he had mouthed such swill as a way of defusing racial tension, with a clear satirical jab and wink of the eye. Now, like ABC Sports' glorious past, those qualities were withering.

Jim Spence has his own story about Cosell in Montreal, where, because of the tragedy in Munich, Canadian Olympic authorities employed extra security. Although Cosell had cursed the Germans for their lax approach to the safety of athletes and visitors, Spence recalled him taking umbrage when his credentials were strictly checked. Impatiently waiting at one checkpoint as a female guard made him wait before entering the Olympic Village, he demanded to be let through. "My dear," he oozed, "I have a very important interview in the village. I am perilously close to being late and I cannot abide tardiness. Now, if you will excuse me." He began to stride through the gate, only to be stopped again. Becoming irate, he barked, "My dear, I'll have you fired. I'm the single most recognizable figure in television today, and I will not tolerate this kind of infantile behavior. Do you understand? This is a ridiculous exercise and I simply do not have time for it."

By then he was trembling, his forefinger jammed almost in the girl's chest, and causing a scene. "Get me someone in authority!" he went on. "The American Broadcasting Company will not be treated this way." Then, almost unbelievably, given what he'd seen in Munich, "You people are treating these young [athletes] as though they are prisoners. Let me remind you, this is not Auschwitz!" It grew so ugly that armed guards had to confront him to quiet him. But as Spence observed, Cosell would merely "shake off with a shrug" incidents like that—not to mention his own blatant hypocrisies—"and quickly turn his attention to someone easier to impress, or, if necessary, steamroller."[15]

BASEBALL SEEMED to be able to reclaim something of the lost Cosell. After selected appearances during the 1977 season's Monday night broadcasts, he was front and center when the network readied for its first-ever World Series, though its coverage was held to a higher standard than it could meet. *Sports Illustrated*'s William Leggett, who had praised the network's handling of the championship series the year before, averred that "ABC showed it still has not learned to cope with baseball's vital nuances. And it insults the intelligence of viewers in a way no other network does: make lots of noise, show a close-up of Barbara Walters sitting in the stands, get tons of publicity for Howard Cosell, send up the blimps, bring on the clowns, show a fire burning in the night sky."[16]

Leggett's last, oblique reference was the first such in the media—but nowhere near the last. Because if Cosell was renowned or reviled for the things he said, his altitude was such that he would become famous for something he *didn't* say. That now infamous line, which has become synonymous with the Rome-like implosion of New York City in the late seventies—"Ladies and gentlemen, the Bronx is burning"—would become soldered to Cosell's legend when it was requisitioned by Jonathan Mahler as the title of his 2004 book, which was then truncated to *The Bronx Is Burning* for the notable 2007 ESPN miniseries taken from it.

Never had a Cosell bon mot seemed more apt for its time as when this one was applied to the crumbling world outside the stadium where the fussin' and feudin' Yankees provided a metaphoric antidote to the ruin all around them by winning the World Series. If John Turturro's movie re-creation of Yankee manager Billy Martin was psychotically memorable—though no less so than his role as Cosell in the TNT cable network movie *Monday Night Mayhem* four years before—the phrase that served up the motif made Cosell a key player, though he was never seen, heard, or portrayed in the film.

That Mahler, and then the ESPN publicists, attributed this quote to Cosell seemed to be good enough; it was something no one doubted he *would have* said. The *New York Times,* in a review of the Mahler book, breathlessly recounted: "It was Game 2 of the 1977 World Series, the Yankees locked in mortal struggle with the Dodgers. As night descended, ABC, broadcasting the game, cut to a helicopter camera for an overhead view of Yankee Stadium and the surrounding neighborhood, where, bizarrely, a large fire raged out of control. Howard Cosell intoned, 'There it is, ladies and gentlemen, the Bronx is burning' . . . Cosell's terse observation gave Jonathan Mahler a catchy title for his first book and a potent metaphor for a city gripped by crisis. The Yankees, powered by an expensive free agent named Reggie Jackson, would win the series and proceed to create a dynasty."[17]

However, all this sheen became problematic when the issue arose as to whether Cosell actually had said such a thing that night. His boothmates, Keith Jackson and Tom Seaver, would say they never heard him say it, and neither did producer Dennis Lewin. The ABC archive might have settled the issue, had not the network brass ordered its video sports library destroyed in the late seventies to make space in its vaults, wiping out much of the network's greatest legacy, as well as Cosell's. Only because Lewin, on his own, heroically salvaged some canisters did anything survive, including early Muhammad Ali fights and selected *Monday Night Football* and Olympics broadcasts—as well as the climactic sixth game of that 1977 World Series when Reggie Jackson clubbed three home runs to nail it down for the Yankees, the last provoking Cosell to eschew balladry and involuntarily yelp, "Oh! What a blow! Oh! What a way to top it off!" and then lay on an extra-thick topping, "How this man has responded to pressure! Oh, what a beam on his face! He's answered the whole world! After all the furor, after all the hassling, it comes down to *this*!" However, the previous games mainly perished.

What was known was that during Game 2, fires indeed burned beyond the right-field wall. But what did Cosell say? It was a mystery until Carl Shimkin, an Internet baseball blogger, tracked down in 2007 the only complete record of the game, the unedited tapes that Major League Baseball had used to compile a recent DVD of the Series. "I couldn't wait to hear Cosell say it," Shimkin says. Instead, "it was Keith Jackson who first points out the massive warehouse fire behind Yankee Stadium during the second inning. The cameras were from ABC helicopters. All Cosell says as ABC cuts to a series of shots of the fire is something like, 'That's exactly the street that President Carter trod on just the week before!'" Shimkin then interviewed the executive producer of *The Bronx Is Burning*, Gordon Greisman, who admitted "he never said it" but argued that it was "harmless baseball legend and lore." Mahler himself would in time admit it, too, confirming that he had conflated Cosell's

natural predilections for literary references and the title of the 1972 documentary *The Bronx Is Burning*, based on New York City firefighter
Dennis Smith's book *Report from Engine Company 82*.[18]

Of course, Cosell did leave his mark on that World Series, though it
was more of a stain for Leggett, who wrote that "Cosell intruded on the
action" and that he "knows little about baseball as it has been played in
the 1960s and '70s, does not particularly care for the game and seemed
to be reading constantly from a set of bubble gum cards extolling the
virtues of the 1953 Brooklyn Dodgers."[19] Still, when the final out of
Game 6 fell into Jackson's glove, Cosell was primed. As the camera isolated on Reggie racing for the dugout through jubilant Yankee fans, Keith
Jackson was saying, "The New York Yankees win the World Series!"
Cosell, however, cut him short to croon, "We've traced the season for
you, the ups and downs, the emotions on the playing field, the way they
came from behind to beat the Red Sox and the Birds, the way they came
from behind to beat the Royals . . ."[20] On and on it went, for a good minute, before Jackson had the microphone back. In the end, making his and
his beloved network's first World Series memorable, he had the last word
on the season. He would have accepted nothing less.

NONETHELESS, EVEN these baseball milestones could not break the
yoke *Monday Night Football* had on him. They could only bring fleeting
relief from the dread he felt going back to the program that had been
central to the general fortunes of ABC. And fortunes they were. The
1976–77 prime-time TV season climaxed the network's long, hard climb
to the top of the Nielsen ratings, the Monday night cross-promotions of
ABC programming having helped to cement the success of shows like
*Happy Days, Laverne and Shirley, Mork and Mindy*, and *Starsky and
Hutch*. While Cosell considered himself, with good cause, the fulcrum of
*MNF*, when NBC looked to lure another of the show's big talents, it was
not him. Rather, the vaunted peacock came for the man who had guided
the show to its apogee, Don Ohlmeyer, with an offer to jump ship and
produce the 1980 Moscow Olympics three years hence. And Ohlmeyer
was more than ready to listen.

Prosperous as *MNF* was, living under the gun of so many negative crosscurrents and psychodramas had worn Ohlmeyer down. Like Cosell and Arledge, he felt stunted, confined. The half a million dollars NBC president Herb Schlosser offered him helped make the decision for him. But graduating from Roone's cohort to executive producer of the Olympics was the clincher. "It was really like leaving the womb," is how he puts it.[21]

It couldn't have come at a worse time for Arledge, who was being squeezed in every direction. For the 1977 season, Pete Rozelle had driven a hard bargain with the networks. With the league going to a sixteen-game schedule, he upped its TV rights fees to then-stratospheric levels. All three networks were gouged, but ABC was the victim of its own success; having paid the lowest toll for NFL games, it now had to pay the highest, $232 million, a sevenfold increase since 1970. Not only that, Rozelle pushed four extra games on ABC the next season, split between Sunday and Thursday nights, which were unable to borrow the Monday night aesthetic or numbers.

If anything helped to counterbalance the scales for Arledge, it was that, with the '77 season approaching, *he* was able to play poacher himself, when word was floated that Dandy Don Meredith was not happy after three years at NBC. Despite being given a number of acting assignments by the network—including a cowboy pilot called *Banjo Hackett: Roamin' Free* that mercifully never made it—he had grown unhappy in his football announcing duties. Teamed with the earnest Curt Gowdy on Sunday afternoons, the entire dynamic was different. It was less loose and ad-lib, more rock-rib football—with nowhere near the attention quotient. Friends could hardly believe it when they saw him boning up for games by actually studying playbooks, which he did sullenly. Not even calling two Super Bowls could stop him pining for the old traveling freak show, as Meredith himself called *MNF*, that had required so little preparation, work, or thought but brought him so much attention.

Early in 1977, with his contract expiring, he had his agent, Ed Hookstratten, verbally accept a new NBC offer that would pay him $400,000. But then Meredith and his wife joined his old buddy Frank Gifford and his newlywed bride on a vacation to Europe, and when he got back, not

surprisingly, he wanted back in at *Monday Night Football*. Feeling like a
fool, Hookstratten quit on him, NBC threatened to sue if Meredith
walked on them, and ABC said *they* would sue if he *didn't*.

In time, emotions cooled, nobody sued anybody, and Meredith came
home, in effect traded one-for-one for Ohlmeyer. ABC matched the salary offer, paying him $400,000, only slightly below Cosell's overall salary.
And Cosell felt relieved at the retrenchment, having come to believe that
*MNF* had lost its edge, still able to amass big ratings but a boring chore
for him, his malaise evident by his clipped conversations with Alex Karras. When Meredith came back, Cosell figured it would restore the old
pizzazz. However, it wouldn't take long before Cosell was again bridling
that Gifford and Meredith, the two jocks who he liked to note were
"thick as thieves," were forming an even stronger axis against him.

When speaking about Meredith, Cosell would become exceedingly
nasty. Meredith, he would write, had left *MNF* out of professional jealousy of him, with a fixation to be a star. While Dandy Don reckoned he
had proven he was one during the NBC years, Cosell disagreed. During
Meredith's absence, he boasted publicly that "I made that fool" and ridiculed Meredith for trying to throw off the "Dandy Don" label, one that
Cosell maintained would typecast him for life.[22] When Meredith
returned, Cosell ventured that he should be grateful to ABC for rescuing
his career.

Clearly, what rankled Cosell was that people at the network were still
in thrall to Meredith, while at the same time taking him for granted, this
despite his own star growing higher in the sky and his dutifully signing a
new contract with ABC every four years. As Hilton said, no doubt reflecting his famous brother's sentiments, "You know what ABC stands for? It
stands for Atta Boy, Cosell." Indeed, Cosell may have gotten grouchy and
petulant, losing many of his endearing qualities, but much of the national
media still doted on him. When *The New Yorker* found him again after
twenty years, in October 1975, he was for writer Michael J. Arlen a lonely
voice in the new TV wilderness, holding back nearly alone a spreading
tedium that had turned TV into "another utility, like the telephone," even
if the Cosell method was "popular and telegenic sadism." Similarly, in the

July 1977 *Atlantic,* Benjamin DeMott pegged Cosell as the classic celebrity—famous for being a celebrity, as a "kind of joke—weightless, thoughtless, theatrical, semigenuine."[23]

Harsh as these judgments were, the attention was enough. In 1979, he would even make it into *Cosmopolitan,* along with Emmy, who begged to differ with the assumption that her husband was a bully. "People think Howard's all a matter of blacks and whites, that there are no grays to the guy," she said. "But he's vastly more complicated than they think." The writer, Jane Howard, noted, "It's hard to think of anyone more pompous, or more high-minded, or more bombastic, or more devoted to his family, or more generous, or more impassioned . . . Funny he doesn't seem more relaxed about [his fame]. Funny he remains, at sixty-one, so driven."[24]

Meredith's return, with all the unresolved issues and ego challenges between them, only seemed to make Cosell more driven to *be* Cosell. Certainly, he was more embittered about Meredith's Emmy—and, for that matter, the one won by Gifford in 1977 as Outstanding Sports Personality. But refusing to take a backseat, as if he could, meant any game he called had great moments of high drama and low comedy—when compelled to fill the air with not punditry but pedantry, out could come something like, as he said of 49ers quarterback Tom Owen during one game, "I'm impressed by the continuity of his physical presence." However, there was little amusing about the *lack* of continuity in the booth, where the old black magic seemed lost.

Dennis Lewin, who had been called back to produce when Ohlmeyer left, felt as if he were now among strangers. "Howard and Don were different, they were a lot more serious, egotistical. The chemistry wasn't the same, they were less fun, and when they were with each other it was tense. In the early days they loved doing something completely new and different. It was all uncharted territory. Now, it was like there *was* nothing new anymore, and nothing funny to say. And they each thought the other was the problem."[25]

Neither was Meredith happy with ABC, which had promised to continue his forays into TV shows and movies but didn't follow through. In 1978, when the NFL schedule was expanded to sixteen games, and the

*Monday Night Football* package to twenty, including the four Thursday and Sunday night games, Meredith demurred that his contract only called for him to work fourteen games a season, which while technically true was a trivial matter to everyone else under contract. Having ABC over a barrel, Meredith was left to pass up those extra games,—leading Cosell to claim that those were the best *MNF* broadcasts of all, with him and Gifford "marvelously in tune." He quoted Gifford as proclaiming, "We're a hit, Howard! We're much better alone!"[26]

Such talk, he knew, would make both Gifford and Meredith wince, given their fraternity, and might even help drive a wedge between them. In truth, he had little good to say about Gifford, either. Soon he would be calling him "an apologist, constantly making excuses for players who fumbled or dropped passes, and coaches who made rotten decisions," and, with palpable envy, a "Teflon man" never held accountable for his many mistakes on the air, one reason for which he said was Gifford's close friendship with Arledge.[27]

The envy and resentment he had for both of his boothmates had come to obsess him, breeding more paranoia. Meredith, whom he had once seen as a man of deep thought and high moral fiber, struck him now as a would-be con man, more leech than friend to Gifford, to whom he was becoming "increasingly subservient," his reward being that Gifford "helped Meredith secure very profitable commercial work." Cosell had soured as well, for various reasons, on Arledge, carrying his grudge since Munich back into the *MNF* booth. The man who had made, and saved, him was in his mind responsible for making a monster out of Gifford and an ingrate out of Meredith. So paranoid had Cosell become that he swore Arledge had "a game plan to keep me in my place. Keep me insecure," making it easier for the two jocks to gang up on him.[28]

Of course, anyone who knew him might have wondered whether any game plan was necessary to keep Cosell insecure; that was surely one thing he did quite well by himself. As a result, things deteriorated rapidly in the *Monday Night Football* booth. By the turn of the show's second decade, the most famous broadcasting team in the history of American sports, and especially the loudest one, no longer believed they were involved in a milestone. As Frank Sinatra might have said, it was indeed a millstone.

LIKE MUHAMMAD ALI, Cosell was still capable of transcending his ennui. He could still make the effort to perform at a level he knew was required of him. In fact, having Ali fights to call was always such a stimulus, provided they weren't of the sleepwalk variety, and if they were he would be the first to criticize Ali for them. For some time now, he had known Ali would soon have to seriously consider retiring. Every time he stepped into a ring, he was pushing his luck. His time was obviously past, as was that of his most recent contemporaries. Joe Frazier hadn't fought since 1976, when he was destroyed again by George Foreman in five rounds. When Foreman lost a decision to Jimmy Young a year later, he claimed God told him to redirect his life, whereupon he became a born-again Christian and went into a ten-year exile from the ring.

When Ali defended the title on February 15, 1978, few could have foreseen any trouble. He would face Leon Spinks, who was ranked as the top heavyweight contender but seemed too young and green for Ali. For the gap-toothed Spinks, whose gold medal victory as a light-heavyweight at the Montreal Olympics was called by Cosell, it was just his eighth pro bout, one of which was a draw against the lamentable Scott LeDoux.

Ali took the fight, as Joe Frazier had Foreman in Jamaica, as a quick, reliable payday, and because he could still sell tickets it was broadcast live on closed-circuit TV in theaters. But as soon as Ali entered the ring at Caesars Palace in Las Vegas, he appeared old, jiggly, and pallid. It took only one round for him to seem exhausted, and as the fight stretched out he was a stationary target for the sprightly Spinks. In the fifteenth and final round, knowing he was being beaten, he tried to knock Spinks out, but the younger man beat him to the punch and had Ali wobbling at the end. As the bell rang, Ali, in a telltale gesture, tapped his glove lightly on Spinks's shoulder before walking forlornly back to his corner, signaling the transition of power that was made official when Spinks was announced as the winner by split decision and given the belt.

Ali's defeat reopened the same sore that had made "an unholy mess" of the U.S. Boxing Championships. While it was obvious to any boxing fan that Ali was logically the No. 1–ranked contender, Don King acted again. With his bankroll now behind Ken Norton, and given his influence on the World Boxing Council, he had the organization name Norton as the top contender. When Spinks said his next fight would be an Ali rematch, the WBC stripped him of its belt, retroactively named Norton its champ by virtue of his recent victory over Jimmy Young, and mandated a Norton fight against the King-affiliated Larry Holmes for the title (Spinks still was WBA champ).

Cosell didn't object to the sleight of hand, either because he was too resigned to care now about such shenanigans in boxing, or because ABC bought TV rights to carry the fight for a live broadcast. Dutifully, he was at ringside in Las Vegas for the match on June 9, 1978, and if much about boxing nauseated him, the sport could still tickle him, mainly the burlesque of bluster he could so easily instigate in fighters seemingly with nothing more than his presence. When he interviewed Norton and Holmes at poolside at the same Caesars Palace before the match, the colloquy went like this:

COSELL: Larry, do you have anything to say about your opponent?
HOLMES: Yes. I think Kenny has been a great fighter and great champion, but I think now is my time!"
COSELL: How about you, Kenny, what do you think about Larry?
NORTON (looking Holmes up and down for a few seconds, then sneering): I think he is a little pinhead![29]

For the fight, which would be broadcast live in prime time, Roone Arledge, against Cosell's wishes, wanted to dress up the show by pairing him with a color analyst, the recently retired former referee Arthur Mercante, who had never done any television work before. Mercante, who had known him for twenty years, recalled that Cosell was gracious when he greeted him, but soon was telling him, "You know, Arthur, I'm a professional announcer and I don't need guys like you to work with me."[30] During the fight, Cosell would continually cut short Mercante's observations, if he let him be heard at all.

The fight actually needed little embellishment. It was a gem, a torrid battle of attrition that saw momentum swing back and forth with each round between the smooth, left-jab-pumping boxer and the awkward puncher with the odd crablike stance. After fifteen magnificent rounds, the last a toe-to-toe slugfest, Holmes was awarded the title in an extremely close split decision. The spectacular nature of the fight—in 2001, *Ring* called the final three minutes the seventh most exciting round in boxing history—seemed to presage that Holmes had arrived as the next big thing in boxing, and that Muhammad Ali was past tense.

The Ali-Spinks rematch, which most regarded as a battle for the real heavyweight championship, was made for September 15, 1978, in the cavernous Louisiana Superdome. Drumming up ticket sales, Ali promised it would be his last fight, which if he was successful would punctuate a career that would end with him as the first man to ever win the title thrice, and the first black man to ever retire as champ. But although he trained hard for the match, he seemed overly subdued in New Orleans. Only hours before the fight, Cosell interviewed him for ABC in his dressing room. It was a ritual he had performed countless times since their first meeting in 1962, when Ali was young and irresistible, prompting Cosell to sense that he had found his muse. Now he looked merely old. His face was rounder and plumpish; puffy bags sat under the eyes. His speech was slower, some words slurring and almost incomprehensible. Perhaps, having come so far with him, Cosell saw his own mortality in that face.

After asking Ali to expound on his feelings before "what is to be your last fight, forevermore," he said to him, "You sound tired, and the fight's at hand. Have you debilitated yourself getting down to 218 pounds?"

Not easing into the normal Ali mode, with the old-time bravado and faux outrage in response to a Cosell pinprick, Ali mumbled, "I'm not tired. I'm in top shape." Making a minimum effort to preen, he vowed to "do the impossible," declaring that "I'm not the greatest of all time if I can't get this title from a man like Spinks." He then pointed his finger at the camera and tried to turn back the clock, braying, "I will destroy Spinks."

It all seemed by the numbers, and Cosell took his place at ringside

prepared for the last fight of Ali's career to end in the gutter of ignomini-
ous defeat for a second time to a comparative amateur. Spinks thought it
was a sure thing. Now it was *he* who took the fight lightly, spending most
of his training partying with his retinue late into the night on Bourbon
Street. But was it cosmically possible for a man like Leon Spinks to beat
a man like Muhammad Ali again? Doing so would mean beating the
power of destiny and of the Ali legacy. Still, the thought occurred to
more than a few that a man as blissfully ingenuous and insentient about
such modes of grandeur might just be suited to the task.

An enormous crowd turned out for the fight, nearly filling the seventy-
thousand-seat Superdome. Their deafening noise was more like that at a
soccer game, "a positive madhouse," Cosell put it, never letting up all
night. Cosell at times could barely be heard, forcing him to turn up his
own volume to a sustained shout. Seconds before the bell, the ref was
seen looking at something in Spinks's corner. Somehow communicating
with Angelo Dundee twenty feet away, Cosell could report, almost
instantaneously, "They were checking a brown bottle in Spinks's corner,
at the request of Angelo Dundee." In round one, noting a much crisper
Ali—"the man with the classic face, no longer youthful"—he approvingly
spoke of "Ali moving, on his toes . . . there'll be no Rope-a-Dope, he
says." Spinks, "an alley fighter" and "a wild man," kept boring in, at times
"mauling the older man." In round two, Cosell wondered of Ali, "Where
is the left jab?" and said Ali was "fighting from memory . . . missing his
punches."

Before round ten, he returned to the scoop he had begun the fight
with, to snuff it out, saying, "The commission checked the contents of the
brown bottle in Leon Spinks's corner and apparently found nothing
undue." By now, Ali had eased into a comfortable rhythm, bouncing on
his toes, gliding across the ring, jabbing and scoring at will as Spinks fell
over himself trying to get to him. At one point he executed a brief churning of his feet. "Even a little bit of a shuffle!" Cosell boomed. "That shows
how he feels. He's in command of this fight! He said he would destroy
Leon Spinks, and he seems to be doing it! What an extraordinary career!
What an extraordinary man he has been! In every way."

Clearly, Cosell had lost his reason, his slavish exultation being over the top, as the timeless old champ seemed to defy the laws of nature. One could hardly blame Cosell. Ali, as he said, "is the story." Having amassed a wide lead in points, this time there was no toe-to-toe fifteenth round. Spinks got no closer to landing a big shot, and as Cosell counted down the last seconds, he intoned, with a perfect minimalist sense of drama, "The fight is . . . *over*!"

Cosell, indeed not as young as *he* used to be, was reluctant to make his usual foray into the ring, as he was practically being trampled by a mob of lackeys, media people, and security cops in combat gear. "There is a wild surge into the ring," he said, one that forced Ali to drop to the canvas as he had in Zaire and Manila, and cover his head for his own protection. "The police are surrounding the ring—they're trying to protect people!" Then, gearing up, "I'm going to try and go into the ring. It may not be possible," and he clawed his way through the throng as Chris Schenkel, the host of the broadcast, took over.

Of course, the crowd always seemed to part like the Red Sea for Cosell, who was soon next to the spent Ali, who could barely speak a coherent sentence. Not pressing him, Cosell stood aside and, as everyone waited for the decision to be announced, began to recite from the Bob Dylan song "Forever Young," concluding of his old compeer, "He remains, I suppose, forever young. Over to Chris Schenkel." Out of anyone else's mouth, it would have been painfully turgid; out of his, it was remarkably affecting.[31]

Minutes later, as the unanimous decision was announced, only feet away was a bizarre sight—a tuxedoed Don King, beaming, trying to get as close as he could to the new champ, whom he had tried to keep from this very fight by removing half of its title sanction. That was the first sign that this would perhaps not be Ali's swan song after all, not if King had a big enough payday for him to fight Larry Holmes for what stood to be a chance for him to win his *fourth* crown, by regaining the now semiofficial heavyweight crown, that of the WBC.

As it was, Ali raised a gloved hand in victory and began blowing kisses to the crowd. He knew just by looking around at the seventy thousand people packed into a football stadium what was possible. The fight would clear a $50 million gate, even with *no* closed-circuit showing. ABC would gain its largest rating ever for a boxing telecast, with a 61 percent share, considerably beating out the previous high, the 43 share for the taped broadcast of the Ali-Frazier "Thrilla in Manila." Muhammad Ali still meant money, and for Cosell the lingering intoxication of shared glory. But, for both, time was running out. Looking at each other's faces, they may have known it themselves.

# HOWARD COSELL
# WHY I SUPPORT THE
# ERA

*To those who follow football, he's Monday* wages and coequal treatment in physical
*Night; to those who like variety shows, he's the* education programs in college.

Never shy about taking a stand on any controversial issue, Cosell was a
high-profile backer of women's rights causes. In 1975, declaring himself
in favor of the ill-fated Equal Rights Amendment in this article in the
feminist magazine *Ms.* magazine, he wrote: "It's long since past time in
this country that women were treated coequally with men." *(Used by
permission of* Ms. *magazine)*

The last time Cosell enjoyed broadcasting boxing was when Sugar Ray Leonard
emerged as an Ali redux in the late 1970s. Here, after Leonard knocked out
challenger Bruce Finch in a February 1982 bout, Cosell shares some laughs with
the welterweight champ and his son. But he would find little about the sport to
make him smile thereafter. *(Bettmann/Corbis)*

Cosell's growing disdain for boxing is evident moments after Roberto Duran defeated Sugar Ray Leonard for the welterweight title on June 20, 1980. As Duran flaunts a fistful of dollars given him as a bonus by promoter Don King, Cosell looks anything but amused. Two and a half years later, after calling the brutal Larry Holmes–Tex Cobb mismatch, Cosell walked away from the sport that first made him famous and endlessly crusaded against it. *(Bettmann/Corbis)*

For years, an ever-faithful Emmy Cosell accompanied her husband almost everywhere he went. By the 1980s, the constant pressures and battles had clearly taken a toll on both of them. As can be seen by the stress and strain on their faces at a 1982 MS Dinner of Champions at New York's Waldorf-Astoria Hotel, their health was in decline. *(Ron Galella / Getty Images)*

Despite constant chafing during his fourteen-year run on *Monday Night Football*, he stayed the course, posing in this mid-1970s publicity shot with Frank Gifford and a new boothmate replacing Don Meredith, ex-lineman Alex Karras. But a careless Cosell remark in 1983, when he called Redskins receiver Alvin Garrett "a little monkey," caused such a controversy that he quit the show in disgust. *(Bettmann/Corbis)*

Although Cosell was a longtime Democrat, politics always receded when he could rub elbows with a VIP such as Ronald Reagan. Having interviewed him on *Monday Night Football* when Reagan was governor of California, Cosell was on hand and all smiles when, as president, Reagan received the American Sportscasters Association's first Graham McNamee Award at the White House on October 25, 1984. *(Bettmann/Corbis)*

Without boxing and football to broadcast, Cosell's last remaining responsibility at ABC Sports as host of the weekend magazine show *SportsBeat*. He was rightly proud of the program's format of hard journalism, calling it his finest achievement, yet it never found an audience, and when the show was canceled in 1985, Howard Cosell's tumultuous four-decade career at the network was over. *(Photo by RM Lewis Jr. / NBCU Photo Bank via AP Images)*

His broadcasting days over, and with little demand for his services, Cosell "lowered" himself by writing a sports column for the *New York Daily News*, ironically filling page space once ruled by his longtime nemesis, Dick Young. In his debut column, on May 4, 1986, he officially began to sleep with the "enemy," but the uneasy alliance lasted only two years before the paper terminated his byline. (© *New York Daily News, L.P., used with permission*)

Near the end, the stress and madness of being the most famous sportscaster in history and a perpetual lightning rod for controversy had taken a grievous toll on Howard Cosell. Here, in one of the last photos of him, wearing a polo shirt, his brow furrowed, he seems lost in thought, and perhaps in the glorious past that was gradually being forgotten by sports fans. (*Focus on Sports / Getty Images*)

In April 1992, Cosell and Muhammad Ali posed together at a luncheon at which Ali received a humanitarian award. Both had survived too many battles and suffered too many blows, and for Cosell time was growing short. Devastated by Emmy's death, and battered by numerous ailments, he held on until April 23, 1995, when he died at age seventy-seven, taking to the grave the fabled era he dominated. (*AP Photo / Lederhandler*)

# 17

## "A SAD WAY TO END"

HOWARD WILLIAM COSELL, son of Isidore and Nellie Cohen, father of two and grandfather of four, a.k.a. "the Coach," was still an immensely well known figure in American popular culture as another decade, the 1980s, loomed. As he took stock of himself, with not a little delusion, he was still a hard-bitten journalist; for many others, he was a caricature. So total at the time was Cosell's saturation of culture that Irwin Weiner, an ABC Sports vice president for twenty years, once came up with a concept for a Saturday morning kids' series called *Monday Night Football: The Cartoon*, one that would turn Cosell, Gifford, and Meredith into animated characters. This wasn't as bad an idea as it sounds, given the success of the Beatles' *Yellow Submarine* and the animation of Bill Cosby's *Fat Albert* and *The Harlem Globetrotters*.

Weiner was told the first person he needed to get approval from was Cosell. Having never met him, Weiner swallowed hard and set up a meeting at Cosell's office. But he had barely begun to pitch the project when he was silenced.

"Young man," he was asked, "do you know whom you're speaking to? I am the biggest name in show business today. And you want to make a cartoon character out of me?"[1]

The show got nowhere, but to Weiner the biggest pity was that Howard Cosell didn't appreciate the irony of his statement—he already *was* a
cartoon character.

Not everyone appreciated the parodic nature of his celebrity. A
decade after the debut of *MNF* and two decades after his unpopular
defense of Muhammad Ali, Cosell still was often escorted into stadiums
on Monday nights by armed guards, due to fresh threats against him.
Frighteningly, during the 1979 World Series, deranged or drunk fans surrounded him and Emmy as they sat in their limousine outside Baltimore's
Memorial Stadium, shouting obscenities and rocking the car back and
forth—a scene not unlike the one Cosell narrated in *Bananas*, only with
him in the role of El Presidente. It was not the first time; he and Emmy
had survived similar incidents in parking lots in Washington, D.C., and
Houston. "Howard," said Frank Deford, "just could make people act
insanely, even dangerously, especially in a group dynamic, with thousands of other like-minded people getting mad at him at once."[2]

Much of the flak aimed at him, of course, came from the press, whom
as a group he held in lower regard than the "bad apple" fans he could
pass off far more easily. He still devoured every negative notice that
appeared in a paper anywhere. And he still created needless confronta-
tions over picayune matters with writers he admired, not to convince
them of his greatness so much as to convince himself. Jerry Izenberg
recalls a bizarre episode when Cosell, two decades after the fact, was still
recycling old delusions to boost himself. "We were both in San Francisco
for some event, I don't even remember what, sitting in the bar of the
Fairmont Hotel, and we were having our usual argument about TV versus the print media. We're going back and forth and suddenly he says,
'Listen, I saved your ass. Remember when I saved the Grambling show?'

"I said, 'Oh, really?' You have to understand, I had never called Howard on that, and he'd said it many times through the years. This time, I
said, okay, that's it, and told him to have the maître d' bring a phone over
and call a guy who had edited the show.

"Howard said, 'Why do you want me to call him?' I said, 'Because we
never touched a goddamn frame of that show. Not one frame.' And we
hadn't, we just made Howard think we did. 'I don't believe you,' he said.

"I told him, 'Okay, call.' And he picks up the phone, then puts it back. He takes out twenty, forty bucks, whatever it was, puts it on the table and says, 'I'll see you later,' and he walks out. For Howard, that was his way of saying, 'You got me,' which is something he could never say."[3]

Never could he, or would he, say this to Dick Young, who was still a burr under his saddle. In 1977, after Joe Namath, by his own request, had been given his release so he could sign with the L.A. Rams, Cosell called it "the best thing that could have happened" to the Jets, who he believed would be improved for it. Months later, as the team was taking a beating on *Monday Night Football*, Cosell mused, "Joe Namath must be thinking to himself, "How fortunate I am to be gone.'" Young, who seemed to live for ways to skewer him, pounced on this typical Cosell flip-flop in a column titled "Howie's Mouth Babbles On."

It often struck observers that when Cosell and Young were covering a fight, they were at least as adversarial as the fighters. Just before the September 16, 1981, "Superfight" between Sugar Ray Leonard and Thomas "Hit Man" Hearns, when Leonard would unify the welterweight title with a hard-won decision, a young pair of honeymooners accosted Cosell at the Caesars Palace arena, pleading for him to sign their program. "Of course, my dear," he said, "I'll gladly sign it. What are your names?" He signed, then kissed the bride on her cheek, causing her to squeal in delight and Cosell to bray, "This must be a bigger thrill than the honeymoon itself!" Young, squirming, shook his head.

"You're an egotistical maniac, Howard!" he shouted to Cosell.

"And you're just a jealous bastard!" came the reply.[4]

The exchange was meant to be good-natured; it didn't sound like it was. But if Cosell could still allow Young to distract him beyond all logic, he could do nothing about him. At ABC, however, he could wage subterranean war on those who inadvertently got on his wrong side. The most obvious example was Terry O'Neil, the onetime factotum who had shot up the company ladder, perhaps just a bit too swiftly for Cosell. In the autumn of 1980, the then thirty-one-year-old O'Neil replaced Dennis Lewin as executive producer of *Monday Night Football*, with marching orders from Roone Arledge to sharpen the journalistic focus of the show, and to somehow blunt Cosell's ego. Summoning O'Neil, Arledge told him,

"We just have to make a change. It's out of hand. I spend half my time listening to the announcers bitch about each other," and "the biggest problem is Howard. He's out of control. If you ask him, he thinks he can produce, direct, do the commentary, and play quarterback for both teams."[5]

O'Neil wasted no time trying to steer him from complaining to reporting. Before the final preseason game in 1980, between the New England Patriots and Philadelphia Eagles, O'Neil saw a story to plumb in the joint holdout of four Patriot players orchestrated by their agent, Howard Slusher. Getting together an extended halftime feature on the brouhaha, O'Neil figured it was a natural for Cosell's prosecutorial instincts, as did Cosell. He taped an interview with Slusher, who alleged that Patriots owner Chuck Sullivan had a conflict of interest in negotiating with the players, since he was chairman of the NFL Management Council, and thus, as Cosell put it, "working for the NFL, not the Patriots." According to O'Neil, Cosell was excited, saying, "We're going to have a superb piece." O'Neil agreed, envisioning headlines that would begin, "Howard Cosell reported yesterday . . ." As O'Neil said, "How he loved that."[6]

The next day, before the game, Cosell was to tape a final comment about Sullivan's conflict. He took his seat before the camera, got the cue from Chet Forte, then . . . nothing. For long, uneasy minutes, he sat, silent. Then he addressed his remarks to an increasingly nervous O'Neil. "Terry," he began, "I've spent a lifetime in this business. I've probably been in this business more years than you've lived. In that time, I've formed some relationships that are more important to me than any of your goddamn halftime pieces or your goddamn friend Howard Slusher." O'Neil was stunned. "My *friend*, Howard?" he said. "That's right, your friend," Cosell replied, then moved toward his knockout blow. "And I'll tell you who my friends are. I've known the Sullivans since they came into football in 1959." He went on rhapsodizing the family, then lowered the boom on O'Neil, saying, "And I'm not going to put my voice on something that's so biased and unfair to them. You can get somebody else."[7]

O'Neil's face flushed, his blood running cold. Apparently, he had not known that Chuck Sullivan's father, Billy, had sold Cosell his Westhampton beach house. However, given Cosell's long years of currying favor with sports' ownership class, hard-eyed reporter or not, making merry with men like Al Davis, Wellington Mara, Sonny Werblin, Leonard Tose, Carroll Rosenbloom, and George Steinbrenner—virtually *every* owner in the wide world of sports—O'Neil clearly should have seen Cosell's betrayal coming. He made the fatal mistake—he trusted Howard Cosell.

Left hanging, O'Neil was able to convince Cosell to say whatever he wanted about the Patriot dispute, to fill the airtime, and he did so even-handedly but without any mention of a Sullivan conflict of interest. But for the producer, this was only the first shock, since Cosell had, for reasons known only to him, determined that O'Neil needed to be severed from *MNF*. If Cosell had been partial to the young man before, he had apparently made a snap judgment that O'Neil was a little too hard-edged, too aggressive, or moving too fast. Even though Cosell himself had agreed with the thrust of O'Neil's previous reporting, all bets were now off. Suddenly, upon further review, O'Neil's work, he let it be known, was "biased" against one of the privileged set before whom Cosell genuflected.

Jim Lampley, another upstart who had often teamed with O'Neil on college football assignments, watched this ludicrous one-act drama play out, and muses about the torturous treatment of his cohort, "Terry was the anointed one at ABC Sports. He was going to be the king of the world, and for good reason. Terry had done amazing work—and it all unraveled on one weekend, because Terry got entangled with Howard on a story he was working. And as with Alex Wallau, Terry was right and Howard couldn't stand it."[8]

O'Neil got wind of this in the days after the game when Frank Gifford told him, "They're after you, my man. Howard and Chet. They want you out."

O'Neil incredulously asked, "Chet, too?"

"Oh, yeah," said Gifford of Cosell's gin rummy partner. "He's a very talented director, but I wouldn't trust him as far as I could throw him."

What's more, even Chuck Sullivan told him, "I've heard some people are trying to get you. I hope you survive it."[9]

They were both right. A week later, the Friday before the season's first game, O'Neil was called into Jim Spence's office, where he and fellow ABC Sports vice president John Martin waited, looking grim. Unbeknownst to O'Neil, Cosell had lobbied both men against him on the bias charge, his case aided by the fact that Spence, perhaps seeing a challenger to his own throne in the near future, detested O'Neil, for whom the feeling was mutual. In *his* entry in the memoir derby, *The Game Behind the Game*, published in 1989, O'Neil wrote, "I had never trusted Spence since 1971," believing he had no convictions other than the bottom line and placating Arledge and Cosell. That impression was now confirmed when Spence told him he was out as producer of *Monday Night Football*, the immediate reason being that Sullivan-Slusher piece.

O'Neil was floored, having drawn praise from both Sullivan and Slusher—and Cosell, before he turned. The only logical explanation was that Cosell wanted him out. "In Spence's world," O'Neil said, "it didn't matter why." It seemed inconceivable that Roone Arledge, had he not been distracted by running the news division, could have allowed it to come to this, nor that he would allow Cosell's personal pique to leave the franchise without its producer three days before the start of the season. But it was also true that Arledge had no personal attachment to him. In fact, there was not a single mention of O'Neil or the Sullivan-Slusher matter in the voluminous *Roone*, or by Cosell in any of his memoirs, for that matter. Roone simply let Spence fire O'Neil and looked the other way.

Being known as Cosell's sacrificial lamb was a stigma he didn't need. A few months later, when his ABC contract expired, he accepted an offer by CBS Sports president Van Gordon Sauter to be executive producer of that network's own weekend sports anthology show. There, O'Neil succeeded in raiding a number of sports production people from ABC, regarding each as another bone extracted from Roone Arledge's anatomy. As the years moved on, and O'Neil kept moving up at CBS, he never was quite able to put behind him that lost weekend in 1980, nor cast Arledge, Spence, and Cosell as anything but a malignant troika that let the past glory and power of ABC Sports slip away as the decade progressed.

By then, O'Neil would say, Arledge and Spence had "fostered Cosell's evolution to gorilla size," and he accused Arledge of turning a blind eye to Cosell's "regular drinking in the *Monday Night Football* booth," adding, "Under such blind eyes do 'anchor monsters' grow big and strong." As for the monster in question, O'Neil, dripping bitterness, believed

Cosell had actually "squandered scores of potential *Monday Night Football* viewers with his ignorance and disdain for the game," and "to this day, the series has struggled under Cosell's heritage of scorn."[10]

AS THE 1980s began, there were ominous portents everywhere. While the information highway was not yet a superhighway, more lanes were carrying more traffic. On June 1, 1980, Ted Turner's Cable News Network hit the air, presaging a new reality—the twenty-four-hour news cycle, with sports news pulled into a maw of instant reportage of events. ESPN was already on, having debuted the previous September, with a daylong parade of sports anchors, videotape, and opinion. Suddenly, it was unnecessary to consult a newspaper or wait for the evening news to be in the flow of news and sports, with the added immediacy of pictures and video.

Howard Cosell, of course, had been a key to the evolution of hard sports news and commentary, his voice a breeder of a new generation of self-glorifying, camera-hungry sportscasters seeking to extract real news from a little boy's games. Yet Cosell, like a Lear figure, was slowly ebbing, as the new world order began to diminish the size and command of entrenched media lions like him.

As fate had it, Cosell himself had the duty of announcing the literal demise of another icon, and one he considered, with typical overstatement, a confidant. The date was December 8, and remains one of those sadly famous days in popular culture. A horrifying concentration of events began at around 10 P.M. when by sheer luck an ABC TV producer, Alan Weiss, who had gone to Roosevelt Hospital on the Upper West Side of Manhattan after a motorcycle accident, watched police officers begin talking about a victim of gunshot wounds they had just brought in. He overheard the name "John Lennon."

Weiss, ignoring his own injury, asked the cops what had happened to Lennon and was told of the shooting outside Lennon's Central Park West apartment building, the Dakota. They told Weiss he had been rushed into the emergency room, blood gushing from wounds to his back. Running to a pay phone in those pre-cell-phone days, Weiss called the office.

Soon after, the news that Lennon had died was announced by a Lennon aide. The nightly news shows were still half an hour away. In an age before instantaneous, twenty-four-hour cable news and the Internet, the only thing live on American television was a football game between the New England Patriots and Miami Dolphins.

Having gotten the news about Lennon, the skeletal ABC News staff on West Sixty-ninth Street called the truck outside the Orange Bowl. When he was told of the shooting, producer Bob Goodrich relayed the news to Roone Arledge, who told him *not* to tell Cosell while the game was on the air. He said that Cosell was a friend of Lennon and it might upset him. Goodrich waited until an impending commercial came on, then broke it to Cosell, who in turn told Frank Gifford and Fran Tarkenton, the former Viking and Giants quarterback who filled in for Don Meredith on the games he took off.

"He was shot outside his apartment, the Dakota apartment building," Cosell said.

"Oh boy" was all a shocked Gifford could say.

Cosell's immediate reaction wasn't shock or grief but reluctance about announcing it when the commercial was over. With the game tied 6–6, he worried that the drama and flow would be interrupted. A play might even be run without a call if he couldn't squeeze it in, and a story of this magnitude couldn't be tossed off in a line or two. Amazingly for the self-identified journalist, a man who had been so crushed when Arledge refused to allow him to go live in Munich, his inclination was to say nothing about Lennon, leaving it to the news people.

"Fellas, I just don't know," he hemmed. "I'd like your opinion. I can't see this game situation allowing for that news flash, can you?"

Gifford—the jock who in Cosell's regard was out of his element beyond a gridiron—was the one who demonstrated the best news judgment and decisiveness. "Absolutely. I can see it."

"You can?"

"You betcha. You've got to. If we know it, we've got to do it."

Sighing, and far from convinced, Cosell said, "Alright."

Gifford dispensed some advice. "Don't hang on it. It's a tragic moment and this is going to shake up the whole world."

"Alright. I will get it in. Let Giff call this play and then I'll get it in."[11]

When the game resumed, the first lull came when the Patriots moved into field goal range and called a time-out. As kicker John Smith was shown warming up his leg on the sideline, Gifford tried to find a comfortable transition, awkwardly saying, "John Smith is on the line. And I don't care what's on the line, Howard, you have got to say what we know in the booth."

Given his cue, Cosell was now in almost the exact situation Jim McKay had been in Munich. "Yes, we have to say it, " he began. "Remember, this is just a football game, no matter who wins or loses." The juxtaposition between reverie and reality, with Smith on camera trotting onto the field for his field goal attempt, was particularly bizarre as Cosell continued, cutting sentences into fragmentary phrases.

"An unspeakable tragedy. Confirmed to us by ABC News in New York City. John Lennon, outside of his apartment building on the West Side of New York City, the most famous, perhaps, of all of the Beatles. Shot twice in the back. Rushed to Roosevelt Hospital."

A pause, then, in a slow rhythm, "Dead . . . on . . . arrival."

It would be yet another indelible marker of his rendezvous with popular history, three words spoken as deliberately and profoundly as those by McKay on that black early morning in Munich when he intoned, "They're all gone."

"Dead . . . on . . . arrival." Other than "Down goes Frazier," he had never spoken three more powerful words in his life. Knowing it himself, and almost winded, he let out a breath before going on, "Hard to get back to the game after that news flash, which in duty bound we have to tell you. Frank." Gifford could only append, "Indeed it is."[12]

The game proceeded, its outcome the height of triviality to millions of viewers, and to the men in the booth. A few minutes later, given breathing room, Cosell repeated the news, injecting an epilogue, movingly reciting from Keats's "Ode to a Nightingale": "My heart aches, and a drowsy numbness pains my sense." Within an hour of Cosell breaking the news to the world, word spread like a brush fire through the canyons of the city. By midnight, thousands had gathered in Central Park, sharing grief and Beatles songs that had now become dirges. Though he had not wanted to go on the air with the news, his spontaneous eloquence became his vindication for his outrage at being kept off the air in Munich. And for that, he owed Frank Gifford.


SEEN THROUGH a periscope, Cosell may as well have been announcing his own impending obituary. The culture that would find no place for him was gathering force, becoming almost dizzying with the added elements of visual enhancement. In 1981, MTV was born, seeding a new era of visual punch, superficially rendering video content. Cosell had been ahead of the curve in one respect—in retrospect, his melodramatic *Monday Night Football* halftime highlights can be seen now as a forerunner of frenetic video imagery, perfectly tailored to the coming age of limited attention spans. Thus, it was not as if he had no place in that age. If he was a dinosaur, he was quite capable of causing trouble.

Muhammad Ali's own professional demise proved portentous. The morning after the champ's third resurrection against Leon Spinks, Ali told Cosell that he was going to "sit down for six or eight months and think about it," meaning his retirement. Sure enough, in September 1979 he passed word to Cosell that he was done, whereupon a special farewell show was arranged on *Wide World of Sports*. Cosell would go on, of course, but it was unmistakable that a big piece of his own life was being retired as well. Ali's long career was presented on the show in familiar taped flashbacks of his dialogues with Cosell over the years. They then sat down for a final time with Ali as champ, not to joke around but for Ali to say, "Everybody gets old," and that he was "so glad it was over." Cosell, still earning his pay, asked if what he had heard was true, that Bob Arum had paid Herbert Muhammad $300,000 in exchange for Ali giving up the WBA title so that Arum could promote a championship bout—in effect, buying Ali's retirement. It was a jarring question, and Ali made news by denying it, nonetheless revealing that he had in fact been given "a great sum of money" to hold a retirement party in L.A., "but can't nobody pay me to retire."

More touchingly, he said that he was glad he was still "intelligent enough to speak," answering those who had begun to mention his deteriorating speech. He then had words of gratitude for his host. "I'm glad I got to know you," he said. "And thank you for all the backing. I remember when the Vietnam crisis was going, you'd go on television and say, 'If you don't believe Muhammad Ali is champion, then get in the ring with him.' I want to say that helped me during my exile."

Lapping it up like honey, Cosell beamed, and assuaged him, "You are the greatest, aren't you?"

A thin smile. "I try to be. Maybe it's just you thinking."

"Good luck to you," Cosell said. "And it's not a good-bye. It's *au revoir*, my friend."[13]

For all this heavy schmaltz, though, they were not done with each other, just yet. Either too bored or in need of capital, Ali indeed listened to the breathless jive of Don King, who owned Larry Holmes, having installed his longtime associate Richie Giachetti as Holmes's manager and trainer of record. King came to Ali with a payday no sane person could have refused: $8 million, more money than he had ever seen in one shot, for a chance to win the title for a *fourth* time, extending his own record string of three. It was a bad idea on so many levels—age, the year layoff, the corrosion of his faculties, the peril of physical harm, and the potential humiliation of ending his career beaten to a pulp—but to Ali it seemed almost too easy, such was his disdain for his old sparring partner Larry Holmes, whose victory over Ken Norton seemed to Ali like devouring table scraps.

To Ali, Holmes was the same novice he had beaten up in training camps. Unlike Frazier, Foreman, and Spinks, Holmes had not won a gold medal. Since he patterned himself after Ali, who better than the real thing to show him how it's done? Ali would be a huge underdog, but he could "shake up the world" again, as if reprising his fight against Sonny Liston in Miami Beach, only with the age differences reversed.

When Ali yet again announced his return in the early summer of 1980, Cosell felt that he had been used as a prop to help hype the next big fight, one he feared might end up in severe punishment for Ali. He was hardly alone in that concern. The giant sports agency IMG, which was in the process of putting together commercial projects and a world tour for Ali, pulled out when he signed to fight Holmes, who himself would rather have fought anyone else but his hero and former boss. But he had no choice when King put it together, with $2.3 million for Holmes. Ali's mother, Odessa Clay, spoke for many when she said, "I don't want to see him fighting anymore." When Cosell caught up with Ali, he asked him why he had gone back on his word. Ali said he had no real answer other than that he had been serious *at that moment* when he had said it. Actually, there was no answer besides the explanation Ali had for Marge Thomas, a bookkeeper in his management circle: "There's nothing like the sound of the crowd when you come down the aisle and they're yelling, 'Ali! Ali!' You'd give your life to hear it."[14]

Witnessing Ali's resurrection, Cosell was so eager for another hot story line that his judgment about the fight was clouded. Not incidentally, ABC quickly moved in and snapped up the rights to a tape delay of the match, putting Cosell at ringside to call it. The bout was set for October 2, 1980, at Caesars Palace in Las Vegas. The demand for seats necessitated the construction of a temporary twenty-four-thousand-seat arena in the parking lot. Cosell arrived a few days before in a kind of deluded haze, believing that he and Ali were sharing the secret of how Ali would prevail—that Holmes was vulnerable to a right hand. The "old master," he said, was going to "do it one more time."

Out of grave concern that Ali's age and impairment might lead to serious damage, the Las Vegas Athletic Commission required that he go to the Mayo Clinic for an examination. The clinic pronounced him "in excellent general medical health," but a deeper reading of the report revealed "difficulty with his speech and memory and perhaps a very slight degree with his coordination." It was good enough for Nevada. Thus spared, Ali wheezed through the old burlesque, dubbing Holmes "the Peanut," for the shape of his head. Evoking old times, he promised to "destroy" Holmes with a ninth-round knockout—"He'll be mine in nine." But while Ali appeared fit and trim, having starved his way down from 260 pounds, he now was like a walking cadaver, his eyes blank, his gait unsteady. When he stepped in the ring, the night would take him closer to the "living death" he had spoken about after the third Frazier fight, with each passing round taking on the appearance of, as one columnist would put it, a game of "Russian roulette played with a pump-action shotgun."[15]

At ringside, Cosell's cockeyed optimism about Ali vanished as soon as Holmes began teeing off on a nearly inanimate Ali too timorous to do anything but keep his forearms up around his head or lean back against the ropes. He was not recycling the Rope-a-Dope as much as merely trying to survive. Cosell, against the backdrop of a subdued crowd, was funereal in tone. So fatigued was Ali by round nine that, unable to keep his gloves up, he was taking constant battering, leaving Cosell to wearily say, "It is sad to see this." When Ali tottered: "Oh, he's ready to go. This must be stopped. It is a sad way to end." Recalling some of his great fights, Cosell asked rhetorically, "And now this?" Then, "Legends die hard, and Ali is learning that even he cannot be forever young. His hands are no longer busy, his feet are no longer swift."[16]

Now it was Ali who looked like so many of his victims had, a bloody cut under one eye, the other swollen shut. Somehow, he made it through the tenth, with Holmes now visibly upset at having to keep pounding his idol. But Angelo Dundee had seen enough, and so had Herbert Muhammad, who gave Dundee the sign to have the fight stopped. As Drew "Bundini" Brown argued with him, Dundee barked at referee Richard Steele, "The ball game's over. I'm the chief second, I stop the fight!"— thus recreating, in reverse, the way Eddie Futch had thrown in the towel in Manila. There was no mob in the ring this time, only a mournful procession of people to console Ali—including Holmes, who movingly threw his arms around him as he sat on his stool, defeated, Bundini standing over him weeping, as were many in the hall. "It is a sad way to see this man's career end," Cosell concluded, "but it seemed inevitable." Or at least it had to nearly everyone in Las Vegas—except him.

It was eerily reminiscent of Floyd Patterson after his last match against Ali, with Cosell's description of Patterson—"pathetic"—no less apropos of the man who had humiliated him that night. On this night, the historic transition of the sport was now complete. Holmes would go on to become the second-longest-reigning heavyweight champion in the history of boxing, behind Joe Louis. Ali, meanwhile, found a way to bow out even more pathetically. Saying he did not want to go out sitting on his stool, he spoke of one last, final, end-of-the-line fight. He had only lost to Holmes, he said, because he came in too light and didn't "breathe right."

The truth was, he needed money. As well, his credibility took a hit, unfairly, when in early 1981 a business associate using his name on a questionable charity venture went to jail after embezzling over $21 million from Wells Fargo Bank.[17] When a low-level promoter named James Cornelius offered him $1 million to fight Jamaican-born Canadian heavyweight Trevor Berbick, who had recently lost a decision to Holmes, Ali announced yet another comeback.

The fight, on December 11, 1981, in Nassau, was a monument, but sadly not to his greatness. "The Drama in the Bahamas," as it was billed, sold out eleven thousand seats on makeshift stands erected on a baseball field, but on the undercard that night, fighters had to borrow gloves from others who had already fought. Moreover, nobody remembered to bring a ring bell, so rounds began and ended with the comic tinkle of a cowbell. Shaken badly by what he had witnessed in Las Vegas, Cosell could not bring himself to watch the fight, which ABC refused to carry, wisely, as a blubbery Ali was just as unable and unwilling to mix it up and lost a ten-round unanimous decision. In the end, Ali stood in the ring for the last time, lamenting that Berbick wasn't really what beat him. "Father Time caught up with me," he said, adding, "But at least I didn't go down. No pictures of me on the floor, no pictures of me falling through the ropes, no broken teeth, no blood. I'm happy I'm still pretty. I came out all right for an old man. We all lose sometimes. We all grow old."[18]

Before the fight, Ali's teenage daughter, Maryum Ali, had come to dread her father going into the ring. "You know how, when you're a kid and you go to the doctor and smell alcohol, you know you're going to get a shot?" she told Tom Hauser in *Muhammad Ali: His Life and Times*. "Well, after a while when I was a kid, every time I heard Howard Cosell's voice on television, I'd start to shake because I knew, 'Oh, boy, here it comes again.' "[19] Finally she could rest easy. As 1982 began, Muhammad Ali was finally through with boxing, now for good. Cosell wasn't, not quite yet, and Ali seemed envious. When they met at a banquet in L.A. a few weeks after the fight, Cosell would later recall, "once a symphony of metaphors and rhymes, his speech was now thick, and he spoke in half-completed whisperings. Too many blows to the head and body had transformed him into somebody I no longer knew."

Ali put an arm around him and said, "I'm gone, and you're still on top." "Don't ever say that to me again, Muhammad," Cosell told him. "You're part of American history. You'll never be gone."[20]

INELUCTABLY NEARING his own requiem, Howard Cosell at age sixty-three was still hungry for a good lead and a good angle, and Arledge indulged those instincts in late 1981 by giving him another Sunday late-afternoon show, the half-hour *ABC SportsBeat*. The show was conceived as a sports analog of *60 Minutes*, with on-location segments about hot-button issues, the first such in-depth exposition of sports topics to be done on TV. For Cosell, it was intended to be no less a TV benchmark than the legendary Ed Murrow's *See It Now*. He explained his mission this way: "Sports journalism on television has to be enterprise journalism. It shouldn't be reactive. It should be creative . . . It's an unending task of information and education." At least he *hoped* it would be endless, since he was already sure that "*SportsBeat* will be my legacy."[21]

The high-minded concept seemed to justify an even more imperious sense of self. Running it like a private duchy, as if independent from the ABC Sports domain, Cosell reached way back into his past and hired as his coproducer Ed Silverman, who had produced his first venture in television in the 1950s. Given a budget for a staff of eleven, he conscripted mainly young go-getters whom he hoped to be able to mold and control. That was as good a reason as any why his first hire was none other than Alex Wallau, who of course had gotten under his skin at the time of the ill-fated U.S. Boxing Championships, but whose work he respected. Also on the payroll, as managing editor, was a recent Yale graduate, Alexis Denny, whom he had plucked from the classroom during his course there and made his assistant, touting her as "my little genius," and two sports-writers, Peter Bonventre of *Inside Sports* magazine and *New York Post* boxing columnist Mike Marley, the latter of whom had no inkling Cosell was interested in him until after he ran across him, in a typical Cosell pose, one night in Las Vegas.

"I was there covering a fight and I saw Howard sitting at the hotel bar with Frank Sinatra and the Perlman brothers, who ran Caesars Palace.

That was the company Howard rolled with, and believe me, when he was with people like that, they always made a fuss over him, which he loved. Anyway, Howard brought me over to his table—Sinatra was gone by then—and I had a drink or two or three with him, then left, thinking nothing of it. Then, days later, I picked up the phone and heard, 'This is Howard Cosell.' I said, 'Not a bad impression, but who is this really?' Long story short, I went up to meet with him and he hired me, which I thought was weird because at the same time he was railing about sports-writers being what's wrong with sports, he hired me and Pete Bonventre. And what were we? Sportswriters."[22]

Cosell, seeking high-visibility on-air reporters, gave a job to Arthur Ashe, the former tennis champion and the first black man to win a Grand Slam event and a Wimbledon title. Ashe's career was cut short after a 1979 heart attack and quadruple bypass surgery, and he turned to writing and TV journalism before he would require another bypass, during which he contracted the HIV virus through a blood transfusion that would kill him in 1993. For much of the on-camera work, Cosell brought aboard the telegenic Jim Lampley, who came to appreciate his roving-reporter assignments for the show, given the alternative of being with Cosell at close range, close enough to recall him today as a man of "wild gyrations and inconsistencies," one day close, the next day distant.[23] Such mood swings caused Wallau to leave the show after only a few weeks, incurring Cosell's everlasting wrath for his lack of blind loyalty.

At the same time, Cosell's relations with the ABC Sports brass were deteriorating, from both sides. Jim Spence had grown tired of placating Cosell, whom he now saw as "one of the unhappiest human beings on the planet . . . increasingly vicious, bitter, even at times downright venomous, one of the most insecure human beings I have ever met." While Spence and his wife were dining, as they often had done through the years, with the Cosells in the early 1980s at the ritzy Upper East Side eatery Le Boeuf à la Mode, Spence was taken aback when Cosell leaned over and began to whisper, with childlike glee.

"Look!" he said. "Those people are staring at me. They recognize me, they really do. They know who I am."

As usual, it was Emmy who brought him back to earth. "Just take off that hairpiece of yours," she said, "and they'll never recognize you."[24]

For Spence, the dinners would soon end. As was the case even with Cosell's close friends, these rituals were no longer worth the price of the embarrassment they caused.

SPORTSBEAT, WHICH premiered on August 30, 1981, rapidly fulfilled Cosell's assertion that it would be the only regularly scheduled network program devoted solely to sports journalism. It soon became outsized in its influence. The things people said on the show would often make news, such as an early scoop with tennis star Wojtek Fibak revealing his search for his displaced father in Poland.

Much of *SportsBeat* would be given over to the ongoing soap opera of Raiders owner Al Davis trying to move the team from its rabid fan base in Oakland—who had just seen the team win the Super Bowl in 1980—for greener economic pastures in Los Angeles, which had lost the Rams to Anaheim. This would become a blood war between Davis the dead-end kid from Brooklyn, whom Cosell had euphemized as "distant and different," and Pete Rozelle the patrician commissioner, with the host siding with his old friend Davis after the NFL voted to keep him in Oakland. In the process, Cosell's cordial relationship with many league owners crumbled. The Chargers' Gene Klein, seeing Cosell in a restaurant where he was having dinner with his daughter Jill, came to his table and screamed, "You're a goddamned whore! You're Davis's whore!" (Wryly, Cosell, recalling the incident, mused that Klein "wanted me to be a whore for the NFL. That would've been fine.")[25]

So too did his relationship with Rozelle collapse into personal, even vicious enmity. Rozelle accused him of enabling Davis's sedition, which carried the worst of implications for Cosell—that he was less than objective in his reportage, something Roone Arledge also suspected. Rozelle even sent Cosell an angry letter, in which he sarcastically wrote that "the man who originated the term 'telling it like it is' and who has been a constant critic of the so-called 'carpetbagging' aspects of professional sports has stamped his personal imprimatur" on the Davis move, the first-ever franchise shift in the NFL. Rozelle blithely ascribed Cosell's motives to his "personal relationship" with Davis.[26]

Cosell sought in vain to explain his position, which was that morally the Raiders' move was unconscionable, but legally was justified because the NFL had selectively changed its bylaws to keep the team in Oakland. He also believed that Rozelle conveniently looked the other way when the Giants moved across the Hudson River to the New Jersey Meadow-lands in 1976. But Rozelle, he would say, "heard only what he wanted to hear, a condition born of arrogance," which hardly helped to heal the rift between them.[27] In the end, Davis—and Cosell—proved to be correct when in May 1982 a circuit court jury hearing the Davis case ruled the league had practiced unfair restraint of trade, freeing the Raiders to move to L.A., where they won another Super Bowl that very year. Two years later, when the U.S. Supreme Court refused to hear the NFL's appeal, it was Cosell, learning about it first, who delivered the good news to Davis, waking him up with an early-morning phone call.

Cosell's relationship with Rozelle was in tatters and they had stopped speaking, save for a 1983 interview of Rozelle on *SportsBeat*. Rozelle would endure as the high priest of the NFL until 1989. During that time, he would take more heat from Cosell, now for doing nothing to *stop* other teams from jumping. In 1984 alone, two teams did so: The Jets fol-lowed the Giants to the Meadowlands, and the Colts left Baltimore for Indianapolis. If this seemed maddeningly contradictory to Rozelle, for Cosell it was elementary—only the Raiders had had legal justification for moving.

The irony was that the NFL, which had fought so hard to keep Davis in place, now giddily began playing the game of musical franchises— with Davis, amazingly, not through yet. Finding L.A. something short of Nirvana, and unable to gain approval for a new stadium, he soon floated the idea of taking his Raiders *back* to Oakland. Cosell, as if needing to demonstrate that he was no Davis lickspittle, now nailed *Davis* on *SportsBeat*. As Mike Marley recalls, "Howard asked me to write a very strong editorial rapping Davis. And I was a little shocked because he and Davis were friendly, which I always thought was based on their mutual hatred of Pete Rozelle. So I wrote a vicious thing about the Raiders' motto going from 'Pride and Poise' to 'Greed and Cash,' and Howard read it word for word on the show. Then the red emergency phone rang and I picked up and it was Roone. I thought, uh-oh, the shit's gonna hit the fan, I went too far, Howard's gonna blame me. But Roone just wanted to compliment Howard on it."[28]

For Cosell, that approbation from Arledge was a little late—about a decade so. He could take it as a very belated recognition that, on the serious and complicated issues, he had indeed brought about a transformation in sports journalism. The pity was, he was still the only working journalist who seemed to be able to do it right, if at all. As for his tricky relationship with Al Davis, they would remain close no matter how critical he could be of the tempestuous owner. In 1991, when the last of the Cosell tetralogy, *What's Wrong with Sports*, was published, it had a foreword by Davis. At that juncture, Cosell believed Davis was too content in balmy L.A. to move back to Oakland. Still, he wrote, "keep in mind that with Al, the future is always uncertain. The man is a football business genius; without a doubt, the smartest operator in sports."[29] Four years later, the year Cosell died, Davis signed a new deal—to go back to Oakland.

THE ENTHUSIASM and commitment with which Cosell reported issue-oriented segments on *SportsBeat* was in marked contrast with the dread he felt when he had to call yet another boxing match. But for the middleweight division, where post-Ali the buzz had been transferred with the rise of Sugar Ray Leonard and his unforgettable bouts against Roberto Duran, Thomas "Hit Man" Hearns, and, later in the decade, Marvin Hagler, most fights had become a drab tapestry, one indistinguishable from the next. While the viewership of *SportsBeat* was a small fraction of the audience for any fight ABC broadcast, Cosell imperiously disregarded the sport that had ushered him to fame as increasingly unworthy of his attention.

With this as background, the latest heavyweight match took place, with Larry Holmes, who had beaten four challengers since the Ali fight, making his next title defense against Randall "Tex" Cobb, who, while undefeated in twenty-three fights, was chosen by Don King as a soft touch who would be an easy payday for the champ. The bout was booked for November 26, 1982, at the Houston Astrodome, in Cobb's native Lone Star State, with ABC doing a live broadcast in prime time.

Cosell approached the match as just another exercise in boredom, but not until thirteen days before the fight did he see it as a prime example of what had become his biggest gripe against boxing in the wake of Ali's deterioration: glaring mismatches and a lack of proper medical oversight that placed fighters' health in peril. Or their lives. On November 13, lightweight champ Ray "Boom Boom" Mancini faced Korean challenger Duk Koo Kim—who despite a mediocre record was ranked No. 1. In round thirteen, Mancini hit Kim with thirty-nine punches in a row. After Kim was floored in the next round, he would fall into a coma, and die four days later due to brain trauma.

Cosell had campaigned for rigorous prefight examinations of fighters (something that only happened after Kim's death, when boxing had fighters submit to electrocardiograms and brain and lung tests, and truncated fights from fifteen to twelve rounds). In hindsight, similar to the cover he took about the U.S. Boxing Championships, he would explain that he only called the fight because "I was contractually bound to work it." Yet Jim Spence would recall that "Howard [did] not raise a single objection, nor even a question about the [Holmes-Cobb] match, before it took place."[30]

When the bell rang, however, his fanfaronade threatened to blow the Astrodome roof off its hinges. Dripping contempt and self-righteousness, Cosell seemed too oblivious to care that he was violating the first rule of a sportscaster by tailoring his call to fit his opinion. He pronounced the match one pitting "a class professional against a club fighter." When Cobb awkwardly waded in and began taking punishment, he wailed, "Not a pretty thing to see, is it?" Then, "This is brutalization. I think the referee should think about stopping this fight, fast." By the fifteenth round, Cobb, his face now a bloody mash, still would not go down, and Cosell howled, "I just can't believe this referee! It's outrageous! I wonder if that referee is an advertisement for the abolition of the very sport that he is a part of?"[31]

The fight, a near-shutout Holmes victory, was an instant cause célè-bre, not least because of Cosell's unrelenting scolding of boxing, his con-demnation of the sport's "apologists" seemingly including everyone involved in the broadcast, even his own network. It wasn't that he was wrong; it was that he had turned the bout into a diatribe, ignoring as well the fact that he had been previously complicit in many of boxing's most bloody encounters. While there was universal agreement that the fight was a stark mismatch, ring doctors had checked Cobb all during the fight. He never was dazed nor close to going down. Surely it would be folly to say the fight was the biggest mismatch of all time, as many would, mainly because of how Cosell had called it. Indeed, even after it had ended, he was still petulant, refusing to scramble up into the ring as usual, explaining on the air that "I will not dignify this fight with any interviews. I think what you have seen tonight speaks for itself."

The next day, viewer and critical reaction to Cosell's call, and behav-ior, was split among those who credited him with telling the harsh truth and those who reviled him for self-indulgence. Tellingly, at ABC Sports, the reaction lined up against Cosell, with some concerned that promoters like Don King might avoid selling fights to ABC if Cosell would be at the mike—which, in itself, might have been a validation of Cosell's case. Spence would say of the performance, "I can't recall in all my years of television anyone hammering and hammering and *hammering* a point like Cosell did that night. It got to the point where you just wanted to scream, not about the fight but about Howard's behavior over it."[32]

A few days later, Spence said, when he was in Acapulco for an affili-ates meeting, he ran into Leonard Goldenson on the golf course, and the chairman asked him, "What was wrong with Howard during the boxing telecast the other night? He just ruined the whole telecast for the viewers at home. Why does he do that? Why does he *feel* he has to do that?" For his part, Cosell would also drop Goldenson's name in regard to the Holmes-Cobb fight, in the manner he always did—the chairman, he swore, had actually *thanked* him for "preserving the integrity of the network." Only Goldenson, who died in 1999, knew which was the cor-rect version, or if neither was. But Spence then returned to New York, called Cosell into his office and told him he had been "out of control" in

Houston. Incensed that anyone could affront him like that, Cosell flew into a rage.

"What do you mean I dominated the event?" he shouted. "I saved your ass is what I did! I'm not the one responsible for putting that mismatch on the air. You people, you geniuses on the twenty-eighth floor, *you* put it on the air and I saved your ass!"

Spence, technically Cosell's boss, could only sit there. Catching ire and spit from Cosell's mouth, Spence listened as he went on for another five minutes, insisting that "my credibility is at stake" and "you'll not strip me of my integrity. The people know me, Mr. Spence. They rely on me to tell it like it is."

It was another bravura performance, the kind that could be amusing had he not been addressing whom he was. As Spence would say, "That was Howard Cosell's way of dismissing, almost with a flick of his hand, the professional opinion on an important broadcasting issue of the senior vice-president of ABC Sports." But then, as Mike Marley notes, Cosell often took pleasure telling the *SportsBeat* staff, "I answer to no one but Leonard Goldenson."[33]

As it happened, ABC was spared having to choose between Cosell and the promoters they had to keep doing business with. It was on that same morning that Cosell, after tongue-lashing Spence, called John Martin, who sympathized with him. Cosell told him, "John, I've made a decision. I am never going to call another professional fight." When Martin reminded him that he was bound to the network for all championship fights, he replied, "I'm not going to do them, and the company has a perfect right to fire me."[34] He then caught a flight for Tampa, for *Monday Night Football*, having seemingly dared ABC to relieve him of his job.

The news that Cosell had actually quit boxing broke in newspapers all over the country. Cobb, a good-humored man who later would do some acting, offered the quip that it was his "gift to boxing," adding that "I'd go 15 more rounds with Holmes if I thought it would get Cosell off football broadcasts."[35] More than just a good line, it was a fair barometer that boxing had become at least as weary of Cosell as he was of it, with the same syllogism applying to the ABC Sports brass. Indeed, the ill feelings and snide barbs being exchanged between Cosell and the network honchos may well have been as big a factor in his decision to give up boxing—as a feeler and a first step in a mutual divorce with the network, something that now seemed inevitable.

In the weeks following the Holmes-Cobb debacle, rumors persisted that he would change his mind, under pressure from ABC. But, in contrast to previous years, there was no real pressure. To the contrary, ABC was quite happy to leave him be. Had Cosell chosen to return, the executives would have had to accommodate him, something no one was eager to do now. This being the situation, Roone Arledge could afford to humor him. Ringing up Cosell one day, he said coyly, "I understand you're not doing any more professional fights."

When Cosell assented, Arledge, even more coyly, asked, "You've read your contract recently?"

"Yes," Cosell said, "and I know I'm in breach of contract, Roone, and I understand that you have every right to dismiss me from the company."

Arledge, biting his lip, assured him, "Are you crazy? I think you've done the right thing. Congratulations!"[36]

Arledge had reason to be so complimentary. For him, and all of ABC Sports, the "right thing" was Cosell so purposefully lifting from them the burden of having to dismiss him.

# 18

## EBB TIDE

B
Y THE mid-1980s, a good deal of American sports, and sports broadcasting, had been defined according to how sports had been seen through Cosell's eyes over the last quarter century. Yet many younger fans, and perhaps some older ones, needed to be reminded of his oracular visions and reportorial judgments. Thus, though he was clearly in decline, there would be periodic tributes to his work in the press. In 1982, *Sports Illustrated* honored him twice, first in a piece by William Taaffe touting the integrity of *SportsBeat*, balancing a mandatory swipe at the host as "a self-promoter on football and a know-nothing on baseball" with props for "remain[ing] a whiz at serious journalism."[1]

Taaffe also praised Hilary Cosell, for her Emmy-nominated NBC "Sports Journal" segments that year, writing, "Except for the Cosells, the networks have given up on sports journalism." This rare bauble for his younger daughter had to be especially satisfying to him, maybe as much as it was for her, given the immense difficulties of growing up in his massive shadow. Indeed, those pitfalls may have been even greater for Hilary and Jill than they were for their mother, whose own life had been turned upside down being his wife. Already Hilary had been exposed to the underbelly of his controversial career, reading not only the withering criticism of him in the press but also the death threats. If his cachet opened a door at NBC, where Don Ohlmeyer saw fit to hire her on merit, she and her father both understood how great the pressure would be for her to succeed on her own; thus Taaffe's laudation was a comforting balm to the entire family.

The other bouquet, a profile triumphantly titled "I've Won. I've Beat Them," came courtesy of Frank Deford, an unabashed admirer of Cosell. Deford swooned: "One thinks then of Nureyev, who once said to a carper, 'I may get tired of playing Romeo, but Romeo doesn't get tired of having me play him.' . . . Cosell isn't television. He's not audio. Howard Cosell is sports in our time. Feel sorry for the people who turn off the sound. The poor bastards missed the game."

Deford's warm and fuzzy billet-doux wasn't merely splendidly written; these sentiments were completely accurate. Not only about his eminence and significance, but about the darker truths that lay behind. For example, Deford at one point quoted Hilary saying of her father, "He has almost a childlike inability to comprehend that he won't make friends everywhere." Deford added: "[He] seems almost to court animosity, after all these years still never showing the slightest tendency to be mollescent in those familiar places where he infuriates—stepping on lines, big-wording, declaiming, dropping diminutives, nailing his law degree to every wall."[2]

These were the most insightful observations about Cosell ever to be written, and stand in marked contrast to a far more one-sided view of him that was seen that year, by David Halberstam in the December *Playboy.* A decade after Cosell had considered, then rejected him to cowrite his first book, the Pulitzer Prize–winning author wrote the article with a poison pen, identifying himself as a "second generation" Cosell hater, one of those who, unlike the first generation, "had once been favorably inclined toward him but now saw him in a new light, as a symbol of the excess that television had wrought upon sports, of the assault upon civility and texture." Linking him with the "McEnroes, Steinbrenners, Reggies and Billys," Halberstam insisted that Cosell "had become the cartoon his enemies had much earlier drawn of him," no longer challenging the sports establishment but "shill[ing] shamelessly for his network, for its principal event, *Monday Night Football*, and for his boss, Roone Arledge," and craving affection from winners to expel his own insecurities: "With the powerful and the victorious he [feels] confident; with the defeated, he [feels] vulnerable."

Such pseudo-psychological diagnosis of the man having become common, Halberstam's was that he was a narcissist, one of those "joyless men and women who cannot love anyone but spend their lives desperately seeking admiration to counteract their feelings of inner emptiness."[3]

It was an open question now of who was more shameless, and who would stoop lower, Cosell or his harshest critics, many of whom were arguably narcissists themselves. And still, there was no debate about his capacity for cruelty. Alexis Denny, who beside her *SportsBeat* duties was put to work writing his *Monday Night Football* halftime highlights, Cosell having tired of virtually ad-libbing them, was a trusted aide-de-camp only until she accepted an offer from ABC Sports to work the 1984 Summer Olympics in Los Angeles—which, save for the 1988 Winter Games, would be the last Olympics broadcast on the network. For Cosell, as with Alex Wallau's exit from the show, it was a direct slap at him. When she severed the knot, it was without so much as a good-bye from the boss for his "little genius." Whatever else Cosell was, he was, to the end, all or nothing when it came to loyalty.

THINGS HAD only gotten worse on *Monday Night Football* since Don Meredith's return, something that seemed impossible given that in 1979 they were so bad that Cosell had threatened to quit—and actually meant it. That happened after he, Meredith, and Gifford had an impromptu meeting with Roone Arledge at the Beverly Wilshire Hotel the afternoon before a Monday night game. Airing their grievances against Cosell, Meredith argued that "I have things to say, points to make, and Howard keeps getting in my way." Gifford chimed in that "Howard seems to be angry in the booth, and he's making us uncomfortable." Cosell, believing this was proof that they had "teamed up against me," later said he was "outraged," steaming that "I had busted my ass for them, and for what? So they could turn on me?"[4]

Arledge was his usual cipher when it came to these squabbles. "Howard," he told him, by rote, "just keep doing what you're doing, and everything will work itself out." Cosell's *MNF* contract was up after that season, and he had his attorney, Bob Schulman, inform ABC entertainment president Fred Pierce that he wanted out of the show. Pierce assured him, "You mean too much to too many people. I'd hate to see you leave *Monday Night Football*. Let's face it, Howard, you *are Monday Night Football*." Arledge, he added, reminded him that the show "is a part of you, and you need that forum." Roone then applied the clincher, knowing exactly what to say that would bring him back.

"Howard," he said, "think of the company."

When he signed a new contract, Pierce shook his hand and said, "Here's to a whole new beginning."[5]

But nothing changed for the better, and once again it was Meredith whom ABC executives seemed to pander to. Negotiating a new, three-year deal, he was still at home in Beverly Hills the day before the first game of the 1982 season, but that night, once he got his deal, he flew to the game. That season, however, the NFL players went on strike, for fifty-seven days, shaving the *MNF* schedule from twenty-one to twelve games. All three networks took a beating that year, having combined to pay the league $2.1 billion the year before; even when the strike was over, ratings were down for the next few years.

ABC still had to be happy that, by paying the league $655 million, they landed the first-ever Super Bowl broadcast on the network, in January 1984. By then, there would be a number of changes. Because Meredith still took off six games a year, his place for those games was taken first by Fran Tarkenton, then, a year later, in 1983, by O. J. Simpson, who had retired from the game in 1979. Cosell found himself much more at ease with the smooth-talking Simpson, to whom he was close personally and who had once said that doing *Monday Night Football* with Cosell was "the dream of my life" and that Cosell was "my dear friend."[6] Indeed, their super-sized egos seemed to mesh in a way that presaged great heights and great depths for each, though no one could have foreseen the depth of Simpson's eventual fall.

But Cosell's mood was generally sour about the show, and had been for years. By now, Cosell had interacted with virtually every major sports figure of the last forty years of the twentieth century, perhaps more than any other man. On the eve of the 1981 season, no longer eager to carry on the drudgery of it all, he had vented to Robert Friedman of *Inside Sports*, "Do you think I actually *like* doing this? You think I actually take any of this seriously?"

"Why not quit, then?" Friedman asked.

Singing a now-old tune, he explained, "Because I'm contractually obligated to ABC. Because I like Roone too much to walk out on him. Because I'm well paid. And besides, what would I do?"

Friedman asked the obvious question: How much longer could he go on? Ducking it, Cosell dove into self-parody, saying, "I thought you were a man of intelligence. You're just like the rest of them. You want me to say I'm going to quit after this season. That I've had it with *Monday Night Football*. Are you really going to stoop to that level of journalism? Young man, take my advice and get out of the business before it corrupts you any further."[7]

Now, two years later, he *had* had it with *MNF*. Mostly because the "redundancy" and "sameness" he had spoken of years before had gotten to him. As Arledge later said, "He'd turned from being provocative, outrageous, and entertaining to being bitter, vindictive, and paranoid—mostly, I thought, because he was bored. Bored with football and fans, bored with sports, bored with an occupation he felt—maybe rightly—was beneath him."[8]

Cosell himself had dropped hints in the Frank Deford article that he might perhaps cut back on his *MNF* duties, or even quit the show entirely. And he meant it. "If I didn't quit soon," he later said, "they'd have to cart me into the booth in a wheelchair. It was time for me to take cognizance of my age and my health, and there was really nothing left for me to accomplish in broadcasting."[9] As it happened, the very first game of 1983 made the decision for him. That game, on September 5, between the Dallas Cowboys and Washington Redskins at RFK Stadium, is of course today fixed in history as Howard Cosell's Waterloo—a far, far greater mark of distinction than it deserves—for a single phrase he uttered late in the second quarter. With the Redskins soaring to a 21–3 lead mainly because of a hardy passing attack featuring a diminutive, quicksilver receiver, Alvin Garrett, a leaping catch by Garrett prompted Cosell to say that Skins coach Joe Gibbs, who had been an assistant on one of the two teams that had previously cut Garrett, "wanted to get this kid, and that little monkey gets loose, doesn't he?"[10]

This was not a metaphor a wise man would have used to describe a black man—a better choice would have been "Smurf," as the Redskins receiving corps was known as "the Smurfs"—and Cosell was surely guilty of poor judgment. Perhaps the stress and the personal travails had begun to cloud his brain and his ability to censor this kind of inner thought, not that he was ever perfect at doing that. To be certain, he had crossed over into such objectionable territory with racially insensitive remarks through the years, in jest, confident that his labors on behalf of Muhammad Ali, Curt Flood, and African American causes made his intentions clear. Though perhaps assuming too much, he had reason to think anything he said with even the most tenuous racial element would carry that same impunity. Indeed, in this case, one need only to have been around Cosell to know that he often called his grandchildren "little monkeys." He had also used the phrase before on *Monday Night Football*, about a sawed-off Kansas City Chiefs running back, Mike Adamle, but no one raised an eyebrow at the time. Adamle, of course, was white.

In the truck, no one gave it a second thought until later in the game when ABC Sports publicity man Irv Brodsky reported to Bob Goodrich that sportswriters were going "all bullshit about what Howard said." By then, at least one viewer had complained—an important viewer, Reverend Joseph Lowery, president of the Southern Christian Leadership Conference, who fired off a telegram to Cosell that he also forwarded to the wire services demanding that Cosell apologize for his "racist" remark. With the press clamoring for a statement from ABC Sports, Goodrich called up to Cosell in the booth and informed him of the brush fire.

At first, Cosell didn't remember making the statement. "I didn't say it," he told Goodrich.

"Yeah, I think you did, Howard," said the producer.[11]

Since neither Gifford nor Meredith had picked up on the trivial phrase either, Cosell issued a brief statement on the air that "according to the reporters," he had made the remark about Garrett, but actually had done "nothing of the sort and you fellows know it." Gifford, coming to the aid of a teammate, added, "I don't know who they were listening to. One thing Howard is not, my God, is a racist."[12]

Because the game had such a thrilling ending—the Cowboys rallying for a 31–30 win—Cosell thought the tempest was forgotten, only to run into *Washington Post* reporter Leonard Shapiro in the press elevator, who reminded him of Lowery's demand. Exasperated, Cosell angrily told him, "If anybody writes about me negatively with regard to black athletes, they've got to be out of their minds, and they're in for trouble."

"I know, Howard," Shapiro sympathized. "It's ridiculous."

Outside the stadium he and Peter Jennings, who had attended the game, shared a limo ride to the hotel. Seeing how bothered Cosell was, Jennings said, "You really expect trouble, don't you?"

"Yes, I do. The sportswriters will blow this thing up beyond all proportion."

"Don't worry about it," Jennings assured him. "Everybody knows where you stand."

"You just watch, Peter."

As it happened, the firestorm was concentrated, stoked mainly by an unsympathetic Shapiro, who wrote a story in the next day's *Post* titled "Cosell's Remark Raises Ire." Actually, it hadn't; aside from Lowery, Shapiro's own story noted, only around twenty viewers had called in to complain about what Cosell said, which in the Cosell calculus was not even a hiccup. But Shapiro had also quoted Alvin Garrett as saying, "It doesn't offend me because Howard is always shooting off his mouth. Half the time he doesn't know what he's talking about. I think *he* looks like a monkey." When Roone Arledge called Cosell later in the day, he seemed unconcerned, saying, "What a bunch of shit," and calling Lowery "an old fool."[13]

The vast bulk of the press agreed. Even Dick Young knew how absurd it would be to nail him as a racist. Arledge released his own statement judiciously admitting that the "monkey" utterance was "unfortunate" but that, in light of Cosell's "superlative and continuing record of promoting harmonious race relations," it obviously was "intended as an expression of affection."[14] The black community quickly rallied to Cosell's defense. Rachel Robinson added her own statement of support, as did notable African Americans as diverse as Bill Cosby, Willie Mays, Georgetown basketball coach John Thompson, Reverends Jesse Jackson and Ralph Abernathy, and activist educator Harry Edwards.

Cosell reiterated his long record of defending black athletes on his *Speaking of Sports* radio show that day. By then, the Redskins had put out a press release from Alvin Garrett himself, who on second thought, and with the encouragement of owner Jack Kent Cooke, once a Cosell detractor but now a crony, pronounced, "Howard Cosell is just great," adding, "I do not take exception to anything he said about me." Garrett said he was "pleased he singled me out for such favorable attention." Gratified by the patronage, Cosell was mortified that Shapiro continued fanning the dying flames, writing a column with a headline that read "Come On, Howard, Say You're Sorry" and absurdly labeling the remark "one of the worst moments" in the history of the show. Reverend Lowery, too, refused to end the matter. (Several years later, Cosell quoted Lowery as admitting to him that the brouhaha, utilizing Cosell as a scapegoat, was intended to shame ABC into hiring more black producers and directors.)

The manufactured controversy—which Cosell called "grotesque" and "absurd" but was placed in historical perspective as what the *Economist*, no less, pinpointed as "an early skirmish in the political-correctness wars" in Cosell's obituary—died out after a few weeks. By then, he was so unconcerned about it that, when he met up with Garrett in the locker room, they clasped hands and Cosell ribbed him, "How does it feel shaking hands with a racist?"

"C'mon, Howard," Garrett said, "you were just fixing me up," meaning praising him.

Rather than race, the real core of the matter was that, to the press that loathed him, the aging lion was now even more vulnerable to criticism. In its wake, Cosell said, "The whole thing sickened me . . . My spirits were sorely taxed, and it even affected me physically. I felt awful. The very thought of going back into the booth depressed me."[15]

He soon began to float the rumor himself that, as he had boxing, he would quit the show after the season, sparking constant questions from the media about it, which he'd answer by repeating the same threat. Because his talk about quitting the show in the past had always been in-house, ABC honchos took this one seriously, and according to Cosell, Leonard Goldenson hastened to preemptively talk him out of it. "You're part of the family here," the chairman told him with the usual placation, "and we'll always want you with us."[16]

Cosell's contract with the network would expire after the next summer's Olympics, and he had no hesitation coupling that fact with his possible exodus from *MNF.* For now, he rode out the 1983 season, but with a dour, unpleasant self-pity that turned the air in the booth acrid. During this stretch, O. J. Simpson was speaking at a luncheon the afternoon of an *MNF* tilt in Buffalo and took a few playfully intended jabs at Cosell—a right he thought he had earned through years of friendship with him—saying that the Coach perhaps did not know as much about football as he believed he did. The comments made the local newspaper, meaning of course that Cosell, who obsessively read everything, saw them, and winced. Subsequently *Sports Illustrated* quoted Simpson saying of Cosell, "To be honest, I've found I can tease him a little more off-camera than I can on-camera."

These were among the mildest things ever said about him, yet Cosell took them as insults, of his knowledge of the game and his uptight nature on the air. He was no longer in a state of mind where he could brush aside such criticism. The worst insult, though, seemed to be, as he would later write, "never once did [Simpson] knock either Gifford or Meredith. The ex-jocks are members of the same fraternity, and they stick together." After reading the rumors of Cosell leaving the show, Simpson called and told him, "Without you, there is no *Monday Night Football.*" Cosell wasn't moved. "That's not what I've been reading in the newspapers," he said. Mortified, Simpson stammered the usual athletes' refrain about being taken out of context. Cosell cut him short with "I don't want to talk to you, Juice. It's over between us."[17]

Of course, he was doing to Simpson exactly what had been done, unfairly, to him when he was blistered for the "little monkey" remark, reacting blindly, in anger, ignoring the intent of what was said. Simpson did take it hard, though Cosell's recollection that Simpson, one of the two or three greatest running backs of all time, "broke down and cried" at being de-friended by Howard Cosell may be the product of an overactive imagination. While they would soon be back on speaking terms, they were never again close, and the tension between them in the booth that season was just as unpleasant as when Meredith had been there.

COSELL DIDN'T officially announce that he was done with *MNF*, but the rumor that he himself had spread made for a good running story line as the season moved along. Some antagonists in the press were already writing pre-obituaries, based on the show's low ratings that had nothing at all to do with Cosell. One, Shirley Povich, the septuagenarian *Washington Post* sports columnist, and a congenital Cosell critic, lodged the claim that the fans had "finally had enough" of the man Povich had ragged on for years[18]—though only days before the column ran, a humdrum game between the Lions and Vikings pulled a 21 rating and 34 share. Cosell decided to pass up the season finale, a Cowboys-49ers game in San Francisco. His last game in the booth came three days before— ironically, a *Friday* night—for a December 16 Jets-Dolphins clash in Miami's Orange Bowl. Choleric as ever, he spent most of the telecast assailing the hapless Jets coach, Joe Walton. He left the air that night with no valedictory comments, no teary verses, not a word about it being his last *MNF* broadcast.

And that's where things sat. Remarkably, over the winter and into the summer, nothing was resolved about whether his *MNF* tenure was, in Cosellian parlance, "Over! It is over!" Arledge, as if in fear that Cosell would take back his self-imposed vow not to return, refrained from contacting him at all. That meant nothing could be done about his contract situation in general. Smoldering more with each passing day that he was being snubbed, Cosell, in frustration, went public on the *MNF* issue. Just after he had done his normal turn calling the boxing at the summer Olympics, he was told by *Los Angeles Times* television sports critic Larry Stewart, "I understand that it's official, Howard. You're not doing *Monday Night Football* anymore." Assuming that Stewart had gotten a tip from someone at ABC to that effect, Cosell replied, "When a man gets into his midsixties, it's time to cut back. As for *Monday Night Football*, it's the end of a chapter."[19]

Stewart, though, had not gotten a tip; he was merely bluffing, and Cosell fell for it. When the headline broke the next day, Arledge—redefining duplicity—was, or at least *pretended* to be, highly upset that Cosell had breached network protocol by quitting before Arledge could meet with him, never mind that he had avoided doing so for nearly nine months. Actually, Cosell had said essentially the same thing when he took questions during a July appearance at the National Press Club in Washington, D.C. For public consumption, he was nothing but consistent: He was through with football; he simply couldn't make it official until he met with Arledge. He would insist that even if Arledge asked him to come back to the booth, he would have said, "No, Roone—and you can take it to the bank." Only he knew if he meant that. But he was entitled to his ire when Tony Thomopolous, the powerful president of the ABC Broadcast Group, informed him that Arledge was "pissed" that Cosell had quit before telling him.

"Arledge can go shit in a hat," Cosell replied.[20]

The truth is, Roone could not have gotten a better gift, as he no longer needed to tiptoe around the subject. In his mind, Cosell had taken himself off *Monday Night Football*, irrevocably. Which of course gave Arledge more license to keep ignoring him, leaving Cosell out on a limb, still laboring at ABC but with no contract. Finally, they met, by accident, while outside the "21" Club in early September. They eyed each other warily, leaving it to Emmy to take the initiative, telling Arledge to "stop this nonsense with Howard" and "get together with him and work out a new contract." Arledge, with a frozen smile, assured her, "There's nothing to worry about. I have no problems with Howard." He then exchanged a few cordial words with Cosell and got into a cab and left, to go on ignoring him.[21]

Meanwhile, Gifford, Meredith, and Simpson became ensconced in the *MNF* booth, though there *still* was no official announcement that Cosell was out, feeding regular scuttlebutt that he would be back, now *because* of the continuing low ratings. Cosell, still consistent, denied he would return, and focused his energies on *SportsBeat*. It took until the first week of *1985*—a year after Cosell's contract expired—before Arledge met with him, prefacing the finalization of the deal. As it happened, this coincided with the run-up to the first ABC broadcast of the Super Bowl, and new speculation arose that Cosell would now be part of the coverage. The network may have even offered him the opportunity. As Cosell would recall, Leonard Goldenson himself asked him if he would consider it. He told the chairman to ask Emmy, who was emphatic.

"I'm sorry, Leonard," she said, "but we're through with the NFL. I really don't want Howard to be any part of it. And I'm sure he feels the same way."[22]

If the conversation did happen that way, then only one thing mattered—if Emmy was through with the NFL, Howard Cosell certainly was. There never was an official declaration. None was needed. After fourteen years, Cosell's "Stygian burden" was lifted. A large piece of the show went with him, and the first ABC Super Bowl broadcast was, in Cosell's judgment, "lackluster" without him. Yet around ABC Sports, there was nothing but relief that he was gone.

MORE AND more, the penthouse apartment in the Imperial House, with its terrace overlooking a sweeping view of the city, became his refuge and conservatory. During the hot summers, he and Emmy would go off to the beach house in Westhampton Beach. There, nestled between Moniebogue Bay and the Atlantic Ocean, he could escape the angst of those last few years, staring at the peaceful ocean with Emmy, or surrounding himself with his four grandchildren. But these homey diversions never could thaw a perpetually foul mood or dissuade him from off-putting behavior when he would have to go back to work.

Emmy would accompany him as usual wherever he went, but no longer as a buffer that could temper his irascible impulses and save him from public embarrassment with a well-chosen phrase. In the midseventies, his fame had overflowed onto her, earning her a profile in, perhaps appropriately, *Today's Health* magazine, titled "She Loves the Man Everyone Loves to Hate." Now, worn down by decades of Hamlet-like diversions from reality about enemies and their conspiracies against him, she came to see many of the same enemies and conspiracies.

"I think it all got to Emmy, all the abuse he got, the gauntlet they had to run," says Jerry Izenberg. "I happened to see that incident in Baltimore when the crowd surged around them. She just couldn't take it anymore. I think she was having a breakdown. Later that night, she told me, 'Well, now you got what you guys wanted,' meaning the writers, that we wanted to see violence perpetrated against Howard. And I said to myself, 'He's even got her brainwashed now.' In the end she got to be like him. It was a very sad thing to see."[23]

Frank Deford agrees. "About that time, I remember Howard went off on one of his tirades, and I could see Emmy was waiting for him to finish. And I was thinking, okay, Emmy's gonna put him in his place, put out the fire like she always does. And he finished and she said, 'Well, Howard, the reality is, they just don't know how to treat a star.' And I went, 'Oh, God, now the fire extinguisher is gone.'"[24]

Cosell would need her buttressing more than ever when he chose to burn his last bridges at ABC, even as he was still drawing a company paycheck. Late in 1984, he had signed up to write his third memoir, with a $100,000 advance from William Morrow. In a foul mood, and aware of how he was being regarded at ABC Sports, he decided the time had arrived to go public with all the grudges he had stored up for so long. It would indeed take a book to give him enough space to dredge up each one. After hiring the former *Newsweek* and *Inside Sports* editor Peter Bonventre, who was working with him on *SportsBeat*, to help him write it, he spent a year pouring out his bile. The result, *I Never Played the Game*, was scheduled for a fall 1985 publication date.


KNOWING WHAT the reaction would be, it was perhaps preemptive that he stopped playing good soldier at ABC Sports. That guaranteed there would be more trouble with Jim Spence. Convinced as Cosell was that Roone Arledge had never utilized his full potential, because Arledge was himself systematically withdrawing from the affairs of ABC Sports, it was Spence, as senior vice president, whom he held responsible for wanting him gone.

In fact, Cosell had issues with Spence dating back to the late seventies, long before the Holmes-Cobb fight, when Spence swallowed his pride and tried to resolve the one-sided feud. In a heartfelt letter to Cosell, he wrote that "the two most important people in my life are Howard Cosell and my wife," and that "I would like to reestablish our personal relationship." The two then met for a drink at the Dorset Hotel bar, and Cosell told Spence, "You know, Jimmy, you and I don't have any problems." That was typical, pretending his self-made problem didn't exist, and confirmed Spence's belief that Cosell "wanted no part of a confrontation"; rather, he was more comfortable sliming someone behind his back. This indeed seemed to be true when, in 1984, Cosell was quoted in a New York newspaper calling Spence an "errand boy," though he denied having said it. [25]

It was inevitable that Cosell would fall out with Arledge and Spence, maintains Don Ohlmeyer, who by 1982 had moved on from NBC and formed his own production company, Ohlmeyer Communications, producing television movies and series. He posits that he remained friends with Cosell only because he had left the network: "I worked with Howard on a day-to-day basis for ten years and there were strains between us, but Roone and Jim worked with Howard on a day-to-day basis for over twenty-five years. That took a bigger toll on them, and him." [26]

IN LATE summer of 1985, excerpts from *I Never Played the Game* appeared in *TV Guide*, mainly the ones that crucified Meredith and Gifford, setting into motion the polemic that would define the book and all discussion about it from here on in. During an October appearance on *Late Night with David Letterman* to plug the book, Cosell joked to the host, referring to the latter's running feud with *Today* anchor Bryant Gumbel, "You've reached that stage in life where your aim is no longer to win but to get even"—a sentiment that more aptly applied to himself. [27]

Issuing heavy fire against powerful people in the industry, he knew, required some self-inoculation. Prefacing his criticism of the ever-popular Gifford, he had written that "in no way should this be miscon-strued as a personal attack against Frank"; rather, it was "as measured and forthright an assessment as I can make" about an old friend. To Let-terman, he insisted, "I say more good things about Frank Gifford than I say bad things." He also acknowledged that his free exercise of opinion might well be cause for his dismissal, but it was a risk he had to take. Such caveats did him no good. The reaction was, predictably, and over-whelmingly, negative. Typical was Ralph Novak's review in *People*, dis-missing the work as "full of paranoia, condescension and hypocrisy."[28]

Even years later, the stigma of those pages remains. In recalling the book's vindictive tone, Larry Merchant laments, "The way he went after Gifford, I mean, why? You can be kind with the truth, you can be funny with the truth. He was neither. Look, none of us could be Frank Gifford, who was a gorgeous man, an All-American All-Pro, and a good guy. Whatever Howard thought of him, he was a colleague. That counts for something, or should. I've bitten the hand that fed me, too, and it tastes good. But you can be a good reporter, you can be honest. You don't always have to be a contrarian all the time, unless you need to create straw men so you can tear them down and say they deserved it."[29]

For Arledge, the book was irrelevant. From where he sat, Cosell's departure from *Monday Night Football* was really when for all intents and purposes he ceased to exist at ABC. Arledge felt no urgent need to even look at *I Never Played the Game*—fortunately, since when he eventually did, he could perceive himself, unlike Gifford and Meredith, portrayed as "the villain" of the story, slimed as a man who had taken credit for telecasts "he has little if anything to do with" and who "cares more about news than sports," causing ABC Sports to suffer from "a dearth of leadership."

Still, in neglecting the book as he did, Arledge managed to affront Cosell as much as with any decision he ever made at ABC Sports. As Arledge later wrote, the latter would have simply been business, but the former was "a personal betrayal," the worst crime of all for Cosell. Dur-ing one of their rare meetings over lunch that fall, all Cosell seemed to want to know was what Roone thought of the book. Arledge told him matter-of-factly that he hadn't read it.

"I don't believe you, Arledge!" he barked. "Come on, you're pulling my leg, aren't you? You've read it."

"No, really," Arledge insisted.

"You really haven't read my book?

"I just haven't gotten to it yet."

An hour later, when they had left the restaurant, Cosell was still grumbling about it. "I can't believe it," he repeated. "You couldn't have resisted reading it."[30]

Beneath his protests, he knew there was an implicit truth: His long-time patron and enabler no longer felt he needed to hear, or even read, what he had to say.

Gifford and Meredith, meanwhile, chose not to get into a spitting match with him, Gifford calling the incendiary passages "petty." But Cosell had given his enemies an open field, and there came a wave of almost involuntary vilification of him that must have made Dick Young giddy. To some who were more sympathetic, he was surely Lear-like now, a mighty king fallen, oblivious to everything but his own remaining delusions. Don Ohlmeyer, who shuddered when he read the book, recalls it now as "the beginning of Howard's tragic period," when he seemed to no longer care whom he offended, nor that he invited what Ohlmeyer calls a "public stoning" by enemies far and wide.[31] The stoning, in fact, was in full force even before the release of the book, which would hit the best-seller lists as soon as it came out in November and not drop off for six months thereafter. At once, its appearance jeopardized Cosell's scheduled turn at the 1985 World Series.

It did not help Cosell that he had been burning his baseball bridge, too. The TV critics had never warmed to his work covering the sport. His performances were always cocksure but seriously uninformed at times—the standard being established in 1978 when he began to extol Atlanta Braves second baseman Chico Ruiz, relating his long career in the game, only this was not the same Chico Ruiz; *that* Ruiz was killed in a car accident in 1972. What he lacked in knowledge he tried to make up in brow-beating. "He was just so anti everything," recalls Dennis Lewin, still a baseball producer. "He was anti everything that moved."[32]

No one was exempt. Once, when Cosell appeared on ABC's late-night news show *Nightline,* an executive at Budweiser—owned by venerable St. Louis Cardinals owner August Busch and one of the network's biggest advertisers—called to tell him he'd erred on a few facts. Cosell exploded, raging at the executive, "You little pipsqueak! I don't give a shit about your company's advertising!"[33] But, of course, ABC did.

During the 1984 American League Championship Series between the Detroit Tigers and the Kansas City Royals, Cosell and play-by-play man Al Michaels took to sniping at each other, though what viewers didn't know was that Cosell had been drinking during the game. After Michaels disagreed with a point he made, believing Cosell's explanation of a baseball strategy "made no sense," Cosell waited until after the game before telling the even then respected announcer that he would never be a good broadcaster until he "learned to take a stand," implying the latter was too soft on tough issues and on players and owners. Michaels, who personally liked Cosell, snapped back, "You're drunk . . . You're ruining the fucking telecast," adding, "You ever come in like that again, I'm not gonna work with you." Needing a good stiff belt himself, he then went into the press room and asked for a large vodka. The apologetic bartender poured the glass only a quarter full—all Cosell had left him.

The next day, Michaels's agent, Barry Frank, called Jim Spence and said his client could no longer "tolerate" Cosell. Spence, who maintained in his memoirs that he had often pulled Cosell out of such a fire, with scarce gratitude in return, did what he and Arledge always did about such flare-ups: nothing.[34]

There was still tension between him and Michaels when Cosell did several *Monday Night Baseball* games during the 1985 season. Then, with the World Series days away, and Cosell taunting ABC on a near-daily basis as he promoted *I Never Played the Game,* Spence at long last had had enough. If Arledge had ducked out on dealing with Cosell, Spence could no longer let him slide. While ABC had never allowed the baseball or football establishment to have a veto on broadcasters, Cosell for years could count on Bowie Kuhn, who, inversely to Pete Rozelle, had gone from critic to crony. But Kuhn had been fired by the owners in September 1984, and his replacement, travel industry CEO and Olympic organizer Peter Ueberroth, had little affinity for Cosell, who clearly had

used up all his chits. Another factor was that, according to Cosell's contract, he was to be paid $20,000 for every baseball game he broadcast.
*That* was something Arledge suddenly thought important; in an April
memo to Bob Apter, ABC's financial controller, he wrote: "Howard may
be too expensive for our B.B. package."[35]

In the end, Spence made the call: Cosell would not be used for the
World Series, played between Gussie Busch's Cardinals and the cross-
state Kansas City Royals. His place as analyst would be taken by Tim
McCarver, the former Cardinals and Phillies catcher who was moved up
from working as a roving grandstand reporter. McCarver was a personable, keenly perceptive, and articulate man who broke Cosell's stereotypical "dumb jock" mold, and with his entrance as a full-time color
analyst, few mourned or noticed Cosell's exit. As a result, says Dennis
Lewin, "I don't think Howard was ever fired. He half resigned and was
half forced out."

After the Series, Lewin was quoted by *USA Today* TV critic Rudy
Martzke as saying the broadcasts were better without Cosell. Aghast
when he saw the quotes attributed to him, Lewin immediately called
Cosell and told him he'd been badly misquoted. Disinterestedly, Cosell
told him, "I don't care what you said," and hung up. "I think," Lewin
concludes, "by then Howard thought calling games of any kind was
beneath him, and accordingly, any criticism. I also think he had started
ending friendships with people like me."[36]

In Cosell's humble opinion, he still possessed big-time star quality.
Only months before, in April, he had hosted an episode of *Saturday
Night Live*, which reunited him with his "protégés" Billy Crystal and
Christopher Guest. In his publicity campaign for *Never Played*, he was
interviewed in the weekly newsmagazines, including *U.S. News & World
Report*. Could any other sportscaster claim such diverse and impressive
credits? Even with the eddy he'd created at ABC, even with no major
sports events to call anymore, he figured that, he was far, far bigger than
anyone who existed in his shadow. But while his shadow did indeed still
loom large, he no longer had any real ability to see his own reflection.

THE LAST thread Cosell maintained with ABC was *SportsBeat*, which had pressed on for four years with Cosell hailing it as his finest work, far outdistancing what he'd done announcing boxing or football. That his profile had fallen dramatically somehow was ameliorated by the rush the little-seen show gave him. Indeed, he was able to use it to continue irritating Pete Rozelle, not to mention his own network, by defending another challenge to the NFL, this time by the United States Football League. This, the latest attempt to cash in on the game's massive popularity, began play in 1983 amid a flush of excitement, with some high-rolling owners, including Donald Trump, luring some key players away from the NFL. But, drowning in red ink, its only option was to force a merger, which it tried to do by filing a $567 million antitrust lawsuit against the older league. While Cosell turned *SportsBeat* into a virtual amicus brief for the new league, the USFL lost the lawsuit in 1986 and promptly went out of business.

Clearly, says Mike Marley, *SportsBeat* was Cosell's "bully pulpit, where he always thought he was doing his most important work." Other favored topics included racism and steroid abuse. "Howard was uncompromising, really tough, sometimes too much. One time he sent me out with Arthur Ashe to Kansas City to do a story about Bill Robinzine, an NBA player who after his career ended went into his garage and killed himself. I brought his widow, Claudia, to New York to be interviewed by Howard and I told him, 'Be gentle with this lady,' because you know how Howard could be. And then his first question is 'Claudia, I don't want to invade your area of personal privacy but what were the contents of the suicide note?' Oh, my God, I nearly fell down when I heard that. But that was Cosell."[37]

Unfortunately, the show was as doomed as the USFL. As much as ABC tried to find a time slot that would draw viewers, nothing seemed to work. At one point, Marley says, not far from the truth, the show's only competition was the religious show *Lamp unto My Feet* that at dawn began the television day in New York. No matter where it was slotted, the network was losing a million dollars a year on the show. In the past, Cosell could rightly assume that any time his position was tenuous, Roone Arledge would shore him up, both his position and his ego. But by now, with the network's new owner, Capital Cities, having ordered Arledge to give up his presidency of ABC Sports to focus entirely on the news division, he couldn't have intervened on his behalf in any capacity other than employing him as a news reporter or anchor—something he had emphatically ruled out. And Jim Spence was a bridge that Cosell had burned long ago.

ABC unceremoniously sent out the pink slip for *SportsBeat* on October 20, 1985. The last show would run on December 15. Posthumously, it would win three Emmy Awards, though none specifically for Cosell, who wouldn't be given one until after he was dead. But there was no residual goodwill for him to soak up. Having invested so much of his enduring swagger in the show, he had lost more than a high-quality platform. He had lost his network.

Not long before, Arledge had implored him to "think about the network," but now no one at the network wanted to think about him. If his "biggest defender" at the network, according to him, Leonard Goldenson, had any objection, he kept it to himself. Seen in the cold light of reality, quite plainly Cosell was no different than anyone else in his business. As an on-air personality, he had had to remodel himself many years before to look and seem younger than he was. Now, at sixty-seven, there was no remodeling that could obscure the fact that he had outlived even his aura, and his usefulness. Many huge stars before him had arrived at the stage where their network readied a gold watch for them. Now it was time for Howard Cosell.

After *SportsBeat* was canceled, he and Dennis Lewin would walk together to the ABC building, but with actual work awaiting only the director. As they made their way through the streets of Manhattan, a despondent Cosell, perhaps wondering why he was making the trip, would say, "Nobody cares about me," meaning at ABC.

Recalls Lewin: "I'd tell him, 'Howard, nobody in the history of this business has had a better opportunity to say what he thinks than you. You had every platform known to mankind to speak your mind. If people aren't watching, it has nothing to do with the network.' But Howard couldn't see it that way. He would just keep saying, 'No, the network's never cared about me.' And to me, that was pathetic."[38]

# 19

## REQUIEM
## FOR A HEAVYWEIGHT

FTER A very agitated thirty years, the adjournment of Howard
Cosell as the virtual face and voice of ABC television, and
American sports, didn't happen with a final bang, nor a whimper. Though
he had been scheduled to be on ABC's coverage of the Kentucky Derby
and the Preakness in 1986, as well as the Tournament of Champions tennis event at Forest Hills, he and ABC simply faded away from each other,
his lawyers and their lawyers working out a contract settlement. His utter
loathing for the network was apparent when Jim Spence arranged a farewell dinner for him that would be televised and include guest celebrities
who would give him a royal send-off. Thinking Cosell would be flattered
by the idea, Spence rang him up.

"We'd like to honor you," he began, before Cosell cut him off.

"I don't want to be honored," he said bitingly. "If you want to talk
about my departure, talk to my lawyer, Bob Schulman."[1]

The grand farewell, proffered, as both men knew, as much to mitigate
ABC's guilt as to genuinely honor Cosell, never took place. And, as if
affirming Cosell's judgment that such contrived rites of mawkish tribute
masked the savage fratricide of the network sports game, Spence himself
soon became the next casualty. Such was the cannibalistic atmosphere of

high-stakes corporate television, as it still is today. Spence had been expecting Roone Arledge to back him as his replacement as president of ABC Sports, but Arledge instead got behind Capital Cities' choice, Dennis Swanson, a ten-year ABC Sports veteran and an ex-marine who was thought to be better equipped to establish some rare discipline in the department. Spence, feeling every bit as betrayed by Arledge as was Cosell, resigned in March, actually predating Cosell's own exit by a few weeks. Swanson would run the place like a veritable drill sergeant, in time souring on Jim Lampley, who was being groomed to replace Jim McKay on *Wide World of Sports* until Swanson bought him out of his contract in 1987.[2] Both Spence and Lampley would land on their feet. Spence, with his wife, formed his own production and marketing company, Sports Television International, while Lampley went to NBC, hosting the Olympics every four years until 2010, and of course calling fights in the pugnacious style of Howard Cosell on HBO's long-running boxing package, his main assignment today.

For Cosell, there were still some empty good-bye gestures, which he took as an insincere laying on of network hands. These were similar to Don Meredith having sent him a Christmas card the year before that read: "It's not the same without you. We miss you terribly." He hadn't heard from Meredith since. There were, too, appropriate, if not front-page, notices in the press about his exit. In *Time*'s January 6 issue, writer Tom Callahan called it "an occasion of both joy and wistfulness, good news for the national eardrum but bad news for news," and sadly noted that "he had hoped to become Walter Cronkite or at least Hugh Downs (for a hilarious few weeks in 1975, even Ed Sullivan), but that was so long ago."[3] For Cosell, though, a farewell to arms and ABC wasn't sad as much as liberating, or so he wanted to believe, *had* to believe. Now he was free to accept what he trusted would be an endless chain of offers for movies, books, and projects that would, once and for all, put the mundane world of sports behind him.

He saw himself doing talk shows, producing documentaries. Financially, he reasoned, he might well do better now that he was free of the ABC ball and chain—for all the revenue he generated for the network, all the ratings that turned into a golden goose, he had never cleared a yearly salary of $1,000,000 until his last few years, and had never made an extra dime for his *Monday Night Football* work; that was just part of his overall "contractual obligations." Not that he was hurting any, having made wise investments through the years and a nice profit from the sale of his books and the Pound Ridge home, and his outside work on TV shows, movies, commercials, and appearances.

But the question he had to face was not "What will I do first?" but rather "Where are the offers?" The horizon seemed less sunny than he had initially imagined. Few came in, and Cosell sightings began to get rare. In May 1986, he decided to accept a job he clearly didn't want but reasoned he needed to keep his profile elevated, writing a twice-weekly sports column for the *Daily News*. It was indeed small potatoes for him. Although the famous paper was read around the country, its circulation was a fraction of what it had been in its heyday, and it had nearly gone bankrupt in 1982.

After commanding a national TV audience for decades, Cosell was down now to his Sunday night radio network show *Speaking of Everything*, his *Speaking of Sports* local radio cut-ins, and a column in a local tabloid. On the other hand, he could encroach on the sacred turf of those he hated most, the sportswriters, with no doubt he would now show them how it was supposed to be done. And he would now be plying his opinions on the very pages once owned by his personal Javert, Dick Young, who in 1981 left to write for the rival *Post*.

After a massive ad campaign, including TV commercials pairing him with the paper's main sports columnist, Mike Lupica, the first column was splashed across the top of the back page, or the front page for sports, on May 4, its lead reading portentously:

> Cosell a *writer*. Cosell a print guy, a newspaperman. It's hard to believe. After all those years spent vigorously criticizing them time and time again . . . Cosell jumps to join print. The announcement is made and indignation mounts. How could he? Why did he? How *dare* he?[4]

Actually, almost no one could be heard asking those questions. As much as he believed his audience was those who "came of age in the '60s and early '70s" and "are not disposed to believe that life begins and ends on the playing fields," that generation had moved past him.

Over the coming weeks, in his stuffy, lawyerly style of writing, he would have at sports' impotent reaction to drug use—"The Terrorism of Drugs," blared the headline of one column—a conservative Supreme Court hostile to antitrust issues, and occasional off-beat topics such as "Harness Racing's Dark Days." The target audience of twenty- and thirty-somethings barely noticed. No matter what he wrote about, he seemed a musty relic, such as when he would use the quaint phrase "this reporter" in his columns. Getting so little reaction and failing to ignite any real discussion, he could harbor only one conclusion—it was the *News's* fault, for having such a small audience.

For Cosell, blame was something toxic, and he needed to toss it onto someone else in order to content himself. However, no one at the *News*, not shockingly since he treated the staff as beneath him, blamed anyone but him. The paper's wry sports editor, Vic Ziegel, one of the younger writers in the early sixties who dug Cosell when the old guard was vilifying him, had gladly signed off on Cosell's hiring. But Ziegel agreed with the other editors that his ramblings were now supercilious and vapid, and was relieved when he and Cosell agreed in 1988 to terminate the column and part company, leaving behind an experience best left forgotten.

Now Cosell could be defined in 20/20 hindsight by men he despised who had followed him out the ABC door. When Jim Spence came forth with his memoir in 1989, he skewered Cosell for many things, most seriously his unchecked alcoholism, an especially hurtful public comment since Cosell was very much alive. Echoing Cosell's not very convincing conscience qualm in *I Never Played the Game*, Spence wrote, "I've debated whether to bring this out . . . but I cannot write a book like this without telling it like it *really* is," which was that Cosell's drinking "became a major problem," that vodka had been "available for him in the booth," and that at ABC there had been a "network cover-up" about it for years. Spence, however, could hardly have been telling it like it was by insisting he and Arledge never knew the extent of Cosell's drinking until the incident with Al Michaels in 1984. In fact, three years earlier, Bob Goodrich had become so alarmed by Cosell's boozing during *Monday*

*Night Football* that on a cold night in Pittsburgh he ordered production assistants who had been acting as "runners" filling Cosell's needs to "cut him off the booze." One of those runners later said he had poured him "about six drinks, vodka, straight up" and that Cosell was "obviously in the bag."[5]

In truth, however, perhaps the least of Cosell's problems was booze; making the same point Dennis Lewin does about such elbow-bending being nothing out of the usual for those times, Jim Lampley advises one to "think *Mad Men*," referring of course to the AMC series about early-sixties New York advertising men, all of whom drink heavily. "Howard was certainly not the only guy at ABC Sports who was having two or three martinis at lunch," Lampley says. "He shouldn't be singled out for that." Indeed, there were far more serious rumors at ABC about Don Meredith and cocaine, a subject left untouched by Spence. Moreover, as Lampley notes with a good giggle, "Go back and watch the fourth quarter of a Pat Summerall–Tom Brookshier game on CBS. Those boys were lucky to make it to the finish line a lot of times."[6]

HANGING ON to his fading celebrity in the late 1980s, Cosell could reap none of the invitations that once came streaming in from every network. One of the few he got, he hurried to do—actress Shelley Duvall's syndicated children's show *Tall Tales and Legends*, in a reenactment of *Casey at the Bat*. He would still name-drop Frank and Dino and Bob—his "groupies," Jerry Izenberg calls them—and if these names no longer dominated public consciousness, to Cosell they still mattered, and so did he. In many ways, he was reprising a male version of Norma Desmond in *Sunset Boulevard*, drawing comfort from a luminous time, now so long ago, when he had been a center-ring star.

During this time, Cosell's "Joe Gillis"—the writer befriended by Norma Desmond and kept virtually entombed in her mansion—was Mike Marley, who after *SportsBeat* gained a law degree from Fordham but found himself constantly drawn back to Cosell's world, which was becoming progressively rooted in the past.

"The first time I was ever in his apartment," recalls Marley, "I asked who else lived in the building. Howard said, drawing out the words, 'Liza—with a Z,' meaning of course Liza Minnelli. 'She lives five floors below me,' and he pointed to her apartment just to establish that he was on a higher floor and had a better apartment than Liza Minnelli. Those kind of things were important to him."[7]

Even so, he had become an island, essentially alone, his former world as removed as Desmond's silent screen was in the early 1950s. For a time, his closest friend seemed to be none other than Bowie Kuhn, his old foil-turned-crony whose typically timid leadership during baseball's labor convulsions led to his being forced out as commissioner in 1984. The two warhorses frequently had dinner together—or rather, drank dinner together, both men having prodigious capacities for alcohol. Kuhn even bought a summer house nearby Cosell's in Westhampton. However, when Kuhn's New Jersey law firm closed, he moved to Florida and the relationship ended.

Meanwhile, his wife, the "only Emmy I'll ever need," after so many years of being joined at the hip with him, now preferred staying home rather than going through the usual madness he always seemed to generate. Cosell, by contrast, remained addicted to having an audience. Dreading rolling alone, he kept Marley close by. Almost daily, Mike would pick up the phone and hear Cosell bark something like "Come on, kid, we're going to Yankee Stadium!" A limo, Cosell in the back, would fetch him, and the two of them would watch a game from George Steinbrenner's box, then they'd roll on to some of the old boîtes around town for rounds of martinis, hopefully to find some celebrity or another.

"One time," Marley recalls, "Howard called me and Peter Bonventre and we wound up going with him to Elaine's on the Upper East Side. We walked in and Howard saw Farrah Fawcett was there with Ryan O'Neal, whom I knew because he was a boxing guy—he was once a prizefighter, and he was then managing Hedgemon Lewis, a welterweight contender at the time. O'Neal and Fawcett stopped by our table and Cosell tried to engage in showbiz chatter with him. 'Not now, Howard,' O'Neal said. 'I want to talk boxing with Mike and Peter.' I don't think anyone would have ever brushed Howard off like that when he was the king—especially when it came to boxing. Still, Howard didn't bat an eye, he went right on sidling up to Farrah. He didn't care about boxing at that point. He cared about being seen talking to a star."

Unfortunately, most of them now gave him the same treatment O'Neal had. On a cross-country flight to L.A., Cosell found himself in first class with Diana Ross. "I didn't see it," says Marley, "but a flight attendant told me that Howard kept trying to talk to her, kept haranguing her, and she put blankets over her head to shut herself off from him, trying to sleep. By the time the plane landed, she had eight blankets over her head."[8]

Worse, most of the time he was snappish, easily provoked into discomfiting public outbursts, even with people who had been partial to him. One of those was Phil Pepe, whose lengthy stint with the *Daily News* had landed him his own column in the 1980s. Pepe had long been one of Cosell's few consistent allies in the press corps, and Cosell returned the favor by giving him a job writing copy for the *Speaking of Sports* show for the duration of a protracted strike that shut down the New York dailies. But "Little Philly," as he called him, tripped Cosell's wire for not having preemptively protested another gross ring mismatch, Larry Holmes's one-round knockout of Joe Frazier's son Marvis. When Pepe took NBC, which carried the fight, to task for "brainwashing" him into believing Frazier had a chance, Cosell rabbit-punched him on *SportsBeat*, saying, "One wonders how the nation's largest-circulation tabloid can entrust a column to a man who can't control his own mind."[9]

Several years later, on one of his Yankee Stadium jaunts, he and Pepe apparently had it out in the press box. As Marley recalls it, "Howard kind of gave Pepe a half slap across the face. It might have been a playful thing, but I had to be a sort of unofficial bodyguard so I jumped between them. I said, 'Phil, if you're gonna hit Howard, you're gonna have to go through me.' Nothing came of it, and it was nonsensical, but things were getting frayed with Howard. He just seemed angry at everybody." (Pepe says this version of the incident is "absolutely not true. Howard liked to joke around and pretend he was angry, but that never happened. At least if it did, it wasn't serious.")

That he could still get himself worked up, even in semiretirement, by what someone wrote in the papers seemed to Marley to be a colossal waste of Cosell's dwindling time. "He would just go on and on about things like what Rudy Martzke wrote in *USA Today*. Howard resented that Chet Forte and all those guys at ABC were currying favor with Martzke. He'd say, 'This moron, they let him sit in the truck, they kiss his ass, when this guy doesn't know anything about television.' And I'd hear this and I'd tell him, 'Come on, is Rudy Martzke that significant, Howard?' I mean, he was seventy years old now, you'd think he'd turn his attention to other things. But Howard always had to have targets to rail against, especially so when he had so little to occupy his time."[10]

Don Ohlmeyer, noticing the same thing, came to Cosell late in 1987 with a vehicle for his return to television, putting his considerable clout behind a syndicated weekly television talk show that would cadge the title and concept of *Speaking of Everything*, showcasing Cosell's adept, provocative interviewing. Ohlmeyer, who would produce, got hundreds of independent stations across the country to carry it, and on Friday night, January 1, 1988, the show hit the air with veteran actor Jack Lemmon and Billy Crystal as guests. There would be other heavy names to come, including Jerry Lewis, George Steinbrenner, attorney Alan Dershowitz, David Letterman, columnists Jimmy Breslin and George Will, New York mayor Ed Koch—and, perhaps most significant of all for Cosell, Roone Arledge. But, reminiscent of the star-stuffed *Saturday Night*, the show never found an audience. Worse, Cosell never found his legs as a TV interviewer, and each week was more of a chore.

"It was really sad for me because I loved the guy," says Ohlmeyer. "It was painful for me to see him in so much pain. I couldn't bring myself to tell him how bad the show was, and he was. Howard was just so bitter by that time, because of the whole thing with the book and the fact that everybody piled on. No one in the press would give him his due. They never said, 'Well, you know, Howard, we had our differences but you made a difference in broadcasting.' Instead, it was, 'Howard, you're an asshole.' That hurt him. He never recovered from it."[11]

The show was peremptorily canceled after sixteen weeks, leaving him only with his two radio shows, which were increasingly forgotten as *Monday Night Football* moved ahead, the ratings rarely spiking to Cosell-era levels but consistently profitable. Don Meredith had stuck it out only one year longer than Cosell, retiring after the 1984 season and living a life of quiet leisure until his death in late 2010 after a brain hemorrhage at age seventy-two. Frank Gifford, the last of the signature cast that had molded the show, soldiered on, though in 1986 he was switched to color analyst, replaced as play-by-play man by Al Michaels, with ex–St. Louis Cardinals lineman Dan Dierdorf added as the third wheel in 1987. Periodically, there would be columns about whether *MNF* was better or worse without the mouth that had roared. Normally, opinion on this broke down along old demarcation lines.

Still, something about *MNF* was missing, something few seemed prepared to say. One who did was the Atlanta curmudgeon Lewis Grizzard, who in 1991, three years before the writer's death, penned a column titled "America Owes Howard Cosell an Apology"—for what Grizzard called a drastically muffled Monday night: "Very few people liked Howard Cosell . . . but that's the point. America learned to love to hate Howard, and once he left the broadcast to pretenders, the broadcast became deathly dull." Added Grizzard, in an epitaph to become common, "I can still hear him."[12]

The debate would persist, with lessening frequency until it hardly mattered. To Cosell, it could not have mattered less. He rarely had anything to say about the show he made famous. If he said anything about sports it was about boxing, which he had now taken to saying was less credible than professional wrestling. Mike Tyson's constant skirmishes with the law and the many indictments of Don King on extortion charges, though he was never convicted, only made Cosell look ever more oracular. Not only had he testified before Congress in favor of the abolition of the sport, he took to belittling anyone within its scope. Once close with King, he now turned on him, saying he was "furious" that while Ali was once forbidden to fight in all fifty states, "that piece of scum Don King hasn't been barred by one. What does that tell you about government, boxing, and the past twenty-five years in America? I wonder how it could have happened in this country."[13]

Larry Merchant had known what a gratuitous Cosell dagger felt like. In 1974, during the second Ali-Frazier fight, Cosell noted that Merchant had Ali way ahead in the late rounds and snidely cracked, "But then again, Larry Merchant had Ali way ahead at this stage of the first fight." Back then, being called out by Cosell like this was a publicity bonanza. Later on, after Merchant had gravitated to HBO as its premier boxing analyst, Cosell didn't have nearly the same éclat as he went about "putting down the whole sport," as Merchant says. "Well, where was he for fifteen years before that, to tell us about all this now? And, now, why should anyone care what he says?"[14]

Ferdie Pacheco, who moved from Ali's corner to ringside as a boxing analyst for NBC, recalls that Cosell had often been to his Miami home during the Ali years, but in later years disparaged Pacheco as a "so-called boxing expert." Today, the "Fight Doctor" remembers him as a "nothing, a joke, a self-imposed windbag," and worse, much worse.[15]

Cosell nursed any number of old grudges, none stronger than against Alex Wallau, who after quitting *SportsBeat* gave Cosell more reason to despise him when he became an ABC Sports boxing analyst. Cosell would wonder aloud how Wallau could lower himself like that. Even after Wallau had ascended the company ladder, becoming a network vice president in the nineties and its president from 2000 to 2004, Cosell could only see Wallau as the young producer who refused to bow before him. In 1998, Wallau was walking down a Manhattan street when he ran into Sal Marchiano, the sports news anchor for New York TV station WPIX. During their conversation, Wallau confided that he had been diagnosed with throat cancer. Later that day, Marchiano ran into Cosell and said, "Isn't it horrible about Alex?" When Cosell didn't know what he meant, Marchiano told him. Cosell barely blinked an eyelash.

"He deserves it," he said, with no emotion, between puffs of his cigar.

Marchiano would relate the story to Mike Marley, who was hardly surprised by Cosell's reaction. "I don't think Howard meant it exactly that way, but he and Alex had a really bad falling-out," he says. The news about Wallau was reported in the media, but both Marley and Marchiano gave Cosell protection he perhaps did not deserve. Says Marley, "Sal never revealed what Howard said until after Howard had died. Howard had angered enough people, and I'm sure he regretted saying that."[16] The story still got around, underground, and every time people would hear of it, they'd roll their eyes and shrug. That's what Howard Cosell had become.

Such churlishness seemed to be a last refuge for him. Cosell was at a cocktail party on August 30, 1987, when someone mentioned that Dick Young had died after intestinal surgery at age sixty-nine. According to a man who was there, Cosell was beaming as he walked around the room, saying over and over, "This is the happiest day of my life. Dick Young is dead." The whole room got suddenly quiet, with some whispering about the sorry spectacle of a man prancing around like a child, saying how happy he was that another man had died.[17]

AMAZINGLY FOR a man so effortlessly cruel, he could dissolve easily into a soft, sentimental slob, growing teary-eyed at any moment when someone he got along with died. Four days after Billy Martin was killed in an automobile accident on Christmas 1989, Cosell delivered the eulogy at the funeral held at St. Patrick's Cathedral—as he had four years before, standing at the same altar for Roger Maris's funeral service. He referred to himself these days as the sports world's "mourner in chief." However, other than being invited into his coveted place in a cathedral pulpit when a eulogy was needed, Cosell himself was all but a memory. By the early nineties, obituaries and eulogies were being written for *him*, to be kept at the ready just in case.

So too was the world he had dominated and stamped dying out. By the mideighties, when Capital Cities had supplanted the long-entrenched cast, sending Leonard Goldenson into retirement, the old gang at ABC Sports was practically gone, the only survivor being Jim McKay. Roone Arledge, meanwhile, would endure as president of ABC News until 1997 when he was put out to pasture with the title of chairman; he retired a year later, and died in 2002 of prostate cancer at age seventy-one, a year before his memoir was posthumously published.

Chet Forte, his card-playing partner and oldest crony, and at whose wedding he had been best man, paid the piper for years of compulsive gambling that no one at ABC Sports, including Cosell, believed serious enough to do anything about—Jim Spence, who found Cosell's martinis so cataclysmic, never mentioned Forte's gambling in his memoir. But by the mideighties, he was blowing $20,000 a game on football, sometimes losing $100,000 on any given Sunday, and betting $20,000 on Monday night games he was directing. His debt had reached a staggering $1 million when in 1986 "Little Chester," who won nine Emmys and earned $900,000 a year at his peak, took a buyout on the last year of his contract and left the network, soon to lose his house and be indicted by a federal grand jury for mail fraud and tax evasion. He cooperated with the government on a gambling investigation, joined Gamblers Anonymous, and was let off easy, with five years' probation. He then directed Roller Derby contests and was a radio sports talk show host, before a heart attack killed him in May 1996 at age sixty.

Frank Gifford stayed in the *Monday Night Football* booth until 1997 when he retired, or was retired by ABC. Still and forever the all-American boy in his seventies, he stayed on the high road about Cosell, parrying lingering questions about the nasty things in *I Never Played the Game* with good-natured ribbing such as "Howard Cosell has written four books—one for each face." One thing Gifford knew after spending all those Monday nights beside him was that "Howard Cosell is the most complex person ever to walk into my life . . . He was basically two personalities. Howard was like the little girl with the little curl. When he was good, he was very good, and when he was bad, he was horrid."[18]

COSELL HAD started to break down physically, an inevitability given his decades of cigarette and cigar smoking and habitual drinking—which, because Emmy was a chain-smoker and heavy drinker as well, made their apartment seem like the lounge at the Friars Club. And it was she, who had spent so much of her life bolstering him, who broke down first. In the spring of 1988, she was diagnosed with lung cancer. Before she went in for long and delicate surgery, she wrote farewell letters to Jill and Hilary, telling them to take care of their father. Worried sick she wouldn't survive, Cosell regularly told friends that if Emmy were to die, he didn't want to live. Indeed, no one doubted that Cosell wanted to go first to the grave, that without her he would have little to live for. Thus, when Emmy made it through the operation, he resolved to dote on her every minute of the day; for months, he waited on her hand and foot, not allowing her to do the simplest of chores, willing her back to health. Soon, she was free of cancer.

Relieved and regenerated, he gathered up his energy and outrage once more to write his fourth book, for Simon & Schuster, titled *What's Wrong with Sports*, for which he enlisted ABC Radio writer-producer Shelby Whitfield as coauthor. However, his spirit, and his own will to live, would be fatally broken only eight days after he turned in the completed manuscript. It happened without forewarning, though he would later admit that his wife's death was "something that I've always feared."[19] Not aware of its imminence, he felt he could take a one-day trip to speak at a charity function in Kansas City. He had arrived the night of November 17, 1990, and checked into a hotel. At around six o'clock the next morning, he was awakened by a phone call from his daughter Hilary, who had been staying in the apartment. Crying, she told him that Emmy had suffered a massive heart attack an hour before. An ambulance was summoned, but she never regained consciousness and was pronounced dead. Letting the phone drop from his hands, he sat on the edge of the bed, first too stunned to react, then wailing in grief.

Not being with her as she died was something he could not forgive himself for, just as he never had for not being with Isidore Cohen when he died, hundreds of miles from home. He flew home that morning, staring into space, and dutifully made arrangements for her funeral. After a week in seclusion with the family at the apartment, he returned to his *Speaking of Everything* radio show; with no guests, he spent the hour speaking of Emmy. He began by saying, "This is the most difficult broadcast I have ever had to do in my whole life . . . I have lost the treasure of my life." He eulogized her as "warm, compassionate, . . . valiant" and "the better half of my life," and said that "it will be difficult to go on without her, but go on I must." He then recited from "Ode to a Nightingale," as he had when John Lennon died: "My heart aches, and a drowsy numbness pains my sense, as though of hemlock I had drunk, or tasted of flora or some sweet Provençal song." His voice now quivered; tears streamed from his eyes. Between sobs, he concluded, "And so I say in memory of my glorious wife, my heart aches and a drowsy numbness pains my sense, and I thank whatever gods may be, Emmy, for your unconquerable soul."[20]

It was genuinely affecting, but it also presented a glimpse into his shattered state. For nearly half a century, Emmy had been the only isle of tranquility in his life, and if he felt not a little guilty that a woman of such rare intellect and taste had merged her life into that of the "arrogant" Jewish kid from Brooklyn, and ultimately merged her own identity into his, he was also merged into her. As both of them liked to say, with no care if anyone believed it, they could not have lived without each other. And now, it was he who had to.

As Mike Marley puts it, "That was when Howard went off the cliff."[21] He seemed to exist in a daze, with long periods of silence and a faraway look interrupted by sudden bursts of animated bonhomie. He was that way at the funeral, when hundreds of people came to the All Souls Unitarian Church on Lexington Avenue to hear eulogies given by John Cardinal O'Connor and ex–New York Giant great Andy Robustelli, and at Westhampton Cemetery, where Emmy's ashes were interred. A headstone was unveiled with her name on the left, an untouched part on the right for where his name would go when he joined her. Indeed, he seemed now to be preparing for that moment.

Against this background of loss, melancholy, and almost complete alienation, *What's Wrong with Sports* was published in June 1991, with a brief last chapter added as a paean to Emmy. Intended as an updated lecture about issues he believed were turning sports and broadcasting into a swamp, much of it was simply more tongue-lashing. One typical review, by Russ White of the *Orlando Sentinel*, commented that he "manages to be "pompous, often boring, wretchedly insensitive and naturally egotistical." Perhaps because he had left few industry foils standing in *I Never Played the Game*, his new ones were mainly athletes. Former Dodger first baseman Steve Garvey was "a phony." Pete Rose, recently banished from the game for betting on his team's games as manager of the Cincinnati Reds, was "a little lowlife." He approvingly quoted Pete Hamill's description of Dave Winfield, who seemed a victim when George Steinbrenner paid a gambler to dig up dirt on his star left fielder during a money dispute, as "a sleaze." But few of his opinions seemed to matter much in the grand scale of sports.[22]

In the book, Cosell wrote, with vehemence, "I find it disturbing when

I hear or read that some poor, misguided soul has accused me of being a bitter old man, a venomous old man, a sad caricature of myself. What bull!" He added, "I am an elder statesman, and will continue to be one, but don't expect me to be quiet or dishonest."[23] Yet he was too frail now to go on a tour pitching a book, or even to continue his radio shows, which he gave up early in 1992. By then, he'd had surgery to remove a cancerous tumor in his chest. He also had several minor strokes and was diagnosed with heart and kidney disease and Parkinson's, the last the same condition that had cost Muhammad Ali his motor reflexes and ability to speak coherently.

For both of those once glorious entertainers, it was the cruelest irony there could be, but one Cosell had foreseen for his old confrere before the first Spinks fight. Now, his fears proven out, he could hardly bear to see him. In 1990, as they waited backstage at Radio City Music Hall before participating in a *Night of 100 Stars* show, Cosell watched silently as Ali's friend photographer Howard Bingham fed him as he would a child. "At least some of the time," Cosell would say, "the great man's condition is pitiful."[24]

Their unique friendship was truly enduring, and Ali was about the only person in the world who could rouse him from his ennui and get him out of the apartment. When ABC ran a special marking Ali's fiftieth birthday, Cosell did what he would not for his own proposed TV tribute; he went to L.A. to tape the show, which would run on March 1, 1992. There, he was among an endless stream of celebrities offering personal tributes from the stage to Ali, who sat in a front-row seat, smiling and quaking.

But so too was Cosell near debilitation now. Prefacing his appearance, a compilation of old film clips ran of them over the years exchanging their familiar lines, both again so much younger and more imposing. Now, as they both walked unsteadily onto the stage, for Cosell to deliver a few trembling, heartfelt sentences, they seemed something like Sunshine Boys, stooped, one taking his last bows, invoking only nostalgia and pity. Teary from the first word, Cosell eschewed Keats this time for a simple, uncluttered panegyric.

"It's hard to believe," he began, "all the years, everything that's passed between us. It's so hard to believe and so memorable, and now it's time to say to you, Muhammad, God bless you, and happy birthday to you. Fifty years old! I never thought *that* could happen, not to you. But it has, and you are something. You are exactly who you said you are. You never wavered. You are free to be who you want to be. I love you. Happy birthday." He was openly crying when he finished, as were many in the hall. When the camera cut to Ali, tears were streaming down his face, almost assuredly not for himself but for the old partner and foil, for whom time was running out.[25]

The last months were especially painful for those with the longest memories of him. "When he lost Emmy," says Jerry Izenberg, "I could tell he was gone. He was out of his skull."[26]

Frank Gifford, generally one to let bygones be such, had called Cosell in the hospital when he had his cancer surgery, and found he still had spunk. Cosell graciously thanked him for mentioning Emmy's death on a *Monday Night Football* game, then told him, "I've got the Big C, but I'm going to beat it." Gifford recalled that he told him he and his wife, Kathie Lee Gifford, were praying for him. "Giffer, that's so kind of you," Cosell said.

"Howard," Gifford replied, his timing perfect, "I didn't say which way we're praying."

Two years later, Gifford saw him when Cosell walked in, uninvited, to a sports banquet at the Waldorf-Astoria Hotel, looking "terribly shrunken and frail. I had read that he was going in for more cancer surgery in a few days. God, I felt sorry for him." That night, Gifford said, "only a handful of people bothered to shake his hand. After a while, he turned and walked toward the doors . . . a shrunken-up old man walking down an empty hallway." That was the last time he saw him, and the vitriol of the past dissolved in pity. "I feel nothing but compassion for him," Gifford wrote in his autobiography.[27]

Now another two years of almost unendurable pain had extracted every ounce of Cosell's spunk. He nearly literally was alone. This was partly by his choice, as if with his remaining sense of pride he wanted to avoid any pity parties by dismissing anyone who cared about him. Mike Marley called to offer his condolences after Emmy died. "I was in Atlantic City doing a fight, stuck in a blizzard," he says, "and I think the funeral was the next day so I wouldn't be able to attend. I told him how sorry I was, that Emmy was a great lady. And Howard paused and said, 'Let me get this straight. You won't be at the funeral.' I said, 'Howard, I can't possibly get there.' He said, 'That's good.' Click. That was the last time I ever spoke with Howard."[28]

A day after his seventy-fifth birthday in 1993, he allowed the *New York Times*'s Robert Lipsyte, whom he had employed so long ago on *Saturday Night*, to visit him. The result was a surreal portrait of living death. Lipsyte wrote of a man doped up on medications, dressed in a "fine blue suit and a rich Christmas tie," his toupee "broadcast ready," sitting in a chair in his living room, smoking cigarettes, waiting for the phone to ring like in the old days, so he could write off yet someone else, or turn down out of hand the rare request for an interview or radio or TV appearance. Cosell, anticipating his own demise, told the writer it would happen "sooner or later."

"C'mon, you're only 75," Lipsyte assured him. " People run marathons at 75. You'll be back on the air driving people nuts again."

"Frankly," Cosell said, "I don't give a damn."[29]

So concerned were his devoted daughters that they generally forbade him from leaving the apartment on his own. In Emmy's farewell letters to them, she implored them to take care of him, saying that he had never paid a bill, that he wouldn't even know how to do it, and would wind up on the street if they didn't do these mundane chores for him. To help care for, or guard, him they hired a nurse named Cecilia Bonner. When he did get out, for a doctor or dentist appointment, or lunch at the Friars, he would be genuinely overjoyed by people still recognizing him and shouting out his name.

Frank Deford was also given entry to the apartment near the end. "Hilary didn't want him in public, and when I went there I could see why. He was just so far gone. The television was on but he wasn't watching it, and he couldn't hold a conversation or focus on anything. It was very painful for me. I mean, that sort of thing is common for older people but you don't expect it from a Howard Cosell, or a Muhammad Ali. These are the brightest people in the world. You want to remember them that way, not how I remember Howard at the end."[30]

The final honors he lived to see came when he was inducted both into the American Sportscasters Hall of Fame and the Academy of Television Arts and Sciences Hall of Fame in 1994, and then presented with the Arthur Ashe Award for Courage at an ESPN awards show in February 1995. Cosell appeared at none of these rites; the Ashe Award was accepted in his stead by Bill Cosby. In the early spring of 1995, his condition worsened. He had lost so much weight that he was down to around 120 pounds and was being force-fed.

In mid-April, he fell in the apartment and broke his hip, and was taken to NYU's Hospital for Joint Diseases on Seventeenth Street for hip replacement surgery. He came out of anesthesia but was so weak and fragile, his immune system so depressed, that he drifted in and out of consciousness for days. His family began a deathbed vigil. One day he woke up with some of the old Cosell pep and watched a New York Rangers hockey game with his grandsons Justin and Colin.

But the only thing anyone could do for him was pray. When Robustelli came to see him and found him barely sentient, he asked Cosell if he wanted John Cardinal O'Connor, the archbishop of New York City, to come and pray for him at his bedside. Cosell, who knew the cardinal well because of all the eulogies he had done at St. Patrick's Cathedral, nodded yes. Within an hour, O'Connor was in the room, praying for the soul of the Jewish man from Brooklyn. It was not quite a deathbed conversion, but nonetheless underscored that not even at the end had Howard Cosell resolved his ambivalence about his own faith.

ON THE morning of April 23, 1995, exactly forty years after he won his first notice in the media as a man worthy of being the talk of the town with his "hornswoggling and pettifoggery," he suffered a heart embolism. Doctors were unable to resuscitate him and pronounced him dead, a month after he turned seventy-seven. For many, it came as a relief, given the grievous toll life had taken on him.

It was mandatory that the first reaction include Muhammad Ali, who released a statement reading: "Howard Cosell was a good man and he lived a good life. I have been interviewed by many people, but I enjoyed interviews with Howard the best. We always put on a good show. I hope to meet him one day in the hereafter. I can hear Howard now saying, 'Muhammad, you're not the man you used to be.' I pray that he is in God's hands. I will miss him."

The media he had tangled with from the beginning reported the news in a somewhat muted fashion, with little of the beatification it would bestow on Jim McKay when he died thirteen years later. Of the major newspapers, only the *Washington Post* put it on the front page, with an obituary written by Leonard Shapiro, one of Cosell's legion of print villains, for having stoked the "little monkey" story. The *New York Times* stuck their obit on page B20, *Time* in the "Milestones" column with other celebrity deaths. *Newsweek* ran a brief notice headlined "Mighty Mouth." Perhaps trained by Cosell himself, some could not let him rest in peace. The *Daily News*'s sports TV critic, Bob Raissman, wrote: "Howard Cosell died 10 years too late. And that's just telling it like it is." Roone Arledge, the man who created the monster, when called for a comment, responded without emotion that Cosell was an "original" and a "giant by telling the truth in an industry that was not used to hearing it and considered it revolutionary."[31]

The entertainment crowd was far more kind. If one could find it in the tiny print of the *Times* obituaries the day after he died, a notice read:

> *The Officers, Governors and Members of The New York Friars Club mourn the loss of their esteemed and dedicated member, who served as an Honorary Member. Friar Howard Cosell. . . . He well be sorely missed.*

> FRANK SINATRA, Abbot
> FREDDIE ROMAN, Deacon

There were also notices from the Hebrew University of Jerusalem, of which Cosell was a trustee and where he held an honorary fellowship, and the Jewish Sports Council, of whose advisory board he was a member. Yet by his own wishes, stipulated in his will, the funeral was held, a week later, not at a synagogue but at the United Methodist Church of St. Paul and St.

Andrew on West Eighty-sixth Street. The mourners included the requisite
A-listers—Muhammad Ali, Joe Frazier, Floyd Patterson, Sinatra, Dan
Rather, Tom Brokaw, and Peter Jennings. Roone Arledge was there. Mayor
Rudy Giuliani and his predecessors Ed Koch and David Dinkins also
attended. So did Al Davis, George Steinbrenner, and Rachel Robinson.
Frank Deford was there, he jokes now, as "the one from the media." Many
of them took turns giving brief eulogies, Davis telling how Cosell had come
to his wife Carol's own hospital bedside when *she* had a near-fatal heart
attack some years before, stood over her as she lay in a coma and gave her
a pep talk, then barked at her doctors, "Get this girl well!" Davis called her
recovery a miracle—"and don't think Howard didn't take credit."

His ashes were interred next to Emmy's and his name etched beside
hers on the headstone at Westhampton Cemetery, the line from "Ode to a
Nightingale" he had used in times of tragedy for others—"My heart aches,
and a drowsy numbness pains my sense"—forever memorializing him. A
year after he went to his grave, he was finally awarded a posthumous
Emmy for lifetime achievement. It was an egregious and shameful omission that only in death was he deemed worthy of the honor. Still, the tributes on and after the day he died were restrained; no one would have dared
make the case that Cosell was beloved. After all, he wasn't Jim McKay.

As the years kept on creating a wider distance between Cosell and
American culture, he was never completely lost in the nation's rearview
mirror. Here and there, the name would be invoked, as a parable perhaps, but also as a tale of paradise lost. On December 26, 2005, a decade
after his death, when the final of 555 *Monday Night Football* telecasts to
be carried by ABC was played, knowing fans at the New England
Patriots–New York Jets game at Giants Stadium wore Cosell face masks,
proof for *New York Times* media columnist Richard Sandomir that "for
fans of a certain age, Monday night has never been the same since the
days of Gifford, Cosell and Meredith." For them, he noted, "the Cosell-
Meredith pairing seems frozen in showbiz amber."[32]

The dissenting view of Terry O'Neil that Cosell's contribution to the
series amounted to a "legacy of scorn" would seem to disregard that
*Monday Night Football* is today the second-longest-running series in history after *60 Minutes*. No longer does it own those gaudy 20 ratings and

40 shares. In the smaller universe of cable TV, however, it still thrives, garnering seven of the top ten biggest audiences in cable history. That it lives so powerfully is, of course, a quantifiable Cosell legacy.

The other sport he had renounced, with far more bitterness, tried to do him a make-good, inducting him in June 2010 into the International Boxing Hall of Fame. Cosell's grandson Colin accepted the honor, saying, "The boxing world was very good to us. With his trademark modesty, I'm sure Howard would say he was very good to the world of boxing as well—tongue in cheek, of course." Mike Marley got a good laugh out of that; in his column for the *Examiner.com* Web site, he wrote: "Cosell's induction into the Boxing Hall, deserved based on the excitement and drama he brought to the sport for so many years, reminds me of the Groucho Marx crack about 'not wanting to join any club that would have me as a member.' His grandson may not know but I do. Cosell would have refused to participate in his own IBHOF induction."[33]

In the end, Cosell was right in foreseeing that his style would not survive him, and for all his caviling about the lack of journalism in sports journalism, he may have wanted to take an era of journalism with him to his grave. The pity was that he didn't live to see many of the battles he fought becoming, in the end, victories, or the consequences of those battles—which can be extrapolated almost beyond imagination. In this telltale way, Maury Allen makes an outlandish but not totally inapt comment: "I think in a way, we have a black president because Howard Cosell supported Muhammad Ali. He was a very big part of American culture, a cultural link from Jackie Robinson to Ali to Barack Obama."[34]

Not everyone will agree that Cosell had that level of imperium. But whoever he was, however long was his reach, few before him or after him have ever, given the power of television, brought more incitement to the eye and the ear. His coda, more than anything else, is his singularity—a long-lost quality in the postmodern culture that has wiped men like him off the slate. Of him, we can fairly say that a hugely gifted and highly imperfect man arrived just when he was most needed and made himself rigidly, belligerently, narcissistically, unforgettably, and eternally Howard Cosell.

# ACKNOWLEDGMENTS

Many people helped move the ball down the field during the making of this book, some moving it in yards, others in inches. All share in its actualization. The prime movers were those who personally witnessed and were privy to the epic, Homeric odyssey of Howard Cosell, and thus offered not only intimate and priceless details and anecdotage of his life but also a broad perspective of the man and his legacy. For providing that, my deep and profound acknowledgment is extended in particular to Don Ohlmeyer, Jerry Izenberg, Frank Deford, Angelo Dundee, Ferdie Pacheco, Dennis Lewin, Lou Volpicelli, Monte Irvin, Ralph Branca, Larry Merchant, Maury Allen, Phil Pepe, Jim Lampley, Ray Robinson, Mike Marley, Carl Shimkin, Stuart Hample, and Melissa Tomjanovich, Woody Allen's assistant.

Because reclaiming an important life from the scrap heap of history requires aid, assistance, and guidance, I am grateful to the gang in the wondrous Microforms Room of the New York Public Library's Stephen A. Schwarzman Building, Nancy Cricco at the NYU Archives Department, the staff at the Paley Center for Media, and Phil Gries of Archival Television Audio, Inc.

Because believing in a project means everything to an author, I would like to thank Bob Weil, executive editor at Norton, who saw the pressing need for this book before Cosell's legacy grew any colder and tirelessly ushered it into print with a fine eye for the art of good writing and good journalism, more than a little insistent that it would be nothing less than both. Thanks as well to Bob's right hand, Phil Marino, for keeping on top of all the little details, and to India Cooper for skillful and meticulous copyediting. Finally, for their indefatigable efforts to find this book a proper home, a well-deserved shout-out goes to my agent, Michael Dorr, president of LitPub Ink., and his colleague Sean Lavin.

# NOTES

**INTRODUCTION: A GIFTED ONE**

1. Michael J. Arlen, "Neutrality at the Empty Center," *The New Yorker*, October 21, 1975.

2. *The Odd Couple*, "Your Mother Wears Army Boots" episode, January 16, 1975.

3. Jerry Kirshenbaum, "Scorecard: Rating the National Pastime," *Sports Illustrated*, November 2, 1981, p. 25.

4. Myron Cope, "Would You Let This Man Interview You?" *Sports Illustrated*, March 13, 1967, p. 75.

5. "Sports Is Life," *Newsweek*, June 3, 1968, p. 98.

6. Howard Cosell, *Cosell* (Chicago: Playboy Press, 1973), p. 117.

7. "When TV Makes Full Use of Howard Cosell," *Mad*, April 1972, p. 53.

8. Martin Kane, "Scorecard: The Hanging Judge," *Sports Illustrated*, September 11, 1972, p. 13.

9. Claire Safran, "She Loves the Man Everyone Loves to Hate," *Today's Health*, February 1975, p. 49.

10. Lawrence Linderman, "*Playboy* Interview: A Candid Conversation with the Fustian Oracle of Sport," *Playboy*, May 1972.

11. Frank Deford, "I've Won. I've Beat Them," *Sports Illustrated*, August 8, 1983, p. 73.

12. Ibid., p. 79.

13. "Monday Night Madness," *Inside Sports*, October 31, 1980, p. 27.

14. "They Said It," *Sports Illustrated*, February 8, 1984, p. 8.

15. Cosell, *Cosell*, p. 215.

16. David Halberstam, "The Mouth That Roared," *Playboy*, December 1982, pp. 130–31.

17. David Shields, "The Wound and the Bow," *Believer*, December 2003/January 2004, http://www.believermag.com/issues/200312/?read=article_shields; reviewer, Ralph Novak, *People*, December 9, 1985; Howard Cosell, *I Never Played the Game* (New York: William Morrow, 1985), p. 147.

CHAPTER 1: "INSECURITIES IN YOU THAT LIVE FOREVER"

1. Rex Lardner, "Voorloper," *The New Yorker*, June 11, 1955, p. 26.

2. Ibid., p. 27.

3. Ray Robinson interview.

4. Howard Cosell, *Cosell* (Chicago: Playboy Press, 1973), p. 177; Hilary in *Howard Cosell: Telling It Like It Is*, HBO documentary, November 1, 1999; Hilton in Jane Howard, "Howard Cosell: Tower of Babble," *Cosmopolitan*, August 1979, p. 216.

5. 1920 U.S. Census records.

6. Howard Cosell, *Like It Is* (Chicago: Playboy Press, 1974), p. 272.

7. Ibid.

8. Addresses as given on 1920, 1924, 1928 U.S. Census records and in Cosell, *Like It Is*, pp. 263–74.

9. Cosell, *Like It Is*, pp. 271, 294.

10. Howard, "Howard Cosell: Tower of Babble," p. 216.

11. Cosell, *Like It Is*, p. 274.

12. Ibid., pp. 274–75.

13. Frank Deford interview.

14. Cosell, *Cosell*, p. 122.

15. Cosell, *Like It Is*, pp. 269, 285; Dave Kindred, *Sound and Fury* (New York: Free Press, 2006), p. 18.

16. Joe Marshall, "Howard Cosell Is Just Another Pretty Face," *Esquire*, October 1972, p. 215.

17. Ibid.

18. Howard, "Howard Cosell: Tower of Babble," p. 246.

19. Cosell, *Cosell*, p. 119.

20. Howard, "Howard Cosell: Tower of Babble," p. 216.

21. Cosell, *Cosell*, p. 118; Howard, "Howard Cosell: Tower of Babble," p. 246.

22. Nick Thimmesch, "Howard the Humble," *Saturday Evening Post*, August/September 1974, p. 134; Howard, "Howard Cosell: Tower of Babble," p. 217.

23. Cosell, *Cosell*, p. 119.

24. Cosell, *Like It Is*, p. 273.

25. Claire Safran, "She Loves the Man Everyone Loves to Hate," *Today's Health*, February 1975, p. 49.

26. Kindred, *Sound and Fury*, p. 16.

27. Cosell, *Cosell*, p. 118; Howard, "Howard Cosell: Tower of Babble," p. 217.

28. Cosell, *Cosell*, p. 126.

29. Jerry Izenberg interview.

## CHAPTER 2: AN OBVIOUS MAVERICK

1. Jane Howard, "Howard Cosell: Tower of Babble," *Cosmopolitan*, August 1979, p. 216.

2. Ibid.

3. *NYU Law Review*, 1939–40.

4. Howard, "Howard Cosell: Tower of Babble," p. 216.

5. Howard Cosell, *Cosell* (Chicago: Playboy Press, 1973), p. 120.

6. Howard, "Howard Cosell: Tower of Babble," p. 217.

7. Ibid.

8. Frank Deford interview.

9. Frank Deford, "I've Won. I've Beat Them," *Sports Illustrated*, August 8, 1983, p. 77.

10. Cosell, *Cosell*, pp. 122, 121.

11. Jerry Izenberg interview.

12. *Howard Cosell: Telling It Like It Is*, HBO documentary, November 1, 1999.

13. Cosell, *Cosell*, pp. 130–31.

14. Ibid., p. 123.

15. Ibid.

16. *Howard Cosell: Telling It Like It Is*.

17. Howard, "Howard Cosell: Tower of Babble," p. 217.

18. Deford, "I've Won," p. 77.

19. Cosell, *Cosell*, p. 121.

20. Ibid.

21. Deford, "I've Won," p. 78.

22. Ibid.

23. Cosell, *Cosell*, p. 122.

24. Joe Marshall, "Howard Cosell Is Just Another Pretty Face," *Esquire*, October 1972, p. 215.


CHAPTER 3: BEING THERE

1. Ray Robinson interview.

2. Frank Deford, "I've Won. I've Beaten Them," *Sports Illustrated*, August 8, 1983, p. 74.

3. Charles V. Bagli, "A New Light on a Fight to Integrate Stuyvesant Town," *New York Times*, November 22, 2010.

4. "Medical Journal Raps Kid Ball as Delinquency Cure," *Sporting News*, August 17, 1955; "Little League Record Needs No Apology," *Sporting News*, September 5, 1956.

5. *Howard Cosell: Telling It Like It Is*, HBO documentary, November 1, 1999.

6. Ray Robinson interview; Dave Kindred, *Sound and Fury* (New York: Free Press, 2006), p. 24.

7. Monte Irvin interview.

8. "This Month in Walter O'Malley History: April," http://walteromalley.com/thisday_04_15.php.

9. Pauley obituary, *New York Times*, May 13, 2009.

10. Howard Cosell, *Cosell* (Chicago: Playboy Press, 1973), p. 125.

11. Harry Phillips, "Memo from the Publisher," *Sports Illustrated*, July 9, 1956, p. 4.

12. Cosell, *Cosell*, p. 125.

13. *The Tomorrow Show*, June 3, 1977.

14. Details from Isidore Cohen's death certificate.

15. Cosell, *Cosell*, p. 124.

16. Deford, "I've Won," p. 77.

17. Ray Robinson interview.

18. Myron Cope, "Would You Let This Man Interview You?" *Sports Illustrated*, March 13, 1967, p. 106.

19. Ibid.

20. Cosell, *Cosell*, p. 127.

21. Jerry Izenberg interview.

22. Cosell, *Cosell*, p. 86.

23. Ibid., p. 131.

24. Jerry Izenberg interview.

25. Frank Gifford, *The Whole Ten Yards* (New York: Random House, 1993), p. 12.

26. Ibid.

27. Cope, "Would You Let This Man Interview You?" p. 106.


CHAPTER 4: MOMENTARY MOMENTS OF CHAGRIN

1. Jerry Izenberg interview.

2. Howard Cosell, *Cosell* (Chicago: Playboy Press, 1973), p. 128.

3. Donald E. Kimberlin, "Telling It Like It Was," *Oldradio.com*, April 27, 1995, http://www.oldradio.com/archives/people/dk-cos.htm.

4. Dave Kindred, *Sound and Fury* (New York: Free Press, 2006), p. 25.

5. Newsreel of Robinson-Basilio fight.

6. "They Said It," *Sports Illustrated*, May 11, 1959, p. 30; Cosell, *Cosell*, pp. 167, 153, 154.

7. Ibid., p. 155.

8. Ibid., p. 172.

9. Ibid., p. 171.

10. Kindred, *Sound and Fury*, p. 28; Martin Kane, "Boxing Greets Its New Dawn," *Sports Illustrated*, July 6, 1959, p. 14.

11. Newsreel of Patterson-Johansson fight; Cosell, *Cosell*, p. 160.

12. Gilbert Rogin, "The Drama in Miami," *Sports Illustrated*, March 20, 1961, p. 18.

13. Ibid.

14. Cosell, *Cosell*, p. 134.

15. Ron Powers, *Supertube* (New York: Coward-McCann, 1984), p. 149.

16. Ibid., p. 154.

17. Wikipedia, "Roone Arledge," http://en.wikipedia.org/wiki/Roone_Arledge.

18. Cosell, *Cosell*, p. 136.

19. Cosell, *Cosell*, pp. 136, 133.

20. Jerry Izenberg interview.

21. Scherick obituary, Reuters, December 3, 2002.

22. Powers, *Supertube*, p. 200; Cosell, *Cosell*, p. 135.

23. Cosell, *Cosell*, p. 135.

24. Ibid., p. 136.

25. Ray Robinson interview.

26. Jerry Izenberg interview.

27. *The Tomorrow Show*, June 3, 1977.

28. Cosell, *Cosell*, p. 126.

29. Larry Merchant interview.

30. Phil Pepe interview.

31. Young obituary, *New York Times*, September 2, 1987.

CHAPTER 5: "LET GO OF THE MIKE, CASSIUS"

1. Ralph Branca interview.

2. Joe Marshall, "Howard Cosell Is Just Another Pretty Face," *Esquire*, October 1972, p. 216.

3. Ralph Branca interview.

4. Lawrence Linderman, "*Playboy* Interview: A Candid Conversation with the Fustian Oracle of Sport," *Playboy*, May 1972.

5. Maury Allen interview.

6. Ibid.

7. Myron Cope, "Would You Let This Man Interview You?" *Sports Illustrated*, March 13, 1967, p. 82.

8. Ibid.

9. Howard Cosell, *Cosell* (Chicago: Playboy Press, 1973), p. 162.

10. Ibid.

11. Ibid., p. 163.

12. Ibid., pp. 172–73.

13. Dave Anderson, "The *Sport* Interview," *Sport*, January 1979, p. 52.

14. Ferdie Pacheco interview.

15. Angelo Dundee interview.

16. Cosell, *Cosell*, pp. 167, 179.

17. Linderman, "*Playboy* Interview."

18. Angelo Dundee interview.

19. Ibid.

20. Ibid.

21. Linderman, "*Playboy* Interview."

22. Ibid.

23. Cosell, *Cosell*, pp. 173–74.

24. Prefight interviews and fight narration taken from broadcast tape of Clay-Liston fight, February 25, 1964.

25. Angelo Dundee interview.

CHAPTER 6: "BEDLAM, CHAOS, CONFUSION"

1. *New York Times,* February 27, 1964.

2. Malcolm X, *The Autobiography of Malcolm X* (New York: Grove Press, 1965), p. 124.

3. Thomas Hauser, *Muhammad Ali: His Life and Times* (New York: Harper-Collins, 1998), pp. 156–57.

4. Ibid., p. 65.

5. Howard Cosell, *Cosell* (Chicago: Playboy Press, 1973), p. 177, 176.

6. Ibid., p. 176.

7. Ibid., p. 178.

8. Myron Cope, "Would You Let This Man Interview You?" *Sports Illustrated,* March 13, 1967, p. 73.

9. Cosell, *Cosell,* 178, 177.

10. "Scorecard: The Black Muslim Hope," *Sports Illustrated,* March 16, 1964, p. 8; *New York Daily News,* February 27, 1964.

11. Cosell, *Cosell,* p. 175.

12. Broadcast tape of Clay-Liston fight, February 25, 1964.

13. Jerry Izenberg interview.

14. Roone Arledge, *Roone* (New York: HarperCollins, 2003), p. 25.

15. *New York Daily News,* February 15, 1964.

16. Cosell, *Cosell,* p. 178.

17. Hauser, *Muhammad Ali,* p. 158.

18. Ibid., p. 157.

19. Jim Spence, *Up Close and Personal* (New York: Atheneum, 1988), p. 101.

20. Larry Merchant interview.

21. Jim Lampley interview.

22. Cosell, *Cosell,* p. 179.

23. Jerry Izenberg interview.

24. Frank Deford interview.

25. Hauser, *Muhammad Ali,* p. 157.

26. Newsreel of Ali-Liston fight.

27. *Wide World of Sports,* May 30, 1965; Cosell, *Cosell,* pp. 181, 182.

28. Cosell, *Cosell,* p. 181.

29. Arledge, *Roone,* p. 92.

30. Ibid., p. 93.

31. Ibid.

**CHAPTER 7: AN ELECTRONIC FIRST**

1. Howard Cosell, *Cosell* (Chicago: Playboy Press, 1973), pp. 138–39.

2. Ibid., pp. 102, 105, 103.

3. Ibid., p. 95.

4. Ibid, p. 106.

5. *Mount Vernon Daily Argus*, August 8, 1964.

6. Jerry Izenberg interview.

7. Thomas Hauser, *Muhammad Ali: His Life and Times* (New York: Harper-Collins, 1998), pp. 139, 133, 204.

8. *Wide World of Sports*, November 20, 1966.

9. *New York Times*, November 23, 1965.

10. Cosell, *Cosell*, p. 182.

11. *Wide World of Sports*, November 27, 1965.

12. Floyd Patterson, "In Defense of Cassius Clay," *Esquire*, August 1966; Cosell, *Cosell*, p. 164.

13. For an explanation of how the famous "Vietcong" quote came about, see Hauser, *Muhammad Ali*, p. 145.

14. Smith in *New York Herald Tribune*, February 23, 1966; Cannon in *New York Journal-American*, February 23, 1966.

15. Cosell, *Cosell*, p. 191; Brian London—British HW Champ 1958–59 thread, Boxing Record Archive, http://boxrec.com/forum/viewtopic.php?f=4&t=116834.

16. Cosell, *Cosell*, p. 196.

17. Ibid., p. 188.

18. Ibid., pp. 184–86.

19. Ibid., pp. 187, 191.

20. Dan Jenkins, "The Sweet Life of Swinging Joe," *Sports Illustrated*, October 17, 1966, p. 44.

21. Phil Pepe interview.

22. Myron Cope, "Would You Let This Man Interview You?" *Sports Illustrated*, March 13, 1967, p. 72.

23. Audiotape, *Speaking of Sports*, WABC, January 15, 1967.

24. Ibid., January 16, 1967.

25. Cope, "Would You Let This Man Interview You?" p. 95.

26. *Sports Illustrated*, February 13, 1967; *New York World Journal & Telegram*, February 7–8, 1967.

27. Cosell, *Cosell*, p. 197.

28. *Wide World of Sports*, February 11, 1967; Cosell, *Cosell*, p. 198.

29. *Wide World of Sports*, March 5, 1967.

30. Morton Sharnik, "Zora Folley Ranks Muhammad Ali as No. 1," *Sports Illustrated*, April 10, 1967, p, 32.

31. Hauser, *Muhammad Ali*, p. 167.

32. Jerry Izenberg interview.

33. Ibid.

34. *Cosell*, pp. 200–201.

CHAPTER 8: A MORAL IMPERATIVE

1. Howard Cosell, *Cosell* (Chicago: Playboy Press, 1973), p. 201.

2. Ibid., p. 203.

3. *New York Post*, June 22, 1967.

4. *The Tomorrow Show*, June 3, 1977.

5. Roone Arledge, *Roone* (New York: HarperCollins, 2003), p. 94.

6. Don Ohlmeyer interview.

7. Cosell, *Cosell*, p. 142.

8. Lawrence Linderman, "*Playboy* Interview: A Candid Conversation with the Fustian Oracle of Sports," *Playboy*, May 1972.

9. Jerry Izenberg interview.

10. Ron Powers, *Supertube* (New York: Coward-McCann, 1984), p. 203.

11. Arledge, *Roone*, p. 94.

12. Ibid., p. 95.

13. Cosell, *Cosell*, pp. 350–51.

14. Don Ohlmeyer interview.

15. Cosell, *Cosell*, p. 56.

16. Arledge, *Roone*, p. 96.

17. Don Ohlmeyer interview.

18. Cosell, *Cosell*, p. 58; Dave Kindred, *Sound and Fury* (New York: Free Press, 2006), p. 145; Erica Mcrae, "Tommie Smith Recalls His 1968 Olympic Protest," September 19, 2008, http://www.blackcollegewire.org/index.php?option=com_ywp_blog&task=view&id=5593; Anne Trubek, "The Oberlin Experiment," *Smart Set* (Drexel University), December 14, 2007, http://www.thesmartset.com/article/article12140702.aspx.

19. Ibid., p. 62.

20. Ibid., pp. 62, 63.

21. Ibid., pp. 63, 64.

22. Wills and *Guinness Book* quoted in Allen Barra, review of *The Muhammad*

*Ali Reader*, ed. Gerald Early (Hopewell, N.J.: Ecco, 1998), *Denver Post*, July 12, 1998.

23. *The Late Late Show with Tom Snyder*, April 25, 1995.

24. "Sports Is Life," *Newsweek*, June 3, 1968, p. 101.

25. Terry Jastrow quoted in Larry Stewart, "Cosell Didn't Always Tell It Like It Was," *Los Angeles Times*, April 28, 1995.

26. Jim Spence, *Up Close and Personal* (New York: Atheneum, 1988), p. 6.

27. Nick Thimmesch, "Howard the Humble," *Saturday Evening Post*, August/September 1974, p. 134; Dave Anderson quote, ibid; Don Ohlmeyer interview.

## CHAPTER 9: A STYGIAN BURDEN

1. Jane Howard, "Howard Cosell: Tower of Babble," *Cosmopolitan*, August 1979, p. 246.

2. ABC telecast of Knicks-Lakers NBA championship series Game 7, May 4, 1970.

3. Roone Arledge, *Roone* (New York: HarperCollins, 2003), p. 95.

4. Howard Cosell, *Cosell* (Chicago: Playboy Press, 1973), p. 207.

5. *Wide World of Sports*, June 28, 1969.

6. Cosell, *Cosell*, p. 206.

7. ABC telecast of Frazier-Ellis fight, February 6, 1970.

8. ABC telecast of Foreman-Waldheim fight, June 23, 1969.

9. Angelo Dundee interview.

10. Mark Kram, "He Moves Like Silk, Hits Like a Ton," *Sports Illustrated*, October 26, 1970, p. 19.

11. Michael Arkush, *The Fight of the Century: Ali vs. Frazier* (Hoboken, N.J.: Wiley, 2007), p. 40.

12. Cosell, *Cosell*, pp. 208, 210.

13. Ibid., p. 210.

14. ABC telecast of Ali-Bonavena fight, December 7, 1970.

15. Arledge, *Roone*, p. 102.

16. Ibid., p. 101.

17. Ibid., p. 108.

18. Don Ohlmeyer interview.

19. Arledge, *Roone*, p. 107.

20. Ibid., p. 104; Cosell, *Cosell*, p. 275.

21. Arledge, *Roone*, p. 109.

22. Cosell, *Cosell*, p. 274.

23. Ibid., p. 278; Arledge, *Roone*, p. 111.

24. Cosell, *Cosell*, pp. 278–79.

25. Don Ohlmeyer interview.

26. Frank Deford, "TV Talk," *Sports Illustrated*, October 5, 1970, p. 9.

27. Robert Creamer, "Scorecard: Mouth to Mouth," *Sports Illustrated*, September 7, 1970, p. 10.

28. Marc Gunther and Bill Carter, *Monday Night Mayhem: The Inside Story of ABC's Monday Night Football* (New York: Beech Tree, 1998), p. 62.

29. *New York Daily News*, September 22, 1970; ABC telecast of Jets-Browns game, September 21, 1970.

30. *New York Daily News*, September 22, 1970.

31. Dennis Lewin interview.

32. Cosell, *Cosell*, p. 286.

33. Arledge, *Roone*, p. 113.

34. Cosell, *Cosell*, p. 294.

35. Gunther and Carter, *Monday Night Mayhem*, p. 70.

36. Arledge, *Roone*, p. 113.

37. Gunther and Carter, *Monday Night Mayhem*, p. 70.

CHAPTER 10: "THAT SON OF A BITCH IS DRUNK!"

1. Marc Gunther and Bill Carter, *Monday Night Mayhem: The Inside Story of ABC's Monday Night Football* (New York: Beech Tree, 1998), p. 72.

2. Howard Cosell, *Cosell* (Chicago: Playboy Press, 1973), p. 290.

3. ABC telecast of Chiefs-Colts game, September 28, 1970; Cosell, *Cosell*, p. 292.

4. Gunther and Carter, *Monday Night Mayhem*, p. 74; Roone Arledge, *Roone* (New York: HarperCollins, 2003), p. 114; Cosell, *Cosell*, p. 294.

5. Cosell, *Cosell*, p. 299.

6. Ibid.

7. Ibid., p. 300.

8. Arledge, *Roone*, p. 114.

9. Lou Volpicelli interview.

10. Jim Spence, *Up Close and Personal* (New York: Atheneum 1988), p. 10; Cosell, *Cosell*, p. 287.

11. ABC telecast of Redskins-Raiders game, October 19, 1970.

12. Cosell, *Cosell*, p. 298.

13. Ibid., 301–2; Gunther and Carter, *Monday Night Mayhem*, pp. 77–78.

14. Lou Volpicelli interview.

15. John Leonard, "Cosell: Milder but Does He Satisfy?" *Life*, November 13, 1970, p. 25.

16. ABC telecast of Cowboys-Cardinals game, November 16, 1970.

17. Cosell, *Cosell*, p. 304; Gunther and Carter, *Monday Night Mayhem*, p. 80.

18. Cosell, *Cosell*, p. 305; Dennis Lewin interview; Gunther and Carter, *Monday Night Mayhem*, p. 80.

19. Lou Volpicelli interview.

20. Gunther and Carter, *Monday Night Mayhem*, pp. 81–82, Cosell, *Cosell*, p. 306.

21. ABC telecast of Giants-Eagles game, November 23, 1970.

22. Spence, *Up Close and Personal*, p. 26.

23. Lou Volpicelli interview.

24. Arledge, *Roone*, p. 116; Cosell, *Cosell*, p. 306.

25. Cosell, *Cosell*, pp. 306–7.

26. Gifford in *Howard Cosell: Telling It Like It Is*, HBO documentary, November 1, 1999.

27. *New York Daily News*, November 27, 1970.

28. Frank Deford, "They Said It," *Sports Illustrated*, May 31, 1971, p. 17; Woody Allen e-mail, March 3, 2010.

29. Lawrence Linderman, "The *Playboy* Interview: A Candid Conversation with the Fustian Oracle of Sport," *Playboy*, March 1972.

30. *Cosell*, pp. 339–40.

CHAPTER 11: LISTING TOWARD BABYLON

1. Michael Arkush, *The Fight of the Century: Ali vs. Frazier* (Hoboken, N.J.: Wiley, 2007), p. 123.

2. Howard Cosell, *Cosell* (Chicago: Playboy Press, 1973), p. 214; George Kimball, "The Last Great Heavyweight Rivalry," lecture given at University of Kansas symposium, March 2006, http://www.cyberboxingzone.com/cbzfo rum/showthread.php?10145-The-Last-Great-Heavyweight-Rivalry-Part-1 -Ali-Frazier.

3. Kimball, "Last Great Heavyweight Rivalry."

4. Arkush, *Fight of the Century*, p. 123.

5. Cosell, *Cosell*, pp. 213, 215.

6. Ibid., 216.

7. William Nack, "The Fight's Over, Joe," *Sports Illustrated*, September 30, 1996, p. 58.

8. "The Battered Face of a Winner," *Sports Illustrated*, March 15, 1971, p. 16.

9. Ferdie Pacheco interview.

10. Cosell, *Cosell*, 217; "Battered Face of a Winner."

11. Thomas Hauser, *Muhammad Ali: His Life and Times* (New York: Harper-Collins, 1998), pp. 231, 233.

12. Cosell, *Cosell*, p. 218; Ferdie Pacheco interview; *Wide World of Sports*, March 14, 1971.

13. Cosell, *Cosell*, p. 218.

14. Ibid., p. 219.

15. Ibid.

16. Ibid., p. 214.

17. Robert Creamer, "Scorecard: Goodby, Howard," *Sports Illustrated*, December 7, 1970, p. 9.

18. Cosell, *Cosell*, p. 312.

19. Marc Gunther and Bill Carter, *Monday Night Mayhem: The Inside Story of ABC's Monday Night Football* (Beech Tree, 1998), p. 92.

20. Howard Cosell, *Like It Is* (Chicago: Playboy Press, 1974), pp. 225–26.

21. Robert Daley, "The Man They Love to Hate," *New York Times Magazine*, September 1, 1974, p. 10.

22. Roone Arledge, *Roone* (New York: HarperCollins, 2003), p. 117.

23. Gunther and Carter, *Monday Night Mayhem*. p. 100.

24. Cosell, *Cosell*, p. 316.

25. Ibid.; Arledge, *Roone*, p. 119.

26. ABC broadcast of Giants-Cowboys game, October 11, 1971.

## CHAPTER 12: MUNICH

1. Numerous sources, including James Churchill Jr.'s 1983 book *The Olympic Story*, identify Brundage's pro-Nazi leanings, which were overt. As U.S. Olympic Committee president, Brundage acquiesced to the German government's demands before the Berlin Games by removing the two Jews on the U.S. track team. He also praised Hitler's Third Reich at a Madison Square Garden rally in the mid-1930s, and in 1941 was expelled from the America First Committee because of his pro-German stance. After the 1936 Games, Brundage's construction company was awarded a building contract to build the German Embassy in Washington, D.C., with a letter from Nazi officials acknowledging Brundage's work on behalf of the Third Reich.

2. Roone Arledge, *Roone* (New York: HarperCollins, 2003), p. 124.

3. Howard Cosell, *Cosell* (Chicago: Playboy Press, 1973), p. 2.

4. Ibid., pp. 20–22.

5. Martin Kane, "Scorecard: The Hanging Judge," *Sports Illustrated*, September 11, 1972, p. 13.

6. Cosell, *Cosell*, p. 25.

7. Don Ohlmeyer interview.

8. Cosell, *Cosell*, p. 34.

9. Ibid., pp. 2–3.

10. Arledge, *Roone*, p. 128.

11. Ibid.

12. Dennis Lewin interview.

13. Cosell, *Cosell*, pp. 3–4.

14. McKay's on-air remarks and other details regarding the broadcast are from a video tape of the ABC coverage of the Olympic hostage crisis, September 5–6, 1972.

15. Arledge, *Roone*, p. 131.

16. Cosell, *Cosell*, p. 10.

17. Arledge, *Roone*, p. 136.

18. Ibid., p. 137.

19. Dennis Lewin interview; Don Ohlmeyer interview.

20. Lou Volpicelli interview.

21. Jerry Izenberg interview.

22. Jim McKay, *The Real McKay: My Wide World of Sports* (New York: Dutton, 1998), p. 10.

23. Quoted in Cosell, *Cosell*, p. 12.

24. Ibid.

25. Ibid., pp. 13, ix.

26. Ibid., p. 13.

27. Don Ohlmeyer interview.

28. Cosell, *Cosell*, pp. 1, 4, 13.

29. Jane Howard, "Howard Cosell: Tower of Babble," *Cosmopolitan*, August 1979, p. 246.

30. Cosell, *Cosell*, p. 10.

31. Dennis Lewin interview.

32. Maury Allen interview.

33. Howard Cosell, *Like It Is* (Chicago: Playboy Press, 1974), pp. 119–20.

34. Dennis Lewin interview.

35. Jerry Izenberg interview.

36. "Shall We Rule These TV Egos Guilty of Unnecessary Roughness?" *Today's Health,* December 1971, p. 63.

37. Dennis Lewin interview.

38. Don Ohlmeyer interview.

39. Frank Gifford, *The Whole Ten Yards* (New York: Random House, 1993), pp. 27–28.

40. Don Ohlmeyer interview.


CHAPTER 13: A BIG PROPERTY

1. Edwin [Bud] Shrake, "What Are They Doing with the Sacred Game of Pro Football?" *Sports Illustrated,* October 25, 1971, p. 99.

2. Jerry Izenberg interview.

3. ABC telecast of Raiders-Oilers game, October 9, 1972.

4. Marc Gunther and Bill Carter, *Monday Night Mayhem: The Inside Story of ABC's Monday Night Football* (New York: Beech Tree, 1998), p. 104.

5. Ibid., p. 105.

6. Lou Volpicelli interview.

7. Howard Cosell, *Cosell* (Chicago: Playboy Press, 1973), pp. 74, 84; Don Ohlmeyer interview.

8. Cosell, *Cosell,* p. 85.

9. Lou Volpicelli interview.

10. Frank Deford interview.

11. Howard Cosell, *I Never Played the Game* (New York: William Morrow, 1985), pp. 266–67; Cosell, *Like It Is* (Chicago: Playboy Press, 1974), p. 174.

12. Cosell, *I Never Played the Game,* p. 268.

13. Lou Volpicelli interview.

14. Harold Peterson, "People," *Sports Illustrated,* May 13, 1974, p. 69; Robert Daley, "The Man They Love to Hate," *New York Times Magazine,* September 1, 1974, p. 27.

15. Cosell, *Cosell,* back cover; Jonathan Yardley, "Booktalk: Howard Cosell and Jim McKay—Choose One—Offer Up the ABCs of TV Sport," *Sports Illustrated,* November 5, 1973, p. 14.

16. Tom Mackin, *Brief Encounters: From Einstein to Elvis* (Bloomington, Ind.: AuthorHouse, 2008), p. 321.

17. Daley, "The Man They Love to Hate," p. 27.

18. Lawrence Linderman, "*Playboy* Interview: A Candid Conversation with the Fustian Oracle of Sport," *Playboy,* May 1972.

19. Dennis Lewin interview.

20. Ira Berkow, *Red: A Biography of Red Smith* (New York: Times Books, 2007), p. 175.

21. Ibid., pp. 216–17.

22. Ibid., p. 217.

23. Ibid.

24. Robert Friedman, "Monday Night Madness," *Inside Sports*, October 31, 1980, p. 26.

25. Berkow, *Red*, pp. 218, 220; *60 Minutes* interview with Red Smith, March 15, 1982.

26. "Sport: This Was How-wud Co-sssell," Tom Callahan, *Time*, January 6, 1986.

27. Phil Pepe interview.

28. Cosell, *Cosell*, pp. 344–45.

29. David Halberstam, "The Mouth That Roared," *Playboy*, December 1982, p. 130.

30. Cosell and Herskowitz quoted in Jane Howard, "Howard Cosell: Tower of Babble," *Cosmopolitan*, August 1979, p. 246.

31. Chris Economaki, *Let 'Em All Go! The Story of Auto Racing by the Man Who Was There* (Indianapolis: Argabright, 2006), p. 191.

32. Lou Volpicelli interview.

CHAPTER 14: "DOWN GOES FRAY-ZHUH! DOWN GOES FRAY-ZHUH! DOWN GOES FRAY-ZHUH!"

1. Howard Cosell, *Cosell* (Chicago: Playboy Press, 1973), p. 220.

2. Ibid., p. 221.

3. Ibid., p. 167.

4. Ibid., p. 233.

5. Ibid., pp. 231–32.

6. ABC telecast of Foreman-Frazier fight, January 22, 1973.

7. Jerry Izenberg interview.

8. ABC telecast of Norton-Ali fight, March 31, 1973.

9. Thomas Hauser, *Muhammad Ali: His Life and Times* (New York: Harper-Collins, 1998), p. 253.

10. Ibid.

11. ABC *Wide World of Sports*, January 23, 1974; Hauser, *Muhammad Ali*, pp. 255–57.

12. ABC telecast of Ali-Frazier fight, January 28, 1974.

13. Cosell, *Cosell* (paperback, New York: Pocket Books, 1974), p. 255.

14. Jack Newfield, *The Life and Crimes of Don King: The Shame of Boxing in America* (New York: William Morrow, 1985), p. 82.

15. *Tyson*, documentary film written and directed by James Toback (Sony Pictures Classics, 2009).

16. Howard Cosell, *Like It Is* (Chicago: Playboy Press, 1974), p. 62.

17. Halberstam, "Mouth That Roared," p. 242.

18. Jerry Izenberg interview.

19. Cosell, *Like It Is*, p. 31.

20. Robert Daley, "The Man They Love to Hate," *New York Times Magazine*, September 1, 1974, p. 30.

21. Ibid.

22. Ibid.

23. Cosell, *Cosell*, p. 215.

24. Hauser, *Muhammad Ali*, pp. 265, 270.

25. ABC coverage of Ali-Foreman fight, October 30, 1974.

26. *Wide World of Sports*, May 16, 1975.

CHAPTER 15: "THINGS BEGAN TO TURN SOUR"

1. ABC telecast of Packers-49ers game, November 26, 1973.

2. *O. J. Simpson: Juice on the Loose*, documentary directed by George A. Romero (ABC, 1974).

3. Robert Daley, "The Man They Love to Hate," *New York Times Magazine*, September 1, 1974, p. 27.

4. *Howard Cosell: Telling It Like It Is*, HBO documentary, November 1, 1999.

5. Frank Gifford, *The Whole Ten Yards* (New York: Random House, 1993), p. 15.

6. Dennis Lewin interview.

7. Mike Fish, "Cosell Was a Primetime Target for Threats," CNNSI.com, January 10, 2002, http://sportsillustrated.cnn.com/football/news/2002/01/10/cosell_fbi_file.

8. Marc Gunther and Bill Carter, *Monday Night Mayhem: The Inside Story of ABC's Monday Night Football* (New York: Beech Tree, 1998), p. 146.

9. Don Ohlmeyer interview.

10. Fish, "Cosell Was a Primetime Target."

11. Gunther and Carter, *Monday Night Mayhem*, p. 147.

12. Ibid., p. 143.

13. Dennis Lewin interview.

14. ABC telecast of Raiders-Broncos game, October 22, 1973; Howard Cosell, *Like It Is* (Chicago: Playboy Press, 1974), p. 8.

15. Cosell, *Like It Is*, p. 8.

16. Ibid., p. 10.

17. Roone Arledge, *Roone* (New York: HarperCollins, 2003), p. 146.

18. Cosell, *Like It Is*, p. 13; Howard Cosell, *I Never Played the Game* (New York: William Morrow, 1985), p. 147.

19. Ibid., p. 149.

20. Gunther and Carter, *Monday Night Mayhem*, p. 152.

21. Jerry Izenberg interview; Larry Merchant interview.

22. Cosell, *Like It Is*, p. 25; Gunther and Carter, *Monday Night Mayhem*, p. 165.

23. Gunther and Carter, *Monday Night Mayhem*, p. 164.

24. Ibid., p. 167.

25. Anne Trubek, "The Oberlin Experiment," *Smart Set* (Drexel University), December 14, 2007, http://www.thesmartset.com/article/article12140702.aspx.

26. *Ms.*, "Why I Support the ERA," October 1975, pp. 78–79.

27. David Shields, "The Wound and the Bow," *Believer*, December 2003/January 2004, http://www.believermag.com/issues/200312/?read=article_shields.

28. Dennis Lewin interview.

29. Cosell, *I Never Played the Game*, p. 356.

30. Mark Goodman, "Hyping Howie," *People*, September 29, 1975, p. 20.

31. Cosell, *I Never Played the Game*, p. 361.

32. Ibid., p. 362.

33. Ibid., pp. 362–63.

34. John J. O'Connor, "Cosell, the Unpredictable, Opens New Series," *New York Times*, September 22, 1975.

35. *Wide World of Sports*, October 5, 1975.

36. Don Mischer interview, Archive of American Television, November 7, 2008, http://emmytvlegends.org/interviews/people/don-mischer.

37. Goodman, "Hyping Howie," p. 22; Cosell, *I Never Played the Game*, p. 355.

38. "*Saturday Night Live with Howard Cosell*," http://www.tvguide.com/tvshows/saturday-night-live/204224.

39. Arledge, *Roone*, p. 148; Cosell, *I Never Played the Game*, pp. 354–57.

40. Cosell, *I Never Played the Game*, p. 356.

41. Arledge, *Roone*, p. 149.

42. Ibid.

43. Ibid., p. 150.

44. Cosell, *I Never Played the Game*, p. 269.

45. William Leggett, "Show Biz vs. Know Biz," *Sports Illustrated*, November 1, 1976, p. 58.

46. Dennis Lewin interview.

47. ABC telecast of Royals-Yankees game, October 14, 1976.

48. Cosell, *I Never Played the Game*, p. 270.

CHAPTER 16: AN UNHOLY MESS

1. *New York Daily News*, December 24, 1975.

2. Howard Cosell, *I Never Played the Game* (New York: William Morrow, 1985), p. 367.

3. Jim Spence, *Up Close and Personal* (New York: Atheneum, 1988), p. 11.

4. Robert Lipsyte, *SportsWorld* (New York: Quadrangle, 1975), p. 242.

5. Thomas Hauser, *Muhammad Ali: His Life and Times* (New York: Harper-Collins, 1998), p. 341.

6. Roone Arledge, *Roone* (New York: HarperCollins, 2003), p. 170.

7. Cosell, *I Never Played the Game*, p. 184.

8. Robert H. Boyle, "Some Very Wrong Numbers," *Sports Illustrated*, May 2, 1977, p. 24.

9. ABC telecast of LeDoux-Boudreau fight, February 13, 1977; Arledge, *Roone*, pp. 171–72.

10. Tom Mackin, *Brief Encounters: From Einstein to Elvis* (Bloomington, Ind.: AuthorHouse, 2008), p. 320; Boyle, "Some Very Wrong Numbers," p. 24.

11. Cosell, *I Never Played the Game*, pp. 183–84; overheard on Spence, Terry O'Neil, *The Game Behind the Game* (New York: HarperCollins, 1989), p. 47.

12. John Byrd, "200 Crowd to See Cosell," *Washington Square News* (NYU), February 6, 1978; Daniel Aquilante, "Student Disrupts Cosell's Class," ibid., April 3, 1978; Aquilante, "Cosell Resigns from Class," ibid., April 10, 1978.

13. Mackin, *Brief Encounters*, p. 327.

14. Ibid., p. 321.

15. Spence, *Up Close and Personal*, pp. 14–15.

16. William Leggett, "TV/Radio: A Need to Learn the ABCs," *Sports Illustrated*, October 24, 1977, p. 52.

17. William Grimes, "A City Gripped by Crisis and Enraptured by the Yankees," *New York Times*, March 30, 2005.

18. Carl Shimkin, "Did Howard Cosell Really Say, 'The Bronx Is Burning'?" *MLBlogs Network*, August 18, 2007; email to the author, April 28, 2010.

19. Leggett, "TV/Radio: Need to Learn the ABCs."

20. ABC telecast of Royals-Yankees game, October 14, 1976.

21. Don Ohlmeyer interview.

22. *Tomorrow Show*, June 3, 1977.

23. Hilton in Jane Howard, "Howard Cosell: Tower of Babble," *Cosmopolitan*, August 1979. p. 246; Michael J. Arlen, "The Air: Neutrality at the Empty Center," *The New Yorker*, October 27, 1975, p. 123; Benjamin DeMott, "Culture Watch: The Celebrity," *Atlantic*, July 1977, p. 82.

24. Howard, "Howard Cosell: Tower of Babble," p. 247.

25. Dennis Lewin interview.

26. Cosell, *I Never Played the Game*, p. 127.

27. Ibid., pp. 143, 142.

28. Ibid., p. 149.

29. ABC telecast of Norton-Holmes fight, June 9, 1978.

30. Arthur Mercante, *Inside the Ropes* (Ithaca, N.Y.: McBooks Press, 2006), p. 150.

31. ABC telecast of Ali-Spinks fight, September 15, 1978.

CHAPTER 17: "A SAD WAY TO END"

1. Marc Gunther and Bill Carter, *Monday Night Mayhem: The Inside Story of ABC's Monday Night Football* (New York: Beech Tree, 1998), p. 203.

2. Frank Deford interview.

3. Jerry Izenberg interview.

4. Randy Gordon, "Superfight: Sugar Ray Leonard vs. Thomas Hearns," *The Sweet Science*, September 16, 2004, http://www.thesweetscience.com/news/articles/851-superfight-sugar-ray-leonard-vs-thomas-hearns.

5. Terry O'Neil, *The Game Behind the Game* (New York: HarperCollins, 1989), p. 55.

6. Ibid., p. 64.

7. Ibid., p. 67.

8. Jim Lampley interview.

9. O'Neil, *Game Behind the Game*, p. 69.

10. Ibid., pp. 270–71.

11. "OTL: The Night John Lennon Died," *ESPN.com*, December 4, 2010.

12. ABC telecast of Patriots-Dolphins game, December 8, 1980.

13. Dave Kindred, *Sound and Fury* (New York: Free Press, 2006), p. 230.

14. Thomas Hauser, *Muhammad Ali: His Life and Times* (New York: HarperCollins, 1998), pp. 399, 400.

15. Ibid., pp. 405–6; "Russian roulette," Hugh McIlvanney quoted in Kindred, *Sound and Fury*, p. 241.

16. ABC telecast of Ali-Holmes fight, October 2, 1980.

17. Hauser, *Muhammad Ali*, p. 422.

18. *New York Times*, December 13, 1981; Hauser, *Muhammad Ali*, p. 430.

19. Hauser, *Muhammad Ali*, p. 429.

20. Cosell, *I Never Played the Game* (New York: William Morrow, 1985), p. 185.

21. William Taaffe, "TV/Radio: They're Waving the White Flag," *Sports Illustrated*, July 26, 1982, p. 54; Frank Deford, "I've Won. I've Beat Them," *Sports Illustrated*, August 8, 1983, p. 82.

22. Mike Marley interview.

23. Jim Lampley interview.

24. Jim Spence, *Up Close and Personal* (New York: Atheneum, 1988), p. 8.

25. Cosell, *I Never Played the Game*, pp. 49, 101.

26. Ibid., p. 98.

27. Ibid., p. 96.

28. Mike Marley interview.

29. Howard Cosell, *What's Wrong with Sports* (New York: Simon & Schuster, 1991), p. 222.

30. Cosell, *I Never Played the Game*, p. 185; Spence, *Up Close and Personal*, p. 17.

31. ABC telecast of Cobb-Holmes fight, November 26, 1982.

32. Spence, *Up Close and Personal*, p. 17.

33. Ibid., pp. 17–18; Mike Marley interview.

34. Cosell, *I Never Played the Game*, pp. 188–89.

35. "They Said It," *Sports Illustrated*, February 8, 1984, p. 8.

36. Cosell, *I Never Played the Game*, pp. 190–91.

CHAPTER 18: EBB TIDE

1. William Taaffe, "They're Waving the White Flag," *Sports Illustrated*, July 26, 1982, p. 54.

2. Frank Deford, "I've Won. I've Beat Them," *Sports Illustrated*, August 8, 1983, p. 82, 70–72.

3. David Halberstam, "The Mouth That Roared," *Playboy*, December 1982, p. 130.

4. Howard Cosell, *I Never Played the Game* (New York: William Morrow, 1985), pp. 137–38.

5. Cosell, *I Never Played the Game*, pp. 139–40; Jim Spence, *Up Close and Personal* (New York: Atheneum, 1988), p. 29.

6. Cosell, *I Never Played the Game*, pp. 154, 161.

7. Robert Friedman, "Monday Night Madness," *Inside Sports*, October 31, 1980, pp. 26–27.

8. Roone Arledge, *Roone* (New York: HarperCollins, 2003), p. 284.

9. Cosell, *I Never Played the Game*, p. 156.

10. ABC telecast of Cowboys-Redskins game, September 5, 1983.

11. Marc Gunther and Bill Carter, *Monday Night Mayhem: The Inside Story of ABC's Monday Night Football* (New York: Beech Tree, 1998), p. 278.

12. ABC telecast.

13. Cosell, *I Never Played the Game*, pp. 333–35.

14. Ibid., p. 335; Arledge, *Roone,* p. 286.

15. Cosell, *I Never Played the Game*, pp. 336, 339, 346–47, 343, 331, 157; *Economist* obituary cited in *Encyclopedia.com*, http://www.encyclopedia.com/topic/Howard_Cosell.aspx.

16. Ibid., p. 165.

17. William Taaffe, "TV/Radio: Fresh Juice but Sour Ratings," *Sports Illustrated*, October 31, 1983, p. 103; Cosell, *I Never Played the Game*, pp. 150, 160–61.

18. Cosell, *I Never Played the Game*, p. 162.

19. Cosell, *I Never Played the Game*, p. 165; Larry Stewart, "Cosell Didn't Always Tell It Like It Was," *Los Angeles Times*, April 28, 1995.

20. Cosell, *I Never Played the Game*, pp. 164, 166.

21. Ibid., p. 167.

22. Ibid., p. 174.

23. Jerry Izenberg interview.

24. Frank Deford interview.

25. Spence, *Up Close and Personal*, p. 23; "errand boy," Stan Isaacs, *Newsday* (New York), September 5, 1984.

26. Don Ohlmeyer interview.

27. *Late Night with David Letterman*, October 31, 1985.

28. Cosell, *I Never Played the Game*, p. 142; *People*, December 9, 1985.

29. Larry Merchant interview.

30. Arledge, *Roone*, p. 294.

31. Don Ohlmeyer interview.

32. Dennis Lewin interview.

33. Arledge, *Roone*, p. 285.

34. Dave Kindred, *Sound and Fury* (New York: Free Press, 2006), pp. 261–62; Spence, *Up Close and Personal*, p. 28.

35. ABC memo, April 2, 1985, in John Bloom, *There You Have It: The Life, Legacy, and Legend of Howard Cosell* (Amherst: University of Massachusetts Press, 2010), p. 173.

36. Dennis Lewin interview.

37. Mike Marley interview.

38. Dennis Lewin interview.

CHAPTER 19: REQUIEM FOR A HEAVYWEIGHT

1. Jim Spence, *Up Close and Personal* (New York: Atheneum, 1988), p. 32.

2. Jim Lampley interview.

3. Howard Cosell, *I Never Played the Game* (New York: William Morrow, 1985), p. 152; Tom Callahan, "This Was How-wud Co-sssell," *Time,* January 6, 1986.

4. Howard Cosell, "Daring to Join the Enemy," *New York Daily News,* May 4, 1986.

5. Spence, *Up Close and Personal,* p. 25; Marc Gunther and Bill Carter, *Monday Night Mayhem: The Inside Story of ABC's Monday Night Football* (New York: Beech Tree, 1998), p. 265.

6. Jim Lampley interview.

7. Mike Marley interview.

8. Mike Marley interview.

9. Cosell, *I Never Played the Game,* p. 209.

10. Mike Marley interview; Phil Pepe interview.

11. Don Ohlmeyer interview.

12. Lewis Grizzard, "America Owes Howard Cosell an Apology," 1991, http://www.lewisgrizzard.com/columns/archive/AmericaOwesHowardCosellAnApology.html.

13. Thomas Hauser, *Muhammad Ali: His Life and Times* (New York: HarperCollins, 1998), p. 173.

14. Larry Merchant interview.

15. Ferdie Pacheco interview.

16. Mike Marley interview.

17. Confidential interview with the author, September 2010.

18. Frank Gifford, *The Whole Ten Yards* (New York: Random House, 1993), p. 11.

19. Howard Cosell, *What's Wrong with Sports* (New York: Simon & Schuster, 1991), p. 331.

20. Ibid., pp. 331–32.

21. Mike Marley interview.

22. Russ White, "Howard Cosell Has a Bad Word for Everyone but Himself," *Orlando Sentinel,* June 30, 1991; Cosell, *What's Wrong with Sports,* pp. 293 (Garvey), 24 (Rose), 259 (Winfield).

23. Cosell, *What's Wrong with Sports,* p. 325.

24. Ibid., p. 241.

25. *Muhammad Ali's 50th Birthday Celebration*, ABC, March 1, 1992.

26. Jerry Izenberg interview.

27. Gifford, *Whole Ten Yards*, p. 18.

28. Mike Marley interview.

29. Robert Lipsyte, "Cosell Turns 75 All Too Quietly," *New York Times*, March 26, 1993.

30. Frank Deford interview.

31. Leonard Shapiro, "Howard Cosell Dies at 77," *Washington Post*, April 24, 1995; Bob Raissman, "Telling It Like He Was: Bitter End to Life of Venom," *New York Daily News*, April 24, 1995.

32. Richard Sandomir, "With a Dandy Curtain Call, ABC Signs Off on 'Monday Night Football,'" *New York Times*, December 27, 2005.

33. Mike Marley, "Howard Cosell Would've Rejected Boxing Hall of Fame Induction," *Examiner.com*, June 15, 2010.

34. Maury Allen interview.

# SELECTED BIBLIOGRAPHY

Anderson, Dave. "The *Sport* Interview." *Sport*, January 1979.

Arkush, Michael. *The Fight of the Century: Ali vs. Frazier.* Hoboken, N.J.: Wiley, 2007.

Arledge, Roone. *Roone.* New York: HarperCollins, 2003.

Arlen, Michael J. "Neutrality at the Empty Center." *The New Yorker*, October 21, 1975.

Bagli, Charles V. "A New Light on a Fight to Integrate Stuyvesant Town," *New York Times*, November 22, 2010.

Barra, Allen. Review of *The Muhammad Ali Reader*, ed. Gerald Early (Hopewell, N.J.: Ecco, 1998). *Denver Post*, July 12, 1998.

"The Battered Face of a Winner." *Sports Illustrated*, March 15, 1971.

Berkow, Ira. *Red: A Biography of Red Smith.* New York: Times Books, 2007.

Boyle, Robert H. "Some Very Wrong Numbers." *Sports Illustrated*, May 2, 1977.

Byrd, John. "200 Crowd to See Cosell." *Washington Square News* (NYU), February 6, 1978.

Callahan, Tom. "This Was How-wud Co-sssell." *Time*, January 6, 1986.

Cope, Myron. "Would You Let This Man Interview You?" *Sports Illustrated*, March 13, 1967.

Cosell, Howard. *Cosell.* Chicago: Playboy Press, 1973.

———. "Daring to Join the Enemy." *New York Daily News*, May 4, 1986.

———. *I Never Played the Game.* New York: William Morrow, 1985.

———. *Like It Is.* Chicago: Playboy Press, 1974.

———. *What's Wrong with Sports.* New York: Simon & Schuster, 1991.

————. "Why I Support the ERA." *Ms.*, October 1975.

"Cosell Calls 'Em as He Sees 'Em." *Mount Vernon* (N.Y.) *Daily Argus*, August 8, 1964.

Creamer, Robert. "Scorecard: Goodby, Howard." *Sports Illustrated*, December 7, 1970.

————. "Scorecard: Mouth to Mouth." *Sports Illustrated*, September 7, 1970.

Daley, Robert. "The Man They Love to Hate." *New York Times Magazine*, September 1, 1974.

Deford, Frank. "I've Won. I've Beat Them." *Sports Illustrated*, August 8, 1983.

DeMott, Benjamin. "Culture Watch: The Celebrity." *Atlantic*, July 1977.

Early, Gerald, ed. *The Muhammad Ali Reader.* Hopewell, N.J.: Ecco, 1998.

Economaki, Chris. *Let 'Em All Go! The Story of Auto Racing by the Man Who Was There.* Indianapolis: Argabright, 2006.

Fish, Mike. "FBI Files: Cosell Was a Primetime Target for Threats." *CNNSI.com*, January 10, 2002. http://sportsillustrated.cnn.com/football/news/2002/01/10/cosell_fbi_file.

Friedman, Robert. "Monday Night Madness." *Inside Sports*, October 31, 1980.

Gifford, Frank. *The Whole Ten Yards.* New York: Random House, 1993.

Goodman, Mark. "Hyping Howie." *People*, September 29, 1975.

Gordon, Randy. "Superfight: Sugar Ray Leonard vs. Thomas Hearns." *The Sweet Science*, September 16, 2004. http://www.thesweetscience.com/news/articles/851-superfight-sugar-ray-leonard-vs-thomas-hearns.

Grimes, William. "A City Gripped by Crisis and Enraptured by the Yankees." *New York Times*, March 30, 2005.

Grizzard, Lewis. "America Owes Howard Cosell an Apology," 1991. http://www.lewisgrizzard.com/columns/archive/AmericaOwesHowardCosellAnApology.html.

Gunther, Marc, and Bill Carter. *Monday Night Mayhem: The Inside Story of ABC's Monday Night Football.* New York: Beech Tree, 1998.

Halberstam, David. "The Mouth That Roared." *Playboy*, December 1982.

Hauser, Thomas. *Muhammad Ali: His Life and Times.* New York: HarperCollins, 1998.

*Howard Cosell: Telling It Like It Is,* HBO documentary, November 1, 1999.

Howard, Jane. "Howard Cosell: Tower of Babble." *Cosmopolitan*, August 1979.

Jenkins, Dan. "The Sweet Life of Swinging Joe." *Sports Illustrated*, October 17, 1966.

Kane, Martin. "Boxing Greets Its New Dawn." *Sports Illustrated*, July 6, 1959.

————. "Scorecard: The Hanging Judge." *Sports Illustrated*, September 11, 1972.

Kimberlin, Donald E. "Telling It Like It Was." *Oldradio.com*, April 27, 1995. http://www.oldradio.com/archives/people/dk-cos.htm.

Kindred, Dave. *Sound and Fury*. New York: Free Press, 2006.

Kirshenbaum, Jerry. "Scorecard: Rating the National Pastime." *Sports Illustrated*, November 2, 1981.

Kram, Mark. "He Moves Like Silk, Hits Like a Ton." *Sports Illustrated*, October 26, 1970.

Lardner, Rex. "Voorloper." *The New Yorker*, June 11, 1955.

Leggett, William. "TV/Radio: A Need to Learn the ABCs." *Sports Illustrated*, October 24, 1977.

Leonard, John. "Cosell: Milder but Does He Satisfy?" *Life*, November 13, 1970.

Linderman, Lawrence. "*Playboy* Interview: A Candid Conversation with the Fustian Oracle of Sport." *Playboy*, May 1972.

Lipsyte, Robert. "Cosell Turns 75 All Too Quietly." *New York Times*, March 26, 1993.

———. *SportsWorld*. New York: Quadrangle, 1975.

Mackin, Tom. *Brief Encounters: From Einstein to Elvis*. Bloomington, Ind.: AuthorHouse, 2008.

Marley, Mike. "Howard Cosell Would've Rejected Boxing Hall of Fame Induction." *Examiner.com*, June 15, 2010. http://www.examiner.com/boxing-in-national/howard-cosell-would-ve-rejected-boxing-hall-of-fame-induction.

Marshall, Joe. "Howard Cosell Is Just Another Pretty Face." *Esquire*, October 1972.

McKay, Jim. *The Real McKay: My Wide World of Sports*. New York: Dutton, 1998.

"Medical Journal Raps Kid Ball as Delinquency Cure." *Sporting News*, August 17, 1955.

Mercante, Arthur. *Inside the Ropes*. Ithaca, N.Y.: McBooks Press, 2006.

Mischer, Don. Interview, Archive of American Television, November 7, 2008. http://emmytvlegends.org/interviews/people/don-mischer.

Nack, William. "The Fight's Over, Joe." *Sports Illustrated*, September 30, 1996.

Newfield, Jack. *The Life and Crimes of Don King: The Shame of Boxing in America*. New York: William Morrow, 1995.

Novak, Ralph. Review of Cosell, *I Never Played the Game*. *People*, December 9, 1985.

O'Neil, Terry. *The Game Behind the Game*. New York: HarperCollins, 1989.

Olsen, Jack. "A Case of Conscience." *Sports Illustrated*, April 11, 1965.

"OTL: The Night John Lennon Died." *ESPN.com*, December 4, 2010. http://espn.go.com/video/clip?id=5884604.

Patterson, Floyd. "In Defense of Cassius Clay." *Esquire*, August 1966.

Powers, Ron. *Supertube*. New York: Coward-McCann, 1984.

Raissman, Bob. "Telling It Like He Was: Bitter End to Life of Venom." *New York Daily News*, April 24, 1995.

Rogin, Gilbert. "The Drama in Miami." *Sports Illustrated*, March 20, 1961.

Ross, Bill. "Ali-Holmes and the Trail of Blood, part 1." *BoxingScene.com*, June 12, 2006. http://www.boxingscene.com/ali-holmes-trail-blood-part-1--4415.

Safran, Claire. "She Loves the Man Everyone Loves to Hate." *Today's Health*, February 1975.

Sandomir, Richard. "With a Dandy Curtain Call, ABC Signs Off on 'Monday Night Football.' " *New York Times*, December 27, 2005.

"Scorecard: The Black Muslim Hope." *Sports Illustrated*, March 16, 1964.

"Shall We Rule These TV Egos Guilty of Unnecessary Roughness?" *Today's Health*, December 1971.

Shapiro, Leonard. "Howard Cosell Dies at 77." *Washington Post*, April 24, 1995.

Shields, David. "The Wound and the Bow." *Believer*, December 2003/January 2004. http://www.believermag.com/issues/200312/?read=article_shields.

Shimkin, Carl. "Did Howard Cosell Really Say, 'The Bronx Is Burning'?" *MLBlogs Network*, August 18, 2007. http://bestblog.mlblogs.com/archives/2007/08/did_howard_cose_1.html.

Shrake, Edwin [Bud]. "The Defection of Dandy Don." *Sports Illustrated*, April 22, 1974.

———. "What Are They Doing with the Sacred Game of Pro Football?" *Sports Illustrated*, October 25, 1971.

Spence, Jim. *Up Close and Personal*. New York: Atheneum, 1988.

Spink, J. G. T. "Looping the Loops." *Sporting News*, August 10, 1955.

"Sports Is Life." *Newsweek*, June 3, 1968.

Stewart, Larry. "Cosell Didn't Always Tell It Like It Was." *Los Angeles Times*, April 28, 1995.

Taaffe, William. "TV/Radio: Fresh Juice but Sour Ratings." *Sports Illustrated*, October 31, 1983.

———. "TV/Radio: They're Waving the White Flag." *Sports Illustrated*, July 26, 1982.

Thimmesch, Nick. "Howard the Humble." *Saturday Evening Post*, August/September 1974.

"This Is Howard Cosell." *Newsweek*, October 2, 1972.

Trubek, Anne. "The Oberlin Experiment." *Smart Set* (Drexel University), December 14, 2007. http://www.thesmartset.com/article/article12140702.aspx.

"When TV Makes Full Use of Howard Cosell." *Mad*, April 1972.

White, Russ. "Howard Cosell Has a Bad Word for Everyone but Himself." *Orlando Sentinel*, June 30, 1991.

X, Malcolm. *The Autobiography of Malcolm X*. New York: Grove Press, 1965.

Yardley, Jonathan. "Booktalk: Howard Cosell and Jim McKay—Choose One—Offer Up the ABCs of TV Sport." *Sports Illustrated*, November 5, 1973.

# INDEX

# ABOUT THE AUTHOR

MARK RIBOWSKY has written eleven highly acclaimed books encompassing a wide range of pop culture topics, including the definitive biographies of Negro League legends Satchel Paige (*Don't Look Back*) and Josh Gibson (*The Power and the Darkness*), maverick Oakland Raiders owner Al Davis (*Slick*), controversial music producer Phil Spector (*He's a Rebel*), and a trilogy of Motown biographies about the Supremes (*The Supremes: A Saga of Motown Dreams, Success, and Betrayal*), Stevie Wonder (*Signed, Sealed, and Delivered*), and the Temptations (*Ain't Too Proud to Beg*). He has also written the exhaustive *A Complete History of the Negro Leagues*, *A Complete History of the Home Run*, and the autobiography of eccentric real estate baron Abe Hirschfeld (*Crazy and in Charge*), as well as hundreds of articles for national magazines including *Playboy*, *Penthouse*, *Sport*, *Inside Sports*, and *TV Guide*, his subjects including Eddie Murphy, David Letterman, Kareem Abdul-Jabbar, Larry Bird, Magic Johnson, Peyton Manning, Charles Barkley, Alex Rodriguez, and O. J. Simpson. He lives in New York City.